INTERNATIONAL PERSPECTIVES ON YOUTH CONFLICT AND DEVELOPMENT

International Perspectives on Youth Conflict and Development

EDITED BY
COLETTE DAIUTE, ZEYNEP BEYKONT,
CRAIG HIGSON-SMITH, AND LARRY NUCCI

OXFORD
UNIVERSITY PRESS

2006

OXFORD
UNIVERSITY PRESS

Oxford University Press, Inc., publishes works that further
Oxford University's objective of excellence
in research, scholarship, and education.

Oxford   New York
Auckland   Cape Town   Dar es Salaam   Hong Kong   Karachi
Kuala Lumpur   Madrid   Melbourne   Mexico City   Nairobi
New Delhi   Shanghai   Taipei   Toronto

With offices in
Argentina   Austria   Brazil   Chile   Czech Republic   France   Greece
Guatemala   Hungary   Italy   Japan   Poland   Portugal   Singapore
South Korea   Switzerland   Thailand   Turkey   Ukraine   Vietnam

Copyright © 2006 by Oxford University Press, Inc.

Published by Oxford University Press, Inc.
198 Madison Avenue, New York, New York 10016

www.oup.com

Oxford is a registered trademark of Oxford University Press

Library of Congress Cataloging-in-Publication Data
International perspectives on youth conflict and development /
edited by Colette Daiute . . . [et al.].
p. cm.
Includes bibliographical references and index.
ISBN-13 978-0-19-517842-5
ISBN 0-19-517842-4
1. Youth and violence—Cross-cultural studies.   2. Children and violence—
Cross-cultural studies.   3. Youth—Social conditions—Cross-cultural studies.
4. Children—Social conditions—Cross-cultural studies.   5. Social
conflict—Cross-cultural studies.   6. Developmental psychology— Cross-cultural
studies.   I. Title: Youth conflict and development. II. Daiute, Colette.
HQ799.2.V56I68 2005
305.235'086'94—dc22   2005005414

9 8 7 6 5 4 3 2 1
Printed in the United States of America
on acid-free paper

For all the young people whose insights
made this book possible,
and
in memory of Jocelyn Solis

ACKNOWLEDGMENTS

The editors and authors of this book are indebted to the Rockefeller Foundation Bellagio Study and Conference Center for their generous support of the international meeting that led to the creation of this book. The meeting in Bellagio allowed for an exchange and development of our own ideas that allowed the book to advance beyond a collection to a more integrated understanding.

The editors also acknowledge Jaicy Hohn, Jana Sladkova, Kimberlee Trudeau, and Moja Ninkovic for their careful assistance on various phases of editing the manuscript. Thanks also to Jennifer Rappaport, our editor at Oxford University Press, for her constructive comments throughout the process.

Colette Daiute thanks Neil Smith, Omar Dahbour, and the Center for Place Culture and Society (at the Graduate Center, CUNY) 2004 Seminar on "War, Patriotism, and Resistance" for introducing relevant scholarship and for their helpful comments on the general introduction of this book.

CONTENTS

CONTRIBUTORS

Dino Abazovic, a sociologist, is director of the Human Rights Center of the University of Sarajevo, and teaching assistant at the Faculty of Political Sciences, University of Sarajevo. His research interests include human rights culture, processes of democratization in postconflict societies, sociology of knowledge, and sociology of religion. He has been the first chairperson of the Steering Board of Balkan Human Rights Network, as well as the secretary general of the Atelier for Philosophy, Social Sciences and Psychoanalysis in Sarajevo. He has published numerous articles. He lives and works in Sarajevo, Bosnia and Herzegovina.

Olayemi Akinwumi, a Nigerian, holds a doctoral degree in African history. He is presently chair of history at Nasarawa State University, in Keffi, Nigeria. He has published books and written articles in many international journals. Some of his publications include *The Colonial Contest for the Nigerian Region 1884–1900: A History of the German Participation* (2002), and *Crises and Conflicts in Nigeria: A Political History since 1960* (2005).

Zeynep F. Beykont conducts research on school language policies and educational programs that support the cultural, linguistic, and academic development of ethnic minority and immigrant youth. Over the past 20 years, she has worked as a researcher and consultant in school-, community-, and museum-based programs designed for language-minority youth in a variety of countries including the United States, Greece, Turkey, and Australia. Dr. Beykont's recent publications include "Refocusing School-Language Policy Discussion," in *International Handbook of Education and Development: Preparing Schools, Students, and Nations for the 21st Century*, edited by Cummins and McGinn, and *Dismantling Language-Based Oppression in Educational Institutions*.

Guozhen Cen is professor of psychology in the Department of Applied Psychology of the Educational Science College at Shanghai Normal University, Shanghai. His major publications focus on issues of developmental and educational psychology, with an emphasis on moral development, socialization, and education. His work has appeared in major psychological and educational journals within China, including *Psychological Sciences* and *Acta Psychologica Sinica.*

William E. Cross, Jr. is one of America's founding theorists and researchers on black identity development across the life span. His book *Shades of Black* (1991) is designed for persons interested in the study of African American identity. Over the course of his career, Dr. Cross has held positions in psychology and African studies at Cornell University, Penn State University, and the University of Massachusetts at Amherst. Currently he is professor and head of the Doctoral Program in Social-Personality Psychology at the Graduate Center, City University of New York. His research interests include the structure and everyday functions of black identity; identity content (nationalist, bicultural, and multicultural) as the primary predictor of identity consequences in everyday life; general personality and reference group orientation as independent predictors of differential self-concept levels; the history or black achievement motivation from slavery to the present; the history of black education from slavery through the late 1940s.

Colette Daiute is professor of psychology at the Graduate Center, City University of New York. She conducts research on social and cognitive development in challenging circumstances, such as urban public schools and nations involved in violent conflict. In her research and practice, Dr. Daiute has focused on young people's uses of literacy and media as activities that promote the development of society and the development of their own social skills. Dr. Daiute's recent books include *Narrative Analysis: Studying the Development of Individuals in Society* (2004, with C. Lightfoot) and *The Development of Literacy through Social Interaction* (1993), and several of her articles on youth conflict have been published in the journal *Narrative Inquiry*, as well as in other journals.

Wolfgang Edelstein is professor and director emeritus of the Max Planck Institute for Human Development in Berlin. He directed the Center for Development and Socialization of the Institute. He was chief scientific advisor to the Icelandic Ministry of Education and in this capacity played a substantial part in the design of school reform, curriculum development, and teacher training in Iceland. His main research interests are in cognitive and sociomoral development, and his educational commitments are constructive learning and school reform.

Sarah Warshauer Freedman is professor of education and senior researcher at the Human Rights Center at the University of California, Berkeley. Her research interests include international education, with a special focus on multicultural or multinational conflicts, issues of multiculturalism and conflict in the teaching and learning of secondary English in U.S. schools, teacher research, participatory action research, and teacher education. Besides numerous articles and chapters, her books include *Inside City Schools: Literacy and Learning in Multicultural Classrooms* (1999), with Elizabeth Simons, Julie Kalnin, Alex Casareno, and the M-CLASS teams, *Exchanging Writing, Exchanging Cultures: Lessons in School Reform from the United States and Great Britain* (1994), and *Response to Student Writing* (1987). She has edited *The Acquisition of Written Language* (1985), and, with Arnetha Ball, *Bakhtinian Perspectives on Language, Literacy and Learning* (2004). She has been a Fellow at the Center for Advanced Study in the Behavioral Sciences at Stanford University, a resident at the Rockefeller Foundation's Bellagio Study and Conference Center, chair of the board of trustees for the National Council of Teachers of English Research Foundation and the NCTE Standing Committee on Research, a board member for the McDonnell Foundation's Cognitive Studies in Educational Practice program, and a member of the national task force of the National Writing Project.

Roger A. Hart is professor of environmental psychology in the Ph.D. Psychology Program of the Graduate School and University Center of the City University of New York and codirector of the Children's Environments Research Group. He is a British citizen; he earned a B.A. from Hull University in England and a Ph.D. from Clark University in Worcester, Massachusetts, both in geography. His research has focused on children's development in relation to the physical environment and on the planning and design of children's environments. He also works with international nongovernmental organizations and UNICEF to further the degree to which children know about their rights and participate in determining their own development and the development of their communities. He edited the quarterly journal *Children's Environments* until 1998. He has written *Children's Experience of Place,* a two-volume work on children's participation, for UNICEF, and coauthored *Cities for Children: Children's Rights, Poverty and Urban Management*, also for UNICEF.

Rachel Hertz-Lazarowitz, Ph.D., is professor of social-educational psychology at the Faculty of Education at the University of Haifa. The social psychological principles of cooperation and empowerment inspire her work, crossing gender, ethnic and national intergroup relationships. She has been working for the last 5 years, with her Arab and Jewish students, on the social and academic *umwelt* of her own campus at the University. She has published widely on cooperative learning and Arab—Jew relationships in the United States, Europe, and Israel. She edited, with Norman Miller, *Interaction in Cooperative Groups: The Theoretical Anatomy of Group Learning* (1992). Recently Hertz-Lazarowitz, with T. Zelniker, C. Stephan-White, and W. Stephan, edited a special issue of *Journal of Social Issues* entitled "Improving Arab—Jewish Relations in Israel: Theory and Practice in Co-existence Programs in Israel" (2004).

Craig Higson-Smith is a research psychologist specializing in traumatic stress and violence. He has also worked as an anti-apartheid activist and in civil conflict situations in Southern and Eastern Africa. He is currently a trainer and researcher with the South African Institute for Traumatic Stress. Craig Higson-Smith is author of the 2002 book *Supporting Communities Affected by Violence: A Casebook for South Africa.*

Alcinda Honwana is the program director of the Social Science Research Council (SSRC) in New York. She has carried out extensive research in Mozambique on the impact of armed conflict on young people. She has published several journal articles on children, youth, and conflict and completed a manuscript on child soldiers in Africa to be published by the University of Pennsylvania Press. Before joining the SSRC, Dr. Honwana worked at the UN in the Office of the Special Representative for Children and Armed Conflict.

Stacey Horn is from the United States and is assistant professor of education at the University of Illinois at Chicago. Her research publications include "Adolescents' Reasoning about Exclusion from Social Groups," *Developmental Psychology* (2003); "The Influence of Group Stereotypes of Adolescents' Moral Reasoning," with M. Killen and C. Stangor, *Journal of Early Adolescence* (2003); "The Multidimensionality of Adolescents' Beliefs about and Attitudes toward Gay and Lesbian Peers in School," with L. Nucci, *Equity and Excellence in Education* (2003). Her research interests are in the areas of adolescent social development, intergroup relations, adolescents' reasoning about stereotyping, prejudice, gay and lesbian issues, and schooling as a context for social development. She teaches courses on adolescent development and education.

In Jae Lee has an Ed.D. from Seoul National University on ethics and moral education (1995). Since 1996, he has taught the theory and practice of moral education at Gwangju National University of Education. He is now associate professor of ethics education at Gwangju National University of Education in South Korea. Dr. Lee has published numerous journal articles and book chapters.

Dan Li is professor of psychology in the Department of Applied Psychology of the Educational Science College at Shanghai Normal University, Shanghai. Her major publications focus on issues of developmental and educational psychology, with an emphasis on sociality development and education. Her work has appeared in major psychology and education journals in China, including *Psychological Sciences* and *Psychological Development and Education.*

Clary Milnitsky is currently head of the CNPq research group, Values Construction, Violence and Identity in Adolescence (CONVIVA), which develops interventions and workshops in schools and other institutions. Her approach to sociomoral issues takes into account culture and context, with methodology that includes ethnographic description and content analysis to ensure the acknowledgement of diversity as well as universality. Dr. Milnitsky studied philosophy at the Federal University of Rio de Janeiro, followed by graduate work in developmental psychology at the Federal University of Rio Grande do Sul, and a Ph.D. at the University of Illinois at Chicago in 1991. She has also been a professor and researcher in the Graduate Program of Developmental Psychology and Social and Institutional Psychology at Porto Alegre.

Rocio Mojica is the program coordinator of Save the Children/UK in Colombia and a member of the Programme Management Team for South America. She is Colombian, with a law degree from Universidad Externado de Colombia and a master's degree in political science from Universidad de Los Andes in Bogota. She has worked in the field of social development, initially emphasizing human rights, and later in the rights of the child, and conducted research studies in these areas. She has designed, implemented, and managed large-scale emergency and reconstruction programs from the perspective of child rights and development programs. The key themes on which she has worked in Colombia are children and conflict, participation and citizenship, child protection, access to quality, inclusive, relevant education, sexual and reproductive health, and emergency prevention, preparation, and protection. She has coauthored several publications, including *Child-Protection Services: Preliminary Analysis in Four South American Countries* and *Children and Violence: Colombia's Case*, for Save the Children/UK and CINDE.

Larry Nucci is professor of education and affiliate professor of psychology at the University of Illinois at Chicago, where he is director of the Office for Studies in Moral Development and Education. His research focuses on children's moral and social development. His recent work has examined the impact of culture on children's concepts of privacy and personal prerogative. Nucci's book *Education in the Moral Domain* has been translated into many languages.

Jocelyn Solis was a postdoctoral fellow at the University of California, Santa Cruz, on leave from her assistant professorship at Brooklyn College, when she passed away at age 30. Having completed her 2002 dissertation on the nature and consequences of undocumented status among children of Mexican immigrants in New York City, Dr. Solis made important contributions in her young life. She was a scholar who contributed to theory and research on immigration psychology, in particular, with a focus on the impact of immigration on the development of children, families, and societies. In addition to her postdoctoral fellowship, Dr. Solis received a fellowship from the Ford Foundation. Publications by Jocelyn Solis appear in *Journal of Social Issues* and edited volumes including *Narrative Analysis: Studying the Development of Individuals in Society*, edited by C. Daiute & C. Lightfoot (2004) and *Mambo Montage: The Latinization of New York* .

Madelene Sta. Maria is currently the chair of the Department of Psychology at De La Salle University in Manila. She earned her doctorate degree in psychology at the University of Cologne, Germany. Her research has focused on the organization of adolescent life in culture and society, the cultural psychological bases of peaceful and conflictual interactions, and culture and emotions. Her recent publications include "Youth in Southeast Asia," in *The World's Youth: Adolescence in eight regions of the World,* edited by Bradford Brown, Reed Larson, and Tharakad Saraswathi (2002), and "The Sociocultural Dimensions of Philippine Conflict," in *Conflict and Conflict Resolution in the Philippines,* edited by Madelene Sta. Maria (2003), "The Phenomenological Approach in Psychological Research," *Philippine Journal of Psychology* (2000), and "Managing Social Conflict: The Peace Zone Experience," *Philippine Journal of Psychology* (2000).

Elliot Turiel is professor of education at the University of California, Berkeley. He is also affiliated with the Department of Psychology and the Institute of Human Development at Berkeley. Currently, he serves as associate dean for academic affairs in the Graduate School of Education. He is the president of the Jean Piaget Society. He has conducted research on moral development, as well as on the distinction made by children, adolescents, and adults between morality and the domains of social convention and personal jurisdiction. Much of his current work is on social and moral opposition and resistance based on perceptions of injustices in cultural practices and societal arrangements. Among other works, Turiel published *The Culture of Morality: Social Development, Context, and Conflict* (2002).

Charles Ukeje, a Nigerian, holds a Ph.D. in International Relations from the Department of International Relations at the Obafemi Awolowo University, Ile-Ife, Nigeria, where he is a senior lecturer. His research interests are in the areas of democratization and governance, conflict and security, and postwar reconstruction initiatives. His geographical areas of specialization are the Niger Delta of Nigeria and West Africa. In addition to his monographs, coedited books, and book chapters, his works have appeared in major peer-reviewed journals such as *Politics, Culture and Society, Issue: A Journal of Opinion, Scandinavian Journal of Development Alternatives and Area Studies, Africa Development, Scientia Militaria, Journal of Terrorism and Political Violence,* and *Oxford Development Studies* (forthcoming).

INTERNATIONAL PERSPECTIVES ON
YOUTH CONFLICT AND DEVELOPMENT

General Introduction

The Problem of Society in Youth Conflict

COLETTE DAIUTE

A child soldier in the Philippines wakes up early to carry a message to a counterinsurgency group fighting some miles away.

Children in Brazil vie for a space to sleep in an alley, knowing that no one passing by will notice.

Young men in a working-class neighborhood in Germany express an angry desire to claim their neighborhoods.

As they fill out a survey, preteens in a U.S. suburb think about how weird it is to be gay.

Arab and Jewish youth attend classes together a few hours after a suicide bomber exploded a bus going to campus, killing or wounding many students.

Black youth in South Africa are discouraged that the world thinks apartheid is over, while they continue to struggle for a place in society.

Young people in Bosnia and Croatia ask their parents and teachers to tell them about what happened in the recent war, but the adults want to forget that time and don't think passing on this history could do any good.

Latino, African American, and recently immigrated children in urban classrooms in the United States tell a story of tolerance to a teacher in a violence prevention program but recount humiliating experiences of discrimination to their friends.

Young women and men in Nigeria look into the eyes of their peers from other ethnic militias, realizing that it is the big oil companies who have made their lives difficult.

These are a few moments in the midst of conflicts involving young people across the earth. In this book, scholars who study youth conflict explain how such moments are embedded in broader social-relational systems. On the basis of the idea that human development is determined by these systems, we, the authors of this book, define "youth conflict" as fighting, social exclusion, and abuse by and among young people from the age when they enter into the public sphere until they are economically independent adults. The hypothesis we consider is that such conflicts, including children's participation in armed conflict, fighting and discrimination among social groups, competition for resources in the streets, and interpersonal acts of violence by youth are embedded in conflicts in the local region, the nation, and international relations. We examine how youth conflict is, thus, not primarily a problem of individual youth, their family cultures, or some developmental stage but a problem in the development of society.

From this perspective, the authors of this book pose a new question about youth conflict: "What is the nature of youth participation in conflict internationally, and what is the relationship of these conflicts to broader social, political, and economic systems?" The chapters are research-based essays discussing salient youth conflicts and developments in 14 countries across seven continents. Analyses focus on the experiences of young people in the context of social, political, and economic processes that play out as inter-group tensions. The collection of case studies is also, however, designed to move beyond the myopia of the local scene. Manifestations of youth conflicts in different places are distinct in important ways, but our examination across contexts is a way to expose processes that may not be as visible in isolated manifestations of youth conflict. By considering the interdependence of the social, historical, and personal scales of conflicts across very different contexts, we seek insights to define youth conflict as a practice embedded in local, national, and international processes that limit and enable young people's development.

Background

Youth involvement in conflict and violence is a global problem, yet research and interventions tend to be isolated to specific manifestations like the participation of children in war, inter-group tensions in the aftermath of war, street living, intergroup fighting, and interpersonal aggression or exclusion. Previous analyses have focused on specific manifestations of conflict, in part because conflicts are grounded in different geopolitical and economic situations that are interesting to researchers in different academic disciplines. Research on young people's involvement in armed conflict has, for example, been studied primarily by anthropologists and therapists working in Africa, the Middle East, South America, and the Balkans (Apfel & Simon, 1996; Brett & McCallin, 1998; Machal, 1996), while psychologists in the United States and Europe have done extensive research on physical and psychological conflicts among peers (Elliot, Hamburg, & Williams, 1998), and a range of social scientists have studied children living in the streets in nations with struggling economies (Brown, Larson, & Saraswathi, 2002).

Focused separately on different manifestations of conflict, previous research has offered informative albeit context-bound explanations of social and antisocial youth development. Previous research shows, for example, that children's involvement in armed conflict tends to occur in countries suffering from extreme poverty (Brett & McCallin, 1998), while children's participation in interpersonal bullying and hate crimes is especially salient in societies with ample resources that are unevenly distributed (chapter 2 here). In the West, moreover, researchers have explained young people's social problems as situated in individual children, cultures, or neighborhoods. When studying child shooters, for example, researchers and clinicians focus on character disorders or cycles of violence in cultural groups (Garbarino, 1999; Giroux, 1996), neighborhoods (Earls & Carlson, 1999), families (Widom, 1989), and peer groups (Astor, 1994).

As a step toward an analysis of youth conflict that is sensitive to local and global processes, this book gathers case studies of various types of youth conflict across geographic, political, and economic contexts. The international examination in this collection of research-based essays brings into view political and economic processes that are not typically considered in child development research. We examine how political instability, unequal access to material resources, and international power relations in military, economic, and health domains create social challenges for young people, lead to their participation in conflicts, and often affect their ability to thrive. This approach is consistent with other recent international projects examining how the cognitive and social activities of young people are influenced by the political-economic position of their society in the world scene (Brown, Larson, & Saraswathi, 2002). Our aim in this book is, thus, to shift analyses away from offering profiles of "violent youth" to describing processes in a "violent world" by examining the interdependent spheres of conflict involving young people.

International Inquiry

Scholars presenting their work in this book are interested in the nature and effects of growing up amid the experience of violence as a social phenomenon. As diverse societies interact via media, commerce, war, migration, and international organizations, definitions and analyses of normative and problematic youth development can better address the dynamics of power relations and inequalities on local and global scales. Problems of racism, economic inequalities, and political instability related to shifting national boundaries are, for example, of interest in the analysis of youth conflict. The experiences of youth of color living in American cities, children living in the streets in Brazil, children involved in armed conflict in Mozambique, Angola, South Africa, and the Philippines, and children socialized to hate those who are different in the United States, Europe, and elsewhere are all our concern, not just as aberrations of an ideal developmental progression but as reflective of human activity in the contemporary world. With the consideration of these conflict activities, the authors of this book extend developmental study from a focus on maturational, behavioral, and personality factors to include political and economic factors across diverse societies.

Authors met in a face-to-face forum as well as in this book. We wrote draft chapters in response to a common set of questions about youth conflicts in our regions and met at the Rockefeller Foundation Bellagio Study and Conference Center in 2003 to share our findings. The essays in this book thus address common questions, designed to foreground national, regional, and international dynamics: "What is the nature of youth participation in conflict in your part of the world? How does youth conflict relate to broader social, political, and economic systems in the area? How do you define 'childhood,' 'youth,' 'conflict,' and the appropriate scale for research to address the salient issues in your area? Why is developmental theory important for understanding and intervening in youth conflict, and how should developmental approaches be expanded or changed? What other questions must be asked about youth conflict in the local area?"

At the conference and in this book, we have sought to generate insights without reproducing the traditional dominance of Western perspectives. Case studies from Mozambique and Angola, South Africa, Nigeria, Korea, China, the Philippines, the Balkans, Mexico, Colombia, Brazil, and Israel offer diverse perspectives for defining youth, conflict, and development that can expand beyond the historically Western-oriented research. The Europe- and U.S.-based research also attempts to raise new perspectives, in particular by considering marginalized groups of youth, such as young gays and lesbians and youth identifying as African American, Latino, and immigrants. This requires a commitment to understand how young people are sensible and adaptive rather than problematic as they become involved in conflicts originating, at least in some way, beyond their personal activity. This stance also involves identifying the complex dynamics of diverse contexts without prejudice against them, not to reduce the issue of conflict to cultural relativism but to examine youth troubles as troubles in societies enmeshed differently in a global system. The analyses presented here are not yet transnational studies of globalization and human development, but they provide foundations for such subsequent research.

The authors are working from diverse perspectives of social science disciplines, including psychology, anthropology, sociology, political science, and education, examining issues of conflict in the field, in nongovernmental organizations, in schools, clinics, and neighborhoods. In their research, these authors used methods including ethnography, participant-observation, interviews, surveys, discourse analyses, archival analyses, and field-based experimental approaches. Some of the scholars grounded their chapters in innovative research designs like youth documentation projects, youth participation in the research, and civic education activities, while others tested theoretical ideas with examples from institutional documents, news media, or data presented in research published by others. These strategies are, moreover, situated at different points in the activity of youth conflict. While those in the field focus on conflicts' events and participants' reflections in the midst of conflict, those in educational and clinical practices focus on young people's interpretations of conflicts—thus on those symbolic actions that govern behavior and development.

This introductory chapter, the part introductions, and the epilogue integrate across the chapters to highlight similarities and differences that place in relief the social forces involved in youth conflict. Some chapters present case studies of children involved in armed conflict and militia battles (chapters 1, 4, 13, 16), in the aftermath of wars (chapters 3, 10), in intergroup school-based violence (chapters 7, 12), and conflicts over sexual preference (chapter 8). Other chapters focus on children living in the midst of long-term ethnic and ideological conflicts (chapters 3, 4, 6), immigrant youth living in foreign lands (chapter 17), youth living in situations of poverty, exploitation, and long-term violence (chapters 1, 11, 14, 15, 16), discrimination, and humiliation (chapters 2, 11, 12, 15), and young people living in nations whose values are undergoing dramatic transformations causing serious lack of understanding and rifts across generations (chapter 9). These and other issues are addressed in relation to educational, clinical, and policy interventions, including violence prevention and peace education (chapters 6, 12, 14), moral reasoning education (chapters 5, 8), sociopolitically and culturally sensitive therapies and practices (chapters 10, 13), and practices of youth self-determination (chapters 1, 10, 14, 17).

The desire to maintain the tension of diversity was also, in part, behind the design of the editorial team. The editors live and work in different countries: Turkey, South Africa, and the United States; they focus on different conflict manifestations related to issues of language and cultural dominance (Beykont, 1997a, 1997b), postwar recovery (Higson-Smith, 2002), moral reasoning about social relations, such as sexual preferences (Nucci, 2001), and issues of ethnicity and power relations (Daiute, 2004a, 2004b). Like the authors', the editors' research is grounded in diverse developmental theories and research practices across different regions.

Defining Youth Conflict

The international analysis in this book begins by proposing definitions. We refer to "youth" as the period from age 8 through the early twenties, blurring the primarily Western distinctions between childhood, adolescence, and adulthood. Although this broad age span is at odds with maturational theories that have convincingly demonstrated socio-cognitive differences across distinct periods of the life space (Piaget, 1968), this age range is consistent with other international projects like the United Nations Convention on the Rights of the Child (Bellamy, 2000; United Nations General Assembly, 1989) and with research that argues for the increased participation of young people in society (Hart, 1999; Sherrod, 2004; Tourney-Purta, Schwille, & Amadeo, 1999). Although some developmental psychologists object to blurring distinctions between children and adolescents, "the truth is that a disproportionate number (if not most) of our images of what happens in adolescence are based on the American and European 'teenager' " (Brown & Larson, 2002, p. 2). Differences in how cultures determine when young people are mature enough to work, to have families, and to take on related autonomous responsibilities seem counter to finer distinctions in stages of childhood. Posing the question "What is child-hood if, in some places, 8-year old children fight adult wars, while in others, people in their late teens are still financially dependent on their parents?" underscores the need to consider international definitions of childhood and youth, as other scholars have argued convincingly in recent years (Nsamenang, 1999). Defining "youth" in terms of local activities requires such breadth.

Instead of relying primarily on chronological age or traditional definitions of socio-cognitive capacities, our project considers social relational processes. Facts of physical maturation like independent mobility and reproduction play a role in defining certain developmental milestones, but the physical and cognitive abilities required in different environments define how young people develop personal abilities in their everyday lives. Children's relative physical and cognitive immaturity are factors, for example, in their recruitment into armed conflict (chapter 1), their facile attachment to strangers (chapter 11), and their seemingly unreflective aggression (chapter 7). Nevertheless, the interactions that result from engaging in sophisticated social practices as soldiers, care-takers, or leaders also blur distinctions of cognitive abilities, like perspective-taking (chapters 3, 5, 8, 12). We know, for example, that some social roles that limit young people's development, such as early child-bearing and confronting social injustices, can also be catalysts to certain kinds of socio-cognitive development (Cross, 1991; Daiute, Buteau, & Rawlins, 2002; Turiel, 2002). For this reason, we use social role as a criterion for defining "youth" as beginning with independent physical movement beyond the home and making a transition to adulthood, characterized by economic independence and self-determination.

For those reasons, as a group, the authors of this book are committed to permeable and context-sensitive definitions of youth development. Nevertheless, we also refer to "children" or "adolescents" to maintain consistency with our prior research. Some authors make distinctions between children and adolescents as is appropriate to their context of study, while others use the terms "childhood" and "youth" interchangeably (as in this introduction).

Just as an international perspective leads us to extend the concept of "youth," we propose a broad definition of "conflict" to include physical and psychological acts of aggression and exclusion motivated by disagreement or competition among groups and individuals. Violence is not confined to physical acts or even death, because its origin may be in state control (Bourdieu, 1998), human emotions (Nordstrom, 2004), and worldview (Brett & McCallin, 1998). Other manifestations of youth conflict, such as intergroup and interpersonal fighting and exclusion, often occur in relation to tensions that lead to or result from wars or other power struggles. Youth conflict also occurs because of injustices, resulting in alienation, anger, and deprivation. Young people, moreover, may practice fighting, social exclusion, and other forms of conflict knowingly to achieve specific ends, or they may enact the intentions of other actors. Cultural practices of play, like sports, or rituals, like physically dangerous rites of passage, are not included in our definition, because they are recognized as normative in their context.

The examination of youth conflict as embedded in social systems also requires defining "society." Society refers to a wide range of affiliations, locations, and identities. Society is often defined in such geopolitical terms as a nation-state or municipality, its laws, values, and practices. Society also refers to communities sharing neighborhoods, public spaces, and institutions like schools, churches, hospitals, and social services (Dahbour, 2003). Societies may span location and time as they apply to ethnic, religious, and other identity groups. Societies may also form outside traditional boundaries, as with undocumented immigrants, the powerful elite, or insurgency groups. Youth involvement in armed conflict tends to occur in societies where political or economic transitions revolve around contested borders, competition for resources, and sovereignty, as in parts of the Balkans and the Middle East.

Youth conflict is thus a social practice—an activity characterized by circumstances, goals, expectations, behaviors, and discourses in particular contexts. It is difficult to think of a society that does not value social harmony, if for no other reason than to maintain the nation, and it is equally difficult to think of a society without conflict. Conflicts in the name of the state, like wars, police violence, or corporal punishment may be accepted as integral to cultural, economic, or political stability, while youth conflicts are often characterized as aberrant or antisocial (Turiel, 2002), even when youth participation in conflict tacitly preserves cultural values or state control. Characterizing youth conflict, instead, as a normative activity, then shifts the unit of analysis to the society. As stated aptly by Solis, "violence pre-exists individuals. . . . [It] has been available historically for individuals, groups, and nations to reach their own goals, such as the constitution or preservation of power" (chapter 17 here, p. 313).

Examining youth conflict as normative in social-relational systems, as we do in this book, is integral to the study of human development. Since conflicts often harm those involved, it is tempting to use medical metaphors like "recovery," "resilience," or "treatment." Nevertheless, if youth conflict is embedded in social practices rather than the result of bad character, misguided, or immature judgment, it seems appropriate to consider conflict, like uncontested social relations, as a developmental process. Conflict is a threat to human development because it causes physical or psychological harm, but uncontested relationships may also threaten the development of those whose rights and resources suffer in unjust peaceful situations.

Since conflicts often require immediate intervention, there tends to be little patience for theory, but this book is based on the idea that developmental theory is crucial for interpreting and intervening in youth conflict.

Developmental Analysis of Youth Conflict

Those who work in clinical, educational, and legal settings argue that theory is useful for crafting interpretations that do not demonize individual youth or societies and for creating interventions that support young people, especially when resources are limited and the conflicts are ongoing (Social Science Research

Council, 2001). Developmental theory progresses from a rich history of examining young people's interactions with the natural, social, and built environments.

In the twentieth century, developmental theorists and researchers explained that people understand the world and those around them differently during successive periods of a life course and that young people are not simply small or inferior adults (Piaget, 1968). Interestingly, however, scholars have found socio-historical analyses of human development to be increasingly important in accounting for the extreme diversity of living conditions within and across contexts (Bronfenbrenner, 1979; Vygotsky, 1978). Scholars concerned about the increasing inequalities revealed by globalization have, moreover, underscored the need to account for how political, economic and cultural factors play a role in individual development (Ong, 1999).

The case studies in this book draw on several major developmental theories that account for social-historical factors, albeit in different ways, to explain youth conflict. Authors draw on a variety of theories, including socio-cognitive developmental theory (Kohlberg, 1969), ecological theory (Bronfenbrenner, 1979), socio-historical theories (Bakhtin, 1986; Erikson, 1968; Vygotsky, 1978), sociomoral reasoning theory (Nucci, 2001; Turiel, 2002), sociological theory (Durkheim, 1968), and critical race/ethnicity theories (Cross, 1991; Matsuda, Lawrence, Delgado, & Crenshaw, 1993).

Extending these theories to explain youth conflict, we offer exemplars illustrating how a society lives in its youth. Since our goal is to broaden the analytic scale of youth conflict, we define development in relation to social history and social justice. Socio-historical analysis (Vygotsky, 1930/1994) explicitly examines development as a process whereby young people internalize the values and practices of social systems. The Russian psychologist Vygotsky explained:

> Every function in the child's cultural development appears twice: first, on the social level, and later, on the individual level; first between people (interpsychological), and then inside the child (intrapsychological). All higher functions originate as actual relations between human individuals. (1978, p. 57)

Grounded in dialectical materialism in this way, the primary unit of analysis in socio-historical theory is activity, represented in discourse, action, and other symbolic relations. Likewise, experience, personality, and thought are explored as social-relational processes rather than as capacities belonging to any single individual (Leont'ev, 1978). According to one theorist presenting a chapter in this book, major sources of conflict, disagreement, and struggle stem from the moral, social, and personal judgments people apply to their existing social conditions (Turiel, chapter 5 here).

The Interdependence of Youth and Society

The chapters in this book explain how youth and society are interdependent. Across a wide range of diverse international scenes, authors offer images of young people as complex intersubjective beings, as individuals who embody the sociopolitical dynamics of their communities and nations, yet whose activities can transform conflict and, eventually, their societies. A child may be given a gun or the name of someone to mistrust, but what the child does with the gun and feelings shared by adults can change the activity and meaning of war.

Our inquiry is, thus, at once devoted to understanding particular circumstances so as not to judge them by external standards and, at the same time, devoted to identifying broader social forces that enable and limit actors and actions in those circumstances. This process of analyzing across scales of activity is similar to that of other researchers seeking justice-sensitive explanations for problematic behavior by oppressed groups (Smith, 1992). By sampling across the personal, interpersonal, and societal scales of conflict, we interpret "the production and reproduction of daily life . . . to resist oppression and exploitation at a higher scale" (Smith, 2000, p. 60). In other words, shifting the analytic gaze beyond individual youth, we are in a better position to identify the foundational and aggravating circumstances of communities, nations, and international dynamics and to avoid blaming individual youth or their families for social problems created originally beyond their personal spheres of activity. Our purpose is not to create universal principles or to absolve young people of responsibility but to reveal processes obscured by examinations focusing on any single scale—global or local.

Some authors of this book locate the causes and effects of youth conflict in political and economic factors. Youth conflict is situated in power struggles to address extreme economic inequality (chapters 4, 11, 15, 16), the globalization of labor (chapters 15, 17), the socialization of youth to assist in armed conflicts (chapter 1), and intergenerational transmission of intergroup conflict (chapters 6, 7, 8). In addition to shifting the analytic focus of youth conflict from the individual to the state, these case studies show how young people's subjective experiences reproduce and transform local social histories (chapter 12).

Some of the case studies offer new concepts of psycho-social interdependence, such as community trauma (chapters 10, 14), undocumented identity (chapter 17), collective memory loss (chapter 3), youth critique (chapter 5), and transformation of society (chapters 1, 5, 12,17). Ukeje summarizes this analytic perspective, as it applies to his case study in Nigeria:

> Understanding the different logics that drive youth militancy and violence therefore requires an acknowledgment of the complex dynamics that young people are daily confronted with—both from within and outside of their immediate domain—and an understanding of how they de/construct these realities and social circumstances by engaging and negotiating with the Nigerian State and multinational oil companies for better opportunities. (chapter 16, pp. 293–294)

The interdependence of youth and society is, moreover, a two-way process. While it is common for psychological or sociological theories of development to examine social reproduction—the influence of society on youth—the case studies in this book also describe adaptive and transformative activities by young people in the face of social disruption, turmoil, and personal tragedy.

These case studies show that when young people think and act in ways consistent with their home cultures, they develop new subjectivities in response to the circumstances and people in their everyday lives. Especially in dynamic conflicts related to injustices, young people's thoughts and actions transform as well as reproduce the ways of the land. Children's identification of injustices (Turiel, 2002), creative uses of cultural genres to achieve social and personal goals (Daiute, 2004b), and personal motivations that lead activities (Stetsenko & Arievitch, 2004) are but a few concepts scholars have proposed to explain young people's agency in the face of historically powerful social and cultural structures.

Such mutual interaction between society and individuals is expressed poignantly in stressful and life-challenging situations where young people's desire for meaningful social connection may lead them into armed conflict, street life, or ethnic gangs. These participations may be at odds with young people's ultimate developmental interests but provide them with opportunities, at least in the short term, to assume some control over their lives and to have some influence on social history. As explained by Sandra, a child soldier in the New People's Army in the Philippines:

> If I have the chance, I want to go to college and study something related to what I did as a medic in the NPA—I was good at what I did, I even used to operate on those who were shot . . . Mama asked me why I wanted to stay with the NPA. I told her that I wanted to experience life as an NPA . . . Back then, I wasn't afraid of dying. . . . At least I had a chance to tell my Mama the reasons why I was going. (chapter 1, p. 35)

Sandra, like other youth, explains how she transformed war activity into an activity to develop skills, identity, and a future direction. This explanation does not justify the exploitation of children but suggests the possibility of youth agency. Ironically, youth participation in civic affairs has only recently become a major focus of developmental research (Sherrod, 2004; Youniss et al., 2002).

Examining youth conflict as an interdependent dynamic of youth and society also reveals the dilemma of youth.

The Dilemma of Youth

When we examine youth conflict as a societal process rather than as a problem of immature, confused, or troubled young people, we expose the dilemma of youth. This dilemma occurs when societies separate their young to protect and prepare them as they mature yet take advantage of youths' separate status to engage them in activities that serve society.

In many contexts, youth is an exception in the life course. During this exceptional phase between the dependence of infancy and the independence of adulthood, young people are defined as emergent and inferior, whether explicitly or implicitly. Although conceptions of youth differ across contexts, most nations and cultures reserve some time between a child's achievement of physical mobility and social independence and his or her economic independence and civic participation as an adult. Circumstances of this liminal era differ by gender, class, and other factors, although most societies provide some period for protection, nurturance, and preparation (Daiute, 2004a). During this exceptional period, young people may be precious, but they are also less than full citizens.

The dilemma of youth is that this separate phase can be limiting as well as nurturing. When separated by their status as minors, young people may receive protections like the right to education or freedom from forced labor, but they are also excluded from participation in citizenship activities, like voting, that exert some determination over the future of the society. In the separate phase when youth are excluded from certain rights and visibility, they are also available for exploitation. Assumptions about their innocence or inability to understand the complexities of social life may unwittingly lead to young people's exclusion from activities where they could contribute or learn. When excluded from full participation as citizens, young people can also become tools or scapegoats for others' purposes. While young people in economically struggling nations may be recruited into wars and illicit activities, like drug trafficking, those in economically rich nations may be recruited as symbols of achievement or blame for troubles that challenge the powerful status quo.

In addition, although young people may be protected, at least in principle, they also serve society (Daiute, 2004a). International efforts to protect young people, like the UN Convention on the Rights of the Child (CRC) (1989) seem to help the plight of some children in extreme circumstances, but efforts like the CRC also underscore the dilemma that separating youth even for protection can also allow for exploitation because the protection exists in the absence of full citizenship rights (Daiute, 2004a). Chapters in this book explain how youth serve functions that adults cannot or do not want to serve, such as being warriors on the front lines of battle and as carriers of ethnic mistrust, hatred, humiliation, or other social exclusions. In contexts where migration or extreme class divisions create conflicts of interest, official or unofficial racism filters to the younger generations, who may express in public discrimination what their parents think is reserved for the privacy of home.

This book also reveals several important ironies of conflict, related to the dilemma of youth. One irony emerging across some of the chapters is that although conflicts often have negative consequences, participation in conflicts can allow young people self-determination and social determination that mainstream institutions like school and government do not. Young people's participation in armed conflicts in the Philippines and Nigeria, for example, afford roles such as medics or messengers, appearing to support development. Another irony is that although youth are often seen as problematic forces in conflicts, young people can express tolerance and flexibility toward historical adversaries and can cooperate toward a collective future.

Excerpts from case studies of youth conflict in Nigeria, the Philippines, Bosnia, Croatia, Germany, South Africa, and New York City illustrate ironies emerging from studying youth conflict as a social system. For example, in very different contexts in Nigeria, the Philippines, and Colombia, young people's lack of resources, maturity, or power makes them vulnerable for recruitment into armed conflict, but their participation in such activities can also lead to increased political awareness and desire for self-determination. Akinwumi reports that in Nigeria, although many youth had joined ethnic militias as a traditional means of survival and identity, 75% of ethnic militia members came to recognize a different source of their problems in the "frustration resulting from lack of jobs and the determination to rectify the injustice perpetrated by Nigerian ruling elites, whether military or civilian, against the masses" (chapter 4, p. 80).

Sta. Maria describes a situation in the Philippines where armed factions in rebellion against the formal government have recruited poor and abandoned children in rural areas to fight with them, which also provided sustenance, a community, rustic shelter, and various conflict-related jobs. Working with NGOs in the area, Sta. Maria reports that violence, conflict, and participation are infused with practices of self-determination as well as limitations, as some children were involved in armed conflict, while others, according to group leaders, acted as messengers, received training in self-defense, and worked on medical teams and in other noncombat activities in the camp.

Another kind of irony emerged from situations where the different experiences of adults and children in local conflicts reversed characteristic sociocognitive capacities. Across two very different contexts, adults' conflict-related knowledge and pain led to reductions in their understanding and reflection, while children sought out information about conflicts and offered explanations about how this information could help them and their society. Based on interviews with children and their parents in two areas of Bosnia and Croatia, for example, Freedman and Abazovic report that both Serb and Croatian children said they wanted to know more about what happened in the war, while their parents wanted to forget the past. One parent said:

> Terrible things happened in Vukovar, horrible things. . . . I have been through a lot and my children have been through a lot only because we are Serbs. That was a dreadful time and I really don't want to talk about it. (chapter 3, p. 65)

The children, in contrast, expressed a need to know; one Croat student told the researchers: "The older ones know what the war was about, but younger generations don't know anything about how this war came about, what were its causes. I believe we should talk about it more" (chapter 3, pp. 65–66). Far away in New York City, children aged 7 through 11 who were identifying with diverse ethnic groups that had a history of conflict in the city and the nation were interested in exploring the feelings and resulting actions of individuals in conflicts, while most of the teachers emphasized resolution, sometimes interrupting discussions of conflict that might have led to greater acquisition of social strategies and mutual understanding (chapter 12 here).

Another irony emerging across the case studies in this book is that institutions designed to serve youth can perpetuate the problems, perhaps because they identify causes in young people rather than in society. In his study of the historical and personal circumstances leading to the orientations of neo-Nazi youth, Edelstein observes:

> In various Western societies . . . recognition and humiliation are woven into the fabric of pedagogy and instruction. They are aspects of teachers' and students' roles, an inevitable part of instruction, of grades and feedback, tests and exercises. What is the involuntary role of the school in development and what is the voluntary influence exerted through grades and the evaluation culture of the school? (chapter 2, pp. 45–46)

Similarly, Higson-Smith found that, while individuals may be willing to move beyond the past, community effects can limit social reorganization because "individuals [are] reluctant to be seen with people and agencies from beyond the community. This isolates the community from important developmental opportunities (community effects). Where this situation exists in numerous communities, social services, including health, welfare, education, and security, become compromised (societal effects)" (chapter 10, p. 184).

In summary, insights from examinations of youth participation in conflict systems echo a paradox observed by Vygotsky, a leader of socio-historical theory:

> the greatest historical paradox of human development [is] that this biological transformation of the human type which is mainly achieved through science, social education, and the rationalization of the entire way of life, does not represent a prerequisite, but instead is a result of the social liberation of man. (1930/1994, p. 183)

By shifting the analytic lens from individual youth to society, we examine youth conflict as normative, thereby also shifting responsibility to social institutions.

Organization of the Book

The chapters in this book are organized into four parts. Part I focuses on psycho-social processes in youth conflict; part II examines the dynamics of conflict across groups of youth within a society; part III presents research seeking to understand youth conflict in the context of interventions; and the chapters in part IV consider broader international processes.

The introduction to each part offers more detail about its case studies and common foci and insights. The editors' epilogue summarizes the major insights of the book about the social-historical dynamics of youth conflict and implications for future research.

Psycho-social Processes in Youth Conflict

The first five chapters zoom in on the psychological dynamics of social histories of conflict, as expressed in young people's thoughts, feelings, and reasoning processes. Grounded in theories of anomie (Durkheim, 1968), cultural meaning (Geertz, 1973), socio-historical discourse (Bakhtin, 1986; Vygotsky, 1978), and sociomoral reasoning, these chapters explain how young people's psychosocial processes echo and contest broader political dynamics and, in turn, guide their perception and action. The interdependence of youth in society is reflected in these detailed essays explaining how young people internalize and transform social histories. Across dramatically different contexts in the Philippines, Germany, Bosnia, Croatia, Nigeria, the United States, and Arab countries, these chapters explain how political and economic instability operates in the everyday subjective experiences of young people.

The chapters in part I explain how young people as a group perceive and respond to diverse circumstances in war, ethnic gangs, postwar reconstruction, and injustices emerging in conflicts beyond any limits or capacities inherent in childhood. The authors of these chapters offer detailed explanations of cycles of humiliation and alienation (chapter 2), youth agency (chapters 1, 4, 2, 7), longing for historical memory (chapter 3), and reasoning about social injustice (chapter 7).

Imagining and Living With the Other

While the chapters in part 1 consider youth as a group, the chapters in part 2 focus on the dynamics of intergroup conflict. Consistent with the examination of conflict as a social system, the chapters in this section identify how young people internationalize and enact divisions in society. Therefore, the authors in this book examine what may appear to be interpersonal issues and aggressions as social processes based in affiliations, such as national, religious, or sexual identities; related prejudices; or cross-generational values.

The group conflicts occur across religious and national identities in Israel (chapter 6), sexual identities in the United States (chapter 8), power groups in Korea (chapter 7), and generations in China (chapter 9). Young people may not be aware of the ethnic, sexual, generational, socioeconomic class, or other identifications that divide them, but society's implicit or explicit reification of groups via unequal practices promotes divisive orientations, as in the case of violence against gay and lesbian youth, women, or nondominant minorities.

Practices of Conflict and Engagement

The chapters in part III echo some of the previous analyses of psycho-social processes and intergroup conflict, but the primary organizing factor of this part is the method of studying young people's conflict knowledge and behavior in the context of practices to promote peace. Some of the interventions presented in these chapters occurred in the aftermath of revolution, others in the midst of years of chronic ethnic, class, or other conflict. These chapters offer insights about youth conflict in the context of interventions to promote peace, like civic participation in Colombia (chapter 14), violence prevention activities in the United States (chapter 12), clinical treatment programs in South Africa (chapter 10), and traditional healing practices in Mozambique and Angola (chapter 13).

Research on youth conflict in the context of practices designed to promote peace highlights the difficulty of any definitive distinction between war and peace; as noted by Nordstrom, "the image of the complete battle, separate from civilian life around it, is antiquated, unreal. . . . So while the study of violence may begin with the direct and immediate carnage, it shouldn't end there" (2004, pp. 58, 60).

Global Processes Involving Youth

The chapters in part IV explicitly address issues beyond the national scale, issues of globalization that are increasingly coming into view in the twenty-first century. The global dynamics across the studies reported in these three chapters span Africa and the United States, Mexico and the United States, and Nigeria and a myriad other locations interested in the oil-rich Niger Delta region. It is not surprising that the United States would be involved across these sites, given its dominance in international markets and military activities. These chapters explain how groups like Mexicans in the United States are exploited for economic gains yet considered "illegal" (chapter 17); how institutions like the popular press and police perpetuate and operate on the myth that black men commit the majority of violence in the United States (chapter 15); and how economic influences far away can transform poverty into ethnic battles that could otherwise be relegated to history (chapter 16).

In addition to organizing the parts in terms of those areas of focus, the chapters in each part present a wide variety of geographic contexts represented. The order of chapters in part I, for example, allows readers to delve into issues of youth conflict first in the Philippines, followed by Germany, the Balkans, Nigeria, and then Middle Eastern contexts. Spanning the globe in this way, as do parts II and III, highlights diverse manifestations of youth conflict and researcher and participant voices expressing those manifestations. Finally, the chapters in part IV assume transnational stances from the perspective of various diasporas.

Readers

This book is designed for readers who work with young people, who create institutions or negotiations for their benefit, who want to understand the challenges facing young people, or who are curious about them. We offer explanations supported by theory and research to communicate to other researchers, educators, and clinicians working across disciplines and contexts of practice. Scholars of international relations, political science, and globalization may also find the book informative in the case studies foregrounding young people's voices, while those in psychology, anthropology, sociology, and education may find new insights in the geopolitical and economic analyses. All are likely to be informed by the diversity of accounts in their local detail, and, we hope, the cross-cutting themes presented in this introduction, the part introductions, and the epilogue. In this process, we ask our readers to suspend belief that youth is a rebellious and irrational stage of life and to consider with us forces that position youth in this way. We attempt to build on previous research in creative ways yet have been serious about scholarly acknowledgments. We hope, in the end, that the case studies in this book foster collective consciousness about youth conflicts across the globe and generate new insights for future analyses of local conflicts, global interdependencies, and interventions. This book is designed to present new ways of thinking about youth conflict and development via a series of case studies, but in addition to this discussion, we offer information about contexts of practice that can support young people and their participation in society.

References

Apfel, R. J., & Simon, B. (1996). *Minefields in their hearts: The mental health of children in war.* New Haven: Yale University Press.

Astor, R. A. (1994). Children's moral reasoning about family and peer violence: The role of provocation and retribution. *Child Development, 65,* 1054–1067.

Bakhtin, J. J. (1986). *Speech genres and other late essays.* Austin: University of Texas Press.

Bellamy, C. (2000). *The state of the world's children, 2000: A vision for the twenty-first century.* New York: UNESCO.

Beykont, Z. (1997a). *Dismantling language-based oppression in educational institutions.* Cambridge, MA: MIT Press.

Beykont, Z. (1997b). Refocusing school-language policy discussion. In W. K. Cummins & N. F. McGinn (Eds.), *International handbook of education and development: Preparing schools, students, and nations for the twenty-first century* (pp. 263–283). New York: Pergamon.

Bourdieu, P. (1998). *Practical reason: On the theory of action.* Stanford: Stanford University Press.

Brett, R., & McCallin, M. (1998). *Children: The invisible soldiers.* Sweden: Radda Barnen.

Bronfenbrenner, U. (1979). *The ecology of human development: Experiments by nature and design.* Cambridge, MA: Harvard University Press.

Brown, B. B., & Larson, R. W. (2002). The kaleidoscope of adolescence: Experiences of the world's youth at the beginning of the twenty-first century. In B. B. Brown, R. W. Larson, & T. S. Saraswathi (Eds.), *The world's youth: Adolescence in eight regions of the globe* (pp. 1–20). New York: Cambridge University Press.

Brown, B. B., Larson, R. W., & Saraswathi, T. S. (2002). *The world's youth: Adolescence in eight regions of the globe.* New York: Cambridge University Press.

Cross, W. E., Jr. (1991). *Shades of black: Diversity in African-American identity.* Philadelphia: Temple University Press.

Dahbour, O. (2003). *Illusion of the peoples: A critique of national self-determination.* New York: Lexington Books.

Daiute, C. (2004a). *Advocacy and developmental theory.* Paper Presented at the 34th Meeting of the Jean Piaget Society Conference, Toronto, Canada, June.

Daiute, C. (2004b). Creative uses of cultural genres. In C. Daiute & C. Lightfoot (Eds.), *Narrative analysis: Studying the development of individuals in society* (pp. 111–133). Thousand Oaks, CA: Sage.

Daiute, C., Buteau, E., & Rawlins, C. (2002). Social relational wisdom: Developmental diversity in children's written narratives about social conflict. *Narrative Inquiry, 11*(2), 1–30.

Durkheim, E. (1968). *The division of labor.* New York: Free Press.

Earls, F., & Carlson, M. (1999). Children at the margins of society. *New Directions in Child and Adolescent Development, 85,* 71–82.

Elliott, D. S., Hamburg, B. A., & Williams, K. R. (1998). *Violence in American schools.* New York: Cambridge University Press.

Erikson, E. (1968). *Identity, youth, and crisis.* New York: Norton.

Garbarino, J. (1999). *Lost boys: Why our sons turn violent and how we can save them.* New York: Free Press.

Geertz, C. (1973). *The interpretation of cultures.* New York: Basic Books.

Giroux, H. A. (1996). *Fugitive cultures: Race, violence, and youth.* New York: Routledge.

Hart, R. A. (1999). *Children's participation: The theory and practice of including young citizens in community development and environmental care.* New York: NY UNICEF.

Higson-Smith, C. (2002). *Supporting communities affected by violence: A casebook for South Africa.* Oxford, UK: Oxfam.

Kohlberg, L. (1969). Stage and sequence: The cognitive-developmental approach to socialization. In D. Goslin (Ed.), *Handbook of socialization theory and research* (pp. 347–480). Chicago: Rand McNally.

Leont'ev, A. N. (1978) *Activity, consciousness, and personality.* Englewood Cliffs, NJ: Prentice-Hall.

Machal, G. (1996). *Impact of armed conflict on children.* New York: United Nations Children's Fund.

Matsuda, M. J., Lawrence, C. R., III, Delgado, R., & Crenshaw, K. W. (1993). *Words that wounded: Critical race theory, assaultive speech, and the First Amendment.* Boulder, CO: Westview.

Nordstrom, C. (2004). *Shadows of war: Violence, power, and international profiteering in the twenty-first Century.* Berkeley: University of California Press.

Nsamenang, A. B. (1999). Eurocentric image of childhood in the context of the world's cultures. *Human Development, 42* (3).

Nucci, L. (2001). *Education in the moral domain.* Cambridge, UK: Cambridge University Press.

Ong, A. (1999). *Flexible citizenship: The cultural logics of transnationality.* Durham, NC: Duke University Press.

Piaget, J. (1968). *Six psychological studies.* New York: Vintage Press.

Smith, N. (1992). Contours of a spatialized politics: Homeless vehicles and the production of geographical scale. *Social Text, 33,* 55–81.

Sherrod, L. (2004, June). *Children's civic participation.* Paper presented at the annual meeting of the Jean Piaget Society, Toronto.

Social Science Research Council. (2001). *Rethinking social science research on the developing world in the twenty-first century: Proceedings sponsored by the International Pre-dissertation Fellowship Program of the SSRC and the American Council of Learned Societies.* New York: Author.

Stetsenko, A., & Arievitch, I. (2004). The self in cultural-historical activity theory: Reclaiming the unity of social and individual dimensions of human development. *Theory and Psychology, 14*(4), 475–503.

Torney-Purta, J., Schwille, J., & Amadeo, J. A (Eds.). (1999). *Civic education across countries: Twenty-four national case studies from the IEA Civic Education project.* Amsterdam: International Association for the Evaluation of Educational Achievement.

Turiel, E. (2002). *The culture of morality.* New York: Cambridge University Press.

United Nations General Assembly. (1989, November 17). *Adoption of a convention on the rights of the child.* New York: United Nations.

Vygotsky, L. S. (1978). *Mind in society.* Cambridge, MA: Harvard University Press.

Vygotsky, L. S. (1994). The socialist alteration of man. In R. Van Der Veer & J. Valsiner (Eds.), *The Vygotsky reader* (pp. 175–184). Malden, MA: Blackwell. (Original work published in 1930)

Widom, C. S. (1989). Does violence beget violence? A critical examination of the literature. *Psychological Bulletin, 106*(1), 3–28.

Youniss, J., Bales, S., Christmas-Best, V., Diversi, M., McLaughlin, M., Silbereisen, R. (2002). Youth civic engagement in the twenty-first century. In R. Larson, B. B. Brown, & J. Mortimer (Eds.), *Adolescents' preparation for the future: Perils and promise* (pp.121–149). Ann Arbor, MI: Society for Research on Adolescence.

PART I

PSYCHO-SOCIAL PROCESSES
IN YOUTH CONFLICT

Introduction to Part I

The myths of adults as protectors and children as innocents are difficult to
sustain under such conditions, but continue to be told and retold in part as
an attempt to conceal the ugly . . . reality in many communities.

—Mamphele Ramphele, South African scholar and leader

In this brief comment, Mamphele Ramphele exposes the powerful myth of
childhood innocence—a myth held in people's values across cultures, a myth
that preserves the possibility of innocence as an ideal, yet a myth that protects
adults. The authors of the first five chapters in this part write, instead, about
how young people who are involved in conflicts, begun by those who would
protect them, think, feel, and express their wisdom about conflicts—those in
which they participate and those in the society where they live. By highlighting psycho-social processes emerging from histories of conflict, these authors
offer different insights related to the dilemma of protection and innocence that
Ramphele describes.

These chapters focus on psycho-social processes wrought by diverse socio-
historical circumstances of conflict. As mentioned in the introduction, young
people's psycho-social processes echo societal formulations of events and relationships. Psycho-social dimensions of youth conflict are also subjective responses to histories of conflict. The psycho-social dynamics emerging from
analyses presented in these chapters include self-determination, agency, alienation, longing for historical memory, moral reasoning, and resistance to injustice. These authors describe how young people internalize conflicts, and these
descriptions bring to life the subjective toll of conflict and motivational possibilities for development through or in spite of conflict.

Drawing on theories that posit the development of individual youth as interdependent with the development of society, the authors of these chapters

recount histories in terms of their effects on young people's lives. A history of civic conflict, for example, strips children in communities with few material resources of the social and emotional supports they need for healthy development, thrusting them into situations where survival organizes their daily activities and relationships (chapters 1, 4). The humiliation of a generation of economically and politically marginalized adults is, in another context, then turned on youth, who respond with anger and bitterness toward others and themselves (chapter 2). Fear and resentment in the aftermath of war lead to repression that haunts the postwar generation, who endure the pain of ignorance and the burden of imagining a future (chapter 3). Recognizing their unequal status and opportunities, women and minorities in other situations become critical of society and work against it in spite of personal risks (chapter 5).

The Case Studies

In chapter 1, Madelene Sta. Maria foregrounds young Filipinos' subjectivities of vulnerability and agency in the context of the recent history of insurgency struggles against the official government in the Philippines. Sta. Maria explains how the lack of social and emotional supports in the face of challenging economic and political circumstances has led to the participation of children as young as 11 in insurgency groups. Based on archival and interview research, she describes the scenario of vulnerability for youth living in poverty and, in many cases, on their own because their parents are dead or away from home in order to find work or fight in the insurgency for other reasons. A highlight of this chapter is the author's analysis, from young people's perspectives, of how insurgency groups offer them sustenance, social connection, and jobs as combatants, couriers, or medics. As Sta. Maria points out, the dilemma is that their participation in such dangerous and uncertain activities locks young people in a "continuous present," while, at the same time, the skills they develop from this participation can become means toward different pathways in their lives. She concludes by underscoring the importance of governmental, nongovernmental organization (NGO), and family leadership in paying attention to the power of the insurgency groups over the lives of children at risk.

In chapter 2, Wolfgang Edelstein offers insights into the psycho-social processes that orient right-wing culture among youth in postunification Germany. Edelstein describes historical processes that affect political and economic structures, family patterns, and related cultural orientations and shape the psychological states, especially of disenfranchised fathers, and in turn their children. Focusing on contemporary interactions of family dynamics and adolescent identity formation, Edelstein identifies "anomie" as a behavioral attitude that constitutes a right-wing rebellion against prevailing social, moral, and political norms. Filling a gap in the analysis of youth conflict, Edelstein makes an important contribution by explaining the problems of modernization in Western social experiences that can cause great damage to young people and to the ongoing development of the society. Given the increasingly numerous nations that are in similarly dramatic transitions since the final decades of the twentieth century, Edelstein's lucid analysis brings to light a genesis of negative psycho-social processes that point toward a need for social change for the benefit of all involved.

In chapter 3, Sarah Warshauer Freedman and Dino Abazovic make it a priority of research and practice to understand how young people's experiences of past wars and ongoing violence might relate to their potential role in reconstructing society after decades of shifting national boundaries in the Balkans. These authors offer poignant quotations from interviews to illuminate the longing of these young people for historical memory in the face of adults' attempts to forget a destructive and painful past. Freedman and Abazovic draw on historical and interview research to document the feelings of apathy, frustration, and desire for knowledge among young people aged 14–16 whom they interviewed in the towns of Mostar in Bosnia and Herzegovina and Vukovar in Croatia, where inter-group tensions continue. Focusing on the psycho-social process of "ideological becoming," Freedman and Abazovic describe a cultural malaise that, regardless of national affiliation or geographic home, young people internalize, feeling abandoned by their parents and teachers and desperately seeking wisdom to orient them toward the future.

In chapter 4, Olayemi Akinwumi recounts the involvement and increasing social consciousness of young people within the history of violence in the Niger Delta oil region. After considering the factors responsible for youth conflict in the country, Akinwumi draws on his research, using the methods of observation, individual and group interviews, and questionnaires, to explain how young Nigerians struggle economically in a land where an elite and the multinational corporations are getting rich while the youth harm each other in violent conflicts around historical ethnoreligious divisions. He offers detail to demonstrate how young people become entangled in the legacy of ethnoreligious conflict, political maneuvers, and economic issues. Underscoring the desire for self-determination he found among the participants in his study, Akinwumi concludes that state leadership should involve young people in creating employment policies that directly affect them instead of treating youth as mere objects to fulfill others' interests.

In a somewhat different mode, Elliot Turiel, in chapter 5, offers a theoretical perspective on social and moral development relevant to discussions of youth conflict and violence. Rejecting the idea that cultures have singular integrated patterns of moral functioning, Turiel explains that a major source of conflict is social hierarchy characterized by dominant and subordinate positions, such as the positions of women and ethnic minority groups across many societies. Turiel reviews research examining conflicts across social developmental domains, in terms of the development of understandings of morality (harm, justice, and rights), social conventions, and personal prerogatives or entitlements. These categories of moral judgment are psycho-social practices that occur across cultures as sources of conflict, disagreement, and struggle. An example of the utility of this theory is its explanation, for example, for why children who are identified as aggressive make moral judgments similar to those of other children but differ in their justifications about retaliation. Turiel also considers examples of group conflicts, including acts of violence, stemming from social hierarchies and cultural practices, such as acts of conflict and resistance by women in contexts in India and Iran where women's freedom of movement and self-determination are much more restricted than men's.

Social Histories of Conflict Internalized by Youth

These chapters offer historical accounts to explain the foundations and circumstances of young people's experiences in local conflicts. These historical accounts foreground forces salient to young people's involvement and create the social relational motivations for psycho-social orientations. Edelstein's analysis reaches back 60 years to World War II Germany and the aftermath as integral to the social orientations of young people and their families in the present time. Akinwumi recounts the interconnected histories of ethnic identities with class divisions as a function of economic domination by oil companies based out the Niger Delta. Sta. Maria presents the recent local history of intranational insurgency movements in the Philippines. Freedman and Abazovic review the conflict history in the Balkans in particular over the past 60 years.

The authors integrate historical methods with psychological techniques like interviewing and surveying to offer their psycho-social analyses. Sta. Maria and Freedman and Abazovic interviewed young people, offering insights as well from ethnographic observations of daily life in camps and schools. Akinwumi used a survey to expand his observations and historical analysis. Edelstein drew on archival research of contemporary youth activity from journalistic accounts to intersect with his longer term historical account. Turiel reviews research supporting his arguments and includes examples from that research.

The authors describe psycho-social processes as developed in these different social histories. To forge this connection, several authors draw on ecological theory (Bronfenbrenner, 1979), which describes how the subjective experiences of individuals and groups are related to broader political and cultural institutions, referred to as "microsystems" and "mesosystems." Across contexts in the Philippines and in Nigeria, Sta. Maria and Akinwumi, in separate chapters, explain how participation in different aspects of insurgency movements or militias may begin for young people as a means of survival but over time become contexts of meaning and development. Sta. Maria offers examples of self-determination out of the labor of conflict, while Akinwumi explains how young militia group members in Nigeria came to realize a struggle for determination of local natural resources for the benefit of the local people.

In contrast, identifying the challenges of stagnation in conflict, Edelstein and Freedman and Abazovic, in separate studies, describe historical processes that exclude youth and the danger of such exclusion. Describing anomie, Edelstein recounts how youth have been alienated through a social history of political-economic disruption, disintegration of individual lives, and humiliation, seeding resentful anger. Drawing on social developmental theories,

Edelstein describes how youth then lash out at their contemporaries as targets of their alienation. Freedman and Abazovic discuss the tensions between repressed and desired memories for social histories of war.

Turiel offers a theoretical context for specific psycho-social processes of moral reasoning that young people apply consistently in the face of injustices.

Consistent with their focus on psycho-social processes motivating and resulting from youth conflict, these authors suggest a variety of strategies for promoting invigorated social spaces for development. These strategies include increased planning by families, community organizations, and the government to involve young people productively in society (Sta. Maria), sustained efforts to create youth employment programs (Akinwumi), the reintroduction of curricula about recent wars and the importance of parents' participation to deal with their painful memories in part by answering children's questions (Freedman and Abazovic), increased understanding of how young people's motivations are negatively affected by modernization, and supporting conversations across institutions affecting social and personal domains (Edelstein).

These psycho-social processes identified in conflict activities extend beyond perspective-taking, which has been the primary socio-cognitive process in conflict-related research from a developmental perspective (rather than from medical or psychodynamic perspectives, which emphasize illness or character disorders) (Elliott, Hamburg, & Williams, 1998). For many years, developmental analyses of conflict have focused on individuals' abilities to understand and empathize with the perspectives of others, especially with adversaries, and, ultimately, to coordinate personal needs with those of others in terms of broader systems of justice (Elliott et al., 1998). Perspective-coordination is an important foundation for social relations, but the chapters in this section of the book identify diverse, context-specific psycho-social dynamics in real-life conflict situations.

Presenting young people's inner lives in the public realm in these ways exposes concealed realities—as Ramphele points out in the epigraph to this introduction. In the process, the representation of "adults as protectors and children as innocents" gradually transforms into a scene with adults and children collaborating to understand the past, themselves, and some possibilities for the future of their society.

References

Bronfenbrenner, U. (1979). *The ecology of human development*. Cambridge, MA: Harvard University Press.

Elliott, D. S., Hamburg, B. A., & Williams, K. R. (1998). *Violence in American schools*. New York: Cambridge University Press.

CHAPTER 1

Paths to Filipino Youth Involvement in Violent Conflict

MADELENE A. STA. MARIA

An interest in the study of youth in conflict arises from two interrelated concerns. One concern centers on the issue of how exposure to or participation in conflict situations can impair development by limiting capacities and resources of the individual for a satisfying emotional and social life. The other concern is about how violent conflict enveloping some of our youth's life today can limit future possibilities for more peaceful and cooperative relations within society (Larson, Wilson, Brown, Furstenberg, & Verma, 2002). The Abu Sayaff phenomenon in the Philippines, for example, could have been averted if researchers, government officials, and nongovernment authorities paid more attention to the Muslim youth exposed to and involved in the armed conflict in the country (Fatmawati Salapuddin, Bangsa Moro leader, personal communication, March 2002). Violent conflict is also said to put the development of young people at risk because these experiences

> deny a clear and predictable path to adulthood [and] throw . . . . the future into uncertainty, leaving the youth without a reliable vision or any confidence in whether they will get into adulthood and what skills are needed. (Larson, 2002, p. 17)

As a UNICEF study cautions, young people's social isolation, violence, diminished opportunities for education, as well as reduced economic potential, will have to be dealt with eventually as consequences of lost years of development due to participation in armed and violent conflict (Azarcon-De la Cruz, 2000).

This chapter examines the reasons for young people's involvement in armed conflict within the country's economic, political, and social contexts. Generally, it is the loss of support from social institutions, exacerbated by economic

29

and political conditions, that leads many of young people to engage in violent conflict activities. It is evident that through their participation in armed activities, youth may be provided with orientations to contribute to society, as they become equipped with the means for personal and group survival, which they perceive to be endangered by existing political and socioeconomic arrangements in society. Their participation, however, may lead to a loosening of the connections between the groups that influence their development (i.e., the family, peer groups, and the armed group). Participation in violence, conditioned by a fragmented and disrupted community life, can also lead to an inability to view the future in its diverse possibilities, thus stunting the young person's development.

The involvement of Filipino youth in violent situations is primarily found in their participation in the armed conflict between rebel movements—primarily the Moro Islamic Liberation Front (MILF), Moro National Liberation Front (MNLF), and New People's Army (NPA)—and the government.[1] Their involvement is likewise evident in the commission of crimes against property (e.g., theft and robbery) and against the person (e.g., homicide and rape) and in their participation in gang and fraternity wars. An attempt is made here to describe the situation of young people who are involved in conflict (specifically, armed conflict) through a review of selected literature and data collected from published and unpublished documents, and from initial interviews and correspondence with various representatives from relevant government and nongovernment agencies. These sources were used to identify the reasons and conditions that shape the participation of young people in violent activities. Likewise, an attempt is made to explore the possible implications for developmental theory.

Forms of Participation in Violence

The forms of young people's involvement in violence largely have been carved out from living in conditions of poverty and sociopolitical marginality. Data gathered in 1996 show a total of 1,380 young persons who were sentenced and detained all over the country (United Nations International Children's Fund [UNICEF], 1998). The youth offenders sampled in this study were predominantly male and had finished or were still at the elementary level of education. Dropping out of school was usually a result of financial difficulties, peer influence, and family problems. The majority of the youth offenders were living either with only one parent or with neither parent. These youth were not living with one or both parents for reasons such as: death of a parent, parents had to leave to work in another place, abandonment by parents, or young people had to leave home to work elsewhere. Most of the youth offenders come from low-income families. The occupations of parents (e.g., as farmers, fishermen, laborers, carpenters, dressmakers, laundry women, or house help) provide young people with an impoverished environment, offering very little prospect for social or economic advancement for the young person and his or her family.

Moreover, a large percentage of the youth offenders were drug users or were addicted to alcohol. Most of them were also gang members, and the influence of peers was evident in the commission of crimes.

A more recent nationwide report ("Situation Analysis," 2003) shows that the profile of the youth offender has remained unchanged. In this report, it was found that the Filipino youth in conflict with the law is usually male, between the ages of 14 to 17 years, a member of a large family, and exposed to drugs and gang influence. The National Council for Social Development (NCSD) reported in 1994 that most of the crimes committed by young people were those against property, which they tended to commit in association with peers or relatives. Offenses against the person and sexual offenses, on the other hand, tended to be perpetrated by one person alone. Many of these youth offenders were members of a peer group gang and had spent most of their time living in the streets.

Recent information on the number of captured or surrendered youth involved in armed conflict (i.e., recruited into the NPA, MILF, or ASG) reveal a total of 135 youth (Office of the Deputy Chief of Staff for Civil Military Operations, Department of National Defense, personal communication, February 11, 2003). In any given community influenced by the rebel groups, an estimated 10–30% are drafted as soldiers (Cagoco-Guiam, 2002). The earliest age of recruitment also is said to be 11 years, and the mean age of a youth combatant is 14 years. Within the rebel movement itself, most members are quite young. Reports, for example, show that the NPA guerrillas are generally aged 16 to 25 years (Mermet & Quere, 2000).

Legal measures have been adopted and formal agreements have been entered to halt the engagement of young people as soldiers. Both the Philippine government and the National Democratic Front, the political body of the NPA, signed a comprehensive agreement on the respect for human rights and International Humanitarian Law. In this agreement, both parties are to ensure the physical and moral integrity of women and children, and to prevent the participation of children in hostilities (Mermet & Quere, 2000).

These agreements and provisions, however, have not produced their intended results. A study done by the International Committee of the Red Cross in 1998 found that the NPA and MILF have recruited children for combat on the basis of reports given by Muslim guerrillas, teachers, and government militiamen (cited in Mermet & Quere, 2000). Military estimates also show that in some regions of the Philippines, 14% of the NPA fighters are children, and that in at least six areas in the country, children form 20–25% of new NPA recruits (Makinano, 2001).

There were similar reports about the MILF and ASG recruiting children to participate in their armed encounters. Mermet and Quere (2000) wrote of teachers in the Islamic schools who were said to be aware that their male students were being recruited to join the MILF. The use of minors from the ages 13 to 16 by the ASG has likewise been confirmed by the military in its various encounters with the group (Makinano, 2001).

Armed groups have denied these forms of participation by young people.

The MILF, for example, has admitted that they have young soldiers but claim that these youth are on reserve, kept confined in their camps, and given schooling (Mermet & Quere, 2000). The MILF claims that the students receive training not for combat but for purposes of self-defense (Makinano, 2001). According to Makinano, the ASG has likewise claimed that the group recruits minors not for combat, but there are reports that reveal that the group would use these children as human shields or as hostages.

Makinano narrates that in the NPA, a youth soldier may be given the position of officer (e.g., liaison officer, commanding officer, squadron leader, or platoon leader), combatant, or assistant with support tasks (e.g., cooking, delivering messages, or spying). In the battlefield, the young person may also be used as a shield to deter military attacks or may be asked to recover weapons from dead soldiers in the field. Young people may also serve in medical missions or as couriers in local areas, through a system called *Pasa Bilis* (literally, "quick pass"), where children are assigned at relay stations to deliver messages or orders scribbled on pieces of paper until the message reaches its destination. Children are also assigned to collect revolutionary taxes from members of the community.

Mermet and Quere (2000) recount that nongovernment organization members working in the conflict areas claim that an MILF policy allows children at the age of 12 years to undergo military training. Training usually occurs in madrasas (religious schools) and in camps. An MILF leader is also reported to have said that young people from age 10 to 16 count among the 300 to 500 men and women who undergo training in one of their camps. The following excerpt illustrates the various tasks engaged in by young men in the MILF:

> When Armin (not his real name) was issued a firearm, he was assigned as foot patrol. He did not receive any training. The instructions were that when ordered to open fire, all recruits were expected to shoot. All his skills were to be gained not through mentors or the group's war veterans, but through direct experience in battle. Experience was therefore to be his only teacher. In the camp, Armin served as a look out. He also was tasked to heat water and to cook. He was, in fact, expected to perform any duty assigned to him. One such duty was to participate in an ambush of a military patrol. ("Children Involved in Hostilities," n.d.)

Machel (2001) recounts that in their involvement in the armed group, girls generally are made to perform many of the same functions as boys, while also being assigned to prepare food, tend to the wounded, and wash clothes. This is evident in the MILF, which is reported to have trained girls to fire M-16 rifles and to prepare for battle. The girls, however, were not allowed to fight, being limited only to cooking, cleaning, and helping in the clinic ("UN Tells Government," 2002, cited in Machel, 2001).

The following is an account of a 17-year-old girl's duties as an NPA combatant:

> Jenny (not her real name) recounted that as she was busy doing kitchen chores, a ranking commander commissioned her to assassinate a military officer. She was

to work as househelp for that military officer. (She) was also directed to conduct perimeter patrol. (De la Cruz & Caliguid, 2002, p. A14)

Concerned groups have tried to repeatedly point out that engaging a young person in noncombatant activities would still be in violation of provisions and agreements preventing the use of young people in armed violence. The definition of a child soldier is not only limited to young people who carry arms in situations of conflict (Action for the Rights of Children [ARC], 2002; see also Machel, 2001, p. 7). This is evident in the Cape Town Principles of 1997, which define the child soldier as

> Any person under 18 years of age who is part of any kind of regular or irregular armed force or armed group in any capacity, including but not limited to cooks, porters, messengers, and those accompanying those groups, other than purely as family members. It includes girls recruited for sexual purposes and forced marriage. (ARC, 2002, p. 7)

Therefore, it is clear that the definition refers to all activities engaged in by young people within the rebel community. The young person in such an environment would still be exposed to the possibility of committing or receiving forms of violent action.

It is now important to examine the conditions that promote the participation of young people in the activities of an armed group or in violent activities influenced by his or her peer group. A survey of these factors will provide a glimpse of the paths that lead to and the contexts that nurture such forms of behavior.

Surveying the Paths to Violence

One path that leads young people to involvement in violent conflict is that of dissolution of support from the young person's social world, weighed down by economic impoverishment. The condition of poverty often transforms the dynamics within the family, as a result of the demands and stresses experienced by each of its members. The young persons who receive no support or protection from the family who are instead relied upon for income and security tend to find comfort in others (usually their peers) outside of their homes (program manager, Child Hope, personal communication, February 3, 2003). A very clear demand on young people is that they assume adult tasks and duties. Unfortunately, when a young people are unable to face up to the adult responsibilities imposed on them by their families for survival, they will attempt to search for safety outside the family, exposing themselves to a life where they learn to be violent in order to survive.

The family and the community have become ineffective as contexts for young people's development, because they perceive or experience the family and community as inadequate in providing them with resources for survival and growth. Moreover, young people are often left with limited opportunities to engage in productive activities within the community. Tolan, Gorman-Smith, and Henry (2003) discuss the importance of community life for the young person's development. They point out that social processes within and structural characteristics of the community are significant elements in the young person's ecology, influencing the microsystems of parenting and peer deviancy, which are directly linked to youth violence. Specifically, they suggest that the ecological elements may bring about the dissolution of family support, which may be evidenced by poor parenting practices. This may, in turn, induce young people's interest in antisocial peer groups or gangs, which leads to greater risks for violent behavior. The lack of support and involvement in productive and collective concerns therefore can facilitate young people's engagement in violent activities.

Another significant path to violence is the experience of war. War severely threatens the community's survival and pushes young people to engage in violent activities to secure the continued existence of their families and communities. Action for the Rights of Children (ARC) in 2002 reported that a majority of children who are involved in armed conflict in almost every country come from the poorest, least educated, and most marginalized sectors of society. The ARC (2002) report emphasizes that when a community becomes an area where armed conflict is conducted, the economic capabilities of its members are severely disrupted, the social life of the community is destroyed, and the educational facilities become nonexistent or extremely limited. The youth's direct experience of family displacement and abuse from the military may lead many of them to join an opposing armed group for the needed security and stability. Often, the young person cannot conceive of an alternative life other than that which is violent and conflict ridden—a life that has experienced during almost the entire period of the young person's existence.

Makinano (2001) reports that Human Rights Watch corroborated this observation when it revealed that Filipino young people most likely to be recruited are those who are poor and are separated from their families. They are also usually displaced from their homes, live in combat zones, have limited access to education, and live in communities that have inadequate social services. The recruitment of young persons is also said to take place in areas with little or no government presence. The life of the family in areas where war is waged may become lost or fragmented, and the fighting exposes young people to constant violence, which may take their sense of order and dignity away from them (Ramos, 2000).

An exposure to a culture of violence within the community can pave the path to young people's participation in conflict situations. The young person may decide to participate in violent activities for the empowerment and the sense of stability these activities may provide them. Being witnesses to the destruction of their communities, they are made fearful and are made to realize that violence may have to be countered by acquiring for themselves the symbols and artifacts of the same violence that which has caused their fear. The young person learns that violence can be used as a potent instrument for survival.

The decision of a youth to join and participate in the activities of the armed group may also be conditioned by a perceived lack of warmth and support from family members, as well as experiences of violence within the family (ARC, 2000). The case of Sandra (not her real name) illustrates how a young person can opt to join armed group in order to escape family imposition and abuse, and as a way to gain control over the abuse being inflicted on a family member.

> Sandra lived with her mother, stepfather and her siblings before she joined the New People's Army. She said that her stepfather did not provide for any of her siblings. Her stepfather would also beat her mother constantly because of jealousy. Her brothers, sisters, and other relatives knew of the beatings and did not do anything about it. Sandra claimed that her stepfather stopped beating her mother when Sandra joined the NPA. (Camacho, Balawon, & Verba, 2001, p. 14)

Sandra had her hopes and dreams, and getting out of the family to join the NPA was a step in achieving these dreams.

> Sandra recounts: "If I have the chance, I want to go to college and study something related to what I did as a medic in the NPA—I was good at what I did, I even used to operate on those who were shot. . . . Mama asked me why I wanted to stay with the NPA. I told her that I wanted to experience life as an NPA. . . . Back then, I wasn't afraid of dying. What will happen will happen. At least I had a chance to tell my Mama the reasons why I was going. It was the first time I told her about how I felt. (pp. 11, 14)

The case of Sandra is illustrative of Machel's (2001) account of those among the young who end up being soldiers particularly when they begin to identify the group as their "new family" and protector. Young people may feel the need to be armed after experiencing continuous and ubiquitous violence within the family and the community.

Families and community leaders may encourage the participation of young people in armed activities to relieve themselves from conditions of poverty. Machel (2001) says that, in general, parents who are impoverished may offer their children for military service, especially when the armed group offers the family remuneration in exchange for their child's "services." Young people themselves may volunteer their services to obtain regular meals, clothing, and medical attention otherwise not provided within their families or in their communities.

Young recruits and other members of the religious community are also said to benefit materially from their involvement in military training. Makinano (2001) reports that the recruits are promised a monthly salary and firearms. The recruits of the ASG are likewise promised a salary after training, firearms, and sometimes scholarships abroad. To convince young Muslims from ages 13 to 25 to join the movement, the MILF is also said to use Muslim elder leaders, who receive a certain amount of money for every new recruit.

Young people are lured by promises of money, weapons, food, and a romanticized rebel lifestyle. The case of Tony (not his real name) is an example of this particular trend that occurs during recruitment:

> When the Abu Sayaff recruited Tony, he was offered a gun and a living, i.e., food and money. He was promised ten thousand pesos, a baby armalite, food in

abundance, and a more comfortable environment. He planned to give the money to his parents; the weapon he thought of keeping for himself. At the age of 12, Tony joined the Abu Sayaff, leaving behind his parents, a brother and a sister. ("Children Involved in Hostilities," n.d.)

It is evident that political systems that promote the use of violence as a means of control exert a powerful influence in the participation of young people in violent activities. The ARC (2000) reports that young people are often recruited into armed activities because of a shortage of adult combatants. According to Makinano (2001), this was particularly true in the Philippines during the 1990s when the NPA suffered a dramatic reduction in membership. This resulted in an intense recruitment of minors.

Other reasons for recruitment have to do mainly with the prevailing notion of childhood and adolescence held in society, which are used by armed groups to justify their use of young people in violent activities. The young are seen by these groups to be adventurous, quick to learn fighting skills, and less costly to support than adults. Makinano reports that some commanders prefer child soldiers because "they are more obedient, do not question orders and [are] easier to manipulate than adult soldiers" (2001, p. 17). These young recruits also can effectively pose a moral challenge for enemies (ARC, 2000). Young people also are perceived as possessing greater stamina and physical strength that enables them to accomplish dangerous combat duties more efficiently. The NPA was said, for example, to be successful in a raid because the police in the town "cannot put up a fight against these very young rebels" (Mallari & Zuasola, 2002, p. A14). An NPA spokesperson of a command in a southern Philippines province was also reported to have said that their young recruits are "idealistic and ready to fight for the revolution" and "have remarkably high resistance power" (p. A14).

However, children are also widely perceived as dispensable commodities (ARC, 2000; Makinano, 2001). This view is said to permit the employment of children in the front line of the armed conflict with little or no training. In the case of those among young people who have committed crimes, public perception is said to be conditioned to view these young people as no longer useful to society. An NGO program officer was reported to have mentioned that even the mothers of murdered youth offenders think that their children deserved to die. This program officer said, "I can never forget one mother who told me that at least she no longer had a problem because her child was dead" (Conde, 2002, p. A4). Young people involved in criminal activities are easily labeled as "society's problems" and become "scapegoats for the community's troubles" (p. A4). Therefore, young people are used in dangerous violent activities because of their strength and sense of adventurism, but at the same time, their involvement ostracizes them from and renders them dispensable in the eyes of the larger society.

Aside from the perceived notions of childhood and adolescence, another category of reasons for participation, also cultural in nature, have to do with the meanings associated with involvement in armed activities. Young people choose to join armed groups because they have been socialized to revere leaders who hold high positions in the military. Participation in military activities is often glorified, and the bearing of arms reinforces one's feelings of masculinity. Handling weapons is also associated with values of power and control; therefore, some of young people are enticed by the chance of living the romanticized lifestyle of a rebel.

An important explanation for voluntary enrollment in military activities is the belief ingrained in young people that armed struggle is the only way to achieve political or ethnic freedom and social justice (ARC, 2000). They are encouraged to participate in a justified war against more dominant and oppressive forces in society. This set of ideologically based beliefs is further reinforced by young people's personal experiences of abuse against their families and communities. Moreover, parents generally volunteer their children who have reached puberty to join the struggle for independence by undergoing training (Makinano, 2001). Parents are said to view time spent in training as more productive than if it were spent with friends or engaging in sports. There have been reports of parents who willingly give up their children to the armed group to rid their children of drug dependencies.

Young people may also personally volunteer because of the joy and pride that may be derived from the spirituality of the struggle (Makinano, 2001). A director of the Phillipines Department of Social Welfare and Development once commented that young people participate in the struggle because "they see themselves as exercising one of the basic teachings of Islam, to carry on fighting not only for their life, rights, and freedom, but for the whole of the Bangsa Moro people, the Mindanaons" (Azarcon-de la Cruz, 2000, p. A8). Involvement in the struggle provides them with the opportunity to experience the highest form of death, "sabir/sahid," or martyrdom.

Socialization into the armed struggle begins very early in the individual's life. The people of Jolo, the Southern Philippines city that has long been the site of violent conflict, are said to sing songs of revenge as they put their babies to sleep. The governor of the Autonomous Region of Muslim Mindanao was reported to have recently issued a warning against the planned deployment of American combat troops in the capital of Sulu:

> The Tausug [the dominant ethnic group in Jolo], when they lull their babies to sleep, do not sing "Summertime" or "Hush, Little Baby." They sing ballads like, "Go to sleep so you'll be strong so you can avenge the atrocities committed on your father." (Bordadora & Balana, 2003, p. A1)

In summary, young people's participation in violence is marked by intertwining paths. Perceived lack of support and security from social institutions, as well as the threat or experiences of violence in the community, in peer groups, or in the family, form the bases on which paths to violence are paved. Extreme conditions of poverty may turn communities into sterile contexts where resources for growth have been washed out. This may weaken the family and deprive it of the capacity to provide support and stability for the young person. The ability to support the family may be expected of the young person, who, when unable to, will turn to the support and security provided by peer groups, who are also similarly pressured and who may be engaging in antisocial and violent activities.

The experience of war destroys a community's social life and severely restricts the resources needed for its survival. Violence becomes an instrument for survival and security, especially in communities where nonviolent alternatives to achieve these have been made impotent by warring factions. In areas of armed conflict and in areas where there is a recurrence of violence, the young person can feel vulnerable and will need the security provided by the active use and display of arms by a group.

In the Philippines, the participation of young people in violent activities is occasioned by the intensification of armed conflict in the country. The economic and political deprivation and marginalization that are the roots of the conflict produce a sense of dissatisfaction and helplessness that is shared by young people with their social group. Young people are exposed to the view that the survival of their group is constantly threatened, and that the group can only be protected through violent activities. Young people are encouraged to participate actively in the armed struggle because of the characteristics they possess, which are valued in armed combat. They willingly participate for the protection, the glory, and the promise of salvation and freedom from the misery of poverty and persecution. The young person may therefore be given a new sense of agency—an agency that is evident in his or her voluntary involvement in conflict. The agency that was lost as a result of the disruption of family and community life, which represent contexts for normative development, is regained within contexts where violence becomes the norm in the achievement of individual and group goals.

However, protection is not necessarily achieved by young people when they participate in violent activities, because they are viewed to be dispensable and may have their rights violated within the movement. There appears to be little opportunity for young people to form reciprocal relationships during the course of their participation in violent situations. The violent act is a task and is accomplished through collaboration with others within a largely hierarchical social world. Being socialized in a system of relations that lead them to believe that violence is the sole means to achieve group goals, they are inevitably pushed into conditions that trap them in a world of constant danger and disruption. These are the very same conditions that have taken from them their capacity to move on and explore possibilities of growth, the very conditions that may take their sense of agency from them.

Some of these young persons may also lose sight of their rights as individuals within society. They are placed in nonnormative environments that may restrict their chances for future productive adult roles. The account of Boy (not his real name) that follows illustrates this possibility:

> Boy vaguely remembered that children are supposed to go to school, and should be provided shelter and food. That these rights could apply to him never crossed Boy's mind. He felt so far removed from those children. To him, the only reality

was surviving. And to survive, he had to prepare to use his weapon. Boy viewed killing with some sense of detachment. Neither idealistic patriotism nor religious freedom moved him. Killing was a task that he must do, competently and efficiently if he were to survive. Nothing personal, just a job. ("Children Involved in Hostilities," n.d.)

No one is certain how many young people like Boy are produced by conditions of poverty and war. Indeed, it may be difficult to imagine how young people can be locked in the present within contexts of violence. Finally, it may be the absence of the protective shield given by the family, as well as the broken promise of safety and security within the social world, that drives young people to participate in violent conflict.

Intervention efforts from government and nongovernment agencies cover a wide variety of services for youth offenders and for young people involved in armed hostilities. These efforts generally ensure that the rights of young people are protected. The service providers also recognize that young people should be reintegrated into their traditional support systems (Tupas, 2002, p. A16). However, problems are evident in protecting young people in a legal system that is tailored for the adult world (NCSD, 1994). The agencies also remain powerless in improving the economic and social conditions that bring young people to an involvement in conflict (Makinano, 2001).

The intervention strategies have remained strong in efforts to rehabilitate the individual but are severely limited in more micro and macro social aspects of rehabilitation, even as these providers now are made increasingly aware that the process of rehabilitating the person cannot be removed from these contexts of development. Difficulties in achieving intervention success, therefore, are indicated in the persistence of poverty and social inequalities in Philippines society.

Conclusion

The participation of young people in situations of conflict is conditioned by the weakening of the family systems of support, and by the disruption of the ties that weave young people's lives with the life of the community. The sense of stability and protection is lost for these young people. They are led to seek protection, stability, and safety in other social groups that provide them with weapons and life routines that embody power, status, and a sense of stability.

Participation in conflict becomes permissible when it ensures the group's survival. Young people's stamina, strength, adventurism, unquestioning loyalty, obedience, and ability to learn quickly are the traits most valued in their involvement. To prepare for this kind of engagement, the young person is expected to learn to submit to authority and to undertake a variety of dangerous tasks with dexterity and efficiency. Paradoxically, the message for young people seems to be: submit to danger and violence, it is the only means of survival.

Participation in conflict is not justifiable to the social group when it does not serve the needs of that group. This participation is perceived by others as occurring because of young people's vulnerability to unproductive habits and their incessant need for stimulation. To sanction young people, they are isolated and ostracized. They are labeled as problems and rendered invisible. For those who may be "saved," a process of reintegration is necessary. Reintegration, unfortunately, means going back to the conditions that remain unchanged, to the conditions that made them the "failures" they turned out to be. Moreover, reintegration may introduce the young person to certain practices that may not be relevant to his or her participation in community life. For example, the young person may go through rehabilitation and be made to learn a craft, which may not be useful to others in the community. Ironically, the message for young people seems to be: learn to adapt; learn to emerge triumphantly within structures that produce and maintain poverty and social inequality.

Interventions, while attempting to provide young people with dignity and a sense of renewed participation in, and commitment to, society have been limited, because interventions have not been able to penetrate the dynamics that provide the pathways to involvement in conflict. For example, both government and nongovernment agencies remain largely unable to reinvigorate family and community responsibility and family problem-solving capacities. The belief that the boundary between the family and external agencies should not be made permeable (i.e., that the family is a private sphere, that problems within the family cannot be interfered with and that interventions should focus only on the individual) removes the possibility of addressing the core of the problem that leads to young people's involvement in violent situations. Moreover, the continued presence of structural violence and social inequality, made possible through models of social and economic development that are not grounded on Philippines historical and cultural experience, maintain and promote among young people a sense of being "failures" (Villacorta, 2002, p. 6). This deprives young people of any sense of political agency within societal norms and values of peace.

To further understand how social and cultural conditions organize youth conflict, analyses should therefore focus more on the conditions that widen the gap between young people and their families, and between young people and their communities. Many young people caught in situations of violence are trapped in what the bioecological model of human development would call microsystems (e.g., the peer group or the armed group). These microsystems, in the case of young people involved in violent conflict, are made impermeable by the nature of the activities within these contexts. In these cases, the possibilities of identity continuity from one context of interaction to another, for example, from the peer group to the family, are diminished, leading to the shrinking of mesosytems in young people's contexts of development. When such a condition occurs, the young person is denied the possibility of experiencing the self in various contexts of interaction, which, in turn, may impair the development of his or her identity as a social being. Astor, Pitner, and Duncan (1996) remind us of the importance given by the ecological theory to the healthy maintenance of mesosytems for the development of the individual. Specifically, these authors emphasize that a person's awareness of weak mesosytems, or the lack of communication between microsystems, can contribute to the frequency of involvement in aggressive actions.

Finally, the experiences young people go through in their involvement in violent conflict may lock them into a "continuous present," into a world where the possibility of being snuffed off from existence is ever present for themselves and their group. This condition may lead to their being deprived of experiencing the possibilities of the new, the possibilities of change, or what is known as plasticity in human development. Without having the opportunities of exploring the future in the present time through play or other forms of social imagination, or through the exploration of other roles and identities, the young person may be deprived, in fact, of any opportunity for healthy development. Instead of engaging in actions that endanger existence through violence, young people need to be engaged in actions that promote growth through a nurturing of positive mesosystems. This may be possible when the resources for development of the individual and his or her family are preserved and available in community life.

Note

1. The rebel movements referred to here are represented by the three main groups engaged in armed conflict with Philippine government forces. The Moro Islamic Liberation Front (MILF) is a breakaway faction of a former secessionist group called the Moro National Liberation Front (MNLF), which during the early 1990s entered into a peace settlement with the government. The New People's Army (NPA) is the military arm of the Communist Party of the Philippines, an underground peasant revolutionary movement, formed in the early 1970s, that seeks to establish a new social and political order by overthrowing the government. The Abu Sayaff Group (ASG), one of the separatist groups operating in the Southern Philippines, split from the MNLF in the early 1990s, claimed national and international notoriety with its perpetration of community raids and a series of kidnappings of both local and foreign nationals in the Southern Philippines. From time to time, the ASG claims that its motivation is to promote an independent Islamic state in western Mindanao and teh Sulu Archipelago, areas in the Southern Philippines heavily populated by Muslims.

References

Action for the Rights of Children. (2002). *Critical issues: Child soldiers.* Available at http://www.unhor.ch/cgi/texis/vtx/protect/opendoc/pdf?tbl=PROTECTION8id=3f8ed714 (retrieved Nov. 16, 2004).

Astor, R., Pitner, R., & Duncan, B. (1996). Ecological approaches to mental health consultation with teachers on issues related to youth and school violence. *Journal of Negro Education, 65*(3), pp. 336–356.

Azarcon-De la Cruz, P. (2000, October 22). The sorrow of war. *Philippine Daily Inquirer,* p. A8.

Bordadora, N., & Balana, C. (2003, February 27). Jolo babies put to sleep with songs of revenge. *Philippine Daily Inquirer,* pp. A1, A16.

Cagoco-Guiam, R. (2002). *Child soldiers in Central and Western Mindanao: A rapid assessment*. Manila: International Labor Office and International Programme on the Elimination of Child Labor.

Camacho, A., Balawon, F., & Verba, A. (2001). *Children involved in the armed conflict in the Philippines: Case study of child soldiers in NPA*. Manila: UNICEF.

Children involved in hostilities and armed conflict: Case studies of soldiers of the Moro Islamic Liberation Front and the Abu Sayaff. (n.d.). Unpublished manuscript.

Conde, C. (2002, December 25). Poverty, abuse force Davao kids to the streets. *Philippine Daily Inquirer*, p. 4.

De la Cruz, H., & Caliguid, F. (2002, October 6). Pa surrenders two rebel kids. *Philippine Daily Inquirer*, p. A14.

Larson, R. W. (2002). Globalization, societal change, and new technologies: What they mean for the future of adolescence. In R. Larson, B. B. Bacon, & J. Mortimer (Eds.), *Adolescents' preparation for the future: Perils and promise* (pp. 1–30). Ann Arbor, MI: Society for Research on Adolescence.

Larson, R. W., Wilson, S., Brown, B., Furstenberg, F., Jr., & Verma, S. (2002). Changes in adolescents' interpersonal experiences: Are they being prepared for adult relationships in the twenty-first century? In R. Larson, B. B. Brown, & J. Mortimer (Eds.), *Adolescents' preparation for the future: Perils and promise* (pp. 31–68). Ann Arbor, MI: Society for Research on Adolescence.

Machel, G. (2001). *The impact of war on children*. London: C. Hurst.

Makinano, M. (2001). *Child soldiers in the Philippines*. Manila: Department of Labor and Employment.

Mallari, D., & Zuasola, F. (2002, August 30). NPA admits fielding teens in combat. *Philippine Daily Inquirer*, p. A5.

Mermet, J., & Quere, V. (2000). *The use of children as soldiers in Asia and the Pacific*. Unpublished manuscript.

National Council for Social Development. (1994). *Children and youth in conflict with the law*. Manila: Author.

Ramos, M. (2000, June 18). The silent plea of children in Mindanao. *Philippine Daily Inquirer*, p. A7.

Situation analysis of children and women in the Philippines. (2003, November 10). Executive Summary. Available: www.dap.edu.ph.

Tolan, P., Gorman-Smith, D., & Henry, D. (2003). The developmental ecology of urban males' youth violence. *Developmental Psychology, 39*(2), 274–291.

Tupas, J. (2002, December 22). The boy who wants to be a rebel. *Philippine Daily Inquirer*, p. A16.

United Nations International Children's Education Fund. (1998). *Situation analysis on children and youth in conflict with the law*. Manila: Adhikain para sa karapatan pambata [Advocacy for Children's Rights] of the Ateneo Human Rights Center, Ateneo Law School.

Villacorta, W. (2002, May 1). Youth alienation and violence. *Manila Bulletin,* p. 6.

CHAPTER 2

Extremist Youth in Germany

The Role of History, Development, and Cohort Experience

WOLFGANG EDELSTEIN

The Emergence of Right-wing Culture in German Youth

The Situation After Unification

A new extremism in German youth has emerged in the years since unification, in East Germany more intensively than in the West. The main components of this right-wing extremism are xenophobia and nationalism, anti-Semitism and ideological commitment to authoritarianism, racial and political inequality (see the overview in Bromba & Edelstein, 2001). These components do not constitute a conceptual unity. Xenophobia is the lead variable, and, according to surveys, affects about one-third of the total young population and even considerably more locally, especially in the lower social strata. In the recent Civics Study by the International Association for the Evaluation of Educational Achievement, German 15-year-olds held the most xenophobic attitudes among those of the 28 participating countries (Torney-Purta, Lehmann, Oswald, & Schulz, 2001). Anti-Semitism is on the rise, but perhaps rather less so than in some other European countries, and the reasons may, at least partly, derive from the Israeli-Arab conflict and the Israeli military rollback in the Palestinian territories. Due to historical reasons, anti-Semitism is not merely politically incorrect but particularly abhorrent in Germany. It is therefore a more complex phenomenon in Germany than elsewhere, and calls for more conscious resistance (see Sturzbecher & Freytag, 2000).

Every study shows that in East Germany the incidence of right-wing extremism, as measured by various indicators, is about twice as frequent as in the West. More than 50% of all racist, xenophobic, and neo-Nazi incidents and most of all violent incidents have happened in the Eastern provinces, where less than 20% of the German population lives. In this sense, East Germany appears more similar to eastern Europe than to West Germany. In eastern Europe, a neo-Nazi youth movement is definitely a threat to the development of a democratic society.

Psychological Factors

Normatively, right-wing extremism represents moral waywardness in thinking and in action. The concept of moral deprivation or waywardness points to the psycho-social and moral implications of a syndrome that combines economic, familial, educational, and cultural factors in variable ways. The causal relationship of the elements remains moot. Here, I single out the anomic correlates of social dispossession, individualization, and the dissolution of institutional bonds. Adolescents respond to these processes either with wayward hedonism or with rebellion, but more often with moral indifference. Adolescents who wind up unsuccessfully in jobs, or who end up failure-prone in apprenticeships following unsuccessful school careers, may respond with a violent ideological or social reaction that protects the person's self-esteem. Such responses may be extremist, xenophobic, racist, and anti-Semitic, and, in Germany, contentious with the moral conventions that, until very recently, have been the more or less unanimously accepted basis of social action in the Federal Republic. Notably, these existing moral conventions are a consequence of a historical process of social learning, in Germany, about universal human rights and the equality of all human races.

It is the refusal to heed this covenant, generally accepted since the downfall of the Nazi empire in 1945, that turns the youthful rebels into racists and neo-Nazis. Needless to say, an attempt to comprehend the motives for this development does not imply acceptance of the rebels' Nazi convictions or justify their stance out of compassion with the underdogs or a position of solidarity with an emerging underclass. Nonetheless, while opposing the actors and their actions, they must also be seen as victims of their economic, social, and psychological conditions. Drawing on one of Anna Seghers's stories, the questions are: How does a man become a Nazi? Who becomes a Nazi? What kind of person is receptive to Nazi values? What are the conditions and contexts that turn people into Nazis? Finally: are there ways and means to counteract such developments? The first of these questions relates to the present analyses; unfortunately, space restrictions prevent discussion of the last question. In view of the literature, it appears justifiable, however, to substitute the notion of "violence" for the term "Nazi" in the foregoing questions. How does a person become violent? Who becomes violent? What kind of person is receptive to ideologies and/or practices involving violence? What are the conditions and contexts that make young people violent? Are there ways and means to counteract such developments (see Baumeister, 1997, and the literature cited there)?

"A Man Turns Nazi." In Anna Seghers's story (Seghers, 1977), the author reconstructs the socialization of Fritz Müller in humiliated post-Versailles Germany, where soldiers return home devastated and unemployed to bring up their children in misery. These children of losers, in their families, schools, and peer groups, develop corresponding mechanisms of compensation, character traits, and motives of spite and revenge. These conditions ultimately lead them into the ranks of the storm trooper thugs, then into the SS, and finally, during the war in eastern Europe, to their well-known involvements in concentration camps, firing squads, and mass murder in Polish and Russian villages and ghettos (Browning, 2001; Newman & Erber, 2002).

While the picture drawn by Seghers concerns an earlier generation, there are significant similarities with the present. The developmental prerequisites match a set of social opportunities for individual action. All individuals have potential for development, but psycho-social needs and social opportunities determine how individuals use their potential: developing careers ranging from moral exemplar to maladapted neurotic to outright monster (Frey & Rez, 2002). Fritz's brothers join the youth movement of the Communist Party, while Fritz himself joins the Nazis. Beyond the social structures that operate unrecognized behind the individuals' backs, differential opportunity structures decide their fortunes. Among the differential factors, we note social class and family, schools and teachers, and the peer group, all providing differential reinforcement for needs and dispositions. Seghers, in her story, draws a picture of the school experience affecting Fritz Müller: different teachers exert different influences, using contrasting modalities of shaping and modeling the characters of their dependent pupils. There is a liberal and progressive teacher who overtaxes Fritz with his good intentions, and the unintended consequence is to move him closer to his evil destiny. There is a Nazi teacher who recognizes Fritz's restricted potential and instrumentalizes him, promoting Fritz's successful monster's career. Seghers sensitively reconstructs the psychology first of the young, then the adolescent, schoolboy. It might have opened a pathway to a conventional conduct of life, but it may also have opened the gate toward a different type of career, a different kind of normalcy. Seghers describes the collective impoverishment in which Fritz's individual family is placed, and the solidarity of the deprived, where Fritz and his like can earn recognition. When crossing the boundaries to violence and to the exercise of power in the form of terror, they do in fact earn praise from the Nazis. Fritz finds himself master of life and death, rather as a happenstance at first in the early years; but later, as an officer of the German forces in Russia, he metes out death and terror systematically and with full intention.

Role of School

Recognition and humiliation are central dimensions of adolescent experience. In various Western societies, this is an important aspect of school experience.

Recognition and humiliation are woven into the fabric of pedagogy and instruction. They are aspects of teachers' and students' roles, an inevitable part of instruction, of grades and feedback, tests and exercises. What is the involuntary role of school in development and what is the voluntary influence exerted through grades and the evaluation culture of the school? In Germany, school appears to play an important role in the emergence of right-wing extremism; this is corroborated by the data of recent youth surveys (e.g., Deutsche Shell, 2000, 2002; Sturzbecher, 1997, 2001), which specify school-related motives for dissatisfaction among youth, especially in East Germany. The surveys disclose that large numbers of disaffected adolescents are disappointed with school and see little meaning in the subjects they are taught. They are lost and distraught in their schools, do not trust their teachers, hold teachers accountable for their boredom, see teachers as disinterested in their lives and fortunes, and accuse teachers of a humiliating aloofness to their problems. To take a relevant example from an East-German province, up to 40% of students in comprehensive schools and vocational secondary schools in the Land of Brandenburg voice such complaints (Sturzbecher, 2001). It is this segment of the educationally underprivileged who are the breeding ground of right-wing extremism.

The school experience of young people is of interest not so much because the responsibility for the emergence of extreme right-wing positions in youth should be attributed to the school but because we should give the role of the school in the development of educational losers serious thought. We should also think about the role that schools might play in the prevention of such developments: How could one shape school experience to prevent losers from seeking revenge for their failure? How could a culture of the school provide its youthful members with a life-world of experiences that generate immunity from neo-Nazi or other right-wing temptations and impulses to violent action? What can schools do to effectively oppose the active components of the extremist syndrome: xenophobia, anti-Semitism, a racist affirmation of inequality, chauvinism, politically motivated violence? What are the cognitive and affective strategies, the designs of instruction, the modalities of shaping the classroom and school climates that counteract the assimilation of adolescents into extremist or violent subcultures (see Edelstein & Fauser, 2000)? To come up with viable answers to these questions, we need to understand the real causes of violence and right-wing extremism among young people.

Causes and Antecedents: An Account
of Change at the Macro Level

How should we account for the emergence of the extremist youth culture amid the purportedly positive social development unleashed by the reunification of Germany after decades of separation? The basic argument runs as follows. Changes in the macro system with psycho-social consequences produce contexts of experience that interact with developmental vulnerabilities of adolescents. These adolescents, given the specific contingencies of the actual social context, will develop maladaptive behavioral dispositions and, possibly, extremist orientations. Anomie and individualistic modernization are the most important factors in this process at the macro level. They represent psycho-social consequences of "long processes" of social transformation (Braudel, Duby, & Aymard, 1990). On the micro level, adolescent development of negative identity and the dynamics of dismissive attachment in families collectively play a decisive role. Finally, cohort effects effectively trigger the emergence of the new orientations in youth, and thus call for a detailed analysis of their psychological power in individual and social development. Glen Elder's (1974) description of the children of the Great Depression represents a model of this type of analysis, the analogy of which would be the fate of the unification cohort in Germany. (For details of the social and sociomoral life-world of this cohort, see Edelstein, 2002, 2005.)

Let us now turn to the causal and systemic factors. Emile Durkheim (1968b) introduced the notion of *anomie* at the end of the nineteenth century to describe the socio-moral consequences of the breakdown of the traditional social order with its stable social formations, division of labor, rules, and value systems. This breakdown marks the transition to modern society, characterized by the industrial division of labor. Traditional society had been organized through intergenerationally stable rules of "mechanical solidarity," with little room for individual variation and individual influence on the social order; therefore, traditional loyalties and duties prevailed against the onslaught of individual needs, goals, and desires. These antiindividualistic attitudes came to be decisive influences in the market-dominated world of competitive capitalism that succeeded the traditional world of personal bonds, inherited skills, and natural exchange. In the wake of the transition, individual achievement and individual judgment had to provide a foundation for the new and more flexible moral order of "organic solidarity." These are Durkheim's (1968a) terms for the principled cognitive morality required to regulate action in complex industrial societies.

The bleak side of this development of higher order organization and increasing functional differentiation is the resulting fragmentation and disorganization. Social and cognitive conflicts bring about more or less far-reaching structural and psychological disorder and loss of moral consistency, leading to a person's "anomic" withdrawal and narrowly self-referential motivation in several conditions. Such alienation results when social potentials that sustain the division of labor and the individual's functionally required responsibility are disorganized, contradictory, and antagonistic, and when individuals are unable to reconstitute social life in terms of a subjectively meaningful sociomoral order. Durkheim diagnosed anomie as a situation of socially generated individual risk, as a deprivation of the socially sustained meaning of life, and as a retreat from action. In the extreme case, this means depression and even death—the case of anomic suicide. The response to alienation and deprivation of meaning in disorganized social structures may be a strategy of anomic rebellion against society rather than depressive withdrawal from society. Anomic rebellion consists in rejecting the accepted public moral coordinates of action, refusing control, and turning against the prevailing social norms and expectations.

Durkheim (1968a) had interpreted the consequences of the transition from traditional society to modernity in terms of gains made by members of society with regard to individual autonomy and autonomous moral regulation. In addition, he described the negative consequences and correlates of the transition in terms of the failure or inability to practice this autonomy. A century later, his perspective is as relevant as ever. In the industrialized West, the transition is now from the established and consolidated forms of industrialist capitalism to new global forms of capitalist organization, marketing, and finance. Richard Sennett (1999) has convincingly described the structure of depressive anomie under the more proximal condition of contemporaneous capitalism, which has generated moral and mental character crises similar to the transition from mechanical solidarity to the new requirements of individual autonomy. In the new global market, winners in the competition gain autonomy and competence, while losers remain paralyzed in unemployment and prone to alienation and depression. The specific deprivation of meaning suffered by the losers of the present transition represents a loss of motivated orientation toward the future. As a consequence, anomie emerges both on the individual and on the collective level, on the local and on the global plane. Again an available alternative to alienation and depression is an aggressively antisocial, anomic rebellion.

Whether such a transition is taking place outside the industrial West we have only conjectures. Could a similar Durkheimian transition mark the passing of traditional society (Eisenstadt, 1973) to a modern protoindustrial, detraditionalized, semienfranchised world of underdeveloped economies, dominated demographically by young urban populations (Larson, Brown, & Mortimer, 2002; Mortimer & Larson, 2002)?

Anomie in the Transition Cohort

To bring the Durkheimian analysis of anomie to bear on the local and cohort-specific phenomena that characterize the extremist youth rebellion in East Germany, it must be applied to the sudden transition from the rigidly stable and centrally planned organization of the (East) German Democratic Republic to Western-style capitalism in the year 1989. The transition generated a sudden destabilization of individual lives in the parent generation of the adolescent cohorts of the time. Support for organized youth activities ceased at the very moment of unification. Institutions for adolescent training and leisure—formerly supports of the socialist state and of socialist education—were discontinued without substitutes, and a great number of adolescents were left deprived of action opportunities, organization, and perspective.

Consequences of these changes included the following. The disempowerment of the former elites coincided with widespread unemployment in the parent generation, especially among the former elites (state employees, teachers, politically active or loyal groups); this humiliation clearly was perceived and processed by the young. Such experiences disrupted the expectancies and normative orientations of many people. This was followed, in the more vulnerable young cohorts, by a lack of trust in the new social order, its institutions, and its representatives. The result of discontinuation of public institutions originally designed to channel the activities of youth was widespread disaffection in the young generation.

Surveys showed (and continue to show) lack of confidence concerning the present and the future, regarding both the economy and the integrity of life perspectives. Many young people lost their perspectives, orientations, and expectations and suffered the experience of cohort specific deprivation. In that cohort (between ages 13 and 25, approximately) some individuals reacted with violence. The violence was mainly enacted against foreigners, especially dark-skinned asylum seekers, but even against handicapped or homeless persons, as the putative, real, or symbolic beneficiaries of the welfare system, possibly because the perpetrators believed the welfare system was about to redistribute their entitlements to social parasites, while depriving Germans of their rightful heritage. More probably, however, they were reacting to their own humiliation, and designing a loser's revenge on those they believed were undeserving winners. They would turn their back on the unsatisfactory present and, for the preservation of pride, would look to an imaginary better past, which, due to the failure of socialism, had to be a past *before* socialism. Thus they came to wear the insignia of racial superiority and to use their bullying power to redeem themselves of the status of victims of an uncomprehended development. Vindicating empowerment through appropriation of a mythical past, which is validated by the use of force against whoever opposes the actor, apparently compensates for what is subliminally felt to be the expropriation and dispossession of a failed generation.

I have contrasted the sudden burst of anomie in the postunification cohort in East Germany with the "long process" of anomie generation in the transition from traditional to modern society. Individualistic modernization is a further strand of the long process of transformation. Ulrich Beck (1992) and Anthony Giddens (1991) refer to this process as the second, or reflexive, modernization. Using a concept that has gained wide currency, Beck asserts the emergence of "risk society," because the new type of social order is characterized by weak social organizations that face difficulties and generate problems ("risks") that can be traced to an increasing deinstitutionalization of social conduct and the life course. Heitmeyer and Olk (1990) have analyzed this process in terms of the diminishing stability of the institutions that channel and support the course of individual lives, especially the family. This "corrosion of ligatures" (to borrow Dahrendorf's term) is represented by the gradual loss of the power of social institutions, such as the family, to regulate individual behavior and individual goals and intentions. This process is the outflow of the sustained, continuous, and incontrovertible rise of individualism: weak institutions open a "danger zone" through which the rising generations must travel, while the traditional agents of socialization progressively lose their power of direction and guidance, confronted by an increasing "risk" of loss of moral purpose. Traditions are corroded and diluted in the process, losing their function as "syntactic rules" for the collective conduct of individual lives. Increasing competition among lifestyles, standards, and styles of conduct brings increasing pressure to bear on the integrity of the normative order, the disintegration of which appears to those affected as an achievement of liberation. Simultaneously, the increasing competition maximizes the pressure on the modernization losers, with the consequence of increasing deprivation and alienation. This process appears concretely and visibly in the economy and on the labor market. Family bonds have weakened under the strain of market-driven interests. The failing of family systems results in increasing frequencies of divorce, decreasing birth rates, growing numbers of singles: indicators of new, subinstitutional forms of life. The increasing length of formal education delays the beginning of economic independence and the formation of stable identities among the young, which ironically increases their dependence on the already weakened system. Thus a tension develops between the principle of personal attachment in families and the principle of competition in the school and in the market—a ubiquitous competition concerning achievements and lifestyles, jobs, and leisure activities. The stress emanating from these tensions must be borne by the individuals alone, as the weak institutions cannot provide the normative support that is needed psychologically. Economic modernization and intensified competition put people under pressure from the forces of individualism. For the victims of this process, the nostalgia for strong institutions, a flight into the security and relief of group power, and the surrender of individual moral standards and individual conscience represent a persistent temptation—sometimes denounced as the lure of fun society. In sum, individualization theory and anomie theory join forces to spell out the consequences for the losers of the long processes of social and social-psychological transformation—as evidenced in the West. It is not beyond doubt, of course, whether modernization processes outside the West have any similarity with these processes.

Psychological Processes at the Micro Level

Family Processes

The effects of social change at the macro level affect the contexts of individual development and produce conditions of vulnerability that impact on the situation of individual action in response to these conditions. At the system level, the family mediates between these contexts. It contributes to the vulnerability and adds to the potential for response when certain conditions are met. The theory of individualistic modernization is focused on the family as a weak institution framing strongly motivated individuals. Adorno's once famous theory of the authoritarian personality, following Freud, explained the genesis of the authoritarian character in terms of family dynamics (Adorno, Frenkel-Brunswik, Levinson, & Sanford, 1950). The centerpiece of the theory is the concept of sons' idealization of fathers, whose repression of the sons simultaneously produces authoritarian submission (to the strong father) and authoritarian aggression (against weak others). This is not the place to go into details of the complex psychological mechanisms involved. In a version of the theory expressly brought to bear on the family dynamics of neo-authoritarian individuals (Hopf, Rieker, Sanden-Marcus, & Schmidt, 1995), the Freudian apparatus of libidinal cathexis has been replaced by the much more transparent model of Bowlby's (1969) attachment theory as the basis of character formation. The types of *insecure attachment,* as specified by Bowlby (anxious, ambivalent, disorganized), have recently been complemented by a new type: the indifferent-dismissive or hostile type of insecure attachment (see van Ijzendoorn, 1997). The dismissively attached switch off their feelings for their parents, drain the experiences with parents of their energy, repress memories of pain, conflict, or humiliation, and thus devaluate both the experience and the persons involved. Denial and devaluation generalize to objects of negative cathexis, providing the humiliated subjects with an ample supply of victims who provide them with opportunities to project their feelings of anger and aggression and to compensate their experience of shaming and devaluation.

Identity Development

We owe to Erik Erikson the classical theory of identity formation in the context of historical change (Erikson, 1959, 1975). In that theory, ego identity is the feeling of trust in the reliable unity and continuity of the self, mirrored by supportive others. This feeling provides strength and motivation for action in the present, and hope and perspective for action in the future.

The construction of a viable identity requires successful resolution of the major conflicts that have dominated earlier phases of childhood. Successful resolution of the conflicts is followed by integration of the strengths and gains achieved in earlier phases of development with the help of supportive structures in families, preschools, and schools. Adolescence is a vulnerable phase in the life cycle, which makes it dependent on the social forces, structures, and institutions in which it is embedded. Erikson has shown how a destructive family dynamic, e.g. an authoritarian and repressive relationship between father and son, may threaten the process of identity formation and put the son at risk of identity diffusion, disintegration, or identification with the aggressor (Erikson, 1959, ch. 1). Erikson places the individual case expressly in the context of historical change, using a case approach to bring the psychodynamic origins of a son's (antiauthoritarian) rebellion into the socio-historical and political focus of the present in which, and from the perspective of which, he is writing.

Adolescence sets the stage for the development of a personal identity and for a person's integration into groups that provide strength to the ego, and it plays a decisive role in the development of a person's ideological perspective on self and society. Thus, adolescence, more than earlier phases in the biography, depends on the social context in which a person is immersed. Beyond the family system and classroom peers and beyond social groups and political organizations, ideological movements and socio-historical formations increasingly claim allegiance by adolescents. More than before, then, a person's process of identity formation is affected, and sometimes torn, by the vectors that dominate the macro-micro interface.

Collective Identity

In his collection of essays entitled "Life History and the Social Moment," Erikson (1975) published an essay on the process of collective identity formation in the protest generation of the 1960s and 1970s. The process is defined as "a critical phase marked by the reciprocal aggravation of internal conflict and of societal disorganization" (p. 195) and thus highlights the quality of macro-micro interaction. Erikson describes the changed economic, social, and cultural context of the new generation; its intellectual and experiential ecology; the conditions of a new historical consciousness; a youthful awareness colored by the cognitive egocentrism that is constitutive of adolescent ideological thought. He labels the adolescent mode of thinking as the "all or nothing *totalistic* quality of adolescence, which permits many young people to invest their loyalty in simplistically overdefined ideologies" (1975, p. 204, italics in original). And "the dominant issue for identity formation is that the active, the selective ego is in charge and enabled to be in charge by a social structure which grants a given age group the place it needs, and in which it is needed" (1968, p. 246). What happens when the social situation subverts this vital condition? Perhaps a society may, in a situation of threat or distress, project on the adolescent generation a collective identity charged with a revolutionary function, adopted as constitutive for its identity by a significant segment of that generation. This takes us beyond Erikson's theory, but it might carry some potential for analyzing the ideological dynamics in which young people are involved in various non-Western parts of the world.

Negative Identity

In the West, the "humanistic protest movement" of the 1960s pursued progressive goals of liberation and social justice. But the terms of the theory are not constrained to serve the analysis of "positive" group identity. An important part of Erikson's work was devoted to the clarification of identity diffusion—the psychodynamic, developmental, and social conditions that prevent, impair, or delay a positive resolution of inner conflicts that is conducive to a healthy or equilibrated identity. Unresolved conflicts contribute to the pathography of adolescent failure to develop a stable identity, generating some variety of identity diffusion instead: negative reciprocity, based in early mistrust, guilt and weakness, anger, work paralysis, and depression.

Such symptoms frequently lead to the choice of a *negative identity*. The adolescent replaces the image of a weak and ambivalent parent with a cruel and basically desperate self; he or she replaces threatening exposure to a significant other's exercise of will with an excess of obedience and deference to leadership; he or she replaces the pressure for activity with passive submission; and he or she replaces taxing expectations of achievement with indolence or with offensive acts and norm violations. Transferring these events from the private to the public space, replacing normal sociability with exclusion, affiliation with criminal gangs, absorption into authoritarian group structures, or the adoption of racist ideologies may provide a negative substitute for an integrated identity. Similarly, the availability of a revolutionary ideology may provide the action potentials that, at times, may compensate for a nonintegrated identity and provide subjective meaning to an experience of self based in a negative identity.

Rise of a Culture of Negative Group Identity

Now we can ask whether in the specific situation of Germany after unification "a critical phase marked by a reciprocal aggravation of internal conflict and societal organization" (Erikson, 1975, p. 195) provided an opportunity for a movement of youthful rebels. In fact, a right-wing youth movement emerged in a society that was beset by specific socio-historical vulnerabilities after the downfall of socialism.

"The dominant issue," Erikson says, "is the assurance that the active, the selective, ego is in charge and enabled to be in charge by a social structure which grants a given age group the place it needs—and in which it is needed" (1968, p. 246). What happens when the social situation subverts this vital condition? The social context of adolescent experience following the downfall of the (East) German Democratic Republic hardly did provide the assurance that an active ego was given the place it needed or signal that it indeed was needed. We may presume that this may be a situation that is widely experienced by youth exposed to the consequences of systemic change or involved in societal transitions that hold little promise for their future.

Erikson pursues: "Youth . . . is sensitive to any suggestion that it may be hopelessly determined by what went before in life histories or in history" (1968, p. 247). We understand that a situation of humiliation witnessed or experienced, of opportunities unattained or foregone, of perspectives dimmed or reserved for others, arouses anger and resentment among those affected by, or highly sensitive to, the threat of foreclosure of their future. The corresponding affect is turned against those who, according to the terrible simplifications of the populists, harvest the benefits from an allegedly unfair and biased distribution of welfare (thus, in Germany, refugees, foreigners, Jews, the handicapped). On the other hand, positive cathexis is focused on the Nazis, because the past communist regime in East Germany and the present capitalist society are united in ostracizing them as objects of moral and political shame and collective guilt. In fact, the right-wing rebels refuse to share the public denial that is the essence of civil consensus about Germany's Nazi past. What has been rejected and forbidden returns as an object of identification: an emotionally charged concept of the nation and a chauvinistic national sentiment; a feeling of hostility toward foreigners who allegedly exploit the nation and appropriate for themselves the opportunities illegitimately withheld from their rightful proprietors; feelings and acts of violence and defiance; symbols and behaviors that confront and negate the humiliation, exclusion, and hopelessness to which they are themselves exposed. Neo-Nazi identification, anti-Semitism, and xenophobia thus have become the hallmark, in the German East, of the ideology of a group of dispossessed and disaffected young people who draw strength, if not comfort, from a posture of rebellion and nonalignment with the majority culture. Such groups, moreover, also attract individuals who aspire to their ideological or political leadership.

If we may believe the testimony of Anna Seghers (1977), this recalls the fascist youth of the 1920s, but it also calls to mind the protesters of the 1970s, both of whom, albeit with opposite intentions, rose against the prevailing social norms of their times. What seems to be common to them is the purpose of obtaining control over their own lives and giving it meaning after an experience of weakness, humiliation, and loss of control (Frey & Rez, 2002; Skinner, 1995). Whatever the distal causes and the proximal contexts of that experience, this is the basic developmental function of the formation of identity in youth. And that is a process that, when it fails, brings confusion, and sometimes depression and death; and a process sometimes achieved at the cost of one's life. This appears to be the case in Germany and, other things equal, this is probably the case around the world.

Summary

In this essay I have proposed a model of how the right-wing youth culture in (East) Germany has emerged. The model postulates an interaction among long historical processes at the macro level, conditions of individual development at the micro level, and social and situational factors that precipitate change in the context of a given cohort. Durkheim's theory of anomie and its descendant theories of individualistic modernization, as described by Beck (1992), Giddens (1991), and Heitmeyer and Olk (1990), were used to construct an analogy between the passing of traditional society in the West and the downfall of socialism in East Germany. The long processes pave the way to the rise of anomie and the corrosion, in processes of modernization, of traditions, institutions, and "habits of the heart" (Bellah, 1986). These processes affect the vulnerability of adolescents to ideologies and behaviors that function to compensate for humiliation, alienation, and deprivation of meaning in life. The vulnerability can be traced to family processes that generate flaws in identity formation. The humiliation, alienation, and deprivation to which the adolescents react are linked to local conditions or situational context: The breakdown of socialism suddenly eliminated the life-world structures, value systems and organizational support patterns, modes of living, and future perspectives of the young generation, in conjunction with widespread humiliation of the parent generation as carriers of past value patterns and social structures. This was a humiliation vicariously resented by the young.

The choice of a rebellious and sometimes even violent lifestyle requires the support of certain mechanisms and forms of life that, for reasons of space limitations, I have not been able to describe in this essay. I wish to mention but three major factors: (1) the cohesion of groups that cultivate a common lifestyle (e.g., right-wing music, hard drinking, and violence) and defuse the moral responsibility of the individual, and that maintain the ideological belief system of inequality, racism, and xenophobia, and an authoritarian leadership; (2) the sharing of negatively valued school experience, often rejected as meaningless and thus providing a setting for continuous alienation; and (3) a world of violent media experience that compensates the experience of powerlessness and reinforces the culture of violence in the group.

To understand the nature of the present to which we are exposed as actors and as victims, besides the reconstruction of change processes at the macro level and the ecologies of individual development at the micro level, we certainly need thick descriptions of the forms of life that, for better or for worse, determine the experiences and generate the motives of the actors in our midst.

References

Adorno, T. W., Frenkel-Brunswik, E., Levinson, D. J., & Sanford, R. N., in collaboration with Aron, B., Levinson, M. H., & Morrow, W. (1950). *The authoritarian personality*. New York: Harper and Row.

Baumeister, R. F. (1997). *Evil: Inside human cruelty and violence*. New York: Freeman.

Beck, U. (1992). *Risk society: Towards a new modernity*. London: Sage.

Bellah, R. N. (1986). *Habits of the heart: Individualism and commitment in American life*. New York: Harper and Row.

Bowlby, J. (1969). *Attachment and loss: Vol. 1. Attachment*. New York: Basic Books.

Braudel, F., Duby, G., & Aymard, M. (1990). *Die Welt des Mittelmeeres: Zur Geschichte und Geographie kultureller Lebensformen* [The Mediterranean world: History and geography of cultural forms of life]. Frankfurt: Fischer.

Bromba, M., & Edelstein, W. (2001). *Das anti-demokratische und rechtsextreme Potenzial unter Jugendlichen und jungen Erwachsenen in Deutschland* [The antidemocratic and extremist potential among youth and young adults in Germany]. Bonn: Expertise für das Bundesministerium für Bildung und Forschung.

Browning, C. R. (2001). *Ordinary men: Reserve Police Battalion 101 and the final solution in Poland*. London: Penguin.

Deutsche Shell. (Ed.) (2000). *Jugend 2000* [Youth 2000]. Opladen: Leske und Budrich.

Deutsche Shell. (Ed.) (2002). *Jugend 2002: Zwischen pragmatischem Idealismus und robustem Materialismus* [Youth 2002: Between pragmatic idealism and robust materialism]. Frankfurt: Fischer.

Durkheim, E. (1968a). *The division of labor*. New York: Free Press.

Durkheim, E. (1968b). *Suicide: A study in sociology*. London: Routledge and Kegan Paul.

Edelstein, W. (2002). Die Ausbreitung einer rechten Jugendkultur in Deutschland, mit einigen Vorschlägen zur Prävention [The expansion of a right-wing youth culture in Germany, with some recommendations for prevention]. In F. Büchel, J. Glück, U. Hoffrage, P. Stanat, & J. Wirth (Eds.), *Fremdenfeindlichkeit und Rechtsextremismus.* [Xenophobia and right-wing extremism] (pp. 11–62). Opladen: Leske und Budrich.

Edelstein, W. (2005). The rise of a right-wing culture in German youth: The effects of social transformation, identity construction, and context. In D. B. Pillemer & S. H. White (Eds.), *Developmental psychology and social change* (pp. 314–351). Cambridge, UK: Cambridge University Press.

Edelstein, W., & Fauser, P. (2000). *Demokratie lernen und leben: Gutachten zum pro-*

gramm [Learning and living democracy: Report for the program] Bonn: Materialien zur Bildungsplanung und zur Forschungsförderung, vol. 96.

Eisenstadt, S. N. (1973). *Tradition, change and modernity.* New York: Wiley.

Elder, G. H. (1974). *Children of the Great Depression.* Chicago: University of Chicago Press.

Erikson, E. H. (1959). Identity and the life cycle. New York: International Universities Press. (Originally published in *Psychological Issues, 1*[1])

Erikson, E. H. (1968). *Identity, youth and crisis.* New York: Norton.

Erikson, E. H. (1975). *Life history and the historical moment.* New York: Norton.

Frey, D., & Rez, H. (2002). Population and predators: Preconditions for the Holocaust from the control-theoretical perspective. In L. S. Newman & R. Erber (Eds.), *Understanding genocide: The social psychology of the Holocaust* (pp. 188–221). New York: Oxford University Press.

Giddens, A. (1991). *Modernity and self-identity: Self and society in the late modern age.* Stanford: Stanford University Press.

Heitmeyer, W., & Olk, T. (Eds.). (1990). *Individualisierung von Jugend* [Individualization of youth]. Weinheim: Juventa.

Hopf, C., Rieker, P., Sanden-Marcus, M., & Schmidt, C. (1995). *Familie und Rechtsextremismus: Familiale Sozialisation und rechtsextreme Orientierungen junger Männer* [Family and right-wing extremism: Family socialization and right-wing orientations of young men]. Weinheim: Juventa.

Larson, R., Brown, B. B., & Mortimer, J. (Eds.). (2002). Adolescents' preparation for the future: Perils and promise. *Journal of Research on Adolescence, 12,* 1–166.

Mortimer, J., & Larson, R. (Eds.). (2002). *The changing adolescent experience: Societal trends and the transition to adulthood.* New York: Cambridge University Press.

Newman, S., & Erber, R. (Eds.). (2002). *Understanding genocide: The social psychology of the Holocaust.* New York: Oxford University Press.

Seghers, A. (1977). Ein Mensch wird Nazi [A man becomes Nazi]. In *Gesammelte Werke in Einzelausgaben: Vol. 9. Erzählungen 1926–1944,* pp. 285–298. Berlin: Aufbau,

Sennett, R. (1999). *The corrosion of character: The personal consequences of work in the new capitalism.* New York: Norton.

Skinner, E. A. (1995). *Perceived control, motivation, and coping.* Thousand Oaks: Sage.

Sturzbecher, D. (Ed.) (2001). *Jugend in Ostdeutschland: Lebenssituationen und Delinquenz* [Youth in East Germany. Life situations and delinquency]. Opladen: Leske und Budrich.

Sturzbecher, D. (Ed.) (1997). *Jugend und Gewalt in Ostdeutschland. Lebenserfahrungen in Schule, Freizeit und Familie* [Youth and violence in East Germany. Life experiences in school, leisure and family]. Göttingen: Verlag für Angewandte Psychologie.

Sturzbecher, D., & Freytag, R. (2000). *Antisemitismus unter Jugendlichen: Fakten, Erklärungen, Unterrichtsbausteine* [Anti-Semitism in youth. Facts, explanations, curricular material]. Göttingen: Hogrefe.

Torney-Purta, J., Lehmann, R., Oswald, H., & Schulz, W. (2001). *Citizenship and education in twenty-eight countries: Civic knowledge and engagement at age fourteen.* Amsterdam: International Association for the Evaluation of Educational Achievement.

Van Ijzendoorn, M. H. (1997). Attachment, emergent morality, and aggression. Toward a developmental socioemotional model of anti-social behavior. *International Journal of Behavioral Development, 21,* 703–727.

CHAPTER 3

Growing Up During the Balkan Wars of the 1990s

SARAH WARSHAUER FREEDMAN
AND DINO ABAZOVIC

Overview

The youth today in Bosnia and Herzegovina (BiH) and Croatia have grown up during times of war and chronic unrest. Since the youth will determine the future of the countries in the still unstable Balkan region, it is critical to understand how their experiences of past wars and current, ongoing violence might relate to the role they will play in the reconstruction of their society.

This chapter focuses on what we learned about youth and violence from a study of young people aged 14 to 16 enrolled in secondary schools in the still deeply divided towns of Mostar in BiH and Vukovar in Croatia. It is part of a larger project that focuses on understanding the contributions of schools, as well as other social institutions, to rebuilding societies after mass atrocity (Freedman, Corkala, et al., 2004; Freedman, Kambanda, et al., 2004; Stover & Weinstein, 2004). With parallel studies in the Balkans and Rwanda, the larger project is particularly interested in helping close gaps between official and local perspectives in order to understand the complexities of social reconstruction. It also aims to learn how the international community might best respond in the aftermath of war crimes, crimes against humanity, and genocide.

This chapter shows that many young people in Mostar and Vukovar suffer from a general sense of depression and apathy. These symptoms may not always be clinically significant, and the same youth simultaneously show some resilience, yet their malaise permeates the culture. It also shows that regardless of their national affiliation or where they live, the youth feel abandoned by the adults who are responsible for them, both parents and teachers. Finally, for the most part, the youth do not know how to heal or how to think about a positive future. They are conflicted about whether it would be best to focus on trying to forget the past or on trying to remember it and also about whether they will ever be able to forgive others for what happened.

Background on the Region

The political situation was and continues to be complex. Until the early 1990s, Bosnian Muslims, Croats, and Serbs were part of one nation-state called Yugoslavia. Silber and Little (1996) trace the beginning of the breakup of the country to the rise in the 1980s of Serb nationalism, which Serb leader Slobodan Milosovic harnessed to strengthen his control. By the early 1990s, some non-Serb regions, including those dominated by Croats, openly went to war against Milosovic's Yugoslav National Army (JNA), while others, such as the Bosnian areas, were quickly swept along (pp. 26–27). The breakup of the country led not only to these wars but also to crimes against humanity and genocide. The result was the creation of five new countries: (1) Bosnia and Herzegovina (BiH), which consists of two parts, the Federation of Bosnia and Herzegovina and the Republika Srpska; (2) the Republic of Croatia; (3) Serbia and Montenegro (Kosovo is also part of this republic); (4) the Republic of Slovenia; and (5) the Former Yugoslav Republic of Macedonia (see the map in fig. 3.1).[1]

These new nation-states are working hard to create their own identities. The process remains tense, largely because the division of land did not neatly give each nationalist group a country. Rather, a situation now exists where populations who have been deeply traumatized by the acts of their neighbors who belong to different groups must find ways to coexist again inside these new states.

Both Mostar in BiH and Vukovar in Croatia are deeply divided along national lines: Croats versus Serbs in Vukovar and Bosniaks (Bosnian Muslims) versus Croats in Mostar. Figure 3.1 shows Mostar and Vukovar. Vukovar sits on Croatia's border with Serbia. Clearly visible across the Danube River is Serbian land. Many of the Serbs who live in Vukovar moved there in the 1930s and afterward to work in the Borovo shoe factory. The factory was bombed during the war, an act that effectively destroyed the local economy. Vukovar's Serbs and Croats still live in integrated neighborhoods, but they do all that they can to avoid contact.

Early in the war, the JNA waged a 2-month-long and very bloody siege on Vukovar. The JNA's goal was to create new borders for Yugoslavia cleansed of Croats. After meeting much resistance, the JNA ultimately triumphed on November 18, 1991, and on November 19 eliminated the last pocket of resistance at the hospital, murdering many patients, doctors, and nurses.

Unlike in Vukovar, where Croats and Serbs live unhappily side by side, in Mostar the Croats live mostly on the west side of the Neretva River, while the

FIGURE 3.1 Central Balkan Region

Bosniaks live mostly on the east side. The famous Ottoman bridge, the Stari Most, built in 1566, linked the two sides of the town before it was destroyed by shelling in 1994. At that time the Croat army took the town as it fought to control Croat-dominated land inside Bosnia. According to Maas (1996), the Croat attacks were just as brutal as those mounted by the JNA. The bridge was not rebuilt until 2004, and its ruins served for 10 years as a constant reminder of the division of the population and of the physical, social, and psychological destruction of the recent wars.

Today in Mostar and Vukovar, most young people who belong to one national group have little opportunity to meet young people from other groups. In a society where coffee is central to social life, the cafés are segregated along national lines. The schools are also segregated. In Mostar, the schools on the east side are for the Bosniak population, and those on the west side are for the Croats. A few students cross from one side to the other for specialist training, but they remain rare exceptions to the rule. In Vukovar as well, children go to segregated schools or to the same school but in separate shifts.

People in Mostar and Vukovar also are affected by the fact that much of the Balkan region suffers from an ailing economy. The report of the United Nations Development Program (UNDP) on human development in Bosnia and Herzegovina in 2002 included a chapter on youth and the "brain drain"; between January 1996 and March 2001, 92,000 young people left BiH, and 62%

of those left behind say they would emigrate if they had the chance (United Nations Development Program [UNDP], 2002, pp. 41–42). The youth of BiH suffer from extraordinarily high rates of unemployment; 34.8% of those aged 19–24, 13.4% of those aged 25–49, and only 9.7% of those aged 50–60 are unemployed (p. 36). Since the wars, there also has been a shift in the percentage of students who continue their education past the primary years. Before the wars, 80% went on to secondary school; in 2000–2001, only 56% enrolled in secondary school (p. 39). It was also the case that 58.5% of the population believed that the educational system was corrupt (pp. 26–27). An active drug trade flourishes on the thriving black market, and many of the youth seek the escape provided by drugs or alcohol. The situation is similar in Vukovar.

In interviews and focus groups for our study, students, their parents, and their teachers in both towns describe a context of ongoing volatility and violence. A young Croat girl from Vukovar explained, "There is always some fight." When asked to provide specifics, she recalled a recent "rough fight between Serbs and Croats" that required police intervention. She explained that the fight "started with provocations, though I don't know who started first" and went on to say, "Mostly everyone has something what he or she went through, what troubles him. The temperaments are high." In Mostar, a Croat boy whom we interviewed reported similar types of violence:

> We get together on a Friday evening and go to the park. That's the central place in Mostar, say. And ahh, Muslims come from the right bank and we quarrel. And finally it turns into a battle and we take revenge on each other.

In both Mostar and Vukovar, the significant, unrepaired physical damage from the wars offers a constant reminder of the past violence; many buildings are scarred by the pockmarks of mortar shells, while others sit in ruins. As one Serb mother in Vukovar lamented, "Children live among ruins. The moment you get out of your house you become aware of where you live. These wounds won't disappear." Besides bad memories and these more tangible reminders, the citizens, including the youth, continue to feel ongoing mistrust across national groups and live with deep divisions stemming from past brutalities.

Theoretical Frame

In the Balkans, how the youth respond to the past wars and ongoing violence is intertwined with how they understand and are affected by the many social institutions and relationships in which they participate. An ecological model, in combination with the theories of Lev Vygotsky (1978) and Mikhail Bakhtin and his followers, helps frame their responses (Bakhtin, 1981; Bakhtin/Medvedev, 1978;[2] Voloshinov, as cited in Morris, 1994). The ecological model posits that many interacting factors lead to civil destruction and the processes of social reconstruction (see Fletcher & Weinstein, 2002). It draws from the work of Bronfenbrenner (1979), Sarason (1972), and Kelly (1968) and assumes that we can say little about universals and instead will learn more from paying particular attention to context. For youth violence, the implication is that the focus must move beyond the individual to consider the other social institutions that both affect the individual and that the individual affects.

Most helpful to understanding how the youth understand and are affected by violence in their societies is the Bakhtinian concept of "ideological becoming." Freedman and Ball explain that "in Bakhtinian writings 'ideological becoming' refers to how we develop our way of viewing the world, our system of ideas, what Bakhtin calls an ideological self" (2004, p. 5). The development of ideologies, according to Bakhtin and his circle, is part of the development of the whole person.

According to Bakhtin, as we develop our ideologies, we struggle to assimilate two distinct categories of discourse: (1) authoritative discourse and (2) internally persuasive discourse. Bakhtin defines authoritative discourse as "the word of the fathers. Its authority was already *acknowledged* in the past. . . . for example, the authority of religious dogma, or of acknowledged scientific truth or of a currently fashionable book" (1981, pp. 342–343). The discourse of political authorities would be included as well. Internally persuasive discourse, by contrast, includes everyday discourses. It is "denied all privilege, backed by no authority at all, and is frequently not even acknowledged in society" (p. 342).

For the young people aged 14 to 16 whom we studied, their development of ideologies is intertwined with their identity development. Adolescence is a critical time, when young people are defining who they are, both as individuals and as members of social groups. It also is a critical period for the development of thought about conflictual intergroup relations and has been found to be the most impressionable period for the development of collective memory (Pennebaker & Banasik, 1997).

Some researchers have tried to determine the amount and types of clinically diagnosable psychological abnormality among young people who grow up with war. They have relied on self-reports and some information about the youth from the points of view of their mothers. These studies have found that around 40% of the population they studied exhibit measurable psychological abnormalities, mostly some type of anxiety, aggression, or depression (Cairnes & Dawes, 1996; Punamaki, 1996). The amount of difficulty children experience has been found to be related to their specific wartime experiences, with separation from and lack of support from families and exposure to multiple types of trauma (witnessing violent acts, loss of loved ones, and the like), putting them at increased risk (Garbarino & Kostelny, 1996; Ladd & Cairnes, 1996; Macksoud & Aber, 1996). It also has been found that youth in these very difficult contexts may have reserves of resilience (Garbarino & Kostelny, 1996; Garmazey & Rutter, 1985). It seems important to ask whether one has to exhibit diagnosable abnormalities to have been scarred in ways that matter, whether one can show some resilience but still have lingering difficulties coping. Few studies have looked beyond symptoms to the attitudes and feelings that drive young peoples' decision-making or to the interactions that influence their development from day to day.

In spite of this research literature on youth who have experienced war or who have grown up in politically unstable environments, little is known about the potential consequences for a nation when its adolescents come of age in a post-war society characterized by chronic conflict and ongoing violence. Although it is not possible to determine exact social consequences, it is possible to gain an understanding of the youth that might help one anticipate possible consequences. As we look at young people's experiences of past and ongoing violence and unrest in the context of these broader ecological and socio-historical theories, we consider how the wars and the social structures that remain in their aftermath might affect the development of the youth.

The Study

We do not focus on young people who themselves behave violently so much as on those who have experienced and continue to experience societal violence. Some of these young people lived through the wars, feared for their lives, and witnessed or were victims of horrible atrocities. Some lost parents or other close relatives or have been or are being raised by deeply scarred adults who may have been victims or perpetrators of the atrocities themselves. Some of the children were sent away during the wars or left with their families and now have returned to a society that is vastly different from the one they left. Some have been displaced from their homes and communities. All live in an unstable society where many of the same tensions that led to the wars remain palpable. As they were aged 5 to 8 during the height of the Balkan wars, all have strong memories of that time.

To learn about how young people are responding to ongoing tensions and violence in the society, we talked to students, their teachers, and their parents in Mostar and Vukovar. With local research teams, we conducted 78 interviews and talked to another 140 people in 20 focus groups. Our findings about the young people's responses to violence and unrest and their difficulty moving on are supported by our analysis of transcripts of these interviews and focus groups. The patterns we observed are illustrated with quotations from these transcripts.

We situated our work in the schools because they are a critical social space where many of the tensions within the larger society are replicated. The schools also provide a grand stage where young people can try on different identities and define the groups with which they will affiliate. In this process, they can play out their responses to the wars, violence, and ongoing instability experienced by themselves and the adults who surround them, most especially their parents and their teachers.

We hope to use our study to discover not only the difficulties the youth face but also the kinds of social structures needed to nurture this generation. Through considering issues related to schooling, we examine how the schools as an institution might contribute to the mechanisms of social repair and support the capacities of the youth for resilience. Toward this end, we examine ways teachers, parents, and students think the schools approach issues related to the healing of the youth. The society expects the schools to play a crucial role in their healing process, albeit not the only role.

The Youth's Responses to Violence and Chronic Unrest

Pervasive Apathy

Adults characterize the young people as a quiet and serious generation who had to grow up before their time. A Croat teacher from Mostar describes students today as "a little nervous," carrying bitterness about the past, carrying burdens. In the focus group of Croat teachers from Mostar, a teacher described this generation as suffering from "some kind of inner discontent," and then went on to say, "They are empty. They wait." In a focus group in Mostar, one of the Croat students expressed his fear for the future, given the characteristics of the youth: "We can't make a modern society when we are so withdrawn, so introverted." A Bosnian father from Mostar described psychological symptoms that his children exhibited during the war. They were afraid to sleep alone and generally were fearful, locking doors and the like. He described these symptoms as better now but with some effects still lingering. A Serb mother from Vukovar concluded:

> Children carry deep wounds. . . . We are not even aware of how deep the wounds are. . . . but I think the wounds inflicted in the postwar period go even deeper because they [Serb children] are constantly being told that they are guilty for something, guilty, guilty.

Regardless of their past experiences, as a group, young people in both Mostar and Vukovar have little hope for their futures. Consistent with the findings of the UNDP report for Bosnia and Herzegovina (2002), many say they want to leave the region to escape what they view as severe limits on what they could accomplish with their lives. The economic depression exacerbates young people's psychological problems and their feelings of apathy. Although the economy of Croatia as a country is stronger than the economy of BiH, the Vukovar economy is seriously depressed. A Serb student who lives in Vukovar reveals her hopelessness:

> When you finish college, you can't find a job, and you're still a burden to your parents who have to support you until they die. And when they die, you are finished because you are used to depending on them. It's like with wild animals—if you take a wild animal and take care of it for some time and then let it go, it wouldn't survive because it wouldn't be able to take care of itself.

This student, like many of her peers, including the Croats, sees no way to become a functioning adult in the culture.

These feelings of despair about the economy came up in Mostar as well. In a focus group of Croat girls from Mostar, one explained: "After you graduate from secondary school or university . . . you can't even find a job washing glasses in a cafe." In a focus group of Croat boys from Mostar, the moderator asked outright, "Do you want to go abroad when you finish school?" Three students immediately replied that they did. They pointed to the low salaries and lack of job opportunity in BiH as their main reason. The Bosniaks felt similarly.

In Mostar, especially among the Croats, some of the despair seemed to be related to the students' beliefs that opportunities come not because of merit but because of connections, a finding also consistent with the UNDP (2002) report. In the focus group of Croat boys from Mostar, one explained his despair around university admissions:

> However much you've learned, there's not much chance you'll be able to enroll in university. Everything is through connections now, who you know. Some get in with bad marks. . . . The ones who've found some connection are always the ones who get a place. They'll get in before you do even if you've really spent all those years working hard on your education.

Croat teachers in Mostar felt that views about the importance of connections led to the lack of a work ethic. They also discussed the difficulty of teaching when the job outlook for students is so uncertain.

Abandoned by Adults

The youth in both Mostar and Vukovar, regardless of their national affiliation, said that the adults in their lives, both parents and teachers, did not understand the trauma they experienced during the war or their problems today. The youth felt abandoned by most of these adults because they did not want to talk to the youth about wartime experiences, and they did not recognize the youth's pain. The youth portrayed the adults as incapable of giving them the attention and guidance that they needed. Some said that their parents thought they were too little to remember very much and that their parents thought that they themselves were the ones who really suffered most in the wars. A Bosniak student from Mostar reported:

> Lately the teachers have been saying we [the teachers] are the last generation that suffered from the war and we [the students] hardly remember the war. But in fact that's not true, that we hardly remember it. We remember everything and we suffer from it too. I think it's pointless to say we don't remember the war.

She then related specific memories of how her schooling was interrupted during the war.

A Croat student from Mostar explained that her parents avoid talking with her about difficult subjects related to the recent past: "They avoid the subject too at home. I don't know, when I ask Dad something, 'Can you explain it to me?' It's 'Come on, why are you interested in that? Why are you talking about that at home?' " This student thought that parents in the community generally were abdicating their responsibilities toward their children and that as a result many youth were in trouble:

They [parents] are preoccupied with themselves. I don't know. They do take account of us, but there are plenty of people in the grade, you can see from their parents that they [the parents] are not much interested. . . . There are plenty who are on the wrong path in my grade. Their parents don't see it. . . . There's quite a lot of them who smoke grass, who drink lots of alcohol, even in class. And the parents don't do anything.

By the end of the interview, this student concluded that she suffered because she lacked adult guidance. She suggested that the schools could do a better job in guiding the youth. "Maybe they should bring in someone to give us a bit more guidance about how we should behave towards those other groups. And in class for the teachers to pay a bit more attention to us."

Another Croat student from Mostar explained the importance of talk and communication, across generations and across ethnic divides:

I think that it would be the best that the society and authority organize different seminars for young people, that there they talk openly. With a dialogue, and not some lectures. . . . Ahhh, maybe some debates, maybe some dialogue between younger and older. Or mixed [ethnicities].

Similarly, a Croat student from Vukovar expressed her need for more talk in school about the recent wars:

We should learn about the causes of the war and how disputes should be resolved in order to avoid wars. We should be educated about these things. The older ones know what the war was about, but younger generations don't know anything about how this war came about, what were its causes. I believe we should talk about it more.

In the Croat teachers' focus group in Mostar, one shirked responsibility for responding to the students' needs: "With the times as they are, I think teachers aren't in a position, they aren't to blame that is for being unable to offer what school should offer." Another explained that the schools did not teach moral values because the society does not function according to moral values:

When you teach him, say, respect, that's not welcome anywhere these days. If he's to be honest, realistic, sincere, that doesn't do you any good these days. Everything's back to front these days. It's a real snafu. It does you no good these days to do what God commanded. That doesn't open any doors these days. Who wants an honest trader these days. I don't know for sure. When everyone is based only on how to cheat the other fellow first, who can earn the most the quickest. I mean, it's all very practical and that's life, but there's school too.

Some parents reported talking to their children about the war, although they found it painful; they also said that they held back because they felt a need to try to protect their children. A Serb parent from Vukovar said in her interview that she did not want to talk about the past:

Terrible things happed in Vukovar, horrible things. It's very difficult to answer why they happened because everyone has their own opinion about that. . . . I don't want to talk about it because it has a very negative effect on me. I have been through a lot and my children have been though a lot only because we are Serbs. That was a dreadful time and I really don't want to talk about it.

Another Vukovar parent, this one a Croat, also claimed that her children were fine because she protected them by pretending that all was fine. She embedded this information in her story of what happened to her family during the war:

> That summer [1991] when we left Vukovar, in which fighting was still going on, sociologists and psychologists came to visit us and talk to us, the refugees, in all the places we were living at the time. We always had guilty feelings, because we knew there were people suffering in Vukovar, so we didn't want to talk or laugh thinking that if those people couldn't laugh we wouldn't either. We did our best to hide our feelings from our children. My husband was in the prisoners' camp, and in the daytime I was pretending that everything was all right. I was smiling, spending time with my children. Everybody asked me: "How do you manage to do that?" But nobody knows what my nights were like. I used to smoke a pack of cigarettes a day. I didn't sleep at night. But I never let my children feel that. That's why I don't think my children experience any severe trauma. They know what happened and have their own attitude towards ethnicity issues, but, as I said, we tried to protect them as much as we could.

Particularly poignant were the words of a mother who lived in Vukovar but is neither Serb nor Croat. She is married to a Serb, though, and her children, who went to a Serb school, found that they fit nowhere. When they asked her what nationality they were, she didn't want to answer because she didn't want them to think in these terms. Her inability to answer paralyzed her in trying to help them navigate the world in which they lived.

However, her son faced difficult experiences that made her answer of "It isn't important what you are" unsatisfactory. She recounted an incident he experienced on a handball team that was mostly Croat:

> After three or four trainings he comes home and says, "I'm not going there any more." And I say, "Why darling? Why you are not going?" He says, "Nobody will tell me that I'm Serbian pig." I say, "Who told you that?" He says, "Well some kid there." I say, "Darling, he is still very young. He doesn't know what he is saying. It doesn't matter. Don't pay attention. Go if you like to." But then you have group pressure of children his age. . . . Children act imprudently, which leaves marks on other children.

There are no right or wrong answers in such situations. The problem is with the society as a whole. A miniwar continues, with children as both perpetrators and victims at the same time and with adults too often left in situations where they find themselves powerless to protect their children.

Indeed, the special case of children of binational marriages cannot be ignored because the numbers are significant, in Mostar even more than in Vukovar. The children of binational marriages seem to be caught in some kind of no-man's-land. In BiH some people choose to identify as Bosnians, a supranational identity, distinct from Bosniaks, who are specifically Bosnian Muslims. Although there may be other reasons, in most cases those who choose Bosnian identity are children from so-called binational marriages or those who oppose national identification based on religious origins. Furthermore, Bosnian identity is often related to identification with the state (citizenship), as a clear and strong demonstration against the all-prevailing national divisions in the country.

Paralysis About Moving On—Tensions Surrounding Forgetting and Forgiving

Except for the Vukovar Serbs, who want only to forget about the past, those from other national groups were conflicted about whether it would be best to focus on trying to remember the past and to remind others of it or on trying to put it out of mind and avoid discussing it in schools and elsewhere. Many of the people we talked to were conflicted; they wanted to remember for some reasons but to forget for others. They wanted to remember to learn from past mistakes and to hold on to the memories of those whom they lost or simply because it was not possible to forget such an experience. But they wanted to forget so as to avoid personal pain and trauma and to be able to move on, although some felt that they needed to remember to move on. It is also the case that some connected putting the past out of their minds to forgiving others, while some said that they could keep their memories and still forgive others. Many of the Serbs of Vukovar and some of the Croats of Mostar expressed their need to be forgiven, while the Croats of Vukovar generally did not think they could forgive their neighbors without an apology, which they did not see as forthcoming. The Serbs saw no need to apologize for deeds they did not personally carry out.

A Bosniak student from Mostar voiced conflicts about remembering, presenting contradictory views about keeping memories of the past. At first he claimed that he could forget and that he wanted to forget: "What's past is past. It can be forgotten now." Then later the same student said the past could not and should never be forgotten:

> It would be a good thing for everyone to know what had happened, since it's not some small thing that can be forgotten, is it. . . . During the war I experienced all sorts of things, and I can't say now, "Well, that's that. I'll forget it." I can't. It'll always be there. It's engraved into me.

A Bosniak father said he wrote about his memories of the war so as never to forget them, but he was conflicted, thinking aloud that perhaps it would be better psychologically to try to put the past horrors out of mind, "simply in order to calm down." Then he concluded that children should be taught about the events that transpired so those events would not be forgotten from one generation to the next.

As individuals, the Croats in Mostar feared remembering because, as one student said, "It brings back bad memories for some people and they have some trauma." This student voiced his conflicts as well. At the societal level, he said that he wanted the past to be taught "so that we remember and understand why there was that war, why it shouldn't happen again."

In Vukovar, as was the case in Mostar for both Bosniaks and Croats, Croats voiced internal conflicts about remembering the recent wars. However, the Croats showed intolerance toward Serbs as a group, expressing blame and resentment. This negativity was much stronger than anything voiced by either Bosniaks or Croats in Mostar or by the Serbs in Vukovar. For example, a Croat student from Vukovar said, "As for the Serbs, I don't want to have anything to do with them. I don't need them in my life."

The Croats also wanted to remember only good things about their group. One of the adults talked about not wanting to remember or be reminded of Croats' roles as German collaborators in both world wars. One teacher explained: "I don't think that some questions about Ustashe[3] should be mentioned. . . . Ustashe this, Ustashe that . . . I think that those are stupidities."

Similarly the Serbs did not want to remember or be reminded of the more recent wars. When asked what he thought students should learn about the recent war in Croatia, a Serb student responded: "We shouldn't learn anything about the recent war. . . . These things are meaningless to me. It's pointless to discuss about who is a criminal, about the tribunal. We should . . . forget about these things." A teacher, when asked what he thought parents wanted their children to learn about the recent wars, said he thought they wanted it all to go away, for life to return to what it was before the war: "I'm not sure what the parents think about it, but they might wish that none of that ever happened. Before the war there were many binational marriages in this region. People didn't pay that much attention to ethnic belonging."

With respect to forgiving, the Croats in Vukovar were angry and felt strongly that Serbs would have to take responsibility for their deeds before they could forgive them. A teacher who is a theologian talked a lot about forgiving and in the process explained why the Croats could not forgive the Serbs. An apology was his minimum condition:

> Words that encourage forgiveness and reconciliation have no effect if the vision of the very essence of forgiveness doesn't exist. What I mean is that those who are responsible for what we had to go through in the last eight, nine years should apologize for what they have done and create conditions for healthy relationships in this area. I don't know how to put it differently. If somebody has hurt me, I can forgive that person so that I can have my peace of mind; but in order to achieve peaceful coexistence, the other side has to show the goodwill.

The Serbs tended to blame their leaders and did not understand why they were being asked to take individual responsibility when, as individuals, they felt they did not commit the crimes.

The same teacher also used strong language to characterize the culpability of the Serbs:

> I wouldn't be able to sleep at night if I knew that I had hurt someone, stolen from someone, destroyed someone's life. I think we should be far more humble than we are. The unscrupulousness of the Serbs, their way of presenting things, their statements are not conducive to creating new, democratic, open relationships.

When there is an official void, the opportunity arises for teachers to promote their own interpretations of the events. As a Croat student in Vukovar explained, "We didn't exactly learn about it [the recent conflicts] since these things are not in the textbooks, but we talked about it." He then went on to say, "For instance, we talked about how Serbs, when they finish their schools, find jobs in Vukovar before we do." Similarly, a teacher in a Croat school in Mostar explained that she and her colleagues were teaching the students that they are Croats, not Bosnians: "Casually we are mentioning Croatia, isn't it. We are working on Croatian on the side." The absence of an official curriculum for dealing with the recent past led to the existence of a hidden curriculum, which seemed in many ways to work against reconciliation.

Conclusion

The design of our work allowed us to gain some understanding of the points of view of parents, teachers, and youth on issues related to how the violence of the recent wars and their aftermath affected the youth. Further, it allowed us to examine the youth in relation to their participation in schools and in relation to how a range of social forces affect them. In Bakhtin's terms, these social forces include both the authoritative discourses in the official world of the communities in which they live and also the internally persuasive discourses of their peers and other everyday people. Both types of discourses meet in the schools.

The weak economy and the constant tension between national groups seems to lead to a great deal of distress and ultimately to an overwhelming sense of apathy. Every national group considers itself victimized by the situation in which they live. This general apathy and culture of victimization translates into a kind of apathy that works against the building of a democratic society. If people are apathetic about politics, they will not vote, and democratic processes cannot be built.

The youth seem paralyzed about how to handle their experiences, whether to forgive, and then, if they can forgive, whether they think it best to try to put the past out of mind or to focus on remembering. Only the Vukovar Serbs are certain that they do not want to remember. These tensions around forgiving and trying to forget surface in other Communities in Crisis work in the Balkans with other populations (see Biro et al., 2004). It is also the case that our projects in Rwanda show the complexities of how past memories will influence building the future (Freedman, Kambanda, et al., 2004).

In post-conflict situations, the youth need adult support, but they have difficulty getting the kind of support they need. Isolated teachers talk to the youth in ways that the youth find helpful, and isolated parents are attempting to help the youth navigate very rough social waters. The youth are grateful for any adult support they get, but they need more support than is readily available to them.

Our design and, therefore, our explanations are consistent with an ecological and socio-historical theory that points to how social forces interact and how different members of a culture affect one another. Our goal is to use our findings to recommend positive directions for the future. Everything we have learned points to the fact that this culture of victimization is destructive. Further, the youth need to be able to talk to adults about their experiences. Several young people praised programs sponsored by nongovernmental organizations from other countries that allowed them the occasional opportunity to talk; they wanted more such programs. Since the adults within the culture have difficulty providing these opportunities, it would be good for the international community to consider ways of providing additional opportunities for the youth but, equally important, to offer programs for adults that would support them in being able to talk to the youth about the many difficult experiences of the recent past.

There are tensions surrounding curriculum that would address these issues. There is, first of all, a general absence of a history curriculum, which seems related to the paralysis we found around adult's reluctance to officially discuss the past and the tensions around forgiving and trying to put the past out of mind. We believe that developing a history curriculum is necessary to working through some of the problems the youth face. These notions of forgiving and trying to forget versus trying to remember may lead to context-bound and grounded ways to talk about historical memory and ultimately to give youth the guidance they call for as they develop their ideologies, their ways of viewing their world. In Rwanda, where the schools are integrated and where the government has an official policy promoting unity and reconciliation, we have begun a project with the Ministry of Education to break the 10-year-old moratorium on the teaching of history (Freedman, Weinstein, & Longman, 2003). This kind of work does not yet seem possible in the Balkans; although it remains to be seen how possible it will be to make constructive progress in Rwanda, at least the conversations have begun.

Finally, we think that the schools in Mostar and Vukovar will have to be integrated at some point in the near future, to give the youth an opportunity to get to know and learn about people across national lines. But integration, too, will need to be accompanied by programs that will support both the youth and the adults in managing the transition. Otherwise, integration will only beget more violence.

All in all, the youth of the Balkans have much to overcome, but through their talk and the talk of their parents and teachers, we were able to learn something about the kinds of support that could make their futures brighter. We have recently gathered some new data that show that life in Mostar may be improving for some people in some pockets of the town. An ethnographer for the larger project, in his most recent report, wrote about changes he is seeing. He found that some young people, now in their thirties, are beginning to be able to talk about the war for the first time. When he asked about this change, one young woman explained that some people are beginning new lives and leaving the recent past behind them:

> I asked Maja how she explains the fact that everybody started talking about the war all of a sudden, discussing events about which they had kept silent for ten

years. "People have started new lives. So, now, they can talk about their previous ones," she concluded. (Communities in Crisis, 2002, p. 27)

Symbolically, the reconstruction of the old Ottoman bridge in Mostar marks for many in BiH the psychological end of an era. In Vukovar, the Berkeley Human Rights Center is working with a group of teachers to start a model integrated school. Again, it will take some time to see how that project progresses.

Notes

1. Macedonia is not labeled on the map, but Skopje is in the northern part of Macedonia, and it borders Albania to the west, Greece to the south, and Bulgaria to the east.

2. The question of the authorship of this work is disputed, although according to Morson (personal communication, August 22, 2002), it is now widely believed that this text was written by Medvedev. When we refer to it here, we will use Bakhtin/Medvedev, since this is the authorship ascribed to the text from which we quote.

3. The term *Ustashe* makes reference to a World War II group and a shameful national past. The Ustashe, with Hitler's help, created the so-called Independent State of Croatia during World War II. As a Croatian nationalist terrorist organization, Ustashe served the Germans during World War II and brutally murdered many Jews and Serbs. To call any Croat other than the most radical nationalist a Ustasha is a grave insult.

References

Bakhtin, M. M. (1981). Discourse in the novel. In M. Holquist (Ed.), *The dialogic imagination: Four essays by M. M. Bakhtin* (Caryl Emerson & Michael Holquist, Trans.) (pp. 259–422). Austin: University of Texas Press.

Bakhtin, M. M. / Medvedev, P. N. (1978). *The formal method in literary scholarship: A critical introduction to sociological poetics.* (Albert J. Wehrle, Trans.). Cambridge, MA: Harvard University Press.

Biro, M., Ajdukovic, D., Corkalo, D., Djipa, D., Milin, P., & Weinstein, H. (2004). Attitudes towards justice and social reconstruction in Bosnia and Herzegovina and Croatia. In E. Stover & H. Weinstein (Eds.), *My neighbor, my enemy: Justice and community in the aftermath of mass atrocity* (pp. 183–205). Cambridge, UK: Cambridge University Press.

Bronfenbrenner, U. (1979). *The ecology of human development.* Cambridge, MA: Harvard University Press.

Cairns, E., & Dawes, A. (1996). Children: Ethnic and political violence: A commentary. *Child Development, 67*(1), 129–139.

Communities in Crisis. (May-June, 2002). *Report on the Fourth Stay in Mostar.* (Ethnographer's Report). Berkeley: Human Rights Center.

Fletcher, L., & Weinstein, H. M. (2002). Violence and social repair: Rethinking the contribution of justice to reconciliation. *Human Rights Quarterly, 24*(3), 573–639.

Freedman, S. W., & Ball, A. (2004). Ideological becoming: Bakhtinian concepts to guide the study of language, literacy, and learning. In A. Ball & S. W. Freedman (Eds.), *Bakhtinian perspectives on language, literacy and learning* (pp. 3–33). Cambridge, UK: Cambridge University Press.

Freedman, S. W., Corkalo, D., Levy, N., Abazovic, D., Leebaw, B., Ajdukovic, D., Djipa, D., & Weinstein, H. (2004). Public education and social reconstruction in Bosnia-Herzegovina and Croatia. In E. Stover & H. Weinstein (Eds.), *My neighbor, my enemy: Justice and community in the aftermath of mass atrocity* (pp. 226–247). Cambridge, UK: Cambridge University Press.

Freedman, S. W., Kambanda, D., Samuelson, B., Mugisha, I., Mukashema, I., Mukama, E., Mutabaruka, J., Weinstein, H., & Longman, T. (2004). Confronting the past in Rwandan schools. In E. Stover & H. Weinstein (Eds.), *My neighbor, my enemy: Justice and community in the aftermath of mass atrocity* (pp. 248–265). Cambridge, UK: Cambridge University Press.

Freedman, S. W., Weinstein, H., & Longman, T. (2003). *Education for reconciliation in Rwanda: Creating a history curriculum after genocide.* Proposal to the United States Institute of Peace, Human Rights Center, University of California, Berkeley.

Garbarino, J., & Kostelny, K. (1996). The effects of political violence on Palestinian children's behavior problems: A risk accumulation model. *Child Development, 67* (1), 33–45.

Garmazey, N., & Rutter, M. (1985). Acute reactions to stress. In M. Rutter & L. Hersov (Eds.), *Child and adolescent psychiatry: Modern approaches* (2nd ed., pp. 152–176). Oxford: Blackwell.

Kelly, J. G. (1968). Toward an ecological conception of preventive interventions. In J. W. Carter, Jr. (Ed.), *Research contributions from psychology to community mental health* (pp.75–99). New York: Behavioral.

Ladd, G., & Cairns, E. (1996). Children: Ethnic and political violence. *Child Development, 67*(1), 14–18.

Maas, P. (1996). *Love thy neighbor: A story of war.* New York: Vintage Books.

Macksoud, M., & Aber, J. L. (1996). The war experiences and psychosocial development of children in Lebanon. *Child Development, 67*(1), 70–88.

Morris, P. (Ed.). (1994). *The Bakhtin reader: Selected writings of Bakhtin, Medvedev, Voloshinov.* London: Arnold.

Pennebaker, J., & Banasik, B. (1997). On the creation and maintenance of collective memories: History as social psychology. In J. Pennebaker, D. Paez, & B. Rimé (Eds.), *Collective memory of political events* (pp. 3–19). Mahwah, NJ: Erlbaum.

Punamaki, R. (1996). Can ideological commitment protect children's psychosocial well-being in situations of political violence? *Child Development, 67*(1), 55–69.

Sarason, S. B. (1972). The ecological approach. In S. B. Sarason (Ed.), *Revisiting "The Culture of the School and the Problem of Change"* (pp. 110–137). New York: Teachers College Press.

Silber, L., & Little, A. (1996). *Yugoslavia: Death of a nation.* New York: Penguin Books.

Stover, E., & Weinstein, H. (Eds.). (2004). *My neighbor, my enemy: Justice and community in the aftermath of mass atrocity.* Cambridge, UK: Cambridge University Press.

United Nations Development Programme. (2002). *Human development report 2002, Bosnia and Herzegovina.* Sarajevo: Economics Institute of Sarajevo.

Vygotsky, L. S. (1978). *Mind in society: The development of higher psychological processes* (M. Cole, V. John-Steiner, S. Scribner, & E. Souberman, Eds.). Cambridge, MA: Harvard University Press.

CHAPTER 4

Youth Participation in Violence in Nigeria Since the 1980s

OLAYEMI AKINWUMI

Since the 1980s, Nigeria has continued to witness an unprecedented surge of ethnoreligious violence. The involvement of youth in these civil disturbances or conflicts is very disturbing. They are the foot soldiers, and in some cases "generals," of the various ethnic militia groups that were formed in this period to defend the narrow interests of the various ethnic groups or individuals who established them. The involvement of these young Nigerians has made these conflicts more violent than they would have been because they have the vigor to pursue and sustain violence in their areas of operations. It also has left lasting scars on both the victims and perpetrators of these conflicts, most of whom are the youth themselves; many are still mourning the loss of loved ones in the conflicts and many became homeless because their properties were destroyed. It has led many to conclude that the country has no future if the "leaders of tomorrow," as the youth are referred to in Nigeria, could take delight in both perpetuating violence against their fellow young people from other ethnic groups and destroying government properties or the economic basis of the country, as is the case in the Niger-Delta area.[1] Young people are the perpetrators of the violence in the country now.

This chapter will consider the factors responsible for youth violence in the country. It will also focus on the state reaction and measures to curb youth involvement in violence. The chapter concludes that until the state resolves the fundamental problems with the economy, especially in the area of employment, Nigerian youth will continue to be involved in ethnoreligious conflicts. Second, it is posited that the youth should be involved in creating policies that directly affect them instead of being treated as mere objects of knowledge and policy. As Sheila Brown (1998, p. 3) pointed out in her book, they should be "listened to" rather than "silenced and scapegoated."[2] Third, as recommended by Olutayo (1994), fundamental survival techniques in the country must be dissociated from violence.

Methodology

For this research, I relied on a combination of observation, in-depth interviews, group discussion, and administration of questionnaires in cities where ethnic militias are very prominent. The in-depth interviews were conducted with identified members with adequate knowledge of the workings of the militias. In addition, group discussions were conducted with members and nonmembers (who felt the impact of the militias). Both the in-depth interviews and the group discussions extracted information from them on the workings and changes of the militias.

The case questionnaire method was aimed at identifying the different population variables that determined the dynamics of members of the militias. Such variables include the numbers of graduates, secondary school leavers, and those below them. The questionnaires were administered between 2001 and 2002 in Lagos, Ibadan, Kaduna, Kano, Port Harcourt, and Warri.[3] Two hundred and fifty respondents were randomly selected from these localities, with an overwhelming population of males, with their ages ranging between 17 and 35. Seventy-five percent of those interviewed were unemployed, with those from secondary schools and below constituting the bulk of them. Their perception of the problem correlated with their level of education and exposure to violence. This group represents what one might describe as the nihilists who have little at stake. Nor do they believe in the government having solutions to the problem. The secondary school graduates, who were few when compared with this other group, represent the intellectual powerhouse of the militias.

Working Definitions

Who is a youth? There are many diverse definitions. For example, there are economical, legal, and statistical definitions. In economic terms, according to the International Labor Organization (ILO) Convention no. 138 of 1973, (as cited in Akinwumi, 2002), a youth is defined as somebody aged 15 to 30. In legal terms, somebody is said to be a youth if he or she is between the ages of 18 and 21. For the purpose of this exercise, the statistical definition will be adopted; however, it must be mentioned that it varies. For example, the United Nations defines a youth as somebody between the ages of 15 and 24 (United Nations [UN], 1992, p. 272). Many nations have adopted either of the foregoing definitions, while others have adopted different age categories for the purpose of their policy. In Nigeria, for example, a youth is defined as somebody between the ages of 12 and 30. It is based on the definition that the Federal Government of Nigeria has barred anybody more than 30 years old from participating in the National Youth Service Corp scheme.[4] I am going to use this definition because this chapter is based on youth and violence in Nigeria.[5] Apart from the aforementioned definition, a youth in Nigeria is also defined or conceived, in Moore and Tonry's words, as somebody who is "unformed and still developing" (1998, p. 4). Somebody who is still in a transitional period to adulthood. Somebody who still needs to be guided in decision-making by his or her parents or guardians.

Unlike youth, violence is a concept that is presently attracting attention from scholars and policy-makers across the globe. The concept has been defined by many individuals from diverse perspectives. For the purposes of this chapter, I will consider three definitions. Anifowose, for example, defines violence as "illegitimate use of force by non-governmental individuals and groups" (1982, p. 3). Tamuno explains violence as "unlawful use or threat of force which could be a manifestation of despair and desperation" (1980, p. 4), while Domenach understands violence from three angles, as (a) "psychological: an explosion of force assuming an irrational and often murderous form"; (b) "ethical: an attack on the property and liberty of one's neighbor"; and (c) "political: the use of force to seize power or to misappropriate it for illicit ends" (cited in Oyekunle, 1994, p. 225). On the basis of these three forms of violence, he defines violence as "the use of force—whether overt or covert—in order to wrest from individuals or groups something that they are not willing to give of their own free will" (p. 225).

For this chapter, I will define violence as physical trauma or injury inflicted by individuals or groups of individuals on others to obtain what does not belong to them or to attack what individuals or groups perceive to be their sources of discontent. This definition also includes psychological trauma (Moore & Tonry, 1998).

Before considering the research findings, we need to focus on the ethnic militias, their objectives, and their violent activities, all of which many have considered a threat to the national stability. It is also important to stress that some youth do not belong to any of the militias mentioned here but have been involved in some major conflicts in the country. They have taken the opportunity of any riotous situation in the country to loot and destroy properties. In Lagos and other urban centers in the south of Nigeria, they are referred to as "area boys" or "area girls," terms generally used to describe the street urchins. They are not employed. They live on drugs, begging, extortion, intimidation, harassing, and engaging in violent activities (Akinwumi, 2002). In the north, they are called the *almajirai* (singular: *almajiri*). They are child beggars from the Koranic schools, driven out by their respective teachers (*mallams*) to beg for alms. They have been implicated in all the ethnoreligious conflicts in the northern cities of Nigeria (Albert, 1997). The group known as *Yan tauri*, "sons of evil," could also be classified as the area boys.

Ethnic Militias, Youth, and the Escalation of Violence in Nigeria

The emergence of ethnic militias in Nigeria should be considered within the context of the struggle for political power and scarce economic resources by the various ethnic groups (numbering about 250) in Nigeria. The contest dates back to the colonial period, especially the late 1950s, when it was certain that the British colonial government would hand over power to the Nigerian nationalists in 1960. Ethnicity became a potent weapon to win votes. Since the 1960s, however, the Hausa/Fulani ethnic group, whether under civil or military rules, has dominated the politics of the country and has produced more civil and military heads of state. Consequently, the other ethnic groups had complained of marginalization and unjust distribution of wealth. This issue was partly responsible for the 1967 civil war in the country (Dudley, 1973; Falola, 1999; Tamuno, 1980).

On June 12, 1993, a federal election was conducted and was won by a Yoruba man, Chief M. K. O. Abiola. This election was considered free and fair by internal and external observers and, in fact, was considered the best organized election in the political history of the country. The military government of Ibrahim Babangida annulled this election without any justifiable reason. This action confirmed the suspicion of other ethnic groups, especially the Yoruba, that the Hausa/Fulani elite was determined to hold power perpetually in the country. It was under these circumstances that some members of the Yoruba elite, led by Dr. Frederick Fasheun, established the Oodua People's Congress (OPC) to challenge the annulment, fight for the actualization of the June 12 election, and defend the Yoruba elite, who became objects of attacks because of their stand against the annulment. Some were killed, others imprisoned, and others driven into exile because of the determination of the military dictator, Sanni Abacha, to silence the group. Within the last group was Professor Wole Soyinka, the Nobel laureate in literature.

Some of the stated objectives of the group are as follows (Akinwumi, 2002, p. 12):

1. To commit to the struggle of ensuring that Nigeria is run as a federal republic, where the federating units are allowed to develop at their own pace and manage their resources
2. To struggle for the restructuring of Nigeria on the basis of equality of ethnic nationalities
3. To resist domination of other nationalities by any group or section of the country
4. To protect the interest of Yoruba at home and in the diaspora

The group, according to R.T. Akinyele (2001), had about 2,786 branches in different parts of Yorubaland in 1999. Membership is open to all Yoruba citizens, on the condition that the interested person is ready to be initiated into the group and swear an oath of secrecy.[6] The group has its youth wing. Most of them are between the ages of 15 and 30 and are readily available for recruitment because they are jobless. They have served as the foot soldiers of the group and have been responsible for most of the violence committed by this group. Gani Adam's faction of the OPC has more of these youthful elements than the other factions; this is why this faction is most dreaded.[7] At one time, the federal government declared Gani Adam wanted and a price tag was put on his head because of the involvement of his faction in violent conflicts against the police and members of other ethnic groups (Akinwumi, 2002; Akinyele, 2001).

Some of the violent ethnic clashes involving the OPC included the Yoruba/ Hausa ethnic clashes in Shagamu, Lagos, Ibadan, and Ilorin. On July 17, 1999, the OPC went to Shagamu, a Yoruba community with a considerable number of Hausa settlers, to intervene on behalf of the Yoruba against the Hausa. The conflict was precipitated because of the death of a Hausa woman who violated the taboo restricting women from seeing the Yoruba secret (Oro) cult operating at night. In the conflicts that ensued, about 100 people lost their lives (Akinwumi, 2002; Akinyele, 2001). In Lagos, the OPC engaged the Hausa in several wars in 1999. In October and November 1999, Hausa living in the city, especially where they are concentrated, were killed and their businesses destroyed.

It was not only the Hausa who were attacked by the OPC but also the other ethnic groups, the Igbo and the Ijaw. The Igbo were attacked at the Alaba International Market on July 13, 2000, because of their dominance at the market, while the Ijaw were attacked at the Lagos Port to prevent what Akinyele (2001) called the annexation of the port by the Ijaw. The OPC/Ijaw crisis spilled over to Ajegunle, where there is a considerable population of the Ijaw. Many properties were destroyed, and many were rendered homeless. About 16 people were said to have lost their lives.

In response to the activities of the OPC, the Arewa People's Congress (APC) was inaugurated at the instance of a retired army officer, Captain Sagir Mohammed, to counter the activities of the OPC. According to the founder, the purpose of the APC is to safeguard and protect northern interests (especially the Hausa/Fulani group) in any part of the country and to respond to any attack on any northerner in Lagos. Unlike the OPC, not much is heard from this group except for threats issued through newspapers. The groups that are responsible for all of the ethnoreligious conflicts in the north are the almajirai and the Yan daba, as previously mentioned. The almajirai are mostly in their teens. They have no Western education, are poor, and depend upon the kindness of people around them. This is the reason why it has been possible to manipulate them to commit violent crimes against others in the society, especially the non-Hausa/Fulani groups. The almajirai and Yan daba have been responsible for burning churches and killing many southerners in the north. According to Albert, the Yan daba operated "during the religious, political, and ethnic violence in Kano . . . where their services are needed by their sponsors" (1997, p. 296).

In the eastern region of the country, two major groups emerged. These are the Bakassi Boys and the Movement for the Actualisation of the Sovereign State of Biafra (MASSOB). The former was established to protect the traders in the region from armed robbers that have laid siege to many of the commercial centers. This was necessary because of the failure of the Nigerian police to live up to their responsibility to protect the society. This group is meant to be a vigilante group. The success of this group led many of the eastern states to take over its funding and provide legal backing for it. For example, the Anambra State government took over the funding after the state House of Assembly gave it legal status by changing the name to Anambra Vigilante (Adewale, 2001, p. 7). Allegedly, the Bakassi Boys, made up of Igbo youth, is currently used by political heavyweights in the east to deal with political opponents. The group has been indicted in a series of retaliatory killings of Hausa/Fulani citizens in Aba and other eastern states.[8] The MASSOB, on the other hand, was established to fight for the restoration of the failed Biafra Republic.[9] The group attempted to redeclare the Biafra Republic on May 27, 2000, but failed because of the intervention of the police. Since then, members of the group have been in conflict with the security apparatus of the country.

The Niger Delta region is the only one in Nigeria where there is a proliferation of youth-headed militia groups. This should be understood within the context of the availability of petroleum deposits in the region and the competition for the control of the revenue from the petroleum between the federal and state governments on the one hand, and between the ethnic groups in the region on the other. It should also be understood within the context of poverty in the region. In spite of the fact that the region has provided about 75% of the total revenue of the country, it is still the poorest. In addition, the region is being ravaged by environmental degradation and pollution because of the activities of the multinational petroleum companies in the region. Karl Maier describes the situation in the Niger-Delta thus:

> Over the years, 643 million barrels of oil worth approximately $30 billion had been pumped from Ogoniland [one of the communities in Niger-Delta] alone through a network of ninety-six wells hooked up to five flow stations. The Shell Petroleum Development Corporation (SPDC) ran the system with its joint venture partner, the Nigerian National Petroleum Corporation (NNPC). In return, the Ogonis received much of the harm but few of the benefits the oil industry had to offer. Poverty is epidemic in Ogoniland and the Niger Delta as a whole. Education and health facilities are primitive at best, and few Ogoni homes enjoy the most basic facilities, such as electricity and running water. (2000, p. 80)

As a result, this situation "created a new brand of 'youths' who woke up to a consciousness, which demanded that the Niger Delta people be aware of their human and material rights" (Ekiyor, 2001, p. 221). The youth of the region became confrontational in their approach. For example, some security personnel were killed, some were kidnapped, especially the officials of some of the petroleum companies, and some of the oil installations were destroyed with the objective of sabotaging the economic interest of the country (Ifeka, 2000). The federal government responded by sending about 3,000 troops to flush out the young people responsible for the killing of its security officers at Odi. As a result, Odi was destroyed (Abugu, 1999, p. 1). Many of the young people have been killed, maimed, and arrested by the government security forces. In fact, most of the communities in the region are still under federal government siege (Oyadongha, 2003, p. 6).[10]

Some of the militia groups that have emerged from the region include the Movement for the Survival of the Ogoni People (MOSOP), led by Ken Saro Wiwa, the Chikoko Movement, the Ijaw Youth Forum, the Ijaw Youth Council, and the Egbesu Boys (the most dreaded of the ethnic militia groups in the region). All these militias in the region, as mentioned earlier, are made up by most of the youth of the region. They all have the same objective: the right to control the resources in their communities for the benefit of all their people. It must be stressed, as the research findings reveal, that the situation in the country made the militia groups an attractive option for the youth but also escalated violence in the country. The research findings are considered hereafter.

The Economic Factor

Most of my informants and respondents blame the economic crisis and the implementation of the structural adjustment program for youth violence in the country. The Nigerian economy, which is based solely on the exploitation and exportation of petroleum in the Niger Delta region, crashed in the early 1980s, as a result of: the fall in oil prices (oil glut) in the period under discussion; the policy-makers' lack of foresight; and gross mismanagement of the economy by corrupt leaders, especially the military (Oyekunle, 1994). In order to resolve the economic crisis, different administrations adopted different methods. First, the International Monetary Fund (IMF) "economic pills" were considered by the civilian administration of Shagari, but were rejected by the Buhari military administration. The Babangida military administration reconsidered the IMF pills and adopted a structural adjustment program (SAP) in 1986. (The SAP is a World Bank solution to Third World countries' economic crisis). The SAP policies included "the liberation of trade," "devaluation of overvalued currency," "privatization of public enterprises," and "reduction in the overbloated public services" (Oyekunle, 1994, p. 227). As a result, both the state and private institutions embarked on mass retrenchment of workers. In addition, there was an embargo on further employment. Among the consequences of these measures was mass unemployment of youth, including university graduates.

The unemployment rate in the country is difficult to determine because of the politics associated with any head-counting exercise in the country. However, the Federal Office of Statistics estimated that the unemployment in the period under discussion was 4.3% of the labor force in 1985; by 1987, it had increased to 7%. Furthermore, the Federal Office of Statistics estimated that 35–50% of the unemployed were secondary school dropouts. In addition, this office estimated that 40% of the unemployed in Nigeria urban centers included individuals between the age of 20 to 24 and that 66% were between 15 to 24 years old (Kanyenze, Mhone, & Sparreboom, 2000). These numbers suggest that the youth were those most affected by the economic policies of the 1980s.

Seventy-five percent of the militia members who were interviewed agreed that they joined these groups because of frustration resulting from lack of jobs and the determination to rectify the injustice perpetuated by Nigerian ruling elites, whether military or civilian, against the masses. The frustration has induced violent activities, including drug trafficking and armed robbery. The SAP demonstrations in Nigerian urban centers during 1989 and 1992 were actually led by students in the higher institutions and some of the unemployed youth.[11] Regarding the reaction to the SAP demonstrations, Tamuno wrote:

> As the SAP measures hit Nigerians harder and harder, from their inception in 1986, the reactions to further doses of belt-tightening became more and more violent. The May—June 1989 SAP riots in several cities and towns—notably Benin and Lagos—were more violent and bloodier in their consequences as they brought out more police and troops to restore order, and entailed several deaths and destruction of property. (1980, p. 62)

Policy-makers know about the linkage between unemployment and increasing youth violence in Nigeria. Suffice it to say that provision of jobs will go a long way to discourage violence and reduce the level of recruitment into various militia groups in the country. About 75% of my respondents agreed that they would leave the groups if they could secure good jobs.

Militarization of the Society

The long tenure of military rule has also been attributed to youth violence in the country. This is the opinion held by many of the academic and human rights activists who responded to my queries. According to these respondents, the long military rule has militarized the society to the extent that many have come to believe that force or violence is the only way to attain success or reach the top of the ladder in the country. Two famous Nigerian leaders wrote on the extent to which the society has been militarized. Dr. Frederick Fasheun, the founder of the OPC, wrote:

> We had a type of military government that made itself repressive and malevolently coercive. However, the long exposure to coercion and repression so successfully bastardised our psyche and destroyed our vital values that Nigerians even protested when soldiers were temporarily withdrawn to the barracks, with traditional rulers leading delegations to military administrators to beg for the restoration of military presence in the streets. We no longer felt safe without this undue militarisation. Yet the military personnel delighted in brutalising the "bloody civilian" populace, seizing traders' goods, confiscating their wares and destroying peoples' property and dwellings. Each successive military government created a terror squad by which it became known and remembered. And such squads did nothing but help their founders to perpetuate corruption, militarisation and repression. (2001, p. 190)

Major General Chris Alli, the former chief of army staff under the military dictator General Sani Abacha, also wrote that the Nigerian psyche has been moulded into a frame of militancy and respect for the use of force. . . . The course of jungle law has been promoted by the state through terrorism, torture, murder and by every conceivable means, but due process. (2001, p. 234)

Therefore, it is not surprising that the youth became violent and confrontational in their approach to issues in the country. The path toward confrontation and violence was provided by the formation of the ethnic militias in Nigeria.

As pointed out by Jeffrey Fagan and Deanna L. Wilkinson, "guns play a central role in initiating, sustaining, and elevating the epidemic of youth violence" in the United States (Fagan & Wilkinson, 1998, p. 4); this also occurs in Nigeria, my respondents said. In fact, they agreed on the centrality of guns in the surge of youth violence in the country. Members of the militias, especially the militia groups in the Niger Delta region, are well armed with sophisticated guns like the AK 47. These weapons were obtained illegally from arms dealers; were stolen from the military depots, especially police stations;[12] and acquired from corrupt military personnel who gave out their weapons to these bandits for a price. Investigation reveals that some of these arms are weapons originally held by discharged soldiers who participated in Economic Community Monitoring Group (ECOMOG) exercises in Liberia and Sierra Leone (Akinwumi, 2003). Other weapons are acquired from local manufacturers (blacksmiths) across the country, and others have been imported through the porous borders (Agbo, 2003, p. 36). According to Okechukwu Nwanguma, guns are "so prevalent in the Niger Delta, especially Warri, that the youths [who] hawk [them] on the streets call [them] 'pure water' " (Akinwumi, 2002, p. 14). These guns are used by the militias in shootouts against each other and against the security officials, always with fatal consequences on both sides.

Social Values

The breakdown of societal values and norms has also been attributed to the increase in youth violence in Nigeria. Traditional values have been eroded by Western cultural values. The influence of Western films, music, fashion, and education has destroyed the basis of African culture. As a result, Nigerian youth are not ready to take back seats again and no longer trust their elders' ability to direct or represent them. Today, respect for elders, a core value of African tradition, no longer exists. According to Thelma Ekiyor, the result of this has been "an obvious overturn in the historical social fabric of the community" (2001, p. 122). This is demonstrated in the Niger Delta region, where the various youth-led ethnic militia groups have accused "the elders of complacency" and complained about the "exploitation of the people and environment of the Niger Delta by the oil companies" (p. 122). As a result, the elders of that region could not restrain the various groups from perpetuating violence or crimes.

To a lesser extent, the revival of traditional religion is also attributed to the upsurge in youth violence in Nigeria. All the ethnic militias rely on "traditional medicine" to fortify them in their violent activities. The "medicine," according to some of my informants, "gives them immunity from bullets." The belief in the efficacy of these medicines or amulets has encouraged most youth to be daring in their exploits against their perceived enemies.[13] It is important to stress that this is not particular to militia groups in Nigeria alone. The rebel movements in the civil wars in Sierra Leone and Liberia also relied greatly on traditional medicines for protection against bullets (Ellis, 1999, p. 42).

From the foregoing findings, it is possible to conclude that youth violence in the country is not the result of one factor. In the case of Nigeria, as in other African countries, the "trigger" factor for youth violence could be said to be the economic crisis that gave rise to unemployment and poverty. The economic crisis, according to the report of the Committee on Youth, Street Culture, and Urban Violence in Africa, "drives disoriented and jobless youths to the street (in this case, gangs) where they create peculiar survival strategies and subcultures, venting their anger on society through acts of violence" (Adesanmi, 1997, p. 26).

The State Response to Youth Violence

My respondents condemned the carrot-and-stick policy adapted by the Federal Government of Nigeria toward young people and youth violence. Under the military, the stick policy was arbitrarily used to discourage further violence in the country. For example, many of the young people in the Niger-Delta region have been arrested and detained by the security agents; some have even been killed. The killing of the environmentalist Ken Saro Wiwa and the military occupation of many communities in the Niger Delta region have not deterred other militias from operating against the state or the multinational petroleum companies in the region. Neither the "shoot-at-sight order" nor the destruction of the Odi community in Bayelsea State under the present democratic government has resolved youth violence in the country. Indeed, these repressive measures have further invigorated young people to rebel against the state.

It would be unfair to say that the government did not attempt to solve the problems, especially the unemployment problem, that have precipitated youth violence in the country, but the various attempts have been halfhearted measures and politically motivated. As a result, the measures have failed to meet the expectations of the youth. For example, the National Directorate of Employment (NDE) and other agencies that were established in the 1980s to combat mass unemployment have not been able to solve the problem. The NDE admits that "until recently, the implementation of NDE programs (was) based on political considerations rather than specific needs of the people" (Kanyenze et al., 2000, p. 21).

On the basis of the foregoing, one would conclude, as many participants in the conference on Youth, Street Culture, and Urban Violence in Africa did, that African states have failed in their responsibilities toward youth and are therefore responsible for youth violence (Adesanmi, 1997, pp. 38–40).

Conclusion

I conclude this chapter by making some recommendations for reducing youth violence in Nigeria based on my research findings on this topic. Policy-makers should concentrate on the following.

1. Tackle the unemployment problem in the country.
2. Introduce a new educational system that will train youth to be self-employed instead of relying on government to provide jobs (allied to item 1); it is the failure to provide jobs for thousands of graduates every year that often leads to frustration and the temptation to be involved in violence.
3. Create poverty alleviation policies to be administered by the government.
4. Stop perceiving youth in a negative ways, for example, considering them as threat to the stability of the country. The government should be more responsive to young people.
5. Involve youth in any policy that directly affects them. For example, Richard Curtain has suggested that the "governments and international agencies should empower young people themselves to implement key aspects of a comprehensive employment strategy" (2001, pp. 7–11).
6. Encourage the nongovernmental organizations and the civil society to address youth violence.
7. Mobilize religious leaders to use their pulpits to preach against violence and to promote a culture of self-reliance in view of the government incapacitation.

One of the issues discussed in the research is a link between government's inability to provide for its growing population of young people and their resort to violence. It is my view that present reforms initiated by this government are directed at addressing this problem. Therefore, a study can be done in the future, as soon as these reforms start yielding results, to draw a comparison between what obtains now in terms of youth violence and in the future.

Notes

This chapter was written when I was at Freie Universitat in Berlin. I wish to express my gratitude to the Alexander von Humboldt Foundation for the Alexander von Humboldt Postdoctoral Award to work on postcolonial conflicts in Nigeria. The award has given me the opportunity to be in Europe to participate in the conference on Global Perspectives on Youth Conflict. I also express my gratitude to my host in Berlin, Professor Dr. Georg Elwert, for the discussions we had on youth violence. I am also indebted to Professors Richard Kuba (Frankfurt University A/M), Maria Grahn-Farley (University of California, Irvine, now at Harvard Law School), and Adoyi Onoja (Nasarawa State University, Keffi, Nigeria) for their comments on the first draft.

1. Most of the people I interviewed, especially the elders, expressed this opinion during my personal interviews with them when I was in Nigeria between November and December 2002.
2. Sheila Brown wrote further that "the reframing of 'understanding youth and crime' requires either a dissolution of 'youth' as a special object of knowledge and

policy, or an inclusion of young people in the social enterprise through the legitimation of their voices and a recognition of their potential for citizenship" (1998, p. 3).

3. I thank the following individuals for their assistance with administering the questionnaires in the cities mentioned here: Sanya Aribido, Esther Adegoke, Usman Ibrahim, Ibrahim Suleiman, and Pius Nobei.

4. This was a scheme designed by the federal government to promote unity among the Nigerian youth. It was inaugurated in 1973. Under the scheme, Nigerian youth are expected to serve the nation for a mandatory period of a year after graduation in any of the tertiary institutions in the country. One is posted to another state, not the state of one's birth, to serve. For example, I am from the then Kwara state; I was posted to Sokoto state in 1986 to serve the nation. The extent to which this scheme has achieved its objective is a matter of debate.

5. For details on this, see Curtain (2001, pp. 7–11).

6. In March 2001, I was denied information by some officials of Gani Adam's faction of the OPC in Lagos, with the condition that I must join the OPC and go through the religious oath. Because of my refusal, I was not granted an audience.

7. The OPC broke into two factions, Fasheun's and Gani Adam's, shortly before the 1999 federal election in the country.

8. During the Sharia crises in the northern states, many Christian southerners were killed. The southern militias, especially those in the southeastern region, retaliated by killing the northern Hausa/Fulani citizens who were based in these states.

9. In 1967, the Igbo of the southeastern region of Nigeria seceded and declared the Biafra Republic. The rebellion was crushed in 1970. It was in the wake of those events that MASSOB was established. Since the end of the war, the Igbo have alleged that their group has been marginalized by the other major ethnic groups.

10. A military task force was inaugurated under the last military dispensation. The task force, known as the Rivers State Internal Security Force, consisted of a security and military force. Until recently, the force occupied most of the Niger Delta communities. During the Ogoni crisis, the task force actually occupied Ogoniland. See Oyadongha (2003).

11. The argument here is "the frustration-aggression hypothesis," according to which violence becomes inevitable when there is frustration resulting from the failure to achieve the desired objective.

12. The OPC, for instance, got some of their ammunition through invading police stations that were not very secure or were in isolated areas.

13. In one of my interviews with members of the OPC, amulets were displayed in three different places in the room of our meeting. On one of the collections was written "tested," while the two other collections were labeled as "not tested" and "failed."

References

Abugu, U. (1999, November 27). It's senseless waste of lives. *Vanguard*, p. 1.

Adesanmi, P. (1997). *Report on youth, street culture, and urban violence in Africa.* Ibadan, Nigeria: IFRA.

Adewale, T. (2001). The rise of ethnic militias, de-legitimisation of the state, and the threat to Nigerian Federalism. *West Africa Review, 3* (1), 5–13.

Agbo, A. (2003, October). A garden under siege. *Tell News Magazine*, p.36.

Akinwumi, O. (2002, December 15–18). *From area boys to ethnic militias: Ethnic dimension in Nigeria.* Paper presented in workshop entitled Globalisation, Anti-Globalisation and Civil Society, Institute of Commonwealth Studies, University of London.

Akinwumi, O. (2003). Ethnic militias and violence. In T. Falola & S. Salm (Eds.), *Nigerian Cities* (pp. 347–352). Trenton, NJ: Africa World Press.

Akinyele, R. T. (2001). Ethnic militancy and national stability in Nigeria: A case study of the Oodua People's Congress. *African Affairs, 100*(401), 623–640.

Albert, O. (1997). Kano: Religious fundamentalism and violence. In G. Herault & P. Adesanmi (Eds.), *Report on youth, street and urban violence in Africa* (pp 285–328). Ibadan: IFRA.

Alli, Chris M. (2001). *The Federal Republic of Nigerian Army: The siege of a nation.* Lagos: Malthouse Press.

Anifowose, R. (1982). *Violence and politics: The Tiv and Yoruba experience.* New York: NOK.

Brown, S. (1998). *Understanding youth and crime.* Buckingham, UK: Open University Press.

Curtain, R. (2001, August). Youth and employment: A public policy perspective. *Development Bulletin, 55,* 7–11.

Dudley, B. J. (1973). *Instability and political order: Politics and crisis in Nigeria.* Ibadan, Nigeria: Ibadan University Press.

Ekiyor, T. (2001). Youth in conflict management: The Ogba and Odi link Projects. In O. Albert (Ed.), *Building peace, advancing democracy: Experience with third-party interventions in Nigeria's conflicts* (pp. 120–138). Ibadan, Nigeria: John Archers.

Ellis, S.(1999). *The mask of anarchy: The destruction of Liberia and the religious dimension of an African civil war.* London: Hurst.

Fagan, J. A., & Wilkinson, D. L. (1998). Guns, youth and violence and social identity. In M. H. Moore & M. Tonry, *Youth violence* (pp. 105–188). Chicago: University of Chicago Press.

Falola, T. (1999). *The history of Nigeria.* Westport, CT: Greenwood Press.

Fasheun, F. (2001). *My prison experience.* Lagos: Spectrum.

Ifeka, C. (2000). Nigeria: Conflict, complicity and confusion. *Review of African Economy, 27*(83), 115–123.

Kanyenze, G., Mhone, Guy C. Z., & Sparreboom, Theo. (Eds.). (2000). *Strategies to combat youth unemployment and marginalisation in Anglophone Africa.* Harare, Zimbabwe: International Organization.

Maier, K. (2000). *This house has fallen: Midnight in Nigeria.* New York: Public Affairs.

Moore, M. H., & Tonry, M. (Eds.). (1998). *Youth violence.* Chicago: University of Chicago Press.

Olutayo, A.O. (1994). Youth and urban violence. In I. O. Albert, J. Adisa, T. Agbola, & G. Herault (Eds.), *Urban management and urban violence in Africa* (pp. 35–48). Ibadan, Nigeria: IFRA.

Oyadongha, S. (2003, January 20). Armed youth seize oil rig in Delta. *Vanguard,* p. 6.

Oyekunle, A. (1994). Child labour, urban violence, and environmental degradation. In I. O. Albert, J. Adisa, T. Agbola, & G. Herault (Eds.), *Urban management and urban violence in Africa* (pp. 220–235). Ibadan, Nigeria: IFRA.

Tamuno, T. (1980). *Nigeria since independence.* Ibadan, Nigeria: Ibadan University Press.

United Nations. (1992). Report on the Second Asia-Pacific Intergovernmental Meeting on Human Resources. Bangkok: Development for Youth.

CHAPTER 5

Social Hierarchy, Social Conflicts, and Moral Development

ELLIOT TURIEL

Placing Culture in Contexts

Conflicts and even violence take many forms and occur in a variety of contexts. As Martha Nussbaum puts it,

> women in much of the world lack support for fundamental functions of a human life. They are less well nourished than men, less healthy, more vulnerable to physical violence and sexual abuse. . . . all too often women are not treated as ends in their own right, persons with a dignity that deserves respect from laws and institutions. (2000, pp. 1–2)

One of the consequences of the treatment of women as the instruments of the ends of others is that they are often the victims of violence. Indices of beatings, killings, and rapes are high in many nations. In India, for example, physical assaults connected to dowries are frequent (Heise, 1989). Dowries are regarded as a groom's entitlement, and dissatisfaction with the amounts has led to severe beatings and killings of brides (known as "bride burning" because setting the woman afire is the most frequently used method). Another example of violence that occurs within families is referred to as "honor killings." In some cultures, girls and women are killed by male relatives (fathers, brothers, husbands) when they are regarded to have brought dishonor to their families by engaging in sexual activities (premarital sex, adultery). Although the most common motivation for such killings is the outrage over taboos that are violated and the perceived dishonor brought upon the family (Wikan, 2002), this is selectively applied, since it is almost always the females who have engaged in the violations who are killed. Rape is another type of physical assault that confronts women in most parts of the world (Nussbaum, 2000). In many nations, the legal system favors males at the expense of the interests of females and creates an atmosphere that does not discourage rape (Nussbaum, 2000).

It is not only females who are subjected to violence in the context of relationships of inequality. It occurs among people of different social classes and castes (Fineman, 1990). In several nations, people of higher castes commit acts of violence, including killings and rapes, in large numbers. In a journalistic account of one particularly brutal incident (Fineman, 1990) it was reported that in India, 10,000 atrocities are recorded every year against untouchables and that "the raping and killing of harijans is a daily event" (A9).

The problems around the maltreatment of women (and others in powerless positions), it is important to add, are not restricted to a few cultures and include Western cultures. National surveys show that between 1.8 and 5.7 million women in the United States are beaten in their homes (Okin, 1996). According to Okin,

> not only are these figures shocking, they certainly present a challenge to those who think the positive feelings experienced in families can be relied on to regulate behavior within them. They are even more troubling when we acknowledge that the propensity for family violence is frequently passed down from one generation to the next. (1989, p. 69)

Families are often hierarchically structured, with females in subordinate positions (Nussbaum, 2000; Okin, 1989, 1996). Families, like societies at large, are a combination of harmony and conflict, fulfillment and suffering, affection and naked power. In Western cultures, too, violence associated with social hierarchy has been more widespread than injustices that affect women. It is well known that in the United States (especially in the southern states), blacks have been the victims of beatings, torture, sexual abuse, and killings. There is a long history of such treatment of blacks, dating back to the time of slavery (Butterfield, 1995).

Social hierarchies, in the family and beyond, with their inequalities, have implications for tensions, conflicts, and violence in multilayered ways. As I argue in this essay, the most obvious is that people in dominant positions often inflict violence and suffering (physical and emotional) on those in subordinate positions. People in dominant positions tend to have a sense of entitlement that leads them to impose their wishes on others. The sense of entitlement is part and parcel of social structures and cultural practices that establish contexts for the restriction of freedoms, rights, and individual choices of those in subordinate positions. In turn, those social structures and cultural practices accord freedoms, rights, autonomy, and the power to pursue individual needs to those in dominant positions. Such conditions are also a source of pervasive conflict, because people in subordinate positions, who do perceive the injustices embedded in the cultural practices, engage in acts of resistance and subversion, with the goal of asserting their freedoms and making the social system more just. Conflicts between people in different positions in the social hierarchy are themselves multilayered, since individuals simultaneously hold more than one position. As one example, a male of a lower social class or caste may be in a subordinate position relative to people of higher classes or castes but in a dominant position relative to females within his own class or caste.

Social Conflicts and Social Resistance

Certain conceptions of culture and morality presuppose that conflicts are culturally specific. Consider the frequently made dichotomy between individualist and collectivist cultures, which is supposed to capture sharp contrasts between Western and non-Western cultures, respectively. To put it briefly, it is said that Westerners give primacy to individuals and place at the forefront freedoms, independence, and rights (Markus & Kitayama, 1991). As a consequence, there may be clashes as a result of people's assertion of their own interests and rights. In that view, non-Westerners typically would not get into conflicts. In collectivist cultures, where primary emphasis is presumably given to the group and interdependence, accepting their designated roles, people live in harmony. An example of this type of dichotomy was presented by Rothbaum, Pott, Azuma, Miyake, and Weisz (2000), who explicitly addressed issues of harmony and conflict. They proposed that in Japan, a nation with a collectivist bent, relationships are framed through a lens of accommodation, in which "symbiotic harmony" is most valued. A contrasting lens is said to characterize American society, often producing "generative tension." As a consequence, relationships in Japan (and other places) involve unconditional loyalty between people, a loyalty stemming from clearly established roles and a valuing of commitment. Even though relationships are hierarchically organized, symbiotic harmony results in conditions free of disagreements and conflicts.

The focus of such analyses of non-Western cultures is on community life as a buffer against conflicts, and perhaps violence. It is presumed that people adhere to their roles, accept their positions in the society, and maintain a system of compensations in the context of hierarchy and inequalities (e. g., people in dominant positions care for the interests of those in subordinate positions, who in turn give their due to those in dominant positions; see Shweder, Much, Mahapatra, & Park, 1997).

Two key features of cultures are unrecognized in such "community"-oriented analyses. One is that freedoms, rights, and personal autonomy are part of the culture—but largely accorded to those in positions of dominance. Research in non-Western cultures shows that this is the case. Both among Druze villagers (a traditional, patriarchal culture) living in Israel (Turiel & Wainryb, 2000; Wainryb & Turiel, 1994) and in Mysore, India (Neff, 2001), it has been found that a strong sense of freedom is accorded to males in their relations with females. It is also recognized by individuals that their culture is organized around practices that grant individual autonomy to males (Turiel, 2002; Turiel & Wainryb, 2000). The second feature omitted in "community"-oriented analyses is that there is resistance from people in subordinate positions whose freedoms are

restricted. Agreements about inequalities do not exist among people in varying positions of power. As Okin puts it, "oppressors and oppressed—when the
voice of the latter can be heard at all—often disagree fundamentally" (1989,
p. 67). From an anthropological perspective, Wikan has put forth a similar
idea in criticizing how characterizations of culture have failed to account for
the plight and protests of people in positions low on the social ladder: "the
concept of culture as a seamless whole and society as a bounded group mani-
festing inherently valued order and normatively regulated response, effectively
masked human misery and quenched dissenting voices" (1991, p. 290). People
in subordinate positions are not simply content to accept the perspectives of
those in positions of power. If such fundamental disagreements and the associated conflicts do occur, it does not make sense to characterize cultures
through an orientation meant to portray a general set of perspectives held by
the group.

Conflict and resistance have their source in concerns most people have with
justice, the welfare of persons, and freedoms and rights. As I have discussed
elsewhere (Turiel, 2002, 2003; Turiel & Perkins, 2004), resistance and subversion are part of people's everyday lives. In recent years, there have been several
publicized examples of social opposition to restrictions imposed on people in
countries like Afghanistan and Iran. Women, especially, who are often expected
to adhere to restrictions on many types of activities not imposed on men, are
active individually and in groups attempting to oppose, resist, and change societal norms and cultural practices (see Turiel, 2003, for a discussion of such
events; see also journalistic accounts by Bumiller, 1990, and Goodwin, 1994,
of events in India and several Middle Eastern countries).

The research conducted among the Druze (Turiel & Wainryb, 2000) and in
India (Neff, 2001), like these journalistic reports, supports propositions regarding conflict and resistance in cultural contexts of social hierarchy. In addition
to the recognition of inequalities in societal arrangements, it was found that
adolescent and adult Druze females judge that the inequalities are unfair. Other
research involving close observations of women's activities in traditional cultures has documented that they do act in ways to counter and change restrictions
judged unfair (Abu-Lughod, 1993; Wikan, 1996). Spending considerable time
with Bedouin groups in a small hamlet on the northwest coast of Egypt, Abu-
Lughod observed that women employ a variety of strategies to get around the
unequal restrictions imposed on them by men (husbands, fathers, brothers).
Those strategies pertained to matters like educational opportunities and goals,
arranged marriages, polygamy, and the distribution of resources. Similar acts
of resistance were documented by Wikan (1996) in families of poverty living
in Cairo.

Social Reasoning, Development, and Resistance

I have proposed that cultures cannot be characterized through general orientations to persons or morality, that all understandings are not shared among
members of a culture, and that there are fundamental disagreements, especially

between people in different positions on the social hierarchy, that produce conflicts. These propositions have implications for explanations of children's development, since social experiences are varied. The multifaceted nature of children's social interactions was conveyed by Piaget when he said:

> Socialization in no way constitutes the result of a unidirectional cause such as the pressure of the adult community upon the child through such means as education in the family, and subsequently in the school. Rather . . . it involves the intervention of a multiplicity of interactions of different types and sometimes with opposed effects. (1951/1995, p. 276)

I have also proposed that opposition, resistance, and subversion of societal arrangements and cultural practices judged unfair are part of most people's lives. Activities of resistance and subversion have further implications for explanations of development that are in line with Piaget's propositions (see also Kohlberg, 1969, 1971; Nucci, 2001; Smetana, 1997). That individuals resist and subvert social practices suggests that social development is not a process of compliance or an internalization of norms and practices but a process of constructing judgments about multiple aspects of social relationships. Resistance and subversion involve critical scrutiny of what exists socially, which would include judgments as to how social conditions ought to be different.

Two features stand out in acts of resistance and subversion. Opposition and resistance involve moral judgments about inequalities in status and about the power that some groups have to control the activities of others. In addition, people often engage in protest over activities that are of personal nature. For example, many subversive activities, aimed at countering the restrictions imposed by governmental and religious authorities, have been over recreational activities (such as dress, listening to music, watching movies, etc.). These features of oppositional activities map onto domains of social reasoning that children develop. A large body of research has documented that at a fairly young age, children begin to form distinct judgments in the personal and moral domains, as well as in the domain of social convention (Smetana, 1995; Tisak, 1995; Turiel, 1983, 1998). The theoretical framework and supporting research on the construction of the domains of judgment through individual–environment interactions has been presented in several places (e.g., Nucci, 2001; Turiel, 1998, 2002). For present purposes, I note some of the general features of the domains and how they relate to the origins of opposition and resistance in childhood.

In this perspective, morality refers to understandings of welfare or harm, justice, and rights that are distinct from the uniformities that coordinate social interactions within social systems (conventions). The research has shown that children, adolescents, and adults think about moral issues (e.g., inflicting physical and emotional harm, stealing, destroying another's property, violation of rights) differently from the way they think about social conventions (e.g., pertaining to modes of dress, forms of address, forms of greeting). They judge moral obligations not as contingent on rules or authority and as applicable across social contexts. Moral transgressions, such as hitting or stealing, are not judged by the existence of rules, the directives of authorities, or commonly accepted practices (e.g., the act is wrong even if it were acceptable practice in a culture). Rather, rules pertaining to moral issues are judged as unalterable by agreement, and such acts would be considered wrong even if there were no rules governing them. Instead of rules and authority, moral judgments are grounded in concepts of avoiding harm, protecting people's welfare, and ensuring fairness. At the same time, children do develop understandings of the conventions, including rules and authority, of social organizations (e.g., the conventional rules in the organization of a classroom or school). In contrast with moral issues, conventions are judged to be contingent on rules and authority, and as particular to groups and institutional contexts. Judgments about conventional issues are based on understandings of social organization, including the role of authority, custom, and efficiency in coordinating social interactions.

Understandings of morality and social convention are also, as indicated, distinguished from the domain of personal jurisdiction. When governmental or religious authorities restrict activities like listening to music, dancing, and watching movies, they can come to have moral implications. The restrictions are regarded as unfair infringements on people's freedoms. Similarly, restrictions on matters like dress can come to be seen as moral when they are applied to some groups and not others (e.g., females and not males) and are connected to the domination of one group by another. In many contexts, however, activities of this sort are taken for granted as choices people make at their own discretion. That is, activities that do not entail inflicting harm or violating fairness or rights and that are not regulated in conventional ways are considered part of the personal domain. Activities categorized as personal may vary by context and culture. Many activities that are conventionally regulated in one context are left to personal choice in another. The research (see Nucci, 2001, for a review) has shown that issues like one's choice of friends, the content of one's correspondence, self-expressive works of creativity, many recreational activities, and the state of one's own body are judged to be up to individual choice and within the boundaries of personal jurisdiction.

As delineated by Nucci (1996, 2001), individuals strive for control over activities in the personal domain in order to maintain a sense of agency, and they do so by attempting to control areas of behavioral discretion and privacy:

> These actions make up the private aspects of one's life; they are subject not to considerations of right and wrong, but to preferences and choice. . . . The experience of agency has two aspects. At one level, agency is experienced as an awareness of oneself as the initiator of action. At a second, more fundamental level, agency is experienced as the sense of oneself as having a unique, bounded social identity. Thus individuals endeavor to control areas of conduct that permit them opportunities to engage in self-expression, personal growth, selection of intimates, and zones of privacy. (Nucci & Turiel, 2000, p. 117)

Nucci proposed that conceptions of a personal domain constitute the psychological source of strivings for rights to freedom (see also Gewirth, 1982). Claims to freedoms are balanced with conceptions of moral obligations and conventional regulations. Areas of personal jurisdiction along with moral judgments that individuals maintain are sources of their critical orientations to cultural practices. Therefore, the intersection of judgments in the personal domain and cultural arrangements constitutes a basis for social conflicts. In addition, it has been proposed that excessive control of the personal sphere by parents can result in psychological difficulties, especially during adolescence (Nucci, 2001; Nucci, Hasebe, & Nucci, 1999). Adolescents in Japan and the United States who perceive their parents as exerting excessive control in the personal domain were likely to report experiencing psychological symptoms (e.g., anxiety, paranoia).

Individuals approach societal arrangements and cultural practices with a combination of acceptance and opposition. The origins of opposition are in childhood. For instance, children do not regard adults as the only sources of legitimate authority and do not accept as legitimate an authority's commands to engage in acts that they consider morally wrong (Kim, 1998; Laupa & Turiel, 1986). Moreover, children act in both socially positive and oppositional ways. On the one hand, children act in prosocial ways, cooperate, and express emotions of sympathy and empathy toward others (Dunn, 1987; Eisenberg & Strayer, 1987; Hoffman, 1991). On the other hand, children act in ways that are socially prohibited, engage in disputes with parents, and get into conflicts with siblings and peers (Dunn, 1987; Dunn, Brown, & Maguire, 1995; Dunn & Munn, 1987).

Social Judgments and Social Contexts

Children's positive and oppositional tendencies and the heterogeneity of their social judgments mean that a great deal occurs in social interactions that defies simple characterizations. This is not to say, however, that we cannot make systematic analyses of social judgments and actions. We can do so by considering how individuals apply various types of thinking in interpreting events that have multiple features. In turn, this means that social contexts are important in people's judgments and actions. Within this framework, it is not that the parameters of social situations determine how people think and act. Furthermore, social contexts need to be defined at levels less global than cultural contexts.

As a means of explaining the ideas that social contexts need to be analyzed at levels less global than culture and that social situations do not simply determine how people react, I first consider research on judgments and actions around honesty and deception. Honesty is often portrayed as one of those societal virtues transmitted to children that form part of good character. Yet telling the truth and lying are highly variable for most people. Deception is one of the common means of subverting practices considered unfair and promoting people's welfare. Well-publicized examples of uses of deception to promote welfare and prevent harm come from efforts to save people from concentration camps during World War II. Although the activities of Oscar Schindler and Raoul Wallenberg are well known, many others, including diplomats from several countries (e.g., Japan, Turkey, Holland) and people who were not in official positions, used deception to save lives.

Research on judgments about deception to prevent harm has been conducted in the realm of medicine. In one study, for instance, a group of physicians made judgments about hypothetical stories that depicted doctors who consider deceiving an insurance company as the only means to obtain approval for a treatment or diagnostic procedure for a patient (Freeman, Rathore, Weinfurt, Schulman, & Sulmasy, 1999). The stories depicted medical conditions of different degrees of severity. In the two most severe conditions (life-threatening ones), the majority thought that the doctor was justified in engaging in deception. In other conditions, the percentages accepting of deception were considerably lower (e.g., only 3% thought that deception was legitimate for purposes of cosmetic surgery). We can assume that, in the abstract, the physicians would judge honesty to be good and dishonesty wrong. Nevertheless, many judged deception acceptable in some situations but not others. In some situations, physicians judged it necessary to engage in deception in order to attain the greater good of their patients. (There is evidence that physicians actually do engage in this type of deception; see Wynia, Cummins, VanGeest, & Wilson, 2000.)

It is likely that the physicians' judgments about deception involve a willingness to subvert a system that is perceived to grant undue power to insurance companies and too little power to the medical decisions of physicians. Deception is also sometimes judged to be in the context of social inequalities, such as those that may exist between husbands and wives. In research I have conducted in the United States, adults were presented with several situations involving deceptions in marital contexts. One version of the situations depicted a family in which only the husband works outside the home and a wife who engages in deception; in another version of each situation, only the wife works, and the husband engages in deception. Analyses of the results of this study are still underway, but findings from two situations are informative. In one, a spouse keeps a bank account secret from the working spouse, who controls all the finances. The majority thought that it is acceptable for a wife to have a bank account secret from her working husband who controls the finances, whereas the majority thought that it is not acceptable for a husband to do so, even when it is the wife who works and controls the finances. It appears, therefore, that the structure of power outside the family is taken into account in making these judgments. In other words, a nonworking husband is viewed as having more influence and power than a nonworking wife. In another situation, a spouse with a drinking problem attends meetings of Alcoholics Anonymous without telling the working spouse, who disapproves of attending such meetings. In that case, the large majority judged that deception by both wives and husbands is acceptable. In that situation, like situations involving physicians' deception of insurance companies, judgments about welfare override the value of maintaining honesty.

I should stress that people in the study were not sanguine about deception between spouses—just as physicians are not content that they may sometimes be compelled to deceive insurance companies. They view deception as undesirable but sometimes necessary in order to deal with unfair restrictions, especially restrictions imposed by those in greater power and control. To be sure, deception sometimes occurs for self-serving purposes. However, the reasons people engage in deception are multidimensional, and sometimes they are motivated by moral goals.

Issues of power, control, and honesty are vexing for youth, who struggle with questions as to when to be open with their parents and when to be deceptive. It is common for adolescents to deceive parents about personal choices, both to spare the feelings of parents who may have different views about the activities and to avoid the control that parents might attempt to exert. In one study (Perkins, 2003), it was found that most adolescents judged deception of parents legitimate with regard to imposed activities considered to be in the realm of personal jurisdiction (activities like whom to date and which social club to join). The adolescents also judged it legitimate to deceive parents who attempt to require their children to engage in acts considered morally wrong (e.g., to engage in racial discrimination). By contrast, deception was not accepted by adolescents when parents directed actions regarding prudential matters (e.g., instructing them not to ride a motorcycle). The study also documented that on the same matters, adolescents are less accepting of deception of peers than of parents. For the most part, they judged deception of peers wrong because there should be mutuality among them.

In many ways, issues of honesty are less concrete than issues pertaining to inflicting physical harm or violence upon others. The most clear-cut and consistent moral understandings among young children appear to revolve around harm; young children judge inflicting harm to be wrong in ways that are not contingent on rules and generally applicable. However, even judgments about harm are coordinated with other considerations. Adults participating in experiments (Milgram, 1974) in which they were instructed to inflict pain on another person (by supposedly administering electric shocks) sometimes did so. But sometimes they refused to do so. Whereas in some experimental conditions the majority of the adults went along with the experimenter's instructions to administer the shocks, in most experimental conditions they defied the experimenter. For the most part, participants in these experiments were highly conflicted about inflicting pain (Milgram, 1974). The conflict can be interpreted as generated by moral judgments about the undesirability of inflicting harm and judgments about adhering to conventional authority in social systems (Turiel & Smetana, 1984).

By this interpretation, people who ended up inflicting pain on another still maintained the judgment that it is wrong to do so. In attempting to explain excessive aggressive or violent behaviors among youths, many have presumed that they are deficient in their moral judgments and other social skills (see Astor, 1998, for further discussion). An alternative view is that the actions of aggressive children are more adequately explained through the ways they apply their moral judgments in interpersonal relationships and in certain physical and social contexts. In one study (Astor, 1994), assessments were made of judgments about inflicting physical harm within two types of contexts among children with and without histories of violent activities. In one context, children made judgments about situations depicting unprovoked acts of one child hitting another. Both groups of children, with violent and nonviolent histories, judged the unprovoked acts of physical aggression as wrong, on the grounds that people should not be subjected to pain. A different set of findings was obtained in the second context of judgments assessed. In that case, assessments were made of judgments about situations in which a child hits another after a provocation (name-calling, lying, stealing, and hitting). Approval of violence under those circumstances was greater for all the children, but substantially greater for the children with a background of violence (except in retaliation for hitting). The group with a background of violence judged the provoked acts of violence as acceptable on the grounds that they are fair retribution for unjust acts. The aggressive children tended to see psychological harm in acts of provocation to be as bad or worse than acts of physical retribution.

According to Astor (1998), physical spaces are also connected to perceptions of potential harm and danger. He investigated perceptions of the places in high schools in which acts of violence are expected to occur. He found that violence is expected to occur in particular places within schools (e.g., bathrooms, stairways) and proposed that potential provocations are attributed to events that occur in those places. Since these locations are perceived as having greater risks of physical harm, some individuals are primed for retaliatory actions.

The findings suggest that features in addition to moral judgments are involved in aggressive behaviors. In particular, it is necessary to consider children's understandings of the intentions of others and their judgments about retribution. A connection between aggression and provocation has been shown in other studies, as well (see Coie & Dodge, 1998). It also appears that children who more frequently engage in aggression are more likely than others to attribute hostile intentions to others when those intentions are ambiguous (referred to as hostile attribution bias). Therefore, psychological attributions contribute to the perceived intent of others, which contributes to retaliatory actions. According to Coie and Dodge, children's social circumstances may influence how they interpret other people's actions:

> It is only a short inferential leap to suggest that attributions of hostile intent and experiences of anger in response to current provocative stimuli are more likely if a child is growing up under circumstances of pervasive violence, harm, and deprivation: when provocateurs regularly assault the child; when assaults regularly occur toward the child's family, peer, and ethnic group; when peer groups and family also interpret provocateurs as being hostile. These conditions characterize many environments of poverty and ethnic heterogeneity, and some subcultures (e.g., gangs). In such environments, hypervigilance to hostile cues and attributions of threat may occasionally be adaptive and retaliatory aggression may be common. (p. 796)

Conclusion

I have said only a little about violence and much more about social conflicts—and especially conflicts that are motivated by efforts to attain moral goals. The conflicts I have discussed stem from inequalities embedded in societal arrangements and cultural practices that accord greater freedoms to groups in dominant positions than to those in subordinate positions. Such cultural practices also serve to allow control by those in dominant positions over those in subordinate positions. Much of the conflict and opposition stemming from institutionalized inequalities and control takes the form of disagreements, resistance, and subversion. People in subordinate positions oppose cultural practices because they are judged to be harmful, unjust, and overly restrictive of legitimate freedoms of choice. Often acts of resistance and subversion represent conflicts of nonviolent kinds that may bring about morally positive societal changes.

However, the same social structural features of inequality are connected to infliction of emotional, psychological, and physical harm. One example is the physical violence that is inflicted upon those who contest or protest societal conditions and practices. As another example, acts of resistance do sometimes involve violence. The most obvious and perhaps most often neglected example—neglected in the sense that it is not seen as part of the "problem" of violence in society—is the violence people in positions of greater power inflict upon those of lesser power (violence against women, minority groups, people in lower castes). One of the outcomes of what Okin (1989) refers to as the gendered family (i.e., unjust relations of inequality) is that males form a strong sense of personal entitlements relative to females. Similarly, people in majority groups and higher social classes are likely to form a sense of personal entitlements relative to other groups. Often, the sense of entitlement results in efforts to exert control over others, including the use of physical violence. Even childhood bullying behavior is said to be directed toward interpersonal dominance of certain persons (Coie & Dodge, 1998).

As I have already noted, specifying the positions of individuals on the social hierarchy is a complex matter, since most have multiple roles. Holding multiple roles may have its consequences for aggressive behaviors. An individual (say a male from a lower social class or caste) holds a position of dominance, with its sense of entitlement, in gender relationships, and a subordinate position, with a lack of entitlement, in social class relationships. The effects of such positioning can vary. It may be that being in the subordinate position leads to greater awareness of the perspectives of those with whom he is in a position of dominance. Or it may be that it leads to even greater acceptance of his position of dominance.

No doubt, youth conflicts and violence are of several types and are associated with different types of reasons. Conflicts stemming from social inequalities and injustices are often nonviolent. In a variety of ways, however, violence is associated with inequalities and injustices.

References

Abu-Lughod, L. (1993). *Writing women's worlds: Bedouin stories*. Berkeley: University of California Press.

Astor, R. (1994). Children's moral reasoning about family and peer violence: The role of provocation and retribution. *Child Development, 65,* 1054–1067.

Astor, R. A. (1998). Moral reasoning about school violence: Informational assumptions about harm within school subcontexts. *Educational Psychologist, 33,* 207–221.

Bumiller, E. (1990). *May you be the mother of a hundred sons: A journey among the women of India.* New York: Oxford University Press.

Butterfield, F. (1995). *All God's children: The Boskett family and the American tradition of violence.* New York: Knopf.

Coie, J., & Dodge, K. (1998). Aggression and anti-social behavior. In W. Damon (Ed.), *Handbook of child psychology* (5th ed.): Vol. 3, N. Eisenberg (Ed.), *Social, emotional, and personality development* (pp. 779–862). New York: Wiley.

Dunn, J. (1987). The beginnings of moral understanding: Development in the second year. In J. Kagan & S. Lamb (Eds.), *The emergence of morality in young children* (pp. 91–112). Chicago: University of Chicago Press.

Dunn, J., Brown, J. R., & Maguire, M. (1995). The development of children's moral sensibility: Individual differences and emotion understanding. *Developmental Psychology, 23,* 791–798.

Dunn, J., & Munn, P. (1987). Development of justification in disputes with mother and sibling. *Developmental Psychology, 23,* 791–798.

Eisenberg, N., & Strayer, J. (Eds.). (1987). *Empathy and its development.* Cambridge, UK: Cambridge University Press.

Fineman, M. (1990, May 14). Untouchables: Murder sparks outcry for outcast' rights. *Los Angeles Times,* pp. A1, A9.

Freeman, V. G., Rathore, S. S., Weinfurt, K. P., Schulman, K. A., & Sulmasy, D. P. (1999). Lying for patients: Physician deception of third-party payers. *Archives of Internal Medicine, 159,* 2263–2270.

Gewirth, A. (1982). *Human rights: Essays on justification and applications.* Chicago: University of Chicago Press.

Goodwin, J. (1994). *Price of honor: Muslim women lift the veil of silence on the Islamic world.* New York: Penguin.

Heise, L. (1989, July 2). A world of abuse. *San Francisco Chronicle,* pp. 11–12.

Hoffman, M. L. (1991). Empathy, social cognition, and moral action. In W. M. Kurtines & J. L. Gewirtz (Eds.), *Handbook of moral behavior and development: Vol. 1. Theory* (pp. 275–301). Hillsdale, NJ: Erlbaum.

Kim, J. M. (1998). Korean children's concepts of adult and peer authority and moral reasoning. *Developmental Psychology, 34,* 947–955.

Kohlberg, L. (1969). Stage and sequence: The cognitive-developmental approach to socialization. In D. Goslin (Ed.), *Handbook of socialization theory and research* (pp. 347–480). Chicago: Rand McNally.

Kohlberg, L. (1971). From is to ought: How to commit the naturalistic fallacy and get away with it in the study of moral development. In T. Mischel (Ed.), *Cognitive development and epistemology* (pp. 151–235). New York: Academic Press.

Laupa, M., & Turiel, E. (1986). Children's conceptions of adult and peer authority. *Child Development, 57,* 405–412.

Markus, H. R., & Kitayama, S. (1991). Culture and self: Implications for cognition, emotion, and motivation. *Psychological Review, 98,* 224–253.

Milgram, S. (1974). *Obedience to authority.* New York: Harper and Row.

Neff, K. D. (2001). Judgments of personal autonomy and interpersonal responsibility in the context of Indian spousal relationships: An examination of young people's reasoning in Mysore, India. *British Journal of Developmental Psychology, 19*, 233–257.

Nucci, L. P. (1996). Morality and personal freedom. In E. S. Reed, E. Turiel, & T. Brown (Eds.), *Values and knowledge* (pp. 41–60). Mahwah, NJ: Erlbaum.

Nucci, L. P. (2001). *Education in the moral domain.* Cambridge, UK: Cambridge University Press.

Nucci, L. P., Hasebe, Y., & Nucci, M. S. (1999, April). *Parental overcontrol of the personal domain and psychopathology.* Paper presented at the biennial meeting of the Society for Research in Child Development, Albuquerque, New Mexico.

Nucci, L. P., & Turiel, E. (2000). The moral and the personal: Sources of social conflicts. In L. P. Nucci, G. Saxe, & E. Turiel (Eds.), *Culture, thought, and development* (pp. 115–137). Mahwah, NJ: Erlbaum.

Nussbaum, M. C. (2000). *Women and human development: The capabilities approach.* Cambridge, UK: Cambridge University Press.

Okin, S. M. (1989). *Justice, gender, and the family.* New York: Basic Books.

Okin, S. M. (1996). The gendered family and the development of a sense of justice. In E. S. Reed, E. Turiel, & T. Brown (Eds.), *Values and knowledge* (pp. 61–74). Hillsdale, NJ: Erlbaum.

Perkins, S. A. (2003). *Adolescent reasoning about lying in close relationships.* Unpublished doctoral dissertation, University of California, Berkeley.

Piaget, J. (1995). Egocentric thought and sociocentric thought. In J. Piaget (Ed.), *Sociological studies* (pp. 270–286). London: Routledge. (Original work published 1951)

Rothbaum, F., Pott, M., Azuma, H., Miyake, K., & Weisz, J. (2000). The development of close relationships in Japan and the United States: Paths of symbiotic harmony and generative tension. *Child Development, 71,* 1121–1142.

Shweder, R. A., Much, N. C., Mahapatra, M., & Park, L. (1997). The "big three" of morality (autonomy, community, and diversity) and the "big three" explanations of suffering. In A. Brandt & P. Rozin (Eds.), *Morality and health* (pp. 119–169). New York: Routledge.

Smetana, J. G. (1995). Morality in context: Abstractions, ambiguities, and applications. In R. Vasta (Ed.), *Annals of child development: Vol. 10* (pp. 83–130). London: Jessica Kingsley.

Smetana, J. G. (1997). Parenting and the development of social knowledge reconceptualized: A social domain analysis. In J. E. Grusec & L. Kuczynski (Eds.), *Parenting and children's internalization of values* (pp. 162–192). New York: Wiley.

Tisak, M. S. (1995). Domains of social reasoning and beyond. In R. Vasta (Ed.), *Annals of child development: Vol. 11* (pp. 95–130). London: Jessica Kingsley.

Turiel, E. (1983). *The development of social knowledge: Morality and convention.* Cambridge, UK: Cambridge University Press.

Turiel, E. (1998). The development of morality. In W. Damon (Ed.), *Handbook of child psychology* (5th ed.): *Vol. 3,* N. Eisenberg (Ed.), *Social, emotional, and personality development* (pp. 863–932). New York: Wiley.

Turiel, E. (2002). *The culture of morality: Social development, context, and conflict.* Cambridge, UK: Cambridge University Press.

Turiel, E. (2003). Resistance and subversion in everyday life. *Journal of Moral Education, 32,* 115–130.

Turiel, E., & Perkins, S. A. (2004). Flexibilities of mind: Conflict and culture. *Human Development, 47,* 158–178.

Turiel, E., & Smetana, J. G. (1984). Social knowledge and social action. The coordination of domains. In W. M. Kurtines & J. L. Gewirtz (Eds.), *Morality, moral behavior, and moral development: Basic issues in theory and research* (pp. 261–282). New York: Wiley.

Turiel, E., & Wainryb, C. (2000). Social life in cultures: Judgments, conflicts, and subversion, *Child Development, 71,* 250–256.

Wainryb, C., & Turiel, E. (1994). Dominance, subordination, and concepts of personal entitlements in cultural contexts. *Child Development, 65,* 1701–1722.

Wikan, U. (1991) Toward an experience-near anthropology, *Cultural Anthropology, 6,* 285–305.

Wikan, U. (1996). *Tomorrow, God willing: Self-made destinies in Cairo.* Chicago: University of Chicago Press.

Wikan, U. (2002). *Generous betrayal: Politics of culture in the new Europe.* Chicago: University of Chicago Press.

Wynia, M. K., Cummins, D. S., VanGeest, J. B., & Wilson, I. B. (2000). Physician manipulation of reimbursement rules for patients: Between a rock and a hard place. *Journal of the American Medical Association, 283,* 1858–1865.

PART II

IMAGINING AND LIVING
WITH THE OTHER

Introduction to Part II

We need to make a distinction between peace as a mere absence of war and peace as a state of tranquility founded on the deep sense of security that arises from mutual understanding, tolerance of others' point of view, and respect for their rights.

—His Holiness the Dalai Lama, *Ethics for the New Millennium*

Writing about ethics for the new millennium (1999), the Dalai Lama highlighted issues related to intergroup conflict and mentioned, in particular, three qualities that people worldwide could practice to promote peace. The authors of chapters in this part likewise discuss mutual understanding, tolerance for others' point of view, and respect for everyone's rights in conflicts among youth playing out divisions in their societies.

While the chapters in Part I focused on psycho-social processes of individuals, the next four chapters focus on the dynamics fueling conflicts between groups of youth. These chapters focus on characteristic intergroup conflicts as they represent divisions in society. The chapters bring to light some hidden processes sustaining youth conflicts, where leaders have made efforts to promote intergroup relations, as discussed in the case of Israel and Korea, or where inter-group issues have been suppressed or ignored, as in the case of the United States and China. Young people learn who their adversaries are and then develop ways of dealing with others in terms of these adversarial identities provided in broader societal discourse.

The portraits revealed in the next four chapters bring to life young people's day-to-day interpersonal relations with young people characterized as "others," in the context of diverse national values and social practices. Each chapter describes the social contexts that make these youth conflicts salient in the society and explains the psychological or physical manifestations of these conflicts. In some situations, intergroup relations come into focus as power hierarchies, with one group positioned as more entitled or aggressive and "the other" group as more inferior or intrusive (chapters 6, 8, and 9), but in another situation, these groups have faced each other on more equal terms (chapter 7).

The Case Studies

Rachel Hertz-Lazarowitz explores how young undergraduates identifying as Arabs and Jews perceive their mutual rejection and acceptance in the unique context of coexistence at a nationally and religiously heterogeneous university in Israel. Hertz-Lazarowitz explains that her goal is to understand the factors that support peaceful coexistence and the factors that explain the eruption of conflicts and violent behaviors on campus. Hertz-Lazarowitz supports her argument that students' perceptions of coexistence are sources of conflict and harmony. In interviews where the research team asked students to speak about the full range of their positive and negative experiences as members of national groups on campus, both Arab and the Jewish students highly valued "close relationships" and "cultural diversity," while in terms of negative experiences, Arab students reported "discrimination" and "political tension" more frequently than Jewish students as the main processes of rejection in their lives on campus. On the basis of such findings, Hertz-Lazarowitz challenges the university to increase acceptance and reduce rejection on its heterogeneous campus.

Jae Lee writes about bullying as it occurs within Korean society, focusing on the social nature of bullying, defining it as "collective ostracism" in Korea. Relating his analysis to research elsewhere, Lee writes that collective ostracism is an increasingly serious problem because of its nature, prevalence, and effects among Korean youth. Lee describes the concept, causes, effects, and types of collective ostracism as a complex social, cultural, and psychological phenomenon involving institutions as well as networks of children whose interactions as perpetrators, victims, and bystanders contribute toward the practice. Discussing the motivations, strategies, and effectiveness of collective ostracism in terms of social influence, for example, Lee offers an analysis of bullying as a social phenomenon rather than primarily as an issue of individual children's aggressive tendencies, character flaws, or other antisocial orientations.

Writing about a division with increasing visibility worldwide, Stacey Horn and Larry Nucci review literature on the rates and impact of harassment and violence against gay and lesbian youth in schools across several contexts as a foundation for proposing a new theoretical framework for understanding how high-school-aged youth understand sexual identity. From the perspective of domain theory, Horn and Nucci present results of their research on young people's reasoning about homosexuality and treatment of their gay and lesbian peers. This theory-based analysis reveals intriguing complexities, such as young people's prejudice and intolerance toward gay or lesbian peers when they believe that individuals have control over whether they are gay or lesbian but more accepting and tolerant attitudes regarding homosexuality when they believe people are born gay or lesbian, thus placing sexual orientation beyond the individual's control or moral culpability. On the basis of these and other findings, Horn and Nucci also suggest future directions for research and practice to promote tolerance and development around issues of sexual identity. By presenting an analysis of conflicts about sexual identity, these scholars of human development and education reveal the workings of another mostly hidden fault line in society that affects the development of social collaboration and humanity.

Gouzhen Cen and Dan Li describe intergenerational conflicts in moral and social values resulting from China's shift from a collective to a free market economic system. This analysis highlights divisions across generations of Chinese youth, manifested primarily across time but also in the contemporary context across diverse socioeconomic classes; urban versus rural living, for example. Based primarily on survey data over several decades, Cen and Li offer a detailed explanation of how changes in the Chinese economic system affect the thinking and values of school-aged youth. The authors explain that the change in the economic system has accelerated the polarization of a previously monodimensional society, in particular numerous and dramatic differentiations in income and social status, as a result of the free proliferation of vocations and their legislation. These psychologists propose the complex phenomenon of "social values confusion," reflected in increases in young people's valuing of material wealth, personal happiness, and, not surprisingly, an increase in property crimes, while maintaining pride in their country, concern for others, and valuing of fairness, albeit alongside decreased trust in social institutions. The researchers then propose recommendations for educational research about inter-generational discussion of values and related practice strategies for making moral judgments in the context of dramatic national transformation.

Identity Conflicts as Social Systems

These chapters explain the historical divisions in society that young people reproduce in their ways of perceiving society, their relationships, and themselves. The diverse manifestations of intergroup divisions in these chapters range from a group's uses of physical and intellectual resources, and thus control of society, to acts of physical and psychological aggression toward peers perceived as weak, to values about social harmony, and to ideas about correct choices of gender identity in society.

The case studies presented in these chapters provide histories of social division as the background for intergroup youth conflicts. Hertz-Lazarowitz, for example, describes Haifa Univeristy as unique in Israel as an institution attended by young people identifying as both Arabs and Jews, where in consequence the local history is positioned against the longer term societal division between Jews and Arabs in Israel. Given their choice to attend this university, young people have the intention to move beyond traditional divisions, so Hertz-Lazarowitz's research considers Arab and Jewish students' experiences sharing with each other their college experiences, mutual perceptions, and intentions for a collective future.

Horn and Nucci describe a history that has only recently become salient in the United States in the aftermath of extreme acts of violence against gay and lesbian youth and in the context of legal considerations of the rights of gays and lesbians to marry and to enjoy the attendant economic opportunities. Although homosexuality was not a major topic of discussion in the schools where Horn and Nucci did their research, they found that young people had sophisticated and theoretically predictable thought processes about sexual identity and the treatment of their lesbian and gay peers.

Lee and Cen and Li describe societal divisions that represent breaks with history in Korea and China, respectively. Describing collective ostracism in Korea, Lee briefly recounts the recent history of peer bullying in the context of the long history of consensus and harmony characterizing the society. In this way, elements of social history are transformed to serve new purposes, which Lee explains as a need for social control. Finally, Cen and Li ground their discussion of cross-generational conflicts in the economic and cultural shift from communism to a free market economy, with data from over 20 years of research spanning this shift. These social histories of conflict become salient to young people as they reproduce the values of their families and communities and as they envision or assume their places in society.

Interestingly, all the authors presenting work about intergroup divisions emphasize the role of society in examining the values that reproduce divisions among young people and for creating institutional structures and practices that forge collective activity, identity, and respect. As a result of collectivist values in Korea, Lee's analysis implies that collective ostracism is a kind of disciplining of young people who remain outside peer groups and thus become vulnerable to bullying. Lee asserts, however, that schools where collective ostracism tends to occur bear responsibility for creating a safe environment where youth are seen as equals and for socializing young people to understand and empathize with others. Horn and Nucci urge researchers to do continued research on these issues and say that their study suggests that by not doing anything to address social divisions around issues of sexual preference, schools actually sanction exclusion, teasing, and harassment.

The authors of these chapters used theory-based survey methods to identify the understandings of the different groups involved in their research. In each case, the survey data were also supported by reviews of literature on the related phenomenon and by research in cultural records documenting these highly salient and troubling manifestations of youth conflict.

CHAPTER 6

Acceptance and Rejection as a Source of Youth Conflict

The Case of Haifa University in a Divided Society

RACHEL HERTZ-LAZAROWITZ

When my research students conducted interviews with Arab and Jewish students during the academic year of 2002, they expected to study and understand the source of conflict between Arabs and Jews on Haifa University (HU) campus. Their fellow students were eager to talk about positive and negative experiences they encounter on campus. Their perceptions, feelings, and interpretations are presented here and in table 6.1. They demonstrate the intensity of the feelings and perceptions that are related to the social processes of acceptance and rejection.

An Israeli Jewish student commented:

> I am personally disappointed that the University authorities are not acting more firmly against the Arab students who carry the PLO flag in their demonstrations. . . . Your knowledge about other groups expands. When I became part of HU campus, I understand they have different expectations for instance in religious issues.

The woman quoted here is 27 years old and describes herself as "very nationalistic and patriotic." She lives in the mixed dormitory on campus, and studies literature and human resources (see table 6.1).

An Israeli Arab student commented:

> When I came to the dormitories I was asked with whom I want to share the apartment, Arabs or Jews—I realized then that the distinction is very central. . . . I

107

have friends from many different groups; I lived with Jewish women who were older then me. They gave me many good advises [on] how to study. I learned from their motivation and determination to succeed as a student.

The woman quoted here is a Muslim and is 20 years old. She describes herself as a Circassian, a Muslim, and an Israeli. She says: "My identity is very complex because the situation is very complex." She also lives in the mixed dormitory on campus. She studies general studies and education (see table 6.1).

In Israel, the seven main universities are the most heterogeneous spaces for interaction between Arabs and Jews. With an Arab population of 20% attending alongside Jews, Haifa University is the most heterogeneous campus in Israel and thus has been a main stage for prolonged social coexistence on the one hand and consistent bitter conflicts on the other hand. This chapter presents my analysis of how students at HU during the 2002–2003 academic year perceived their coattendance because, as I argue, these perceptions are central to sources of conflict and harmony. My analysis stems from two theoretical frameworks. One foundational framework is based on *acceptance* (Deutsch, 1994), and prosocial behavior (Eisenberg, Hertz-Lazarowitz, & Fuchs, 1990; Hertz-Lazarowitz, 1989; Staub, 2003), which account for cooperation and peaceful coexistence *interpersonally*. The other foundation is the dramaturgical model (Harré, 1979; Hertz-Lazarowitz, 1988), which explains *rejection* accounting for tensions, conflicts, and violence *between groups* in educational contexts.

The study discussed in this chapter continues prior research to examine sources of conflict (Hertz-Lazarowitz, 1988, 2003) and sources of peaceful coexistence on campus. The study is based on interviews conducted with 47 Jewish and 27 Arab students. My research team asked participants to speak about the full range of their *positive* and *negative* experiences as individuals and as members of national groups on the HU campus. Across interviews with these two groups, 11 common themes emerged, expressing students' perceptions of "acceptance" or "rejection" in either "positive" or "negative" ways. In the positive cluster, both the Arab and Jewish students highly valued "close relationships" and "cultural diversity" as the main processes *of acceptance* in their lives on campus. In the negative cluster, Arab students reported "discrimination" and "political tension" more frequently than Jewish students as the main processes of *rejection* in their lives on campus. On the basis of these findings, I explain that *acceptance/rejection* constitute a duality of perceptions across the student groups and that the persistence of such a duality challenges the responsibility and commitment of the University, in particular to increase acceptance and reduce rejection on its heterogeneous campus.

Background

Schools in highly heterogeneous societies are often at risk of becoming zones of conflict and violence. This risk stems from tendencies within such societies to distribute resources and access to power differentially on the basis of its members' social class, gender, national origin, and religion. Israel is such a multicultural society, divided on many issues that put the country into a constant state of tension (Hertz-Lazarowitz, Zelniker, White, Stephan, & Stephan, 2004).

The seven main universities are the most heterogeneous spaces for contact and interaction among all the different groups in Israeli society. For this reason, attention to the processes by which university students negotiate this heterogeneity may be instructive for how heterogeneous societies may ameliorate or transcend the often attendant conflicts. Because the Israeli educational system from kindergarten to twelfth grade is fully segregated by nation for Arabs and Jews and by religiosity for the Jews, the university is the first educational *umwelt*, defined by Lewin (1935) as the physical environment where different groups meet, connect, and engage in a discourse that touches the important personal and collective issues in the lives of all Israeli youth.

The goal of this chapter is to provide an in-depth analysis of the anatomy of young people's mutual acceptance and rejection in a context of planned coexistence. This analysis will then be the basis for understanding the factors in the university *umwelt* that explain the emergence of peaceful coexistence and integration and the factors that explain the eruption of conflicts, violent behaviors, and segregation on campus. Haifa University is an appropriate context for examining issues of conflict and cooperation among individuals.

In my analysis of life on a heterogeneous campus, I differentiate between social cognitive processes that are the source for interpersonal conflicts and social cognitive processes that are the source of intergroup-collective conflicts. Cooperation, moral reasoning, prosocial behaviors, and empathy direct and provide useful frameworks and actions to account for decreasing rejection and increasing peaceful coexistence interpersonally, because psychological processes of empathy and caring can be designed to take place among the students on the personal level (Stephan & White-Stephan, 2001).

When most members of distinct groups perceive rejection as acts of injustice and domination imposed by the power and authority of the institution, the issue becomes a collective group experience within the given *umwelt* (Fine et al., 2003). In such a context, where minority ethnic groups or oppressed national groups sense feelings of not being recognized or not being respected, the theoretical model of the "social drama" (Harré, 1979; Hertz-Lazarowitz, 1988) can explain tension, conflicts, and violence between groups in general and in educational contexts specifically. The model Harré theorized asserts that conflicting groups can perceive and construe various actions in contradictory dualities. For example, the same events, such as dressing according to one's group's religious standards, can be perceived as respect or contempt by the other groups.

After presenting a general background of the Israel and the University, I will elaborate on the dualities accounted for in the Harré model and discuss the related impact on the *umwelt* of the University.

Haifa University, Israel: A Site for Conflict and Coexistence

After having spent many years involved in research and practice on cooperation and integration in schools and communities (Hertz-Lazarowitz, 1999, 2004), I have recently chosen the university context as a site for studying Jewish-Arab youth in conflict (Hertz-Lazarowitz, 2003). As already mentioned, this setting is appropriate for such study because it offers a unique opportunity within Israeli society to deal with national and religious heterogeneity. To begin, I offer a short description of Israeli society and the HU campus.

Despite its small size and population of about 6 million, Israel, like most societies in the Western world, is becoming ever more diverse economically, socially, and culturally. Social scientists in Israel have identified four major groups in conflict in Israeli society. These conflicting groups revolve around distinctions of nation between Jews (80%) and Arabs (20%); religion between orthodox (14%) and secular Jews; ethnicity between Jews of Middle Eastern origin (Sephardim, about 50%) and Jews of European and American origin (Ashkenazim); and, most recently, distinctions between immigrants, mostly from the former Soviet Union (17%), and nonimmigrants (Horowitz, 2000; Smooha, 1997).

Notwithstanding some changes in the intensity of these various intergroup tensions, such as the constant growing integration of Sephardim and Ashkenazim (40% of intermarriages), the Jewish—Arab rift within Israel has persisted since 1948, the year of the birth of the State of Israel. This intergroup/national tension centers on issues of civic rights, recognition of identity, equality of allocated resources, and legitimization of each group's historical narratives. In general, the Israeli Arabs demand more equality than the Jewish State of Israel gives them. Thus issues of civic equality, loyalty, domination, and oppression are constantly negotiated within Israel (Kalekin-Fishman, 2004; White Stephan et al., 2004).

Within the Arab minority in Israel today, which constitutes 20% of the population, the majority are Muslims (85%), the rest Christians (10%), Druze, and other small groups of non-Jewish citizens (5%). Most Jews and Arabs live in segregated cities or villages and enroll in a fully segregated educational system (Al-Haj, 1998; Mar'i, 1978). The university is the sole place where these populations meet and interact; hence the HU experience is unique for both groups.

With approximately 15,000 students, HU is located in one of the five ethnically mixed cities in Israel, and, for the last three decades, with its liberal arts and social sciences departments, has had the largest Arab student body in Israel (22%). Of the Jews, about a third are Sephardim, and of the Ashkenazi students, 20% are immigrants from the former Soviet Union. The proportion of Arabs at HU equals their proportion in the general population and reflects their aspiration for higher education (Al-Haj, 1998; Mar'i, 1978). While the contribution of HU to the development of the academic and political leadership of Israeli Arabs has been well documented, it has gone hand in hand with the eruption of conflicts on campus (Al-Haj, 1998; Hofman, 1988; Hofman, Beit Hallahmi,

& Hertz-Lazarowitz, 1982). For this reason, HU is a stage set for conflict and coexistence.

Haifa University as an *Umwelt* for Social Drama

With conflicts between Arabs and Jews flaring annually over the years, there is a sense of a predictable "social drama" emerging at HU. This social drama is physically and symbolically expressive in the very architecture at HU: "The structure of a setting may be an icon of the social theory . . . the physical settings are not neutral, they contribute to the action" (Harré, 1979, p. 192). The main and tallest building at HU is the 30-story Eshkol Tower. Whether by design or not, this tower proclaims messages of power, territory, distance and a struggle over recognition and control (Hertz-Lazarowitz, 1988). The tower has three levels of classrooms on floors 5, 6, and 7, with the main library and dining areas also located on those floors. The rest of the floors, up to the 29th floor, are departments' offices, various centers' rooms, and the offices of faculty and administrative staff. The 27th to the 29th floors are where the highest academic and administrative persons reside. On the 30th floor is a gallery room where one can observe a beautiful view of Haifa and northern Israel. All students, Arabs and Jews, spend most of their time on campus on the fifth, sixth, and seventh floors. Nevertheless, it is Arab students who are most salient in their numbers, dress, and language and in their gathering in a large group in the halls of Eshkol Tower. This makes the mass presence of Arabs the most salient *act* relating to "who controls the campus territory." Perhaps because of the salience of Arab students in the tower, some Jewish students estimate that the Arab students on campus are the majority. In addition, Arabic, which is heard predominantly in the halls of the tower, has caused folk culture to label HU "Palestine University" and "Fatahland."

This presence gives Arabs an expressive sense of power and respect, which they do not typically experience in a mixed setting, while conversely it makes many Jews feel threatened by the loss of power and the weakening of the Jewish identity (Hertz-Lazarowitz, 2003; Stephan, 1999). The architecture of HU was significant in the analysis of the social drama that took place in a bloody conflict on campus between Arabs and Jews in 1985 (Hertz-Lazarowitz, 1988). In the last 20 years, several buildings were added to the HU campus, but Eshkol Tower is still the main building on campus. There is currently a social topography of distance and power (Lewin, 1935), expressed in the locations of powerful actors, such as the high authorities, who reside in floors 28 and 29, and the students who are crowded into the very low halls of Eshkol Tower.

In addition to the architectural structure of HU, the conflicts at HU can be analyzed in terms of students' discourses of acceptance and rejection. Officially, HU encourages integration and contact among youth from different races, ethnicities, and cultures. Nevertheless, in their everyday lives in integrated schools, students experience deep discriminations and prejudices that lead to violence and conflicts in all levels of schooling (Fine, 2004; Hertz-Lazarowitz, 2003; Stephan & White-Stephan, 2001).

Full segregation takes place between Arab and Jewish youth until the two national groups integrate at the university (Al Haj, 1998; Hertz-Lazarowitz, 2003; Kalekin-Fishman, 2004). The long-term Israeli Arab—Jew political conflict highlights tensions between the two national groups; thus the educational process is interwoven with larger political issues. This unique context is a natural laboratory for research on the development of social-cognitive processes that can moderate or accelerate prejudice, feelings of discrimination, and open conflicts.

The Dramaturgical Model: A Theoretical Framework for Understanding Youth Conflict

The dramaturgical model of Harré (1979) guides the theoretical analysis of several of my studies on youth conflicts at the HU *umwelt*. Harré focused on interpersonal relationships, but in applying this model to the Israeli situation, I modified his concepts of social dynamics to account for ethnic and national relationships on HU campus. The three central pairs of concepts are the practical/expressive, action/acts, and respect/contempt. Following my own study of the conflict on HU, I added a forth concept, *power/weakness* (Hertz-Lazarowitz, 1988).

The *practical/expressive* contrast refers to aspects of social activity where many of the activities one group views as practical the other group interprets as expressive, and vice versa. For example, Arabs at HU view their speaking of Arabic openly on campus or their socializing in large groups in central areas of Eshkol Tower as natural and *practical social activities*. On the other hand, Jews view these as *expressive* of threat to the Jewish identity of HU and metaphorically to the future of the Jewish homeland.

The *action/acts* relation differentiates an *action*, a sequence of behavior, from an *act*, its interpretation and meaning. Every ritual can be analyzed as a sequence of action types. Every facet of the social drama on campus requires interpretations of behaviors as *action*s and of *actions* as *acts,* "the very stuff of social life" (Harré, 1979, p. 192). This dynamic of the contradictory interpretation of actions and acts is the reflection of expressive activities of people striving to present acceptable and recognized selves. For instance, kissing, handshaking, and nodding are interpretable as the *greeting act*. In the sequential structure of conflict, *actions* such as shouting, catcalling, and fighting during a demonstration constitute either acts violating freedom of speech on campus or acts of war between the minority and majority groups.

The *respect/contempt* duality refers to publicly expressed opinions (e.g., policies, newspapers, and other documentation) and to private feelings (e.g., personal interactions, interviews, and self-reports). Relations between Arabs and Jews on campus are highly motivated by the ritual of *respect* and *contempt*.

For some participants in the drama, these forces may operate unconsciously, and for others, especially the Arab students, it is highly conscious.

The *power/weakness* duality interacts with the respect/contempt duality. We found in analyzing a bloody conflict on campus in 1985 (Hertz-Lazarowitz, 1988) that the duality of *power/weakness* was important to Jews, so I have added this to the model as a fourth conceptual pair. For Jewish students, power is expressed in terms of control and moral legitimacy, and weakness is expressed as threat and fear of losing the homeland that is symbolized by the University *umwelt* (Hertz-Lazarowitz, 1988). A cultural contrast emerged from results indicating that the *respect/contempt* duality had more meaning as an expressive act within the Arab culture (Dwairy, 1998), while *power/weakness* has more meaning as an expressive act in the Jewish culture (Hertz-Lazarowitz, 1988, 2003).

This theoretical model suggests that the dual conceptual perceptions can contribute to the understanding of the complex anatomy of heterogeneous groupings on campus. The interpersonal and group relations are based on a discourse that includes a sequence of verbal and nonverbal behaviors (actions) that (as acts) carry interpretation and meaning relating to acceptance and rejection, integration and segregation, discrimination and privilege, and prejudices and breaking prejudices. Listening to and analyzing the different discourses of the Actors in the social drama can explain the dynamic of periods of civic and peaceful coexistence as contrasted with bitter and violent conflicts on campus. This can further suggest actions to reduce conflicts and enhance peaceful coexistence.

An Analysis of Acceptance and Rejection at Haifa University

In the interviews conducted in 2002 with 74 students (47 Jewish and 27 Arab) at HU, participants were asked to speak about their positive and negative experiences on campus. In doing so, we assumed that such knowledge could alter intergroup relations on campus and off campus and would offer social scientists a new understanding of the interplay between personal and collective factors (Hertz-Lazarowitz, 1988, 2003; Stephan, 1999).

The research questions were, first, "Are students aware of the diversity in the campus and how do they perceive, interpret, and function within this diversity?" and second, "How are students from both nationalities constructing their perceptions about the life within the heterogeneity of the HU campus?"

My research team consisted of a group of students enrolled in a research seminar entitled "Selected Issues in Social Psychology in Educational Contexts." The interview protocol included 13 open-ended questions; each interview was tape-recorded and transcribed for subsequent analysis. Researchers analyzed the transcriptions for 15 categories derived directly from the interview questions (Hertz-Lazarowitz, 2001). These categories included (1) self-presentation of interviewer and interviewee; (2) naming the different groups on

campus by the interviewee; (3) citing *personal positive* qualities of heterogeneity on campus; (4) citing *general positive* qualities of heterogeneity on campus;
(5) citing *personal negative* attributions of heterogeneity on campus; (6) citing
general negative attributions of their experience on campus; (7) mentioning
the salience of heterogeneity issues in courses and classes on campus; (8) mentioning lecturers' discrimination or equality in handling students' affairs; (9)
analyzing an event where the interviewee felt discriminated against; (10) evaluating everyday social life on campus on a range of 1 (highly discriminative) to
10 (highly equality oriented); (11) evaluating everyday academic life on campus on a range of 1 (highly discriminative) to 10 (highly equality oriented);
(12) defining one's political and social self; (13) stating future plans. When
the interviewers created a summary table (see table 6.1), they added two more
items for each interviewee, (14) key quotations to bring the voice in, and (15)
unique elements (Hertz-Lazarowitz, 2001).

We devised a text-table summary form noting the frequencies of 10 categories in each interview; this served for later summaries and data coding across
nationality. A reliability check consisted of achieving 90% agreement by three
Jewish and Arab readers' judgments of each transcript as to its categories (see
table 6.1).

Students' Self-Identity Definitions and Political Orientations

The interviewees' self-descriptions attest to their perceptions of diversity. When
asked to define their identities, most of the participants mentioned several identities, related to various categories such as personal, national, role, ethnic, political, religious, residential, and more. We grouped these identities into two main
categories: *personal identities,* including responses such as "I am a human being," "student," "likes arts"; and *national-ethnic identities,* including responses
such as: Arab and Jew and all variations, for example, Arab-Palestinian national
Jew, Druze, Circassian, Russian, Ethiopian, and more. The main finding is that
the national identity was the dominant identity mentioned by the Arabs (88%),
while among the Jews the variation of identities was much broader.

The political orientations of the Arabs and the Jews (question 13) were similar, in that all defined themselves as moderate or left-wing. The main difference
here was that no Arab defined his or her political stand as right-wing. Arabs
tended less to declare their political stand, by saying "no opinion" (19%) and
by avoiding this question (20%) (Hertz-Lazarowitz & Zelniker, 2004).

Student Interview Findings: The Personal Versus
the General and the Positive Versus the Negative

Table 6.1 presents examples of coding categories for an interview of an Arab
and a Jewish student. As shown in table 6.1, students related distinctively to
the four categories and identified various characteristics of heterogeneity on

Table 6.1 Summary Table for Two Interviews About Heterogeneity on Haifa University Campus

Category	Jewish student	Arab student
Self-presentation	An undergraduate female student 27 years old married and lives with her partner in HU dormitories, studies in the Departments of Literature and Human Resources.	An undergraduate Muslim female student, 20 years old, single, lives in the dormitories. She comes from a large village, studies in the Departments of General Studies and Education.
Awareness	I see the things as they are, and I realize the fact that people different from me study at the same place, they speak a different language, and I am aware they have different needs and desires.	I am very aware of it. I live with them daily on campus, there are different groups and they have different cultures and different religions. I can easily recognize them by language, dress, colors and manners.
Groups	I identify different groups by nationality and ethnic origin within each nationality. Different religions within the Arabs and different level of religiosity of Arabs and Jews. There is diversity by residence, newcomers and locals. There [are] all kinds of nations, colors, and places. A celebration of heterogeneity.	There are Arabs, Christians, Muslims, Druze, Ethiopians, and newcomers from Russia, Jews and also a small group of Circassians that I am part of. . . .
Positive personal	Your knowledge about other groups expands. When I became part of HU campus, I understand they have different expectations for instance in religious issues.	I have friends from many different groups; I lived with Jewish women who were older then me. They gave me [much] good [advice on] how to study. I learned from their motivation and determination to succeed as a student.
Positive general	You see things positively by the opportunity to know different people and different groups. Your knowledge expands.	First of all I think it is very important that we get to know each other because we live in the same country. It helps to understand each other and live in coexistence.
Negative personal	I am personally disappointed that the university authorities are not acting more firmly against the Arab students who carry the PLO flag in their demonstrations. Such students are not legitimate to be friends with, and not to be accepted to the university.	When I came to the dormitories I was asked with whom I want to share the apartment Arabs or Jews—I realized then that the distinction is very central.
Negative general	This heterogeneity brings more troubles than positive things. It seems like it has merit but it does not. There is tremendous tension between Arabs and Jews on the national level, and the effort to reconcile will fail.	Sometimes I feel hatred in the air. The things that happen in Israel, the terror and security issues, make life very complicated for me.

continued

Table 6.1 Continued

Category	Jewish student	Arab student
Identity	I am very nationalistic and patriotic; politically I am for peace and talks with the Palestinians; I do not see a military solution to this problem. I just hope there is someone on the other side that we can talk with.	First of all I am a Circassian, I am Muslim and Israeli. I have moderate political opinions and I want peace. My identity is very complex because the situation is very complex.
Voice	As a person that understands what is going on here from the political aspect and based on the feelings of the people there is a serious problem. This heterogeneity brings more troubles than positive things.	Last year I lived with Jewish students, this year I live with Arab students, before that I lived in a Christian monastery and I learned a lot about their religion. I enjoy learning different and interesting things from people.
Unique elements	[In her interview she gave many problematic examples about her co-residence with Arabs in the highly heterogeneous HU dormitories on campus.]	I belong to a very small group and most people do not know the difference between my ethnic group and other Muslim groups.

campus as nested in the positive and negative and on a personal or a general level.

On the basis of the full interview and the summary tables, we concluded that issues of awareness of heterogeneity and different groups revealed similarities across Arab and Jewish students. Jewish and Arab students were highly aware of the heterogeneity on campus. Students pointed to the main concept of "difference," including many visible differences, such as dress, language, religion, and color, and some nonvisible differences, such as values, norms, need, and desires (see table 6.1, groups and identity sections).

Designed to portray the perceptions of Arab and Jewish students in regard to their life on the HU campus, the interview revealed students' cognitive and socioemotional perceptions. Notably, students used different terms to describe the HU campus, including "heterogeneous student composition," "diversity of ethnic groups," "binational campus," and "a multicultural campus."

The students' perceptions as expressed in the interviews were organized into a four categorization model, positive-negative, personal-general, making it possible to study the origins of tension and harmonization of life at HU. The 11 themes that emerged were coded as *key* statements, namely, statements that were expressed in high frequency among the students in the interviews such as "At HU there are too many political demonstrations." These statements were coded, and percentages of frequencies per statement were calculated.

In the *positive personal domain benefits of heterogeneity* (Question 3) three themes emerged: (1) *personal closeness* (for example, "The context of HU facilitates friendships"), as expressed by Arab (48%) and Jews (49%); (2) *cultural exposure* (for example, "I learned about other and new cultures"), as expressed by Arabs and Jews (33% for each group); (3) *breaking prejudice* (for example, "In every mixed group there is the potential to understand things that in a life time one can not understand elsewhere"), as expressed by Arabs (19%) more than the Jews (9%).

In the *positive general* domain benefits of heterogeneity (Question 4), two themes emerged: (4) *cultural diversity* (for example, "We live together in this country and HU helps us to know each other"), expressed by the Arabs (73%) slightly more than by Jews (63%); (5) *HU as a democratic place* (for example, "HU is a democratic institution as is the State of Israel"), expressed more frequently by Jewish students (33%) than by Arab students (23%).

In the *negative personal* domain characteristics of heterogeneity (Question 5, What are the elements of heterogeneity on HU that are negative and affect your personal life as a student?), three themes emerged, as follows. The theme of (6) *politics and tension* (for example, "Too many political demonstrations") was expressed similarly by Jews (56%) and Arabs (58%), with some variation in certain statements, such as "too many demonstrations on campus" being expressed more by Jews, while other statements, for example, "writing nationality on the registration forms," were expressed more by Arabs. The theme of (7) *discrimination and racism* (for example, "Having feelings of 'Anti' against different groups") was expressed with similar frequency by Arabs (22%) and Jews (19%). Each group gave statements of different directions; for example, the context was perceived as highly discriminative among the Arabs and as highly affirmative among the Jews ("There is too many affirmative acts on campus"). The theme of (8) *feelings of separation* (for example, "No communication between groups") was expressed by Arabs (20%) more frequently than Jews (13%).

In the *negative general* characteristics domain of heterogeneity (Question 6, What are the elements of heterogeneity on HU that are negative and affect your public life as a student?), the same themes as in the personal negative domain emerged, but the frequency was different from those in the negative personal experiences. Because the domain of negative personal creates an antagonistic perception of heterogeneity on campus and will lead to the discussion based on the Harré dramaturgical model, I will present a detailed account of frequencies of statements made by Arabs and Jews.

Several of the most frequent statements differed by nationality. These include: "There is discrimination on campus and it is on behalf of other groups," which was expressed by 23% of Arabs and only 4.5% of the Jews; "Every group is segregated within itself and there is not enough benefit drawn from the diversity," expressed by 24% of the Jews and 14% of the Arabs; and "There is tension in the University that causes conflicts, confrontation, and demonstrations," expressed by 22 % of the Jews and 14% of the Arabs.

Politics and tension at HU (9) included general statements such as: "The HU authorities try to be more than fair toward the Arabs"; "Politics disturbs life on campus"; "Arabs' behaviors are very disturbing during memorial Jewish ceremonies." Overall, the Arabs (27%) perceived conditions relating to this theme as less negative then did the Jews (37%).

Discrimination and racism (10) included statements such as: "The minority is discriminated compared to the majority"; "No attention at HU to respect the Arabs' holidays"; "The presence of the Arabs lowers the academic level of HU," expressed by 27% of the Arabs and 37% of the Jews. Overall, this theme was expressed more often by the Arabs (46%) than by the Jews (14%).

Separation (11) included statements such as: "Each group is closed within itself, and is not taking advantage of the heterogeneity"; "No feeling of a home"; "Alienation grows deeper between Jews and Arabs." This theme overall was expressed less by the Arabs (14%) than by the Jews (26 %).

In summary, Arabs and Jews indicated that they valued the personal and general positive domains of life at HU. Positive statements about close relationships (about 50%), exposure to different cultures (33%), and cultural diversity (over 60%) reflected the significance of personal acquaintances and friendships between students from different national and ethnic groups. Arabs perceived the HU experience as breaking prejudice more frequently then did the Jews. In the general (public) positive aspects of life on campus, both Arabs and Jews valued very highly the way multicultural existence and coexistence between different individuals and diverse groups are facilitated and practiced at HU. Both groups also valued HU as a democratic institution in a democratic state. Arabs referred to multicultural benefits more frequently, and Jews referred to the democratic milieu of the University more frequently.

In relating to the negative aspects of heterogeneity, "political tension" colored dramatically the personal and general domains of experience at HU for both groups, although more frequently (about 55%) in the personal domain, as compared to the general domain (about 30%). Arabs and Jews perceived this as the most negative and disturbing element of their lives on campus. Each group perceived the other group as the source for this tension. This oppositional view was more evident on the personal level, as students felt sad about losing the potential benefits of the heterogeneity of the campus in their personal experience. On the negative personal and general, Arabs more frequently expressed feelings of being discriminated against.

Discussion

The findings clearly showed a more balanced picture on HU campus life then did our study on injustice and surveillance. While we know that youth can encounter injustice individually or as a group every day (Daiute & Fine, 2003), the finding of this study is that the young people interviewed also experienced closeness, help, respect, and being privileged as persons and as group every day.

Because campuses in general are significant symbolic spaces for youth empowerment around the world, for example, in the United States, South Africa, and Israel (Hare, 1985), university campuses have become a stage for political activism, with violent and sometimes nonviolent conflicts. By confronting authorities of power, students are the "actors" "playing" various types of "social being," in order to test and redefine power, status, identity, and majority—minority relations, including the legitimacy of opposing collective narratives. However the positive aspects of life in such a complex and diverse *umwelt* are less studied than the negative aspects and are rarely documented.

The same campus observed in earlier studies emerges in this study as a site for tremendous positive moral, prosocial, and humanistic developmental processes. Many of the interviews were highly powerful and moving in both directions, highlighting the joys and pains of being a student in HU. The students are actors playing various types of social beings within the drama of living in a heterogeneous and diverse university. It seems that the interviewees managed to develop complex and multifaceted perceptions of diversity, and in general perceive it as an enriching experience.

This study continues the inquiry into social developmental processes within HU. An earlier study (Hertz-Lazarowitz, 1988) of the perennial conflicts between Arabs and Jews focused on the physical environment of this *umwelt,* namely, the setting, the sequence of events, and the presentation of the conflict in the public sphere (printed documents). The second study (Hertz-Lazarowitz, 2003) focused on the "social meaning" of the *umwelt,* using interviews asking about experiences of injustice and surveillance as perceived by mainly Arab students and their leaders.

My basic assumption in all the research on HU has been that the university is a space for advantaged and disadvantaged groups of students to achieve academic excellence in a just and moral way. The qualitative data, based on personal interviews in each of the studies, served to conceptualize and discuss the messages and themes voiced by the students. This may further social scientists' understanding of issues of closeness and separation, of exposure to cultures that intensifies positive outcomes and that intensifies racism. No doubt the role of internal and external politics affects the experience of the students and their experimentation with new visions of a more peaceful and diverse social drama on campus.

The Message of Identity

All of the Arab and Jewish students discussed identity as a major issue on campus. Identity is a dynamic field of research (Hofman, 1988; Rouhana, 1997; Smooha, 1997), and research findings point to dramatic changes that took place in the way the Israeli Arabs and the Israeli Jews (the definitions commonly in use since the 1960s) redefine their identities over time. However, the common assumption held in Israel, namely, that national and civic definitions are the same for the Arabs, cannot be taken for granted in respect of young Palestinian citizens of Israel within its 1948 borders. Dramatic political events in Israel and the West Bank and Gaza and the neighboring Arab countries are milestones that have changed the ways Arabs and Jews define their own and others' identities (Hertz-Lazarowitz, Kupermintz, & Lang, 1998). Within this framework, students at HU are significant agents, functioning as seismographs to predict changes in identity definitions. Overall, there is a growing detachment of the Arabs from the Israeli civic identity. As Suleiman (2002) has noted, national identity has become more central to Arab students' self-identification, reflecting their alienation from their civic (Israeli) identity. Suleiman also claims that the fact that the use by Israeli Jews who are experts on Arab issues (known as Arabists in Israel) of the term "Israeli Arabs" to define the minority does not reflect the terms used by indigenous minority members (Suleiman, 2002).

At this stage, we find an incisive dissociation of the Arab students from the civic (Israeli) identity, which may be explained by two processes. The first is rage turned upon civic discrimination, which is not perceived as a personal but as a collective issue. Thus the civic becomes political. Second, the process of delegitimization of the national and political identities is intersected by political ideology. The identity of the minority is interfaced with the political orientations of the majority. The fear of the double identification, national (Arab) and political (Palestinians), should be viewed in the context of Jews' double definitions as Israeli Jews. However, the current meaning of these double definitions for each group calls for further research using qualitative methodologies.

Conclusions

Jewish and Arab students alike are intent on being recognized and respected, as individual and group members. Their academic goals have to be guarded in a caring and just multicultural context. In the university *umwelt,* the political and the personal cannot be separated. Students' reports of personal *negative* characteristics of diversity were mostly concerned with the political tensions that bring conflicts about issues of power, identity, language, and culture to the front line of life on campus. Failure to respect and accept the other person and the other group are the antecedents for disrespect and injustice in multicultural coexistence (Fine, 2004; Hertz-Lazarowitz & Zelniker, 2004).

Education has to be viewed as a personal and general political matter, with positive and negative characteristics. Unfortunately, most of the negative attributions in the study reported in this chapter were related to the power structure in society. Haifa University as an institution can do far more to transform Arab-Jewish relations. On the basis of its diverse student body, and the positive aspects reported by the students, it can build a field of academic knowledge and reduce ignorance about Arabs and Jews (Stephan & White-Stephan, 2001). The University has students who desire to gain and develop knowledge based on their partially positive experiential learning and become change agents in the field.

Haifa University and its students, more than other Israeli universities, undertakes the mighty mission of continuing the dialogue within a reality of conflict; yet it should still be more determined to develop the vision, and the leadership to pursue it. From other work with mixed communities in Israel, it was shown that a spirit of synergy, democracy, coexistence, and academic excellence could inspire a system wide change (Hertz-Lazarowitz, 1999).

Epilogue

Since the time of collecting the interview data (2002) and the presentation of this study (2003) at the "Global Perspectives on Youth Conflict" book project and conference of March 10–14, 2003, in Bellagio, Italy, many dramatic political events have taken place in Israel, the region, and the world: the continuation of the Intifada by Palestinians resisting the Israeli occupation in the West Bank and Gaza; the bipolarization of Jewish opinions in regard to the occupation, the security fence, and the settlements; the United States invasion of Iraq and the war there; the severity of terror in Israel and in other places and recently the withdrawal of Israel from Gaza (August 2005). All of this affects the fabric of life of every person on earth.

Yet, while this reality touches the citizens and the students in many ways, Arab—Jewish relations in Israel have not changed dramatically thus far (Hertz-Lazarowitz et al., 2004). The HU campus is still a unique heterogeneous meeting place for Arabs and Jews. Moreover, within the Arab nation, students from different religious affiliations, such as Muslims, Druze, and Christians, study on campus in increased numbers. Within the Jewish group, students of different ethnic origin, especially Jews from the former Soviet Union and Ethiopian Jews, study together with veteran Jews and the Arabs.

From 2001 to 2004, no major open conflict took place on campus, but the social and political drama relating to recognition and acceptance of the "other" group is continuing. In 2003 and 2004, I have continued the research discussed here at HU. My students, in conducting the research, have become active actors on campus, because they understand better the "social drama" they live in. They become more committed to enhance respect and legitimization of the diverse groups on the HU campus (Hertz-Lazarowitz et al., 2005).

References

Al-Haj, M. (1998). *Education, empowerment and control: The case of the Arabs in Israel.* Albany: SUNY Press.

Daiute, C., & Fine, M. (2003). Re-focusing the gaze of youth violence. *Journal of Social Issues, 59*(1), 51–66.

Deutsch, M. (1994). Constructive conflict resolution: Principals, training and research. *Journal of Social Issues, 50,* 13–32.

Dwairy, M. (1998). *Cross-cultural counseling: The Arab Palestinian case.* New York: Haworth Press.

Eisenberg, N., Hertz-Lazarowitz, R., & Fuchs, I. (1990). Prosocial moral judgment in Israeli kibbutz and city children: A longitudinal study. *Merrill Palmer Quarterly, 36*(2), 273–287.

Fine, M. (2004). The power of the *Brown v. Board of Education* decision: Theorizing threat to sustainability. *American Psychologist, 59*(6), 502–510.

Fine, M., Freudenberg, N., Payne, Y., Perkins, T., Smith, K., & Waltzer, K. (2003). Surveillance of youth in public places. *Journal of Social Issues, 59*(1), 141–159.

Hare, A. P. (1985). *Social interactions as drama: Application from conflict resolution.* Beverly Hills, CA: Sage.

Harré, R. (1979). *Social being.* London: Blackwell.

Hertz-Lazarowitz, R. (1988). Conflict on campus: A social drama perspective. In J. E. Hofman (Ed.), *Arab-Jewish relationships in Israel* (pp. 271–299). Bristol, IN: Wyndham Hall.

Hertz-Lazarowitz, R. (1989). Cooperation and helping in the classroom: A contextual approach. *International Journal of Educational Research, 13* (1), 113–119.

Hertz-Lazarowitz, R. (1999). Cooperative learning and group-investigation in Israels' Jewish and Arabs schools: A community approach. *Theory into Practice, 38*(2), 105–113.

Hertz-Lazarowitz, R. (2001). *Manual for the analysis of students' interviews.* [Hebrew]. Unpublished manuscript, Haifa University, Israel.

Hertz-Lazarowitz, R. (2003). Arab and Jewish youth in Israel: Voicing national injustice on campus. *Journal of Social Issues, 59*(1), 51–66.

Hertz-Lazarowitz, R. (2004). Existence and coexistence in Acre: The power of educational activism. *Journal of Social Issues 60*(2), 357–372.

Hertz-Lazarowitz, R., Kupermintz, H., Azaiza, F., Sharabary, R., & Peretz, H. (2005, July, 11–15). Identity construction by Arab and Jewish students as explaining their perceptions of Haifa University as a zone for coexistence and conflict. Paper presented at the 7th IACCP International Congress, San Sebestian, Basque Country, Spain.

Hertz-Lazarowitz, R., Kupermintz, H., & Lang, J. (1998). Arab—Jewish student encounters: The Beit-Hagefen co-existence program. In E. Weiner (Ed.), *Handbook of interethnic coexistence* (pp. 565–585). New York: Continuum.

Hertz-Lazarowitz, R., & Zelniker, T. (2004, January, 5–7). Can peace education be enhanced via participatory research? Three case studies at Haifa University, 2001–2003. Paper presented at the International Conference on Peace Education for Contemporary Concerns, Jaipur, India.

Hertz-Lazarowitz, R., Zelniker, T., White-Stephan, C., & Stephan, W. (Eds.). (2004). Arab—Jewish co-existence programs. *Journal of Social Issues, 60*(2), 237–452.

Hofman, J. E. (Ed.). (1988). *Arab—Jewish relationships in Israel.* Bristol, IN: Wyndham Hall.

Hofman, J. E., Beit Hallahmi, B., & Hertz-Lazarowitz, R. (1982). Self-concept of Jewish and Arab adolescents in Israel. *Journal of Personality and Social Psychology, 43,* 786–792.

Horowitz, T. (2000). *Violence as a social phenomenon.* [Hebrew]. Jerusalem: Szold Institute'

Kalekin-Fishman, D. (2004). Ideology, policy and practice: Education for immigrants and minorities in Israel today. Norwell, MA: Kluwer Academic.

Lewin, K. (1935). *Principals of topological psychology* (F. & G. E. Heider, Trans.). New York: McGraw Hill.

Mar'i, M. (1978). *Education in Israel.* Syracuse, NY: Syracuse University Press.

Rouhana, N. (1997). *Palestinian citizens in an ethnic Jewish state: Identities and conflict.* New Haven: Yale University Press.

Smooha, S. (1997). Ethnic democracy: Israel as an archetype. *Israel Studies, 2*(2), 198–241.

Staub, E. (2003). *The psychology of good and evil: Why children, adults, and groups help and harm others.* New York: Cambridge University Press.

Stephan, W. (1999). *Reducing prejudice and stereotyping in schools.* New York: Teachers College Press.

Stephan, W. G., & White-Stephan, C. (2001). *Improving intergroup relations.* Thousand Oaks, CA: Sage.

Suleiman, R. (2002). Perception of the minority's collective identities and voting behavior: The case of the Palestinians in Israel. *Journal of Social Psychology, 142*(6), 753–766.

White-Stephan, C., Hertz-Lazarowitz, R., Zelniker, T., & Stephan, W. C. (2004). Introduction to improving Arab—Jewish relations in Israel: Theory and practice in coexistence programs. *Journal of Social Issues, 60* (2), 237–252.

CHAPTER 7

Collective Ostracism Among Youth in Korea

IN JAE LEE

Collective ostracism among Korean youth recently has become a notable social problem. Both covert and persistent since 1997, collective ostracism in Korea has also accelerated in frequency and severity (Barg, Son, & Song, 1998; Gaudy, 1999; Gu, 1997; Kang, Lee, & Yim, 2002; Lee, 2000; Lee & Kwak, 2000). Collective ostracism ranges from trivial conflicts in dissonant human relationships to violent criminal acts. The seriousness of collective ostracism is evident in the lower as well as the upper grades of elementary schools (Lee, 2000; Lee & Kwak, 2000).

Collective ostracism requires study and treatment because it has negative effects on youth and society. In collective ostracism, perpetrators, or "bullies," seek to consolidate and keep their positions of power by excluding those perceived as inferior groups or individuals. Thus, in the broadest sense, collective ostracism is a perversion of values that organize society and maintain its coherence, because contemporary collective ostracism is anticommunitarian and antiethical in orientation. Collective ostracism leads, moreover, to serious youth problems such as melancholia, avoidance of social contact, social phobias, refusal to attend school, or running away from home (Gaudy, 1999; Korean Association of Teachers, 1999; Lee, 2000; Lee & Kwak, 2000). Such negative consequences of collective ostracism can persist into adulthood and have dire results, such as suicide (Astor, Pinter, Meyer, & Vargas, 2000; Gaudy, 1999; Kim, Kim, & Kim, 2004; Kim & Park, 1997; Lee, 2000; Thompson, Arora, & Sharp, 2002). Society thus has a responsibility to address circumstances leading to and resulting from collective ostracism. In particular, social institutions like home and school should cooperate with young people to resolve and prevent collective ostracism.

This chapter describes the concept, causes, effects, and types of collective ostracism. Drawing on various theories and research, I offer a complex conceptualization of collective ostracism as a practice caused by the interaction of social, cultural, and psychological dimensions. My analysis indicates that collective ostracism among Korean youth is caused by the interaction of personal, psychological, educational (teacher, students, curriculum, classroom, and school environment, etc.), and sociocultural (family, social climate, youth's value system or youth culture, etc.) factors. I also explain the practice of collective ostracism in terms of roles, contexts, and responsibilities to overcome it, as well as in terms of insights about the psychological orientations of bullies, victims, and bystanders.

The primary place for analyzing and preventing the fundamentally sociocultural issue of collective ostracism is the school. School is unique because it is the one place where teachers and students spend a significant amount of time together in both structured and unstructured contexts (Gresham, 2004). In a sense, school is the most meaningful context because it is where the problem usually starts, and it is where prevention activities could be facilitated by social agents like teachers and school administrators. Educators, like parents, can act as role models and as mediators for youth involved in the practices of bullies, victims, and bystanders. Therefore, we should try to find some practical activities to make the school a democratic, caring, and stable community, which can be trusted by all because it functions as "a healthy home" and "a sane society" (Lee, 2000). More important than anything else is the partnership between home and school, parents and teachers, in understanding and addressing this problem (Gaudy, 1999; Kim et al., 2004; Lee, 2000).

In this chapter, I first review and synthesize results of recent research (from 1997 to 2003) on collective ostracism among Korean primary, middle, and high school students (Barg et al., 1998; Kang et al., 2002; Lee & Kwak, 2000; Lee, 2000; Lee & Kang, 2003). Then I critically analyze results from these studies and argue for a new understanding of the problem, for devising educational countermeasures, and for making connections to other issues of youth conflicts and violence across cultures. This research addressed several goals. A foundational goal of the research was to identify the concepts and characteristics of collective ostracism in Korean youth as distinct from the problem in other countries. A second goal was to identify the types, complex causes, and ethical effects of collective ostracism. The third goal was to provide insights about the psychological characteristics and activities of bullies, victims, and bystanders; the fourth was to extract from the research results some effective ways to overcome collective ostracism.

Background

Social interaction with peers is important for young people's personal, social, and moral development (Ormrod, 2003; Pellegrini & Bartini, 2000). Through their interactions with peers, young people gain social skills and develop social-relational capacities, and a related range of emotional skills (McDevitt & Ormrod, 2004; Rose & Asher, 1999). While interaction with peers—including some conflict as well as harmony—forms the groundwork for the development of a range of social and cognitive capacities (Ormrod, 2003), exclusion by peers, including antagonism and conflict, can lead to loneliness, sociopsychological problems, feelings of alienation, and so on (Gaudy, 1999; Juvonen & Graham, 2001; Lee & Kwak, 2000; O'Moore & Kirkham, 2001; Ormrod, 2003). In particular, bullying by peers gives rise to hostility in victims, which can in turn have a negative influence on the development of their self-concept and can hinder their development prosocial behavior abilities, such as perspective-taking, caring, and moral judgment (Andreou, 2004; Bandura, Barbaranelli, Caprara, & Astorelli, 1996; Long & Pellegrini, 2003; Ormrod, 2003). Such outcomes of negative peer interactions require us to be concerned with the phenomenon of collective ostracism.

What Is Collective Ostracism?

Collective ostracism in Korean youth is called "Wang-Tha," which is slang for *outsider*. The practice of Wang-Tha is focused on psychological teasing (for example, insulting, ridiculing, disregarding, excluding, etc.) and leads to the alienation and isolation of those who are teased. Wang-Tha is, moreover, often a problem between members belonging to the same group, so it tends to happen among acquaintances (Lee, 2000; Lee & Kwak, 2000). Although adults who observe or know about collective ostracism often ignore it, the problem is not a trifling matter found only in schools but one of the most serious youth problems outside as well as inside schools.

Barg, Son, and Song (1998, pp. 61–62) defined collective ostracism as "the act done individually or collectively that gives others pain repeatedly by assaulting physically or psychologically people who are less powerful than oneself among the members of the group, or who break the tacit rules of the group." Gu (1997) defined it as such verbal and physical acts done by more than two students collectively, thereby excluding victims of collective ostracism from the group and restricting their performance in the group. According to him, these acts disrespect and do harm to a victim's social and psychological status. The term *collective ostracism* in Korea is likely to relate to a range of acts of violence which are occurring between students in or around school, such as: (1) verbal and psychological violence (teasing, slander, threats); (2) physical violence (from a light slap on the cheek to more terrible violence); (3) extortion; (4) coercion to engage in activities that students do not voluntarily practice; and (5) sexual harassment.

Since the late 1970s, there have been systematic studies of school bullying in many other countries around the world. In pioneering research, Olweus (1978, 1993) defined bullying or victimization in the following general way. A student is being bullied or victimized when he or she is exposed, repeatedly and over time, to negative actions on the part of one or more other students. And currently, Olweus (1999, pp. 10–11) writes that "bullying is thus characterized by the following three criteria: it is (1) aggressive behavior or intentional 'harm doing'; (2) carried out repeatedly and over time; (3) an interpersonal relationship characterized by an imbalance of power." Farrington (1993), a criminologist in England, defined bullying as the repeated oppression, psychological or physical, of a less powerful person by a more powerful person. According to Smith and Sharp (1994), it is also bullying when a student is hit, kicked, threatened, locked in side room, or sent nasty notes or when no ever talks to him or her. Thompson, Arora, and Sharp (2002) defined bullying as longstanding violence, physical or psychological, conducted by an individual or group and directed against an individual who is not able to defend himself or herself in the actual situation, with a conscious desire to hurt, threaten, or frighten that individual or put him or her under stress.

Considering the dimensions and types of school bullying, the phenomenon of "Ijime" in Japan is similar to collective ostracism in Korea. However, as Morita, Soeda, and Taki (1999) define it, Ijime differs somewhat from school bullying in other countries, in that it has less of a connotation of physical violence and a relatively greater emphasis on social manipulation.

Although a number of definitions about school bullying differ semantically and have disparate natures, many of them have one similarity, in that bullying is a subset of aggressive behavior. Aggressive behavior, in turn, is often defined as negative acts carried out by physical contact, by words, or in other ways, such as making faces or mean gestures, and intentional exclusion from a group. Of cause, the bullying often occurs without apparent provocation. This definition for bullying is now accepted by many researchers (Smith & Sharp, 1994).

Taking into account the aforementioned definitions, I define collective ostracism as negative acts carried out by peers intentionally to harm another, without apparent provocation, and persistently over time. Interactions connote an imbalance of power, as victims obviously find it difficult to defend themselves. It is not, therefore, collective ostracism when two people of about the same strength have the odd fight or quarrel. The serious social problem of collective ostracism tends to occur out of sight of adults or others who would curb the practice. The bullies appear, moreover, to enjoy their victims' suffering and to be free from guilt over their actions leading to this suffering.

Two additional criteria serve to distinguish collective ostracism as a subset of the broader concept of aggression (Smith, Helen, Ragnar, & Andy, 2002). First, although, as I mentioned earlier, collective ostracism seems unprovoked, it tends to occur when someone does not grasp the tacit rules that guide the peer group's actions and thus breaks the rules, appears to put on airs, disregards others, or commits some socially inappropriate act (Lee & Kwak, 2000). Ostracized students who tell teachers or parents about their plight are ostracized all the more because they violate the tacit rule of the group members: "never publicly expose a message that pertains to the group alone" (Barg et al., 1998). For these reasons, students are reluctant to reveal that they are being bullied.

As several empirical researches indicated, the problem of collective ostracism is pervasive. For example, in a survey of 6,893 Korean elementary, middle and high school children (Barg et al., 1998), 24.2% reported being bullied at least once or twice during one year. In other nationwide surveys (Gaudy, 1999; Lee & Kwak, 2000), more than 30% reported being bullied during the term. But about 60–65% students who reported being bullied in the foregoing surveys respond that they don't know why they have been ostracized. This common lack of awareness suggests we can assume that ostracism is unprovoked or for some "unreasonable or no good reason" (Lee, 2000). So nothing can justify collective ostracism.

Second, collective ostracism originates in the desire to be superior to others by denying or disregarding their presence or identity and by creating situations that weaken them in some way (Barg et al., 1998; Gaudy, 1999; Lee & Kang, 2003). One could be an assaulter to reduce one's own anxiety about social situations or relationships or just to avoid being a victim of collective ostracism oneself (Lee, 2000).

Types of Collective Ostracism

Recent studies on collective ostracism of Korean youth (Barg et al., 1998; Gaudy, 1999; Kim & Park, 1997; Lee, 2000; Lee & Kwak, 2000) identify the following five types:

1. Alienating the other person by intentionally or bluntly disregarding another's greetings or questions, excluding a person from a game, totally ignoring a person, not eating lunch with that person, etc.
2. Abusing or threatening a person by means of abusive terms such as "damn" or "bullshit," saying something like "beat it," or making explicit threats to the person (the most common type of collective ostracism).
3. Mocking, including teasing a person who has a physical handicap or who has an ugly appearance, teasing a person who is bad at school, and teasing a person by calling him or her a coward. It is assumed that this type reflects a trend in Korea to make light of the handicapped.
4. Harming a person's body or possessions, including causing damage to a person's sportswear and shoes, wringing a person's neck, stripping a person of his or her money or clothes, striking or kicking a person, and pinching; occurs when somebody does what he or she wants or likes to do without considering another's position.
5. Coercing a person, including forcing him or her to do another's homework, carry another's bag, show his or her exam papers, and take class materials or a lunch basket.

Gender differences in collective ostracism in Korea occur across these diverse types. Boys tend to actively engage in aggressive behavior such as mocking, abusing, or calling a nickname, vexing a person to anger, provoking a quarrel, and coercing, whereas girls tend to engage in behavior such as not talking or facing each other (Barg et al., 1998; Lee & Kwak, 2000). These gender characteristics in collective ostracism are very similar to those in other countries (Crick & Grotpeter, 1995).

Collective Ostracism in Theoretical Context

The definitions of youth vary with researchers' theoretical perspectives and in relation to different cultures and age groups. Nonetheless, there is a common view about the nature of psychological and social growth in adolescence. Adolescence is a developmental period marked by numerous changes, including physical and ecological changes (Long & Pellegrini, 2003). This study begins with the perspective of seeing youth as adaptable agents who can change themselves in correspondence with their new circumstances.

With regard to why collective ostracism occurs among adolescents, social cognition theory of aggression (Ormrod, 2003) provides a plausible theoretical basis. According to social cognition theory, aggression among children and adolescents is generally divided into two proactive aggressions: a deliberate act of aggression against someone else as a means of obtaining desired goals and reactive aggression as a response of frustration in the face of provocation. Students who exhibit proactive aggression, that is, bullies of collective ostracism, tend to show off in personal relations (Pellegrini, Bartini, & Brooks, 1999). The more narcissistic one is, the more aggressive one is and the less one has self-control. In addition, such a person takes little care of others, in a Machiavellian sense; that is, the person has a psychological tendency to regard others as a means to an end and maneuver them for the sake of his or her own goals. Persons with this tendency are aggressive, coldhearted, egocentric, impulsive, and ostentatious (Andreou, 2004; Sutton & Keogh, 2001). According to Sutton and Keogh (2001), students with strong Machiavellian beliefs make little effort in learning situations and do not conform to classroom rules or follow examples set by teachers in educational or social circumstances. This supports the claim that Korean youth can use collective ostracism in order to show off unrealistically exaggerated powers in overcompetitive and group-oriented situations (Lee & Kang, 2003; Lee & Kwak, 2000). In fact, current collective ostracism in Korean youth appears to make a scapegoat of someone in bullies' pursuit of a feeling of superiority. Bullies' hapless victims often are students who are immature, anxious loners lacking in self-confidence, so they are relatively defenseless in the face of the bullies' harassment.

Developmental psychologists argue that young people are easily brought to a crisis of self-identity and easily fall into utter confusion about their values (Bandura et al., 1996; McDevitt & Ormrod, 2004; Ormrod, 2003; Rose & Asher, 1999). Young people also sometimes feel uneasy and wander in anguish. So they have a defiant, violent, or indifferent attitude about their parents, family, studies, and so on. Violence and misdeeds are, in a sense, calls for help in these unstable psychological states (Gaudy, 1999; Lee, 2000). These days, the young people known as the N-generation (the network, or digital, generation who use the internet or multimedia as a way of life), have a propensity to be egocentric and focused on the pursuit of their own interests. Sometimes an extreme selfishness causes them to treat others as personal conveniences and not to care about the consequences of their actions on other persons. This orientation is also characterized by having temporary rather than lasting relationships with friends, because of a "contact-phobia" and self-involvement (Gaudy, 1999).

Another account of collective ostracism can be found in the mechanisms of *moral disengagement* (Bandura et al., 1996), a term that refers to what is known as the deviation mechanism from moral obligations. The following five processes are included in moral disengagement. First, *moral justification* is a process whereby "detrimental conduct is made personally and socially acceptable by portraying it in the service of valued social or moral purposes" (p. 365). For instance, the following expressions fall under moral justification: hitting or pushing is just fun, and it is permissible to mistreat someone who acts in an inferior way or badly. Second, *advantageous comparison* is the process whereby "injurious conduct can be rendered benign or made to appear to be of little consequence" in comparison with more reprehensible activities (p. 365). The following examples demonstrate this. It is not bad to damage others' possessions, compared with beating others. To bully others is also not to inflict an injury on them. Third, *displacement of responsibility* is a process that operates by viewing detrimental conduct as "springing from the social pressures or dictates of others" (p. 365). Fourth, diffusion of responsibility is a process that can be viewed as doing harm by a division of labor, that is, "different members performing subdivided aspects that seen harmless in themselves but [create a result that is] harmful in its totality" (p. 365). The fifth process is disregarding or distorting the consequences of action by blaming victims for culpable conduct or for being less than human. To consider someone subhuman is to be less sensitive to him or her and to think that he or she should be treated recklessly. Self-censure of detrimental conduct may become blunted by the dehumanization process, in which others are perceived as lacking human qualities or attributes. In the mechanisms of moral disengagement, the detrimental results of one's conduct are validated as righteous, and so agents can be disengaged from self-sanctions. Deviation or disengagement from moral obligations weakens self-censure and reduces prosocial conduct while facilitating assailing conduct.

Causes and Ethical Issues

Collective ostracism occurs as a result of multiple sociocultural, educational, and personal factors rather than as a result of one single factor. Accounting for complex causes, existing research (Barg et al., 1998; Gaudy, 1999; Gu, 1997; Lee, 2000; Lee & Kwak, 2000) suggests that collective ostracism relates to the interaction between collective pressures that create and maintain a cultural climate around youth and various traits that elicit individual orientations of bullies and victims.

Theory and research indicate that nowadays some Korean youth do not feel guilty about their actions, so they bully their classmates without any good reason (Barg et al., 1998; Gaudy, 1999; Lee, 2000). Most important, most students cannot confidently voice their opinion that collective ostracism is not right.

Individuals involved in collective ostracism do not express a guilty conscience because they engage in this practice collectively. Students may also, moreover, be reflecting societal attitudes, when they act without hesitation to ostracize or bully the handicapped and the feebleminded, who are not highly regarded in society. For example, some play darts, targeting the ostracized students; others have the fun of scrubbing the ostracized student's face with a floor-cloth used in the bathroom; others ostracize and bully a specific person just because they feel bad looking at him or her or just for refreshing themselves (Lee, 2000).

The students who participate in or allow collective ostracism to take place excuse themselves from blame without recognizing the negative effects of their acts. Because they know well how to disguise their evil acts and prevent the victims from telling their parents by threatening them with more suffering if they talk about the bullying, teachers and parents remain ignorant of the situation. Therefore, when teachers and parents eventually come to know of the damage to victims of collective ostracism, the victim's hurt may be beyond repair. According to Coles (1997), bullies are miserable, cold-minded, perverse children, who are intelligent but don't use their intelligence ethically. When these bullies' actions go unhindered, the moral seriousness of collective ostracism also jeopardizes the physical and mental well-being of other good students.

Damage caused by collective ostracism extends beyond simple physical injury. Collective ostracism sometimes leads to psychological unrest, impatience, schizophrenia, and suicide (Gaudy, 1999; Lee & Kwak, 2000). Negative psychological outcomes are experienced not only by the victims and bullies but also by the bystanders who witness the attacks (Korean Association of Teachers, 1999; Lee, 2000). The thought process is as follows: if someone is ostracized once, then he or she will be ostracized forever; therefore, he or she must ostracize someone else to avoid being ostracized further. Consequently, the sphere of collective ostracism expands readily (Barg et al., 1998; Gaudy, 1999; Lee, 2000).

Many students who have been victims continue to live with an uneasy state of mind since they expect to be victims of collective ostracism at any time. The student who has been ostracized or mistreated by classmates in adolescence could develop a negative image of people and the world. Perhaps he or she will seek revenge, thereby causing another tragedy and perpetuating the vicious circle of collective ostracism. The practice of collective ostracism may engage individuals in specific roles as bullies, victims, or bystanders persistently over time, as described in the next section.

Psychological Orientations in the
Practice of Collective Ostracism

Although recent research has identified students as primarily only victims or only bullies (Austin & Joseph, 1996), the classification of students as either bullies or victims is simplistic and does not provide a useful conceptual framework for investigating the nature of collective ostracism. Here I would like to divide students into three groups: the bullies, the victims, and the bystanders (Bark et al., 1998; Gaudy, 1999; Korean Association of Teachers, 1999). Because even though it has been recognized in general that bullies (active, initiative-taking perpetrators) and victims (who are repeatedly and systematically harassed) are typical in bullying situations, increasingly we must be looking at the role of watchers or bystanders who support and fuel bullies' drive to show off to peers. Much of the recent research (Espelage & Swearer, 2003; Solberg & Olweus, 2003) on bullying supports a conceptualization of bullying behaviors as dynamic rather than static and argues that students' involvement falls on a continuum such as bully, victim, bully-victim, or bystander. Therefore, to understand the nature of collective ostracism properly, it is necessary for us to abandon the dyadic bias toward bullying and recognize the diversity of experiences along the bully/victim continuum.

Bullies tend to be extroverts who think self-centeredly. They also have a great desire for accomplishment. They exercise their influence over other children, so they have many friends. These students put their stress and dissatisfaction into action and are blind to any sense of another's difficulty or suffering. Bullies have a sense of their own superiority over other students. They are divided into two groups: leaders and supporters. The leader is the so-called jjahng (boss), while the supporters are the students who follow the jjahng's direction or commands. The supporters protect the jjahng's secret. They ostracize the victim by using crowd psychology (Barg et al., 1998; Korean Association of Teachers, 1999). This explanation of bullies' characteristics is consistent with Olweus's analysis (1978) that bullies have a positive attitude toward violence and a strong desire to dominate others while lacking a positive self-concept.

Victims are characterized by autism, defeatism, and, occasionally, the delusion of persecution. They show signs of uneasiness, enervation, anger, depression, and so on. For example, they may be prone to being taciturn, may have difficulty expressing their desires, or may often be left out of group activities. In addition, victims have trouble coping with conflicts between friends and doing anything to win a person's favor. For example, they have difficulty expressing their opinions or thoughts, making jokes, and making decisions. As for their home environments, victims typically lack warm, caring parents or have overprotective parents, and many are children of divorce or circumstances that put them in foster care, which changes frequently. Youth who are victimized also face difficulties in forming harmonious relationship with friends (Gaudy, 1999; Lee, 2000).

Bystanders consistently witness the bullying episodes, and through their behavior in these situations they take a position toward what is going on. This has an effect on the outcome of bullying. Salmivalli (1999) has shown that during the bullying episodes, students take on different roles, depending on their individual dispositions and what the group expects of them. They play the following parts. *Assistants* help and join the bully. Even if they do not actively attack the victim, they offer positively feedback to the bully. *Reinforcers* come to see what's going on and encourage bullying behavior by laughing and commenting on the action. *Outsiders* tend to stay away and don't take sides with anyone. Not even these students are, however, noninvolved. They allow bullying to go on by silently approving it. They are reluctant to intervene because they believe "It's none of my business, and somebody else is reporting it." *Defenders* side with victim, comfort him or her, and try to stop the bullying. They are more likely to be self-confident, popular, and well liked by their peers (Kaiser & Rasminsky, 2003). We can regard defenders as guilty bystanders, in that they look upon the bullies as bad and would like to help the victims, and their behavior is clearly antibullying. Generally speaking, the bystanders and the sympathizers suffer lots of mental conflict about the bullies and victims, but they are reluctant to get involved in these troubles. Many bystanders don't participate in collective ostracism actively, but their inaction against collective ostracism makes the victims feel more helpless. The problem is that bystanders become callous and coldhearted to a friend's suffering, ultimately allowing the behavior to continue. They want to lead an easy life by leaving their friends in the lurch or by participating in the problem rather than leading a difficult life by challenging the peer who is a leader of ostracism (Gaudy, 1999; Lee, 2000).

Strategies for Overcoming Collective Ostracism

Collective ostracism is a complex problem involving various factors that are difficult to address at once in any single way. So it is necessary to recruit the various participants in the practice of collective ostracism into comprehensive and systematic approaches to solve the problem. There is reason to believe that with the cooperation of schools (teacher, students), families (parents), communities (adults' model, moral climate), mass media, institutions, and so on, the problems of collective ostracism could be significantly reduced. Now I will examine methods of overcoming and preventing collective ostracism focused on the roles of the school and home.

The Role of School and Classroom Teachers

The teacher's role is very important because collective ostracism usually happens in schools, and teachers are responsible for students' life guidance. Especially in the case of elementary school, children are relatively less collectivized and less violent than middle and high school students. In addition, teachers spend time with elementary school students all day long in the classroom and thus are a potent influence on the children. So a teacher's careful guidance of younger students could help to reduce or end collective ostracism.

The teacher's cognizance of collective ostracism requires change (Lee, 2000). It is not good for a teacher to take an optimistic view that there is no collective ostracism in his or her class or to disregard it. Otherwise, collective ostracism will go on and systematically progress in secret outside a teacher's notice; and the damage of the ostracism is more serious than is generally understood. Above all, teachers should not overlook the fact that collective ostracism is caused not only by the students but also by teachers' own speech and behavior; teachers might foster collective ostracism by failing to either promote respectful interactions among students or speak out against teasing and other behaviors consistent with ostracism (Espelage & Swearer, 2003). Extant studies have documented that teachers tend to report lower prevalence rates of collective ostracism than do students and don't correctly identify bullies (Barg et al., 1998; Gaudy, 1999; Lee & Kwak, 2000). Therefore, to prevent collective ostracism, teachers, first of all, should not discount or minimize collective ostracism or reports of students, and then they should be positive and fair role models in managing bully/victim relationships. Teachers should also try to help students develop positive self-esteem and enhanced resiliency.

It is best if a teacher is a prudent individual who can take the positions of the bullies, victims, and bystanders into account indiscriminately, because anyone can always be a victim of collective ostracism. A teacher should also persuade students that collective ostracism is a serious encroachment upon personal rights. Teachers and students should cooperate to make "a caring and just class community" in which students can trust and rely on each other.

Finally, teachers should try to prevent collective ostracism by actively using techniques such as small group activities, peer counseling, assistant activity of collective ostracism, one-day experience of collective ostracism, attaching a loving name card to friends, and various applications of rolling paper. Having been quite widely used in preventing and reducing bullying, peer counseling is certainly important, in that the victims get empathic support from their peers. Because the victims' social self-concept is negative, what they need is positive experiences with peers, including peer support. It is suggested that a one-day experience of collective ostracism or rolling paper is very useful to encourage the bully or the bystander to take the victims' perspective and feeling, and to help and empathize with the victim.

Students' Roles

Bullies should put themselves in another's shoes and understand that anyone can be ostracized. To this end, it is recommended that they read about collective ostracism and talk about what collective ostracism is and how it makes their peers feel in role play. There also are good ways that they can draw pictures and write their own stories about collective ostracism, to encourage them to feel some empathy for the victim who is being ostracized and help solve the problem with an idea of their own ("I'll ask him to sit with me," or "I'll tell Will to leave him alone"). They should also try to find the merits of the introverted and timid people, to see that everyone has his or her own merits that the others don't have and so we can't have any right to disregard them, regarding them as inferior. To get bullies to act in these ways successfully, it is very important that we should encourage and accept any positive suggestions they make, and above all, don't accuse them, blame them, or argue with them (Kaiser & Rasminsky, 2003). In addition, schools should have a firm policy with a statement of rights, for example:

Every person at this school has the right to experience positive and respectful relationships between all members of the school community. They also have the right to learn and teach in a happy and safe environment. Bullying is not, therefore, acceptable at this school. (Peterson & Rigby, 1999)

Victims should try to find reasons why they are ostracized by their friends by thinking about their words and actions toward their friends (Gaudy, 1999). They should cope with the situations in a confident manner, rather than adapt themselves to the other students' acts blindly. They must try to correct his wrongdoing by reflecting on his conduct and open his mind first while thinking that others' personalities as well as his own personality are also valuable. If victims can't overcome the situation by themselves, they should be encouraged to ask for help from their parents and teachers. Teachers should tell victims that they will support and protect them, and be careful not to suggest that the bullying is their fault or they deserve it in any way (Kaiser & Rasminsky, 2003).

Bystanders or sympathizers should not be afraid of being ostracized when their friend is ostracized and should help him or her. They should reflect on how they contribute to the ostracism indirectly or directly and should try to explain the merits of the victim to the others. It is hard to bully without support from peers, and their absence will reduce a bully's power base. Therefore, the teacher should teach bystanders that they should not provide an audience for the bully. The teacher should also emphasize that everyone has the responsibility to help and no one has the right to hurt others. Teachers should help bystanders understand that they should play the role of befrienders (Thompson et al., 2002) who can be the buffers or the defenders of victims and can surround victims to offer protection and support.

The Role of Home

Another source of collective ostracism is troubled relationships in families. The parents of children who have been ostracized can be most helpful by remaining calm and analytic. It is important for parents to grasp what position their child has among his or her friends. Parents should encourage their children by saying, "You are so precious and valuable" rather than rebuking their children for being ostracized. Parents also need to put their faith in their child and help him or her understand that he or she is not alone and can get help from his or her parents. Finally, it is important to let the parents of bullies know what has happened and involve them in the process of finding a solution to the problem.

Concluding Thoughts

In Korean schools, collective ostracism, even though it is now an international phenomenon, represents a microcosm of Korean culture. Students' collective ostracism from childhood to adolescence is a complex problem because it is learned and reinforced through different environmental contexts, that is, cultural, societal, school, familial, and individual. Now, above all, it is very important to institute an effective intervention program for reducing collective ostracism and to practice this intervention continuously. The teacher's role, especially, is essential in reducing the occurrence of collective ostracism in the schools. This essay suggests that in conquering collective ostracism, the prevention program will need to be provided systematically from elementary through high school in order to increase teachers' knowledge of collective ostracism intervention skills, support humane relationships between peer groups, and create a safe and caring school environment.

References

Andreou, E. (2004). Bully/victim problems and their association with Machiavellianism and self-efficacy in Greek primary school children. *British Journal of Educational Psychology, 74,* 297–309.

Astor, R. A., Pinter, R. O., Meyer, H. A., & Vargas, L. A. (2000). The most violent event at school: A ripple in the pond. *Child and Schools, 22*(4), 199–216.

Austin, S., & Joseph, S. (1996). Assessment of bully/victim problems in 8- to 11-year-olds. *British Journal of Educational Psychology, 66,* 447–456.

Bandura, A., Barbaranelli, C., Caprara, G. V., & Astorelli, C. (1996). Mechanisms of moral disengagement in the exercise of moral agency. *Journal of Personality and Social Psychology, 71*(2), 364–374.

Barg, G. S., Son, H. G., & Song, H. J. (1998). *Bullying in elementary, middle, and high school.* Seoul: Korean Educational Development Institute.

Coles, R. (1997). *The moral intelligence of children: How to raise a moral child.* New York: Random House.

Crick, N., & Grotpeter, J. (1995). Relational aggression, gender, and psychological adjustment, *Child Development, 66,* 710–722.

Espelage, D. L., & Swearer, S. M. (2003). Research on school bullying and victimization: What have we learned and where do we go from here? *School Psychology Review, 32*(3), 365–383.

Farrington, D. P. (1993). Understanding and preventing bullying. In M. Tony & N. Morris (Eds.), *Crime and justice: An annual review of research* (Vol. 17, pp. 381–458). Chicago: University of Chicago Press.

Gaudy (Company). (1999). *The report of collective ostracism.* Seoul: Uri Education.

Gresham, F. M. (2004). Current status and future directions of school-based behavioral interventions. *School Psychology Review, 33*(3), 326–343.

Gu, B. Y. (1997). The causes and guidance ways of collective ostracism in Korean youth. In *Those who bully, those who are bullied,* The research report of youth counseling problems (Vol. 29, pp. 7–35). Seoul: Plaza of Youth Dialogue.

Juvonen, J., & Graham, S. (2001). *Peer harassment in school: The plight of the vulnerable and victimized.* New York: Guilford Press.

Kaiser, B., & Rasminsky, B. K. (2003). *Challenging behavior in young children: Understanding, preventing, and responding effectively.* New York: Pearson Education.

Kang, U. H., Lee, E. H., & Yim, E. J. (2002). The bullying and psychological Traits. *Korean Journal of Counseling and Psychotherapy, 14*(2), 445–460.

Kim, S. G., Kim, Y. H., & Kim, M. H. (2004). Conquering process of group-bullies among teenagers. *Journal of Korean Academic Nursing, 34*(3), 458–466.

Kim, Y. T., & Park, H. S. (1997). A research on the actual conditions of peer ostracism in youth. In *Those who bully, those who are bullied,* The research report of youth counseling problems (Vol. 29, pp. 7–35). Seoul: Plaza of Youth Dialogue.

Korean Association of Teachers. (1999, August). *A new class* [Special issue]. Seoul: Author.

Lee, C. J., & Kwak, G. J. (2000). *Collective ostracism in school: the actual condition and characteristics.* Seoul: Jib Moon Dang.

Lee, E. H., & Kang, U. H. (2003). Adolescents' dominance, superiority, self-admiration, lack of faith in human nature, bullying, and victimization. *Korean Journal of Health Psychology, 8*(2), 323–353.

Lee, I. J. (2000). A comprehensive understanding of collective ostracism. In Elementary Education Institute, *Issues of elementary education for twenty-first century* (pp. 113–146). Seoul: Gyoyukgwahaksa.

Long, J. D., & Pellegrini, A. D. (2003). Studying change in dominance and bullying with linear mixed models, *School Psychology Review, 32*(3), 401–417.

McDevitt, T. M., & Ormrod, J. E. (2004). *Child development* (2nd ed.). Columbus, OH: Merrill Prentice Hall.

Morita, Y., Soeda, H. K., & Taki, M. (1999). Japan. In P. K. Smith, Y. Morita, J. Junger-Tas, D. Olweus. R. Catalano, & P. Slee (Eds.), *The nature of school bullying: A cross-national perspective* (pp. 309–323). New York: Routledge.

Olweus, D. (1978). *Aggression in the schools: Bullies and whipping boys.* Washington, DC: Hemisphere Press.

Olweus, D. (1993). *Bullying at school: What we know and what we can do.* Oxford: Blackwell.

Olweus, D. (1999). Sweden. In P. K. Smith, Y. Morita, J. Junger-Tas, D. Olweus, R. Catalano, & P. Slee (Eds.), *The nature of school bullying: A cross-national perspective* (pp. 7–27). New York: Routledge.

O'Moore, M., & Kirkham, C. (2001). Self-esteem and its relationship to bullying behavior. *Aggressive Behavior, 27,* 269–283.

Ormrod, J. E. (2003*). Educational Psychology* (4th ed.). NJ: Merrill Prentice Hall.

Pellegrini, A. D., & Bartini, M. (2000). A longitudinal study of bullying, victimization, and peer affiliation during the transition from primary school to middle school. *American Educational Research Journal, 37*(3), 699–725.

Pellegrini, A. D., Bartini, M., & Brooks, F. (1999). School bullies, victims, and aggressive victims: Factors relating to group affiliation and victimization in early adolescence. *Journal of Educational Psychology, 91*(2), 216–224.

Peterson, L., & Rigby, K. (1999). Countering bullying at an Australian secondary school with students as helpers. *Journal of Adolescence, 22,* 481–492.

Rose, A. J., & Asher, S. R. (1999). Children's goals and strategies in response to conflicts within friendship. *Developmental Psychology, 35,* 69–79.

Salmivalli, C. (1999). Participant role approach to school bullying: Implications for interventions. *Journal of Adolescence, 22,* 453–459.

Smith, P. K., Helen, C., Ragnar, F. O., & Andy, P. D. (2002). Definitions of bullying: A comparison of terms used, and age and gender differences, in a fourteen-country international comparison. *Child Development, 73*(4), 1119–1133.

Smith, P. K., & Sharp, S. (Eds.). (1994). *School bullying: Insights and perspectives.* London: Routledge.

Solberg, M. E., & Olweus, D. (2003). Prevalence estimation of school bullying with the Olweus Bully/Victim Questionnaire. *Aggressive Behavior, 29,* 239–268.

Sutton, J., & Keogh, E. (2001). Components of Machiavellian beliefs in children: Relationships with personality. *Personality and Individual Differences, 30,* 137–148.

Thompson, D., Arora, T., & Sharp, S. (2002). *Bullying: Effective strategies for long-term improvement.* London: Routledge.

CHAPTER 8

Harassment of Gay and Lesbian Youth and School Violence in America

An Analysis and Directions for Intervention

STACEY S. HORN AND LARRY NUCCI

Overview

Harassment and violence directed by youth toward lesbian and gay peers is a major problem in many communities throughout the world. This chapter reviews the literature on the rates and impact of harassment and violence directed against lesbian and gay youth in school contexts in Europe and the United States. We discuss the limitations of current research in terms of social cognitive domain theory as an alternative theoretical framework for conducting such research. We then present a recent set of studies using domain theory to uncover high school—aged youths' beliefs and understandings about homosexuality and their judgments about lesbian and gay peers. What the results suggest is that young people draw upon moral, social conventional, and personal knowledge when evaluating the treatment of their gay and lesbian peers. Further, factors such as beliefs about the origins of homosexuality and gender normativity are related to how young people make sense of these issues. Some of the implications of this research for school-based programs to reduce prejudice and maltreatment of lesbian and gay youth are discussed.

On October 6, 1998, two men entered a bar in Laramie, Wyoming, that was known locally as a place where lesbian and gay people often hung out. After surveying the crowd they befriended a 22-year-old University of Wyoming student named Matthew Shephard. Some time later, the two heterosexual men left the bar with Shephard and drove him to an open field, where they severely beat him, tied him to a fencepost, and left him to die in near freezing weather. Eighteen hours later, two cyclists found Shephard, initially thinking he was a scarecrow because of the way his body was positioned on the fence. Shephard died from his injuries in a Colorado hospital several days later ("Gay Victim of Beating Is Dead," 1998).

Shephard's brutal death shocked the national conscience. The incident, however, was hardly unique. Harassment, social exclusion, even physical attack against lesbian and gay youth occur with distressing frequency and are an important and underattended source of youth conflict and violence. The cost of this inattention is considerable, both in terms of the harm caused to lesbian and gay young people and the occasional episodes of retributive violence engaged in by lesbian and gay youth themselves or those perceived to be lesbian and gay.

Estimates of school-based victimization (verbal or physical attack) within the United States of lesbian and gay youths range from 33% to 95%, with the rates being somewhat higher for males than females (Rivers & D' Augelli, 2001; Russell, Franz, & Driscoll, 2001). A recent survey of Massachusetts high school students (Garofalo, Wolf, Kessel, Palfrey & Durant, 1998) found that compared to their heterosexual peers, lesbian, gay, and bisexual (LGB) youth were more likely to report that they had missed school during the prior month because of fear, had been threatened with a weapon at school, had been involved in fights at school, and had had property stolen. Making matters worse, the evidence indicates that very little is done to intervene by teachers, school staff, or other students in these situations (Bochenek & Brown, 2001).

The impact of victimization often goes beyond the immediate psychological or physical trauma and translates into long-term problems with mental health and suicidal behaviors. Hershberger and D'Augelli (1995) found that approximately 40% of their sample of American LGB youths reported having engaged in a past suicide attempt, roughly the same percentage as was reported for a sample of British gay men (Rivers & D' Augelli, 2001). In addition, studies in the United States and the Netherlands report that the rate of attempted suicide of LGB youth is more than three times that reported for other youths (Remafedi, 1999; Vincke & Heeringen, 1998). While the focus of this chapter is upon issues pertaining to youth within the United States, the aforementioned European study would indicate that such conflict persists even within more progressive societies such as the Netherlands, where gay marriage has recently been legalized ("Netherlands Legalizes Gay Marriage," 2000). Needless to say, in areas of the world dominated by religious fundamentalism, the treatment of LGB individuals is considerably less tolerant and may include officially sanctioned public beatings or executions (Amnesty International, 1999).

The anger that naturally arises within youth as a result of such harassment is not always turned inward. Sometimes the victims of harassment engage in violence against others. On April 20, 1999, two male students wearing long, black trench coats opened fire in a suburban high school in Littleton, Colorado, injuring as many as 20 students. In all, 15 were killed, including the two gun-men (Obmascik, 1999). Investigations following the incident uncovered the fact that the two youths had been the victims of considerable harassment by peers because of their *presumed* homosexuality and unconventional dress. It is be-lieved that young people who had been victims of bullying and abuse focusing on their *presumed* homosexuality committed five of the eight school shootings that occurred in the United States between 1996 and 1999. In none of these cases was there ever clear evidence that the young people who engaged in the shootings actually were gay or lesbian (Kimmel & Mahler, 2003). What is clear, however, is that taunting around a young person's sexuality is damaging and can have serious consequences.

The Status of Current Research

While it is certain that LGB youth are the targets of much prejudice and discrim-ination in schools, very little is known about young peoples' attitudes toward and reasoning about issues regarding sexual orientation and prejudice (Herek, 2000; Van de Ven, 1994). One factor contributing to this may be that the prej-udice and fear that leads to the harassment of LGB youth also affects the inter-est or willingness of the child development research community to investigate these issues. In the absence of knowledge about how young people understand issues of sexuality and gender identity, it is unrealistic to expect schools and other agents of socialization to constructively address this source of youth con-flict and violence. A first logical step, then, is to address both the broader dis-interest, as well as the social costs to researchers that have hampered research activity and progress in addressing this educational challenge.

A second factor contributing to the lack of knowledge in this area has been the difficulty in conducting research regarding sexual orientation with minors, as well as a general weakness of theories and methods guiding this work. While a few studies have investigated correlates and prevalence of young peoples' negative attitudes toward lesbian and gay individuals (Baker & Fish-bein, 1998; Marsiglio, 1993; Morrison, McLeod, Morrison, & Anderson, 1997; Price, 1982; Van de Ven, 1994), most of the research in this area has utilized college-aged or adult populations (for reviews see, Herek 1994; 2000). The research on adult attitudes has investigated the correlates of negative attitudes toward lesbian and gay individuals and has delineated some of the functions of individuals' prejudice toward gay men and lesbians (Herek, 1994; 2000); how-ever, there are three major criticisms of research on sexual prejudice (Herek, 2000).[1]

First, Van de Ven (1994) suggests that most of the research on negative at-titudes toward lesbian and gay people has been limited in its scope, in that attitudes have been assessed utilizing a single cognitive evaluative measure. While the measures used in various studies have differed (e.g. Herek's Atti-tudes Toward Gay Men and Lesbians scale; Price's Modified Attitudes Toward Homosexuality Scale), most of the measures create an overall attitude score based on individuals' responses to questions regarding beliefs about the morality and/or naturalness of homosexuality, lesbian and gay rights, and stereotypes about lesbian and gay individuals (e.g., lesbian and gay people seduce young children). Van de Ven (1994) suggests that sexual prejudice is a multifaceted phenomenon and that researchers should use multiple outcome measures that assess individuals' cognitive, affective, and behavioral attitudes toward lesbian and gay people for us to have an understanding of this phenomenon. Further, many of the previous measures have failed to distinguish between individuals' beliefs about homosexuality and/or lesbian and gay individuals, their attitudes about interacting with lesbian and gay others in specific contexts, and their evaluations of the treatment of others based on their sexuality. These distinctions are important to consider, in that individuals may hold negative beliefs about homosexuality (e.g., it is wrong, it is unnatural) while at the same time believing that lesbian and gay individuals have rights and should be treated fairly.

A second criticism of research on sexual prejudice is that the measures assess individuals' attitudes and beliefs devoid of context. While there is a growing body of research on heterosexism in the school context and levels of victimization of LGB students in school (see Bochenek & Brown, 2001; Garofalo et al., 1998; Gay, Lesbian, Sraight Education Network, 2003; Szalacha, 2003), very little of this work attending to context has assessed *individuals'* attitudes and beliefs about homosexuality, or about their gay and lesbian peers. Thus, few studies (for an exception, see Van de Ven, 1994) have investigated the influence of individuals' beliefs and attitudes on their interactions with others in specific contexts like school, even though school is often a context in which negative attitudes and prejudice toward lesbian and gay people are acted out (Bochenek & Brown, 2001; Gay, Lesbian, Sraight Education Network, 2003).

A final criticism of the previous research on attitudes toward homosexuality is that it has failed to make a distinction between attitudes based on sexual orientation and those based on gender nonconformity. Because most measures simply ask questions regarding gay and lesbian individuals, we do not know the extent to which individuals' attitudes are based on their stereotypes of lesbian and gay people as gender nonconforming versus their attitudes and beliefs about homosexuality. Evidence suggests, however, that gender-role attitudes are related to prejudice toward gay men and lesbians (for a review, see Kite & Whitley, 1998).

Social Cognitive Domain Theory: A New Direction for LGB Research

A promising new direction for research in this field is provided by social cognitive domain theory (Nucci, 2001; Turiel, 1998, 2002). The central premise of this theory is that evaluative social judgments are multifaceted and draw from a number of conceptual frameworks or domains rather than a single structure of socio-moral reasoning (e.g., Kohlberg, 1984). The distinctions drawn among conceptual frameworks by domain theory correspond quite well to the components of social judgments uncovered within previous social psychological research on attitudes toward homosexuality, and thus have the potential to address the need for a multifaceted approach to research in this area (Van de Ven, 1994). Three basic conceptual frameworks or domains are posited by domain theory: morality, societal convention, and the personal. Concepts of morality address issues of human welfare, rights, and fairness and are constructed out of the child's early social interactions around events, such as unprovoked hitting and hurting, that have intrinsic effects upon another person (Turiel, 1983, 2002). Morality (defined in terms of justice, welfare, rights) can be distinguished from concepts of social conventions, which are the consensually determined standards of conduct particular to a given social group. Conventions established by social systems, such as norms or standards of dress and how people should address one another, derive their status as correct or incorrect forms of conduct from their embeddedness within a particular shared system of meaning and social interaction. The particular acts have no prescriptive force, in that different or even opposite norms (e.g., dresses for men, pants for women) could be established to achieve the same symbolic or regulatory function (e.g., distinguishing men from women). The importance of conventions lies in the function they serve to coordinate social interaction and discourse within social systems. Finally, while morality and convention deal with aspects of interpersonal regulation, concepts of personal issues refer to actions that make up the private aspects of one's life (e.g. contents of a diary) and issues that are matters of preference and choice (e.g., music, hairstyle) rather than right or wrong. It has been proposed that the establishment of control over the personal domain emerges from the need to delineate boundaries between the self and others, and is critical to the construction of personal autonomy and individual identity (Nucci, 1996).

A final element included within the domain theory account of socio-moral cognition is the role of informational assumptions in the generation of social judgments. Moral judgments, for example, are predicated upon information regarding the effects that actions have upon the welfare of others. In the prototypical moral exemplar of hitting another person for no reason, the information employed to engage in the moral evaluation is readily apparent (the action was not provoked and caused harm). There are other situations, however, in which culturally mediated information forms the basis for our moral judgments. For example, individuals' beliefs about when life begins, which cannot be determined fully by empirical evaluation, are often based on individuals' religious and cultural assumptions about the soul. What is critical to this discussion is that the informational assumptions individuals employ in generating their moral judgments come from cultural sources other than empirical science and include superstitions and religious beliefs that are not subject to empirical evaluation.

If we apply the tenets of domain analysis to judgments and attitudes about homosexuality, we can readily see the utility of domain theory as a paradigm for research on reasoning and attitudes about this multifaceted issue. As we have already mentioned, a research approach employing domain theory is inherently prepared to address the basic criticism that research on reasoning and attitudes about lesbian and gay issues has failed to reflect the heterogeneity presented by the complex moral, societal, and personal choice issues entailed in judgments about sexual orientation (Van de Ven, 1994). More specifically, domain theory affords a coherent framework from which to address the basic limitations described earlier of current research on sexual prejudice. By providing a systematic account of the elements that enter into socio-moral judgments, domain theory affords a basis for teasing out the contributions that informational assumptions and moral, conventional, and personal judgments have upon evaluations of lesbian and gay individuals and treatment of their actions.

In differentiating the informational assumptions individuals maintain about the origins and effects of homosexuality from the subsequent moral and conventional evaluations of lesbian and gay individuals and their sexual behavior, domain theory affords a basis upon which to determine whether the harassment directed at lesbian and gay youth reflects intolerance based on assumptions about the motivations and sources of sexual orientation, or intolerance of the sexual behavior in itself. For example, if, as Jerry Falwell maintains, one's sexual orientation is merely a matter of personal choice, then from a fundamentalist religious perspective, a person with a nonheterosexual orientation has willingly chosen to flaunt what the religious perceive to be the will of God. If, on the other hand, an individual with a culturally or religiously based position against homosexuality also maintains the informational assumption that one's sexual orientation is primarily determined by factors beyond the individual's control, then assigning moral responsibility to the individual becomes problematized and is likely to result either in complex judgments objecting to the behavior while not assigning moral blame to the person (i.e., "hate the sin, but not the sinner"). Thus, a domain approach affords a systematic way to tease out whether the judgments about homosexuality associated with religious affiliation or cultural background are mediated through associated informational assumptions or are determined solely through commitment to cultural or religious conventions and authority.

In addition, the differentiation of moral judgments of human welfare and fairness from nonmoral evaluations based on social convention or other factors provides a basis from which to systematically investigate cases in which individuals maintain objections to homosexual orientations and conduct but are also unwilling to accept harassment or harm to lesbian and gay individuals as morally justified. Such individuals would represent instances of tolerance rather than acceptance of lesbian and gay individuals. The limits of the tolerance displayed toward lesbian and gay youth as a function of context (e.g., public versus private settings) would reflect interactions between moral concerns for fair treatment of others and the claims by individuals (e.g., youth not identified as gay or lesbian) to personal choice regarding whom to associate with.

Finally, by differentiating conceptions of social convention from judgments about sexual orientation, domain theory affords an approach to teasing out whether and to what extent the harassment of lesbian and gay youth stems from objections to their sexual orientation or their violation of gender-based conventions maintained by youth culture. Research concerning more general issues of peer in-group, out-group behavior indicates that the violation of peer conventions of such things as forms of dress is a major factor contributing to the singling out of individuals for exclusion and harassment (Horn, 2002). In sum, social cognitive domain theory offers the prospect of a general theory of social cognitive development that would address the complexities of reasoning and judgments young people apply to evaluations and treatment of lesbian and gay peers.

An Application of Social Cognitive Domain Theory to Adolescents' Reasoning About Lesbian and Gay Peers

In a recently completed set of studies, we employed social cognitive domain theory to investigate adolescents' and young adults' attitudes and beliefs about homosexuality and the treatment of gay and lesbian peers. The data in these studies were generated from questionnaires administered to 109 male and 155 female 10th- and 12th-grade students attending a large suburban high school in the Midwest (10th grade: 44 male, 75 female [*M* age = 15.6]; 12th grade: 65 male, 80 female [*M* age = 17.6]) and 29 male and 57 female college-aged students (predominantly juniors and seniors, *M* age = 24.6) from a medium-sized urban university. We chose these age groups in order to capture developmental shifts in conventional thinking (Nucci, Becker, & Horn, 2004) that may be related to adolescents' judgments and reasoning about these issues. Anonymous questionnaires were employed, because of the sensitive nature of the issues under investigation.

The high school was located in a predominantly middle- to upper-middle-class ethnically diverse suburb. The school had an active gay-straight alliance; same-sex sexuality was discussed in a positive manner in a number of classes, and there were visible gay and lesbian teachers on the faculty. In addition, the school had an antidiscrimination policy that included sexual orientation. The university was located in a large city and enrolled students from the surrounding city and suburban communities. The university had an active gay and lesbian student group and an office specifically for gay, lesbian, bisexual, and transgender concerns, as well as a nondiscrimination policy that included sexual orientation and gender identity.

High school participants were African American (24%), Asian American (4%), European American (56%), Latino/a (5%), and other (11%). The demographic distribution of the sample paralleled that of the school. In terms of religious identification, they were Catholic (17%), Baptist (6%), Protestant (14%), evangelical Christian (19%), Jewish (12%), other (11%), or not identified with any religion (22%). Participants were recruited from the required 10th-grade health or 12th-grade social studies classes (psychology, sociology, philosophy). Only those students receiving parental permission (58%) were surveyed. Those students who did not return the parental permission form (41%)[2] or were not given permission to participate (1%) completed an alternate questionnaire made up of educational games during administration to protect the anonymity of those students participating in the study.

College participants were African American (8%); Asian American (12%); European American (56%); Latino/a (20%) and other (5%). In terms of religious identification they were Catholic (45%), Baptist (8%), Protestant (5%), evangelical Christian (5%), Jewish (4%), other (18%), or not identified with any religion (15%). The demographic distribution of the sample paralleled that of the university. Participants were recruited from two education classes (one required and one elective). Only those students providing consent (100%) were surveyed. One student chose not to complete the survey.

All students providing consent completed a questionnaire in their class. Prior to being given the questionnaire, participants were told that their responses to the questionnaire were confidential, that participation was voluntary, and that they could decide to stop at any time. The questionnaire administration took approximately 45 minutes. Once all students had completed the questionnaire, the researcher answered any questions they had regarding the study.

The first part of the questionnaire obtained demographic information from the participants (gender, grade, ethnicity, religious denomination, and age), as well as information on whether participants had a gay or lesbian friend, their comfort with gay and lesbian peers in different school contexts, their beliefs about how someone becomes gay or lesbian, and their attitudes and reasoning about whether homosexuality is right or wrong.

To measure students' comfort with gay or lesbian peers, they were asked to respond to 10 questions about their attitudes toward having gay and lesbian peers in a variety of school contexts. For example, students responded to questions such as "Having a gay or lesbian student in my English class would be . . ." They could respond using a five-point Likert scale (1 = Okay, it wouldn't bother me at all; 5 = Really bad, it would bother me a lot).

To measure students' beliefs about how someone becomes gay or lesbian (*origins*), they were asked "How do you think someone becomes gay or lesbian?" and provided with a list of eight possible reasons from which they could choose all those that fit their beliefs (i.e., they are born that way, they hang out primarily with people of the opposite gender). The reasons provided in the questionnaire were based on a combination of three considerations: the theoretical model guiding the research (social cognitive domain theory), the results of pilot interviews with 40 college students, and the research reports from prior studies on antigay attitudes. Reasons that were offered in other sections of the questionnaire were generated through consideration of the same three factors. Participants could choose more than one response. Their origins score was calculated based on the proportion of their response that fell into each origins category.

Finally, to measure students' attitudes regarding homosexuality (*attitude judgments*) they were asked "Do you think homosexuality is all right or wrong?" Responses were given on a five-point Likert scale response (1 = completely wrong, 3 = neither right nor wrong, 5 = completely all right). To better understand the reasoning that students used in determining whether homosexuality was right or wrong, students were also asked to choose from a list of 18 statements the reasons that they thought homosexuality was all right or not all right (*attitudes justification*). Participants could choose more than one response. The 18 reasons were collapsed into nine conceptual categories (i.e. religious opposition, individual rights). Participants' attitudes justification scores were calculated based on the proportion of their response that fell into each justification category.

In the second part of the questionnaire, participants were presented with a series of descriptions of individuals who were either male or female, gay or lesbian, and gender conforming or nonconforming in appearance or choice of extracurricular activity. For example:

> Ashley is a lesbian high school student. She plays on the school volley team. She is a "B" student. She dresses and acts differently from most of the other girls at school. For example she acts masculine, has a crew cut, and never wears make-up or dresses.

For each target individual there were five scenarios in which other students at the school excluded, teased, harassed, assaulted, or accepted that individual. For example, "Other students at Ashley's school don't want to hang out with Ashley because she is a lesbian." Participants were asked to evaluate whether or not they thought it was all right or wrong (*treatment judgment*) for the students to exclude, tease, or accept the target individual and to provide a reason for why (*treatment justification*) they thought it was all right or wrong. Judgments were assessed on a five-point Likert scale (1 = completely wrong; 3 = neither right nor wrong; 5 = completely all right).

We assessed participants' reasoning by asking participants to choose, from a set of nine responses, the reasons that best reflected the reason why they thought the action (e.g., exclusion) was all right or wrong. For example, "It is unfair/hurtful to him." The responses used were generated from pilot interviews with 40 college students and based on prior work in social cognitive domain theory (Turiel 1983; Turiel, Hildebrant, & Wainryb, 1991). Interestingly, on the basis these interviews, we determined that two categories of religious justification were necessary. One of the categories referred to the rules or laws of religion (God's law); the other referred to religious principles regarding human equality and the treatment of others (religious human equality). Adolescents could choose more than one response. Their justification score was calculated as the proportion of their response that fell into each justification type. Log-linear transformations were conducted on the proportional scores to adjust for nonnormality (see Winer, Brown, & Michels, 1991).

While the study focused on a number of interesting issues and questions, for the sake of clarity and brevity, we will provide an overview of some of the more compelling results from the studies. To that end, we will focus on four specific questions. First, what general views did the students hold with regard to whether or not homosexuality was right or wrong? Second, what background variables (e.g., age, religious orientation, gender) were associated with particular beliefs about homosexuality? Third, how were individuals' beliefs (informational assumptions) about the origins or causes of an individual's homosexuality related to judgments about the treatment of gay or lesbian peers? Fourth, to what extent and in what ways were judgments about the treatment of others based upon the sexual orientation or gender norm conformity of peers? (For complete technical reports regarding these issues, as well as other results from this work, see Horn, in press; Horn & Hudgens, 2004; Horn & Nucci, 2003.)

Basic Views About Homosexuality

Approximately half of the students in the study expressed views that homosexuality was all right (52%). The remainder of the students expressed views that homosexuality was neither right nor wrong (31%) or wrong (15%). Participants' reasons for why they felt homosexuality was right or wrong centered upon issues of individual or human rights (i.e., sexual orientation as an issue within an individual's personal domain; 35% of responses), the perception that homosexuality was biologically determined (20% of responses), the fact that their religious faith taught the importance of treating all persons with equality (15 % of responses), the opposition to homosexuality as maintained by the precepts of their religion (8% of responses), and the notion that homosexuality violates the natural order (6% of responses).

Relationships Among Adolescents' and Young Adults' Age, Religion, and Gender and Their Beliefs About Homosexuality

In an examination of the relationships among students' background variables (i.e. religion, gender, age) and their judgments about homosexuality, we found a moderate relationship between students' religious denomination and their evaluations of whether homosexuality was all right or wrong.[3] That is, students who identified as being Christian evangelical or Baptist held views that were least accepting of homosexuality, while mainstream Protestants (e.g., Lutherans, Presbyterians) and Catholics were more moderately accepting of homosexuality, and students who identified their religion as Jewish and those who didn't identify any religion were most accepting. These findings were consistent with previous research with adults, indicating that individuals ascribing to fundamental religious beliefs hold more negative attitudes toward lesbian and gay people and are more likely to believe homosexuality is wrong (Herek, 1987, 1994) than are members of mainstream religions or nonreligious people (Marsiglio, 1993). In addition, consistent with previous research, males were slightly less accepting of homosexuality, overall, than females, and younger students (10th-graders) were less accepting of homosexuality than older adolescents or college students.

As already mentioned, our samples were from institutions that are fairly liberal regarding these issues and where the administrators had already taken steps to make the environment one that was relatively safe for and accepting of lesbian and gay students. Thus, we observed fairly positive attitudes being expressed by most students, and an overwhelming rejection of the more serious forms of harassment and harm to gay and lesbian or gender-nonconforming students by all but a very small minority of the participants at this high school (less than 1% endorsed harassment or assault as all right). Nonetheless, even in this relatively safe environment, we saw evidence of the more vitriolic and potentially violent reactions that some young people have toward sexual minority youth. One of our male participants wrote the following on his questionnaire. "All f—ing fags should die!!! Kill all the butt-f—ing faggots!!!"

Beliefs About Origins and Acceptance of Lesbian and Gay Peers

To assess students' informational assumptions about how people become gay or lesbian, we asked students to indicate their beliefs about the origins of homosexuality. What we discovered was that students who believed that people become gay or lesbian through some kind of socialization (5 %) were more likely to believe homosexuality was wrong ($M = 2.88$) than individuals who believed homosexuality was biological ($M = 4.23$). Further, they were also more likely to evaluate exclusion and teasing based on sexuality as all right. This pattern of results was also associated with the belief that homosexuality was the result of a combination of socialization and choice on the part of the individual. This finding suggests that sexual prejudice toward gay or lesbian peers is more easily sustained when individuals hold informational assumptions that people have some control over whether they are gay or lesbian. This is consistent with the notion that moral culpability presumes a conscious choice and the autonomous capacity to engage in wrongful behavior. More positive or accepting attitudes regarding homosexuality, on the other hand, were related to informational assumptions that people are born gay or lesbian, thus placing sexual orientation beyond the individual's control or moral culpability.

What is interesting in this regard are those students who were members of mainstream Christian religions for whom engagement in homosexual conduct is viewed as sinful, *regardless* of the source of the person's homosexuality, and who also maintain the moral dictum that all persons are to be treated with equal respect and compassion. In exploring that aspect of our data more carefully, we determined that many of the college students who identified as Catholic, in particular, presented a pattern of judgments and supporting reasons that amounted to "hate the sin, but love the sinner."[4] Thus, they presented judgments of homosexuality as wrong, because their belief that it countermanded the will of God, but also condemned actions of harassment or abuse of gay or lesbian peers as contrary to religious moral mandates to love all persons equally (for a complete report, see Kurtz, Horn, & Nucci, 2002).

Evaluations of the Treatment of Peers Based on Gender Norm Conformity and Sexual Orientation

Our exploration of gender nonconformity and sexual orientation as factors in judgments about peers provided interesting and somewhat surprising results.[5] Overall, students opposed social exclusion or harassment, irrespective of the characteristics of the peer depicted in the scenario (mean judgments on a scale from 1 = completely wrong to 5 = completely all right: exclusion $M = 2.2$, teasing $M = 1.3$, harassing $M = 1.09$; assault $M = 1.04$). Reasons given for objecting to such actions primarily focused upon the harm or injustice that would result from the action (between 80% and 95% for judgments regarding teasing, harassing, or assaulting someone). Within that overall tendency toward tolerance, however, students were more willing to exclude the gay or lesbian peer than the straight peer. Justifications for social exclusion primarily focused on personal choice, indicating that one should be able to "hang out with whomever you want." Male students, however, indicated that the person it would be most acceptable to socially exclude was the *straight* male who engaged in gender-nonconforming dress. Justifications students gave in support of social exclusion primarily focused upon violations of social convention: "He doesn't dress the way a guy in our society should." While females were generally more accepting of a lesbian peer than males were of a gay peer, they also were more likely to use social norms or conventions as justifications regarding the exclusion of the lesbian peer who did not conform to gender norms in appearance than other target individuals used in the scenarios (e.g., gay, conforming; straight, nonconforming in behavior). What these results indicate is that social exclusion of lesbian and gay youth may not be simply a matter of responding to sexual orientation but may also be a function of more general attention to the conventions that structure peer culture. As was evident in the reports emerging from the spate of school shootings in the 1990s, peer harassment of perceived gender nonconformity in appearance may have as devastating an impact on youth as the harassment that is directed at lesbian and gay peers.

Implications

The statistics presented at the beginning of this chapter make a compelling case for the need for educational interventions to reduce the incidence of peer harassment and violence directed at LGB youth. The results of our initial studies applying domain theory to study this issue suggest that the relationship between negative beliefs about homosexuality and attitudes toward and the treatment of gay, lesbian, and gender-nonconforming peers is complex. These results have important implications for educators and others concerned with reducing sexual prejudice and heterosexism in schools. Before addressing some of those implications, we should reiterate that the results of these initial studies point to the need for further research on the conceptions and judgments young people make about sexual minority youth.

For instance, even though a small minority of our sample exhibited extremely negative violent views toward gay and lesbian peers, it is precisely this minority who are more likely to be responsible for the hate crimes against gay and lesbian people such as the lethal beating of Matthew Shephard. Future research on these young people who hold such extreme views, and the contributing factors and social supports that sustain such hostile and potentially harmful points of view, is critical. In addition, research that more fully investigates the development of sexual prejudice in youth is warranted. What developmental constraints or processes are related to higher or lower levels of sexual prejudice and heterosexism in youth? For example, how is sexual identity or moral development related to youths' attitudes and beliefs about sexuality and the treatment of gay and lesbian peers? In addition, because homosexuality is a controversial and contested issue in most countries and cultures, research on sexual prejudice and heterosexism must investigate the ways in which individuals coordinate conflicting information about homosexuality and gay and lesbian peers. What is the relationship between legal or institutional protections for or sanctions against gay and lesbian people and attitudes and beliefs about homosexuality and the treatment of gay and lesbian youth in schools? Finally, what is the role of context in these processes?

Despite the need for additional research in this understudied area, the results of our initial study on sexual prejudice in youth suggest a number of strategies for reducing this type of youth violence. Understanding the social reasoning that young people use in evaluating the treatment of gay, lesbian, and gender-nonconforming peers may have important implications for understanding the ways the school context or climate might influence young peoples' attitudes toward and evaluations of the treatment of others. For example, in schools in which exclusion, teasing, and harassment based on perceived or actual sexual orientation and gender nonconformity are sanctioned as wrong because of the inherent harm they cause the individual, students may begin to see these issues as moral and may, therefore, be more likely to evaluate them using their moral knowledge. In schools where exclusion, teasing, and harassment are part of the status quo, either through explicit or implicit acceptance of them, young people may come to understand these as legitimate ways to regulate their social worlds and thus be less likely to utilize moral reasoning in thinking about these situations. Recent work on children's and adolescents' reasoning about issues of exclusion and teasing (Killen, McGlothlin, & Lee-Kim, 2002) suggests that because of the multifaceted nature of these issues, we need to help students understand how to negotiate and coordinate group and individual needs with their understanding of fairness and individual rights. In schools where antilesbian and antigay language and behavior is ignored by teachers and other adults, the message that students receive is likely to be that these are legitimate forms of interacting with others. This nonverbal acceptance of less severe forms of sexual prejudice can lead to the legitimization of more severe forms of sexual prejudice such as assault.

In the past decade there has been a marked increase in programs aimed at reducing bullying and social aggression in schools. These programs have included working with individual bullies and victims, but, more important, many of them have directed their efforts at helping young people understand the moral implications of this behavior and have worked to dispel the myth that exclusion and teasing are "just a part of growing up" (see Espelage, 2003). Unfortunately, however, despite the fact that research suggests that bullying in adolescence most often takes the form of sexual harassment targeted toward someone of the same sex (Craig, Peplar, Connolly, & Henderson, 2001), very little of the mainstream work currently being done on preventing bullying has included issues of sexual prejudice as components of programs (Horn, 2003). Interestingly, a number of independent programs aimed at improving the school climate specifically for LGB youth have also been developed in the past 10 to 15 years. While many of these programs have been extremely successful in improving the sexual diversity climate for LGB youth (see Szalacha, 2003) the implementation of these programs is often contingent upon the political climate within a particular school, district, state, or country. Further, many of these programs are aimed at providing support mechanisms and resources (such as support groups) for GLB youth rather than changing the negative attitudes or behaviors toward gay and lesbian people in the school more generally. Thus, to integrate this work more fully into the school culture, efforts should be made to infuse issues of bullying or prejudice related to sexuality or gender nonconformity into mainstream moral education, character development, and bullying reduction programs.

Finally, perhaps the most effective approach toward shifting attitudes and behavior related to sexual orientation and gender nonconformity and to reduce this type of youth violence would be to help students to understand the ways gender norms, gender roles, and heterosexism limit all of us. This can be done through curricular and noncurricular avenues by having students explore the ways gender roles and norms, historically and currently, constrain and limit individuals' abilities to maximize their personal potential and have contributed to systemic and pervasive prejudice and discrimination of certain groups of people.

Conclusion

Violence directed at LGB youth by their peers is not unique to the United States. While we have reports of this type of victimization occurring in other Western countries such as Britain, Ireland, and Canada, we know very little about this topic more globally. One reason for this is the controversial nature and multiplicity of beliefs regarding homosexuality. Because of the current lack of information regarding these issues across the broader international community, developing any type of transcultural research or programmatic agenda would be difficult. What the results of our initial studies point to, however, is that understanding the ways individuals coordinate moral, societal, and personal domains of knowledge regarding these issues and the role that informational assumptions play in this process is an important first step in better understanding the nature of this type of youth violence and what to do about it.

Notes

1. See Herek (2000) for an argument as to why *sexual prejudice* is the most precise term to use when assessing or referring to an individual's attitudes and beliefs about gay and lesbian people.

2. Because we were not allowed to obtain any demographic information on the students who did not return permission forms, we were unable to compare this group to the participants in the study. In addition, we don't know if the students not returning their forms simply forgot about it or selected themselves out of the study for some other reason. In classes in which teachers required that students return the form as part of their course participation, the response rate was close to 100%. In classes where this was not the case, the response rate was typically lower than 30%. While this may suggest that a majority of students simply neglected to return their form, it is possible that some students selected themselves out for other reasons; thus, our sample may be biased toward individual students and families who are more accepting of same-sex sexualities.

3. Tests were conducted using analysis of variance. Mean scores ranged from 2.58 (Baptist) to 4.3 (no religious affiliation) on a five-point Likert scale (1 = completely wrong; 5 = completely all right).

4. Due to low frequencies, we were only able to compare Catholic students to students who identified no religious affiliation.

5. For a complete report of these results, see Horn (in press).

References

Amnesty International. (1999, September). Campaigning for gay and lesbian human rights. *Focus, 29,* 45.

Baker, J., & Fishbein, H. (1998). The development of prejudice towards gays and lesbians by adolescents. *Journal of Homosexuality, 36,* 89–100.

Bochenek, M., & Brown, A. (2001). *Hatred in the hallways: Violence and discrimination against lesbian, gay, bisexual, and transgender students in U.S. schools.* New York: Human Rights Watch.

Craig, W. M., Peplar, D., Connolly, J., & Henderson, K. (2001). Developmental context of peer harassment in early adolescence: The role of puberty and the peer group. In J. Juvonen & S. Graham (Eds.), *Peer harassment in school: The plight of the vulnerable and victimized* (pp. 242–262). New York: Guilford Press.

Espelage, D. (2003). *Bullying in American schools: A social-ecological perspective on prevention and intervention.* Mahwah, NJ: Erlbaum.

Garofalo, R., Wolf, R. C., Kessel, S., Palfrey, J., & DuRant, R. (1998). The association between health risk behavior and sexual orientation among a school-based sample of adolescents. *Pediatrics, 46,* 964–972.

Gay, Lesbian, Sraight Education Network. (2003). *National School Climate Survey.* New York: GLSEN.

"Gay Victim of Beating Is Dead." (1998, October 12). *Chicago Tribune.*

Herek, G. (1987). Religious orientation and prejudice: A comparison of racial and sexual attitudes. *Personality and Social Psychology Bulletin, 13,* 34–44.

Herek, G. (1988). Heterosexuals' attitudes toward lesbians and gay men: Correlates and gender differences. *Journal of Sex Research, 25,* 451–477.

Herek, G. (1994). Assessing heterosexuals' attitudes toward lesbians and gay men: A review of empirical research with the ATLG scale. In B. Greene & G. Herek (Eds.), *Lesbian and gay psychology: Theory, research and clinical applications* (pp. 206–228). Thousand Oaks, CA: Sage.

Herek, G. (2000). Sexual prejudice. *Current Directions in Psychological Science, 9,* 19–22.

Hershberger, S. L., & D' Augelli, A. (1995). The impact of victimization on the mental health and suicidality of lesbian, gay, and bisexual youth. *Developmental Psychology, 31,* 65–74.

Horn, S. S. (2002, November). "Living outside the box": The impact of social norms on adolescents' evaluations of peer exclusion and harassment. Paper presented at the annual meeting of the Association for Moral Education, Chicago.

Horn, S. S. (2003, Spring). The absence of gender identity and sexual orientation in peer harassment research. *SRA Newsletter,* p. 3.

Horn, S. S. (in press). Adolescents' acceptance of same sex peers based on sexual orientation and gender expression. *Journal of Youth and Adolescence.*

Horn, S. S. (2005). Age-related changes in adolescents' and young adults' beliefs and attitudes about homosexuality and the treatment of gay and lesbian peers in school. Manuscript submitted for publication.

Horn, S. S., & Hudgens, S. (2004). Sexual prejudice in youth: Validation of an instrument. Unpublished manuscript, University of Illinois at Chicago.

Horn, S. S., & Nucci, L. P. (2003). The multidimensionality of adolescents' beliefs about and attitudes toward gay and lesbian peers in school. *Equity and Excellence in Education, 36,* 1–12.

Killen, M., McGlothlin, H., & Lee-Kim, J. (2002). Between individuals and culture: Individuals' evaluations of exclusion from social groups. In H. Keller, Y. Poortinga, & A. Schoelmerich (Eds.), *Between biology and culture: Perspectives on ontogenetic development* (pp. 159–190). Cambridge, UK: Cambridge University Press.

Kimmel, D., & Mahler, X. (2003). Adolescent masculinity, homophobia, and violence: Random school shootings, 1982–2001. *American Behavioral Scientist, 46,* 1439–1458.

Kite, M., & Whitley, B. (1998). Do heterosexual women and men differ in their attitudes toward homosexuality? A conceptual and methodological analysis. In G. Herek (Ed.), *Stigma and sexual orientation: Understanding prejudice against lesbians, gay men, and bisexuals* (pp. 39–61). Thousand Oaks, CA: Sage.

Kohlberg, L. (1984). *Essays on moral development: Vol. 2. The psychology of moral development.* San Francisco: Harper and Row.

Kurtz, A., Horn, S. S., & Nucci, L. P. (2002, November). The relationship between religion and judgments of fairness in young adults' beliefs regarding homosexuality. Paper presented at the annual meeting of the Association for Moral Education, Chicago.

Marsiglio, W. (1993). Attitudes toward homosexual activity and gays as friends: A national survey of heterosexual 15- to 19-year-old males. *Journal of Sex Research, 30,* 12–17.

Morrison, T., McLeod, L., Morrison, M., & Anderson, D. (1997). Gender stereotyping, homonegativity and misconceptions about sexually coercive behavior among adolescents. *Youth and Society, 28,* 351–382.

"Netherlands legalizes gay marriage." (2000, September 12). BBC News. Available: news.bbc.co.uk/1/hi/world/europe/921505.stm.

Nucci, L. (1996). Morality and the personal sphere of actions. In E. Reed, E. Turiel, & T. Brown (Eds.), *Values and knowledge* (pp. 41–60). Hillsdale, NJ.: Erlbaum

Nucci, L. (2001). *Education in the moral domain.* Cambridge, UK: Cambridge University Press.

Nucci, L., Becker, K., & Horn, S. S. (2004, June). Assessing the development of adolescent concepts of social convention. Paper presented at the annual meeting of the Jean Piaget Society, Toronto, Canada.

Obmascik, M. (1999, April 21). High school massacre: Columbine bloodbath leaves up to 25 dead. *Denver Post*, p. A1.

Price, J. (1982). High school students' attitudes toward homosexuality. *Journal of School Health, 52*, 469–474.

Remafedi, G. (1999). Sexual orientation and youth suicide. *Journal of the American Medical Association, 282*, 1291–1292.

Rivers, I., & D' Augelli, A. (2001). The vicitmization of lesbian, gay and bisexual youths. In A. D'Augelli & C. Pattreson (Eds.), *Lesbian, gay, and bisexual identities and youth* (pp. 199–223). New York: Oxford University Press.

Russell, S., Franz, B., & Driscoll, A. (2001). Same-sex romantic attraction and experiences of violence in adolescence. *American Journal of Public Health, 91*, 903–906.

Szalacha, L. (2003). Safer sexual diversity climates: Lessons learned from and evaluation of Massachusetts' safe schools program for gay and lesbian youth. *American Journal of Education, 110*, 58–88.

Turiel, E. (1983). *The development of social knowledge: Morality and convention*. Cambridge, UK: Cambridge University Press.

Turiel, E. (1998). The development of morality. In W. Damon (Ed.), *Handbook of child psychology* (5th ed.): *Vol. 3*, N. Eisenberg (Ed.), *Social, emotional, and personality development* (pp. 863–932). New York: Academic Press.

Turiel, E. (2002). *The culture of morality*. Cambridge, UK: Cambridge University Press.

Turiel, E., Hildebrant, C., & Wainryb, C. (1991). Judging social issues: Difficulties, inconsistencies, and consistencies (Serial No. 224). *Monographs of the Society for Research in Child Development, 56*.

Van de Ven, P. (1994). Comparisons among homophobic reactions of undergraduates, high school students, and young offenders. *Journal of Sex Research, 31*, 117–124.

Vincke, J., & van Heeringen, K. (1998, September). Suicidal ideation and behavior among homosexual adolescents and young adults: A comparative study. Paper presented at the Seventh European Symposium on Suicide and Suicidal Behavior, Gent (Belgium).

Winer, B. J., Brown, D. R., & Michels, K. M. (1991). *Statistical principles in empirical design*. New York: McGraw-Hill.

CHAPTER 9

Social Transformation and Values Conflicts Among Youth in Contemporary China

GUOZHEN CEN AND DAN LI

This chapter describes the challenges faced by Chinese youth with respect to their moral and social values that have emerged as a result of China's shift from a command economy to a free market system. We present survey research from a series of studies indicating that Chinese youth have shifted from traditional collectivist values to ones consistent with pursing personal development. Material wealth and personal happiness have become salient values among Chinese youth. Positive virtues of patriotism, concern for others, and fundamental fairness are also evident in the values of contemporary Chinese youth. However, research has demonstrated that there are also some values/moral problems among Chinese youth today. These include less trust of social institutions, expectations that bribery and social influence are associated with success, and a reduced belief that one can resist such forces. These shifts in social values appear to be accompanied by a rise in the national crime rate of robbery and theft. The chapter provides an analysis of the cultural and contextual causes related to the rise of what we term moral and social values confusion. Finally, we offer a set of recommendations for educational research and practice that would ameliorate these problems.

Since the early 1980s, China has undergone a major transformation from a planned economy to a free market system. This movement within the economic system has come with a host of other social transformations that have generally benefited Chinese society. For example, labor productivity has increased rapidly, and peoples' living standards have improved to a great extent, capturing attention from all over the world (Sen, 2001). In viewing these changes, however, we must also be aware of the various destabilizing factors and complicated social conflicts that have accompanied this development process. These more negative aspects of the recent, rapid transformations in China have also exposed Chinese society to a variety of social problems. The focus of this chapter is upon the impact these changes have had upon the moral and social values of Chinese youth.

The main features of the recent period of transformation of Chinese society can be summarized as follows. First, the transformation of the economic system has accelerated the polarization of society and restructured the previously monodimensional social structure. Individuals within different aspects of the social system, vocations, and professions have been clearly differentiated in both earning and social status. Accordingly, this has promoted a new division of social classes, and new social groups such as entrepreneurs, individual business operators, and private property owners have come into existence. These shifts in the balance of roles and access to resources inevitably lead to conflicts emerging between different interest groups. Looking ahead, one can anticipate that continuous escalation of these conflicts will be one of the key causes of many social problems in China during this social transformation period.

Social transformation leads to diversification of people's moral and social values. Multivalue systems tend to make people evaluate things from diverse points of view, and there is no longer an absolute and uniform moral criterion for many issues (Dong, 2002). People who adjust to these shifting social circumstances tend to have increased moral tolerance for certain issues. This is especially the case among the urban population. While diversity is generally a social good, the rapidity with which these processes are occurring within China has meant that old moral and social values have been affected, while the new ones have not as yet been fully established. Thus, the division of social structure and the increasing diversification of social behaviors and value systems have lead to clashes between the old and new values, mindsets, and behaviors. Within such a context, there is a widespread tendency for people to experience frustration and dissatisfaction, which lays the psychological grounds for misconduct and criminal action, hence many of the social disorders emerging within modern China. In the first quarter of 2004, for example, the crime rate in China rose 14.2% over the same period the last year. While the rates for violent crime (arson, murder, rape) either stayed stable or fell, the rates for property crimes of theft and robbery rose dramatically (Chinadaily, 2004).

The recent transformation of Chinese society has also fostered a diversification of approaches and media of moral education. For example, educational information obtained from schools may differ largely from that from parents or the internet. This kind of inconsistent value orientation presents adolescents with a confusing and arguably disordered morality. On the one hand, such value diversity may contribute to adolescents' intellectual and cultural development, particularly for youths growing up within more stable home environments. On the other hand, such a cacophony of moral values and attitudes in the absence of clear adult institutional support may result in disaffection among youth and a general failure to develop the intellectual and social values and skills needed to achieve a fulfilling life.

Research on Values Among Youth in China During the Past 2 Decades

Awareness of the potential impact that the transformation of the economic system and diversification of social structure may have upon Chinese society has led to a considerable amount of research over the past 2 decades. In this section, we explore that research as it pertains to moral and social values among Chinese youth. Work conducted in the 1980s (reported in Sun, Chen, & Peterson, 2002) found that values such as "wisdom," "self-esteem," and "true friendship" were given high priority by Chinese adolescents, while values such as obtaining an "easygoing lifestyle" or an "exciting lifestyle" were considered much less important. The same researchers reported that middle school children also considered "a sense of achievement" an important social value. Kou (1989) found that middle school students reported appreciating spiritual life, interpersonal relations, and self-perfection more than physical comfort or other elements of physical existence.

Within the late 1990s, however, survey research indicated that Chinese adolescents no longer endorsed unconditional forms of the statement "Serve the people, serve the society" that had been a value promoted prior to the transformation to a market economy (Huang, 2001). Instead, this collectivist value had been largely replaced by attention to both individual benefit and social benefit and attention to justice. A recent survey (Huang, 2001) reported the surprising result that when compared with adolescents in Australia and America, contemporary Chinese adolescents took a more critical view of collectivism and attached greater importance to individualism. Money emerged as the first index among Chinese adolescents in their choice of occupation (Huang, 2001), and more and more youths reported being in pursuit of "social status" and "self-perfection." In general, then, the broad trend has been a shift from expression of collectivist emphasis upon the common good to a greater concern for individual achievement and material satisfaction. This is not to say that concern for the general welfare or spiritual growth have disappeared as social values, but that an emphasis upon self-fulfillment and material benefit have emerged as competing value orientations.

These shifts in values would appear to reflect responses to the shifting cultural and economic milieu rather than to a set of fundamental differences in basic age-related trends in Chinese children's moral reasoning. Research conducted over the past 2 decades in China has replicated the broad developmental trends in moral judgment reported by Piaget (Cen, 2002; Liu & Cen, 2000) and other developmental researchers (e.g., Damon, 1977) working in the Western tradition who have examined children's moral concepts of sharing and fair distribution (Cen & Liu, 1988; Li, 1982, 1983). Naturally, this work went beyond the investigation of issues pertaining to justice and fair distribution within contexts typical of Western society to include developmental studies of children's conceptions of public and private ownership and public labor (Cen, 1987) that are germane to life within modern China. This work (Cen, 1987; Cen & Liu, 1988) determined that Chinese children by about age 9 evidence conceptions of fair distribution that attend to issues of equity (providing goods to the needy over the "more capable") rather than strict equality. This progression essentially matches the emergence of distributive justice concepts described for children in Western society (Damon, 1977). Thus, while the particular expression of social values conflict is tied to the contemporary Chinese context, it cannot be readily attributed to something unique about basic processes of social and moral development among Chinese children and youth. In the following sections we will explore in greater detail the nature of current social values among Chinese youth and the moral conflicts that the recent shifts in social values have generated. In subsequent sections, we will revisit some of the factors that may account for these moral conflicts and conclude with a discussion of educational approaches that may ameliorate some of the problems being experienced by today's Chinese youth.

Current Trends in Social and Moral Values
Among Chinese College Students

The work that has been just described has provided evidence that social values are shifting among Chinese youth. In this section, we provide an overview of recent survey research that has explored the broad core values endorsed by contemporary Chinese college students. The following section reviews some of the values conflicts unveiled in these more recent studies.

Put in broad terms, pursuing personal development and individual virtue are the primary moral values of contemporary Chinese youth. A recent survey of college students in Beijing (Yang & Yan, 1997) asked students to respond to the question "What do you think is the most important thing in one's life?" Students were instructed to select their top three choices from a list of 10 descriptors and place them in rank order. The results showed that health (21.2%), knowledge (15.2%), love (13.2%), and money (11.3%) were the top four values, while family (6.5%), status (4.1%), power (2.0%), and reputation (1.7%) made up the bottom four. What is most surprising in those results is the relatively low ranking provided to family, given the historical value placed on family in Chinese society. Similar results were found in a study in which college students were asked to indicate their biggest wish of the next 5 years (reported in Yang & Yan, 1997). In descending order, the replies were: career success (38.8%), achievements in studies (20.6%), ability to earn big money (18.0%), happy life (3.4%), good health (2.3%), ideal companion (1.8%), and family harmony (0.3%). When asked to respond to the question "What do you consider to be the most important factor in choosing a job/work?" the top three responses, in order of priority, were income (33.3%), the chance to apply one's professional expertise (26.0%), and social status (10.7%) (reported in Yang & Yan, 1997).

The full force of the series of studies reported in Yang and Yan (1997) becomes evident when findings regarding the value and purposes of work are examined. A cardinal value of Chinese society prior to the recent period of social transformation has been that one's individual labor was to be viewed as a contribution to the growth and betterment of the nation and larger society. In one investigation, recent college graduates were asked to identify 20 factors that "are motivating to one to work hard." The 10 factors rated highest in descending order were: increasing personal income, giving full play to one's ability, suiting individual interests, free choice in career selection, sense of personal achievement, having the chance to go abroad, personal welfare being increased, personal position being promoted, having a house, and opportunity for unpaid leave to further one's education. All of these factors focused upon personal considerations and personal growth. "Making a contribution for the country " was rated 16th out of the 20 possible priorities.

The six factors that the college-age youth considered to be important to their selection of a profession were as follows: higher pay, match with individual professional interests, higher social status, excellent working conditions, ease of the task, and meeting social needs (Yang & Yan, 1997). The authors note that "meeting social needs" was placed in the sixth (last) position.

In a separate study conducted in Sichuan and Chongqing (Huang, Zhang, & Li, 1994) exploring perceived needs among youth in both locations, the authors concluded that "the needs for personal development were those most valued by the university students" (p. 41). This emphasis upon individual growth does not mean that Chinese youth have become egocentric and disinterested in the common good, but rather that individual needs for personal growth are coming to be more openly expressed and sought after than had been evident prior to the current era. When asked "What do you appreciate as the best virtue that one should possess?" Beijing University students responded with the following items in order of preference: bighearted, amicable, impartial, and honest—all virtues indicative of a respect for others (Yang & Yan, 1997). Moreover, young contemporary Chinese also maintain values of patriotism, devotion to work, and cooperation. When asked to respond on a scale from 0 "not caring about the future of the nation" to 100 "loving one's country as much as one can," the average participant scored 90.4 (Yang & Yan, 1997). Participants in the same study scored an average 91.1 when asked how they would rate themselves "if 0 represents not caring about the future of the nation, while 100 represents caring extremely about the future of the nation."

Perhaps an even better example illustrating that Chinese youth are maintaining an interest in the common good, while paying greater attention to personal goals, comes from a study done during the recent severe acute respiratory syndrome (SARS) outbreak (Cen, Wu, Gu, & Cui, 2004). In this study, five situational stories, implying the five values of justice, care, public responsibility, devotion to duty, and forgiveness, respectively, were used as stimulus materials. These stories were presented to 427 participants who were college and university students and professional youth. The stories were based upon real events occurring during the period in China during the spring of 2003 when the Chinese government actively worked to eradicate SARS. Responses showed concerns ranging from self-interest to social welfare to principled morality. On all the five values, the majority of participant responses were in the form of judgments in favor of society and the general welfare. In descending order of salience, the values employed by participants in response to the SARS situations presented in the stories were: public responsibility, forgiveness (to persons who might have transmitted the disease), justice, care, and devotion to duty. Attention to concerns for personal self-interest fell below these prosocial moral values.

Instances of Social Values/Moral Confusion
Among Youth in China Today

The survey research just described points to the heterogeneity evident in the values maintained by contemporary Chinese youth. This heterogeneity is not unique to China, as is evident in research on social development conducted across many societies (see chapter 5 here). However, the particular sources of social conflict in modern China stemming from the rise in materialism and emphasis upon personal success have raised values issues that are a cause for considerable concern. These are not simply the opinions of adults. In a recent publication, Sun (1998) compiled the results of a series of large-scale surveys conducted with high school and university students in several large urban centers. One such investigation, conducted in Shanghai (Sun, 1998), determined that about 40% of Chinese adolescents endorsed the statement that "today there are some things making it so that people don't know what is right or wrong and don't know how to deal with it." Only 13.9% of participants in the study did not agree with this opinion. When asked to evaluate the moral status of social institutions, the adolescents who were investigated were relatively satisfied with respect to family ethics, with 80% of them judging family ethics and morality positively. However, roughly 40% of the same adolescents rated the ethics of members of professions (e.g., doctors, bankers) as unsatisfactory, and about the same percentage gave low marks to the ethical and moral status of Chinese society more generally (Sun, 1998). Perhaps even more distressing is Sun's (1998) report of a 1992 study in which more than 70% of the adolescent participants reported agreeing with the statement "The honest will come to grief, but the speculator will get rich."

Even though a majority of the youth in these surveys expressed dissatisfaction with the status quo of contemporary Chinese societal and professional morality, there were few who evidenced a willingness to either challenge or keep themselves apart from the very same values and behaviors (Sun, 1998). For example, when asked "Which kind of attitudes do you generally take when unhealthy tendencies happen around you?" the results showed that only 9.04% of the youth surveyed expressed that they would "step forward bravely and condemn it." This relatively tepid response was in line with their responses to other questions: 7.91% of them answered that they would "report a case to the authorities," 11.31% of them indicated that they would "appeal to the mass media to expose it," more than a fourth (27.39%) indicated that they "are incapable of doing anything," even though only 4.93% indicated that such problems "have nothing to do with them" (Sun, 1998). This apparent social-moral passivity uncovered in Sun's (1998) research was corroborated by an investigation in Beijing in 1994 (summarized in Sun, 1998) in which only 24.4% of the adolescent participants surveyed indicated that they would "step forward to prevent an observed act of stealing."

Moreover, a substantial minority of the youths surveyed in the studies summarized by Sun (1998) expressed a willingness to take part in unhealthy tendencies, even though the actions went counter to their own expressed social values. For example, in an investigation conducted in Beijing in 1994, 63.2% of youths surveyed believed that "although bribery is a very bad thing, one has no alternative but to do so in order to be successful." These percentages are in line with perceptions that bribery and insider deals are common practice (a view endorsed by roughly 30% of Chinese youth). So, while on the one hand Chinese adolescents and youth appear to be dissatisfied with the status quo of contemporary professional and societal morality, on the other hand they appear willing to give priority to their own personal goals and benefits rather than maintain such moral demands when applied to their own conduct.

Accounting for Social-Moral Values Conflicts Among Contemporary Chinese Youth

Having provided some detail regarding the values conflicts confronting youth in today's China, we turn again to a more detailed examination of the factors contributing to these shifts in social values. In our view, two main factors are at work. The first is the complex set of influences resulting from the combination of China's entry into a free market economy and the globalization that is affecting societies worldwide. The second is the mixed messages youth are receiving from schools, families, and media and the failure of the Chinese educational system to adapt to these changing social realities.

Confucianism, Globalization, and the Shift to a Free Market Economy

The current moral and values confusion experienced by Chinese youth should be seen in the historical context of a clash or mixture of traditional Chinese culture and the process of modernization. This cultural clash goes deeper than the paradigm differences represented by Western communism and capitalism. Confucianism has been the mainstream within Chinese culture dating back to ancient times. Corresponding to the modern view of "taking the individual person as the cardinal principle among everything," "taking the society as the cardinal principle among everything" was the philosophical basis of Confucianism. It maintained that the needs of individual persons should be submitted to the needs of the whole society and the values of the individual person are themselves attached to the value of society. Confucianism declared that there were three main virtuous goals that are related, respectively, with personal self-cultivation, the relationship between oneself and others, and the relationship between oneself and society. These goals are "cultivating one's moral character and cherishing the people," "attaining modesty, amiability, and comity," and "maintaining filial piety and fraternal duty" (Gu, 1999).

"Cultivating one's moral character and cherishing the people" has several positive personal and social functions. For example, it impels a person to strengthen self-cultivation and to develop consciousness about morality. But this virtue goal also had negative effects on persons in the closed society in China during past times. For example, it came to hold that cherishing the people, especially for one's elders and betters, meant that one had to give up one's own interests and personality. The highest expression of this virtue was to be boundlessly loyal to the supreme ruler.

"Modesty, amiability, and comity" indicated that one should be modest and amiable when engaging in interpersonal interactions with others. Comity should guide one's manner and approach while dealing with the contradictions that naturally occur among a variety of interpersonal relationships. As with the first Confucian virtue, this second set of goals expressed genuinely favorable intentions. However, stringently applying this virtue goal also has dispiriting effects on persons. For example, it came to mean that one should suppress one's own thoughts, ideas, and images and should not express one's own heartfelt viewpoints, nor should one compete fairly in situations in which competition is necessary—solely to maintain friendly and harmonious relations (Gu, 1999).

"Filial piety and fraternal duty" put forward the ethical principles, norms, and demands for families and for the society. It was conducive to the formation of the moral atmosphere of respecting elders and taking good care of younger members in the family and in society. But this virtue goal came to emphasize, in an extreme form, mechanical ranks and absolute obedience in one's life both in family and in society. Under the oppressiveness of the idea of social hierarchy, people became subject to instructions, even to every word, that came from higher authorities or elders. Initiative and responsibility for taking part actively in and experiencing a variety of activities and for actively adjusting a variety of relationships was hindered (Gu, 1999).

As can be seen in this analysis of the social benefits and limitations of traditional Confucian values, one can readily see that it is a system that would impede the development of a person and a society in modern times. Thus, much of what we Chinese are experiencing as values confusion is rooted in the requirement that China move beyond the moral and social values defined by Confucian virtue. The opportunity and challenge to move beyond this traditional framework has been occasioned most forcefully by China's entry into the global marketplace. As we said earlier, during the past 2 decades China has been going through great changes in its progress toward modernization. As a result, China has been drawn into the worldwide trend of information networking and economic globalization. Chinese young people of today are more eager to know about the world than ever before, and at the same time they have been influenced much more than before by cultures of the whole world.

An influential survey research study (Wu, 2002) conducted during the backdrop of China's World Trade Organization entry captured the eagerness of Chinese youth to become better connected to the outside world. The participants in the study were 2,041 young people in Shanghai who ranged in age from 14 to 35. The survey was conducted in 2001. When asked "Have you ever learned or are you learning a foreign language?" 85.8% of the participants gave a positive response. A follow-up question asked: "What is your main motive for learning a foreign language?" In response, 54.7% chose "to find ideal work/job," 26.5% "to better understand the outside world," 9.7% "to go abroad," and 2.5% "out of interest." The survey also asked about participants' "most favorite foreign movie or TV series." In response to this query, 66.4% chose movies from the United States, 12.2% from Japan, 3.9% from western Europe, 2.2% from Russia (former Soviet Union), 1.6% from India, 1.4% from Korea, 0.7% from eastern Europe, and 1.1% from others. The survey also found that a minority (20.6%) of the young people "never" read foreign books, magazines, journals, or newspapers, while a majority (54.5%) of them reported reading them "occasionally," with 21.2% of them reporting reading foreign material often or very often.

Other aspects of the survey explored the views of the young participants regarding direct international and interpersonal contact with other countries and people. A statement within the survey read: "some concepts of ours are very different from those in Western countries; therefore we should avoid getting in touch with them so as to avoid conflicts." In response to this cautious, perhaps even xenophobic, statement, 1.2% of the participants chose to "fully agree," 3.2% of them marked "agree," and 8.0% chose "neutral." However, a majority (60.0%) selected "disagree," and 26.0% selected "strongly disagree." A follow-up probe on the same issue presented the statement "We must reject exchanges with foreign cultures in order to protect Chinese traditional culture relics." Only 1.9% could "fully agree" with this view, 2.4% of them chose "agree," and 3.3% chose "neutral." In line with the openness expressed in other aspects of the survey, 49.4% of the participants selected "disagree," and an additional 41.4% marked "strongly disagree," clearly rejecting this self-protective and closed point of view. In contrast, 40.4% of the people surveyed chose to "fully agree" with a statement saying "We shall welcome more foreigners to China and let them understand our country and people," another 40.4% of the participants chose to mark "agree" to this same welcoming perspective. Among the participants, 25.6% could "fully agree" with the statement that "Frequently chatting with foreign friends would definitely broaden one's view," another 45.9% of them chose "agree," while a minority (21.9%) selected "neutral," 4.2% "disagree," and 0.6% "strongly disagree."

These attitudes of openness to the outside world are matched by recent patterns of social behavior. According to statistics released by the China Internet Information Center (Ke, 2002), there were only 0.62 million internet users in China as of November 1997, while the figure reached 33.7 million by the end of 2001. Among the millions of users, young people between the ages of 18 and 35 formed the major and most active users. The demographic structure of Chinese internet users determined in June 2000, showed that 1.65% were under 18 years old, 46.77% were in the age group between 18 and 24, and 18% were between 25 and 30. Less than 7% of the people over 40 used the internet (Ke, 2002). Thus, much of the most dramatic change in the interface between China and the global information network is occurring among the youth.

In the face of these rapid changes and powerful external influences, the government has made an attempt to maintain some control or guidance of the process of modernization. These efforts may have had some dampening effects upon the potentially disruptive effects of unfettered change. The market economy operates solely on the basis of commodities and profit motives. Thus, the traditional values of collective responsibility face enormous challenge in the face of a system that works on principles of rational self-interest. Adam Smith's invisible hand may be the most effective and efficient way to obtain wealth. However, it places great social strains on the moral fabric of a society when wealth and profit begin to compete with righteousness and social welfare. We have seen in our national crime statistics, and in our surveys of youth, that this rapid shift to a market economy has led some people, including the youth, to pay homage to money and to seek it by fair means or foul.

The direction of Chinese society is clearly toward greater integration with the world economy and greater integration into the information network. The youth are embracing this direction, and China's national future is clearly tied to this liberalization of our society. Yet, as a nation and a culture with a long history and rich tradition, China is faced with the challenge of finding a balance between the rigidity and stagnation of traditional Confucian virtue and the hedonism of the marketing culture. The values confusions being experienced by China's young people reflect the need for balance in this time of rapid transition.

Addressing the Challenge: The Role of Moral and Social Values Education

As we have argued in this chapter, the past 2 decades have created a context of values confusion for youth in China. Meanwhile, the moral and social values education that is offered our youth in school, family, and society has not been up to the needed task. In this final section, we will share some of our thoughts regarding how to address these issues. The arguments we will present are distilled from several decades of work with teachers and schools, as well as our own and others' research on children's moral development. We should note at the outset that the factors at work in creating this value confusion affect all aspects of Chinese society and its institutions. As educational psychologists, our expertise is in areas of child development and pedagogy; however, we wish to limit the focus of our remarks here to the role that schools can play in reducing values confusion and enabling Chinese youth to approach modern life from a coherent moral perspective.

Moral Education

Morality was usually considered to be a matter of personal self-cultivation in China. We discussed this earlier in terms of the first Confucian virtue goal. In modern society, however, morality is not only a matter of personal business but also a matter related to the country and the larger society a person belongs to. The family is the primary social institution for socialization, and stable, harmonious family relationships are central to moral development among children and youth (Chen & Yu, 1990). Beyond the family, however, the main social institution with responsibility and capacity to impact children's moral and social growth is the school. The stated goal of schooling in China is to enable students to develop in an all-around way: morally, intellectually, and physically. In reality, some schools and teachers pay much more attention to intellectual than moral development. Particularly in an era characterized by global market competition, education tends to become centered on high test scores and academic achievement. Moral education can often be neglected or ignored. Schools and teachers should realize, however, that society needs the person not only to have ability in a wide range of knowledge but also to have moral character.

Perhaps the most important thing that schools can contribute is the integration of traditional Chinese values with moral capacities to function well in the China of today. This would include an integration of the values and orientations of other cultures with Chinese moral and social values. The traditional Chinese moral and social values, such as paying attention to manners and courtesy, respecting elders and caring for the young, being honest and keeping promises, industriousness and frugality, unity and helping each other, building an enterprise through arduous effort, and so on, should be carried on and developed further. The excellent values in Western culture, such as humanism, justice, scientific ideals, valuing the legal system, consciousness as a defining aspect of the human being, scrupulously abiding by social ethics, and so on, should be absorbed and learned. In other words, rather than leaving it to the young to struggle to find common ground among traditional values and those of the market society, schools should select among the strengths of Chinese cultural traditions and the humanist, Enlightenment values of the West to provide students with a coherent and ethically defensible values framework. Finally, as developmental psychologists, we would argue that the pace and structure of pedagogy should be sequenced in a manner appropriate to children's age and level of competence.

In order to move in the direction that we suggest, there should be at least three changes in the way moral education is conducted in Chinese schools.

First, the reliance on inculcation as the sole way to develop virtues in youth must be changed. It is very common in schools in China that teachers are *speaking* and students are *listening* while in the context of a course or lesson on morality. This inculcation approach should be changed to a dual one in which not only must students listen to what teachers are speaking but also teachers should listen to what students are thinking. We note with some irony that in some Western democracies (e.g. America), the response of some educators to a perceived moral crisis among youth (Bennett, 1992) has been to promote inculcation (Wynne & Ryan, 1993). Our historical experience with command-based education is that it does not prepare students for life in the modern era. In the absence of student reflection, moral education becomes divorced from the process of moral decision-making. Reflection is the tool by which students can resolve their moral confusions and generate positions from which to tackle the moral challenges of everyday life.

Second, the approach to managing moral conduct and discipline should be changed. It has often been the case that students' conduct has been trained repeatedly, simply, and mechanically. This should be changed. While receiving training in behavior, students should know not only *how* to behave in a particular way but also *why* they should do it that way.

Third, the closed way in which moral education has been carried out should be changed. Typically, moral education has been simply limited to events that take place in the school. This approach, in which students become capable and familiar with moral problem-solving only in school contexts, needs to be changed. Moral education should be opened up to encourage discourse and social experience around a broad spectrum of social issues and contexts, so that the youth can become better able to cope with the broader issues they will confront in modern life.

Finally, the basic nature of moral and social interactions that we are proposing as fundamental to life in schools needs to be carried over into the pattern of parent-child interactions that take place within the family. A majority of parents in China today place great importance on their children's attainment of high academic test scores. We argue that parents need to be paying at least as much attention to their children's moral growth and attending to their child's social values. In concert with our views regarding what needs to change within the school, parents also need to alter their manner of associating with their children. Heeding what an elder or superior says is one of the traditional ways in China. Chinese parents usually have required their child to obey parental requests or commands. However, for effective moral education in today's world, this needs to be changed. Parents and their child should exchange their needs, desires, thoughts, feelings, and so on equally, openly, and frankly with each other.

Directions for Future Research

Given the challenges facing Chinese society, we view it as urgent that attention be paid to further research on children's moral and social growth. First, further research needs to be conducted regarding the real situation of children's and youth's social values and morality today. At this turning period of the social-economic system in China, it is certainly going to be the case that there will be a variety of values among children and youth. In the absence of an ongoing understanding of the real situation regarding the status of the moral and social values of youth, moral education, no matter by whom, where, or how it is carried out, will have limited effectiveness.

Second, we need continued research on how to make moral education effective. The moral education of today should be in keeping with the distinguishing features of modern society. For this, in the opened society of contemporary China, there are two issues that should be researched. One is how to turn the preaching of moral knowledge into the operation of moral practice. The other is how to turn the transmission of specific moral norms into thinking about and exploring moral problems.

Third, research should be conducted about how to get the school, family, and community to play their respective roles in moral education much more efficiently. For the family, issues to be researched are as follows: how to enhance parents' responsibility and sensitivity for moral education, how to raise parents' level of scientific and correct viewpoints and methods in moral education, how to improve parents' coordination and consistency with schools in moral education, and so on. For the school, the issues that should be researched are as follows: how to combine moral education with the regular course of academic teaching, how to compile a variety of learning materials for moral education suited to students at different ages, and how to construct an atmosphere favorable for students' growth in morality through a variety of activities in culture, entertainment, and sports and games. For the community, the issues to be researched include: how to discover and use the resources existing in the community for moral education and how to establish effective relationships with school and family for varied moral activities.

Fourth, research should be conducted about how to integrate the contributions of all of the related people who could be involved in the child's moral development and moral education. Besides teachers, administrative personnel in school, parents, and family elders, we should also include cadres of adult citizens at all levels in different enterprises and organizations. How to organize them and let them play their role well, how to raise their level of consciousness and capacity to contribute to moral education for the child, and so on should be researched. The African notion that "it takes a village to raise a child" (Clinton, 1996) is an idea that resonates with Chinese history and culture. What is needed in the current era is research on how to implement this wise notion in modern Chinese society.

Fifth, we need additional research about how to help a young person reach the ideal state of "self-management" in regard to his or her morality. One's morality should be guided by one's own internalized principles. How to develop internalized moral principles is the core of the self-management component of a person's morality. The course of internalization and the related influencing factors should be researched. In modern society in particular, there are many temptations in daily life. Research should be conducted on what meanings such temptation has for different kinds and ages of children and youth. We cannot presume as adults, having grown up in a different era, to fully understand how youth interpret the events and contexts around them. This basic research also needs to be coordinated with research on how to strengthen the ability of children and youth to resist those things that they perceive to be temptations. Only by knowing and grasping the related influencing conditions and factors can we hope to guide children and youth to reach the ideal state of self-management in morality.

Conclusion

Chinese society is in the midst of a challenging and exciting period of economic and social transformation. As should be clear from other chapters in this book, the forces of globalization and the interconnection of people through the media and internet have posed challenges of various sorts for youth in many parts of the globe. The primary challenge facing youth within the Chinese context is one of reconciling or integrating the social and moral values of traditional Chinese culture with the temptations and opportunities presented by China's entry into the global market. China and its people have benefited greatly from the shift from a command economy to a free market system. However, all major social and economic change carries with it social costs. The challenge to those of us who care about the fate of China's youth is how to make it possible for them to negotiate this period of transition in a manner that allows them to prosper and to grow as moral and ethical citizens of China and the world.

References

Bennett, W. (1992). *The de-valuing of America: The fight for our culture and our children*. New York: Simon and Schuster.

Cen, G. (1987). Research on the development of public labor concepts among primary school students. *Acta Psychologica Sinica, 19*, 321–328.

Cen, G. (2002). A research on the internal justice among children aged 10–16 in China. *Psychological Science, 25*, 14–17.

Cen, G., & Liu, J. (1988). The development of sharing concept of children aged 5–11. *Psychological Science, 11*, 19–23.

Cen, G., Wu, N., Gu, H., & Cui, L. (2004). An investigation on some values during the time of anti-SARS, *Psychological Science* (Shanghai), *27*, 264–266.

Chen, X., & Yu, X. (1990). An investigation on the development of moral judgment and related factors in Chinese adolescents. *Psychological Sciences, 13*, 23–27.

China's crime rate up in 1st quarter. (2004, August 5). Chinadaily. Available: http://Chinadaily.com.cn.

Clinton, H. (1996). *It takes a village to raise a child: And other lessons that children teach us*. New York: Touchstone.

Damon, W. (1977). *The social world of the child*. San Francisco: Jossey-Bass.

Dong, M. (2002). Practical status of moral education to adolescents and pondering about countermeasure. *Contemporary Youth Research, 2,* 9–12.

Gu, R. (Ed.). (1999). *Research on and practice in effective moral education.* Beijing: Chinese Building Material Industry Press.

Huang, X., Zhang, J., & Li, H. (1994). *Values and education among Chinese youth in the contemporary era.* Chengdu: Sichuan Education Press.

Huang, Y. (2001). Examining value orientation of youth by data. *Youth Research, 10,* 35–45.

Ke, T. (2002). The challenges from the internet's development to the fields of culture and ideology in Shanghai. In J. Yin (Ed.), *2002's report on Shanghai society* (pp. 359–376). Shanghai: Shanghia Academy of Social Science Press.

Kou, Y. (1989). An investigation on profession values and its system among middle school students. In Z. Zhang (Ed.), *Exploring for the development of student's morality* (pp. 300–315). Beijing: Press of Beijing Normal University.

Li, B. (1982). An investigation on the development of moral judgment of children aged 5–11 in 18 districts of China. *Psychologial Science, 5,* 22–27.

Li, B. (1983). Survey of the development of children's justice concept. *Psychological Science, 6,* 14–21.

Liu, J., & Cen, G. (2000). The characteristics of "immanent justice" judgment in children aged 10–15. *Acta Psychologica Sinica, 32,* 190–195.

Piaget, J. (1932). *The moral judgment of the child.* New York: Free Press.

Sen, G. (2001). *Post-reform China and the international economy: Economic change and liberalization under sovereign control.* London: First Press.

Sun, B. (1998). *Moral confusions among urban adolescents and educational ways to deal it in China during the social transforming period.* Shanghai: Shanghai Teacher Training Center.

Sun, Y., Chen, X., & Peterson, C. (2002). An investigation of the value system among adolescents in contemporary China. *Contemporary Youth Research, 2,* 9–12.

Wu, Y. (2002). The openness and awareness of Shanghai's youth under the background of China's WTO entry. In J. Yin (Ed.), *2002's report on Shanghai society* (pp. 305–334). Shanghai: Shanghai Academy of Social Science Press.

Wynne, E., & Ryan, K. (1993). Reclaiming our schools: A handbook on teaching character, academics, and discipline. New York: Macmillan.

Yang, D., & Yan, K. (1997). (Eds.). *Research on values among university students in China in the contemporary era.* Shanghai: Shanghai Education Press.

PART III

PRACTICES OF CONFLICT AND ENGAGEMENT

Introduction to Part III

One has to believe that if men and women created the ugly world that they are denouncing, then men and women can create a world that is less discriminating and more humane.

—Paulo Freire, Brazilian educator and liberator

Consistent with the epigraph, the authors of the chapters in this part examine activities to "create a world that is less discriminating and more humane," in educational, clinical, and community practices. These analyses contribute to the mission of this book in several unique ways. The interventions to prevent or remedy youth conflict were based on social analyses of the relevant manifestations of youth conflict and the possibilities for creating institutional contexts that made sense in terms of local resources and existing infrastructures. These interventions are then contexts for examining how young people and those who work with them enact motivations for youth conflict, resolution, and the creation of a collective future.

The practices of recovering from violence and preventing the (re)occurrence of violence involve remaining true to the moments of conflict—remembering them, interpreting them, expelling them. Recovery, prevention, and the transformation of society also require activities that go beyond those moments of pain and disbelief, in particular those practices that create a productive future out of a conflicted past. Interventions in educational contexts, clinics, and community organizations must, as these chapters explain most explicitly, involve young people in practices toward the development of society and self.

The authors presenting in this part of the book conducted practice-based research designed to understand youth conflict in the intervention process. Thus, in their work with young survivors of violence in South Africa, Mozambique, and Angola, children living in the streets in Brazil, young people in the midst of violence in Colombia, and children in schools where members of discriminated minorities in a huge ethnically heterogeneous U.S. city meet, the authors of these chapters understand conflicts in the context of programs designed to address the problems of conflicts.

Craig Higson-Smith analyzes ongoing youth conflict in terms of the situations of fragmentation and disempowerment in apartheid South Africa. Higson-Smith explains that South Africa, like other postcolonial societies, is a fertile context for youth conflict and violence, not solely because of poverty, although societies taken and then abandoned by colonizers are overwhelmingly poor, but also because of social, political, cultural, and economic upheaval that lead many young people into situations of conflict. Drawing on clinical work with young people in group work by the Sinani Programme for Survivors of Violence, Higson-Smith offers insights by interweaving history, statistics, and the personal stories of violence and tragedy, which he says are most important for understanding the complexity of youth conflict.

Young people growing up in South Africa during past decades have had to contend with the collision of traditional African, European, and Asian cultures, massive relocations and urbanization, the militarization of society through the apartheid regime and the liberation movements, and civil conflict between different liberation movements. By describing these changes in detail, Higson-Smith's chapter explores how young people are drawn into violent situations and how their motivations and concerns about political and economic realties offer insights for effective intervention. Research with participants in these groups reveals the dynamics of conflict, such as fragmentation and disempowerment, in contrast to those of coexistence.

Clary Milnitsky writes about vulnerability to violence among young people living in the streets in Brazil, focusing on activities in the public sphere of the streets that make children living there excluded and vulnerable. In a fascinating blend of analysis and intervention, Milnitsky and designers of the Casa Harmonia created an intervention to work within the context of the practices of life outside the typical domestic arrangement. In this way, Milnitsky and her colleagues not only adapt interventions to children's lives in the streets but also learn about the activities, meanings, and obstacles there, as well as possible means of transition to more supportive contexts.

Colette Daiute discusses the significance of storytelling as a developmental process that can exacerbate or recast conflict as it guides the behavior of individuals and social groups. In the context of a literacy-based violence prevention program in schools serving diverse ethnic populations, Daiute demonstrates how historical and individual processes come to life for children aged 7 through 11, as their teachers guide students' perceptions of conflicts and suggest strategies to address conflicts. What emerges is an intricate mosaic that foregrounds the problems of society, when we read stories as social scripts, and the consequences of those societal problems for individuals, when we read the same stories as personal. Daiute also offers examples to show how the intra- and interpersonal dimensions of conflict are intimately tied to intergroup conflicts.

Alcinda Honwana offers critical analysis of much of the interventional practice to promote healing among children who have been involved in armed conflict. Honwana opens the world of children's participation in armed conflict in Mozambique and Angola through her analysis of notions of health, mental health, and healing, explaining how those understandings and practices are also fundamental to the well-being of young people, especially in the recent postwar period. After recounting recent history of war and its consequences for refugees, displaced people, disabled people, orphans, widows, infant soldiers, and abused girls, Honwana offers an ethnographic perspective on the sociospiritual systems that account for children's socialization and development. She reports on how local people understand mental health, its relation to the war, and therapies to deal with social and emotional problems via indigenous therapeutic strategies and healing mechanisms, such as treatments and cleansing and purification rituals carried out by diviners, healers, and healing churches, which in rural areas have often been the only mechanisms available to cope with death, illness, distress, and suffering and to restore health, peace, and harmony in the lives of individuals and groups in the postwar period.

Roger Hart and Rocio Mojica describe efforts in Colombia, a society facing extremely high levels of violence and poverty, yet a society that has been creatively developing new ways of building a more participatory culture of citizenship, including many new ways of working with children and youth. Hart and Mojica explain that with the impetus of the UN Convention on the Rights of the Child, Colombia (among other such societies) has made a commitment to develop the potentials of individual children to participate in the creation of civil society. After recounting the history of civil war, poverty, and crime that has plagued Colombia in modern times, Hart and Mojica describe what they learned about increasing children's self-determination and participation through society-building activities in families, homes, and communities, with reference in particular to how these participations offer specific relief from the effects of chronic violence in the environment and more generally to what these activities augur for the development of the society.

Insights About Youth Conflict in Practice

The unique contribution of these chapters is that all involve in the important work of practical theory (Lewin, 1951). These scholars have applied a range of theories and research methods to analyze specific instances of youth conflict and violence in the streets (Milnitsky), in clinical treatment during and after civil wars (Higson-Smith, Honwana, Milnitsky), in governmental and non-governmental organizations (Milnitsky, Higson-Smith), and in educational institutions (Daiute, Hart and Mojica). Such practice-based research has cultural validity and contextual complexity, and, in spite of the difficulty of maintaining certain kinds of scientific proofs, practice-based research tests interventions as well as understandings and actions related to youth conflict. Addressing these concerns, and given appropriate methods to do so, along with analyzing the circumstances, causes, and consequences of youth conflicts among young people and those around them, this research holds more promise for subsequent intervention and policy than laboratory-based research that may provide more scientific control. The practical theory presented in this part thus offers not only information about youth conflict but also innovative methods for expanding practice as well as theory around youth conflict. Innovative research designs, for example, involving youth in storytelling for understanding and peace (Daiute, Higson-Smith), youth participation in research (Hart & Mojica), and other practice-based methods, are thus in place as interventions, which can be modified on the basis of research results.

The practices designed to remedy and understand conflict described in these chapters include, in Mozambique and Angola, young people's participation in cleansing rituals that protect society from the dead, who, in the minds of the participants, want restitution and peace, as well as release former young combatants of their spiritual and psychological pain (Honwana). Practices in South Africa include clinics designed to work with individuals in ways that will ultimately also heal the community and nation (Higson-Smith) and practices in Brazil redefine the clinic in the terms of children living in the street rather than the other way around (Milnitsky). In the United States, practices involve young people living in ethnically heterogeneous contexts rife with discrimination in documentation projects providing personal and group reflection (Daiute). Moving toward the ultimate participation of young people in the government of their society, Hart and Mojica examine conflicts in Colombia in the context of civic engagement of various kinds.

On the basis of participant-observation research with young survivors of armed conflict, Honwana delves into the world of "truth as it seem[s]" to the people involved when she describes effective means of healing within rites of cleansing and purification rituals in Mozambique and Angola.

In the context of a school-based violence prevention program, Daiute examines how children's narration of conflict in different modes to different audiences reveals and promotes reflection on the range of points of view in conflicts and thus transitions to future coexistence.

Also with a focus on children's participation in the future of society out of conflict, Hart and Mojica offer insights about the systemic nature of conflict in relation to several action-oriented programs in Colombia, a country currently riddled with violence among economic interests.

In relation to the projects they describe, these authors discuss efforts to change "the ugly world that they are denouncing" to create a world that is "less discriminating and more humane," as Freire urges. The authors' descriptions of these interventions and analyses of how participants—children and adults—respond to them, change in relation to them, and transform them—offer insights about not only youth conflict but also social and psychological resources for advancing to new social relations.

CHAPTER 10

Youth Violence in South Africa

The Impact of Political Transition

CRAIG HIGSON-SMITH

In the *World Report on Violence and Health* recently released by the World Health Organization, it is estimated that in 2000, violence claimed the lives of 1.6 million people worldwide. Of these deaths, 91% occurred in low- to middle-income countries. Men are more at risk of dying by violence than women, with males accounting for 77% of homicide victims and over 60% of suicidal deaths. Violent death is particularly common among adolescents and young adults, as is clearly illustrated by the average figures for violent deaths in Africa, as shown in figure 10.1.

The report's chapter on youth violence reveals alarming global trends in this phenomenon. Global figures of homicide rates in males aged 10 to 24 years doubled between 1985 and 1994 and continue to rise. Africa, and Central and South America, are the regions with average annual youth homicide rates greater than 12 deaths per 100,000 population (Krug et al., 2002, pp. 274–275).

A closer look at the South Africa statistics is equally alarming. South Africa's National Injury Mortality Surveillance System estimates that between 65,000 and 80,000 South Africans died as a result of nonnatural causes in the year 2000. Once again, 80% of victims were male, most commonly between 25 and 34 years of age. Homicide accounted for 44% of these deaths, suicide 9%, transport accidents 25%, and other accidents 10%. The cause of death in the remaining 12% was not determined (Matzopoulos, van Niekerk, Marais, & Donson, 2002). In a recent survey of young people in Johannesburg, almost

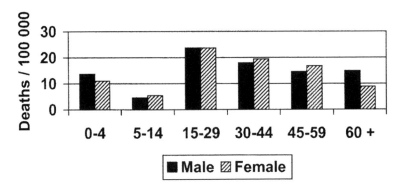

FIGURE 10.1 African Deaths Resulting From Homicide By Age (data from Krug et al., 2002, 274–275)

three out of every ten sexually active males up to the age of 18 admitted having sex with a person without her or his consent. Even more worrying was the fact that 27% of female youth did not consider forced sex with someone known to them to be sexual violence (Andersson et al., 2000).

While statistics about young people and conflict are important, they sometimes mask the diversity of experience that this phenomenon encompasses. The personal stories of violence and tragedy are necessary to understand the complexity of youth conflict. Included throughout this essay are the words of young South Africans collected in group work by the Sinani Programme for Survivors of Violence.[1]

> Thuli witnessed a fight between a girlfriend and boyfriend. The boy shot the girl dead at close range. She couldn't tell anyone what she saw because she was scared.

> The other party tried to drive out the youth, [so] Solly and his friends had to live in the canefield for three months.

> The mother of one of them visited to talk to her son, she was killed when she went home. Now no one feels safe to contact their families.

> He witnessed two friends killing each other because of [different] political affiliation, they were good friends before.

> I saw my sister being raped by a gang, right in front of me. I have never forgotten this image, although we never spoke about it again. I watched as my sister became more and more withdrawn, eventually hardly leaving the house. This made me so angry, and I vowed to revenge. I did not feel able to do this alone, and formed a group of young men willing to assist me. I trained them in fighting skills, and also how to dress and to speak so as to fit in a township setting.

> [Gang members] are so powerful. They can take any women they want. When he saw me, I knew I could hide and avoid him as long as possible, but he would get me eventually.

Social scientists are challenged with identifying what it is about these parts of the world that make them so prone to youth conflict and violence. Although countries in these areas are very often among the poorest in the world, this essay argues that it is not poverty itself but social, political, cultural and economic upheaval that is the best predictor of youth conflict. South Africa is not one of the world's poorest countries, but it is a country where change has led many young people into situations of conflict. Young people growing up in South Africa during past decades have had to contend with the collision of traditional African, European, and Asian cultures, massive relocations and urbanization, the militarization of society through the apartheid regime and the liberation movements, and civil conflict between different liberation movements. By describing these changes in more detail, this chapter explores how young people are drawn into violent situations, and offers some thoughts about more effective intervention.

Collision of Cultures

Early in the sixteenth century, Portuguese sailors, searching for a trade route to India by sea, reached the southernmost tip of Africa. After another 150 years, the first Dutch settlers arrived. Before long, these traders brought in slaves from other parts of Africa and from Southeast Asia. The foundations for a complex multicultural population had been laid, and South Africa would never be the same again. Today, virtually no South African can claim to belong solely to any particular culture. People from rural villages are deeply affected by the values and beliefs of cultures whose origins lie in Europe and America. People whose ancestry is European but whose families have lived in South Africa for several generations find themselves feeling estranged from relatives in the North. In fact, like so much of the world, South Africa is at once a multicultural and an acultural place. In this context, understanding one's own culture often means grappling with the complex, often painful, and ultimately personal issues of identity, loyalty, and belief. The speed with which cultures are changing is such that most young people in South Africa today find their own values and beliefs at odds with those of their parents and grandparents.

With the rapid and ongoing development of communication and travel technology, geographic distance between people is becoming less and less of a barrier between cultures and societies. Although the developing world lags behind many countries of the Northern Hemisphere in this regard, it remains true that diverse cultures are interacting more today than they ever have before.

Stamm, Stamm, Hudnall, and Higson-Smith (2004) have summarized and simplified the process of cultural transformation as it has been repeatedly played out in the past, and is still reenacted today. These authors present cultural transformation as a predictable process that begins in a time of cultural stability before contact with other cultures. Following contact with other cultures, a process of cultural challenge, loss, and reorganization and revitalization ensues.

Eventually this process may result in a new period of cultural stability (see fig. 10.2).

The eras of cultural challenge and loss, with their competing belief systems, disruption of language, culture, and society, changes in economic structure, and so on, contain the seeds for conflict. This model very usefully describes the changes that South African society has experienced since the 17th century, with

Era of cultural stability for "original" culture

- Economy
- Trade
- Government
- Belief system (spirituality)
- Family systems
- Arts/material culture
- Food
- Dress

Cultural clash with "arriving"

Era of cultural clash

- Epidemics or new diseases
- New trade opportunities
- Resource competition
- Warfare with new groups
- Competing belief systems
- Intellectual innovations

Era of cultural loss

- Discontinuity of experience
- Loss of cultural memory
- Loss of language
- Loss of traditional resources
- Poverty
- Poor health care options
- Disruption to families
- Loss of self-rule
- Involuntary relocation

Era of reorganization and revitalization

- Bi- or multi-cultural adaptation
- Choices about self/community
- Protected traditionalism where desired
- Recognized claims on resources
- Recognition of traditional govt.
- Resurgence of language
- Resurgence of spiritual traditions
- Resurgence of cultural symbols
- Increased family stability
- Renewed sense of health

FIGURE 10.2 Modelling cultural change (Stamm, Stamm, Hudnall, and Higson-Smith, 2004)

foreign rule by a colonial power, the dismantling of indigenous social structure and government, and disruption of traditional culture and language. While the developments of the past 10 years—including the change to democratic government, the removal of restrictive and racially based legislation, positive moves toward reconciliation, and the constitutional protection of culture and language—clearly place South Africa within an era of reorganization and revitalization, the legacy of cultural loss in the country's past still resonates through the society as violence.

The Militarization of Society

In 1912, the African National Congress (ANC) was formed with the proclaimed purpose of seeking equality for African people. Under British rule, the Native Land Act of 1913 had begun to restrict land ownership by African people, and legislation was passed to create separate services and amenities for black and white people, and to protect white workers' interests. The National Party, with its mostly Afrikaans-speaking support base, came to power in the elections of 1948. Shortly after coming to power, the National Party government instituted modern apartheid (literally, "apart-ness"). All nonviolent political protests were crushed by the government, and as time went on, the apartheid regime's response to political opposition became more and more brutal.

The apartheid regime and its security forces were not afraid to use their far-reaching powers to effectively silence all opposition within the country. For example, Coleman (1998, p. 14) reports that since 1960, 75,000 persons were detained without trial; of these, at least 25% were children and young people, and 10% were women. Detention might be in solitary confinement and for virtually indefinite periods, with many experiencing detention for as long as 32 months. There is clear evidence of torture in detention. Of course, political repression did not happen only through the formal mechanisms of legislation and legal security force actions. With an extensive network of informants and spies, security forces monitored and harassed suspected political activists and their families. For nearly 35 years, a situation of conflict existed between the liberation movements and the apartheid regime, a conflict that thoroughly militarized South African society and engulfed the lives of virtually all youthful South Africans.

> Sifiso organized a meeting in a church that was surrounded by the police: the police didn't want to listen and started shooting, people ran and some were shot, some were run over by cars. As the person who organized the meeting, he feels to blame.
>
> His brother was killed by police, and Mvume really wanted revenge, but friends talked him out of it.
>
> He witnessed a man being burned by the necklace method.[2] The mob was angry because of the man's action against the community, but it was so cruel to see someone die that way.

An important component of the militarization of South African society was conscription. Until the early 1990s, military service was compulsory for white South African men upon completion of their schooling. For most conscripts, military service consisted of 2 years of basic training, followed by regular military camps for the best part of their adult lives. Military conscripts made up roughly half the full-time forces of the South African Defence Force (SADF).

And yet the militarization of South African society did not only happen through conscription of men into the military. It also occurred through institutions like churches and schools. In 1989, 300,000 white school children participated in school cadet programmes. Evans (1989) lists some topics in cadet training, including: the structure of the SADF, civilian defense, and the nature of the "threat" against South Africa. Training was received in military procedure, as well as various skills of warfare, including concealment and camouflage, firearm training, and tracking.

Most conscripts viewed national service as a rite of passage and as a moral duty to defend their country and religion. At the special hearing for conscripts of the Truth and Reconciliation Commission (TRC), it was convincingly argued that, at the age of 17 or 18, these young men had neither the tools nor the information required to challenge the dominant ideology of the country (Truth and Reconciliation Commission [TRC], 1998, vol. 4, ch. 8).

Militarization of schoolchildren and young adults was also a feature of life for black South Africans. Schoolchildren played a leading role in the Soweto Uprising of 1976, and for the next 15 years young people continued to leave the country to join the ANC in exile, many of them to receive training in guerrilla warfare and return to the country as soldiers of the liberation struggle. The militarization of schools meant that when virtually all South African boys and many girls left school, they had already been groomed to take their place within the military machinery of the apartheid forces or the liberation movements.

Civil Conflict

One form of violence that is seldom spoken about in relation to South Africa is the civil conflict that lasted for nearly 20 years between the followers of the ANC and the Inkatha Freedom Party (IFP). Although this conflict has its roots in KwaZulu-Natal (a province on the country's eastern seaboard), it spilled over into high levels of civil violence in communities around Johannesburg. One of the first acts of the apartheid government was to create separate residential areas for people of different ethnic backgrounds, South Africa's "homelands." One such homeland had been created for the Zulu people and was named KwaZulu. KwaZulu was governed by the KwaZulu Administration under Chief Gatsha Buthelezi, a well known Zulu leader and significant person in the antiapartheid movement. As a result of his participation within government structures, he was perceived to have become more politically moderate, and this placed him at odds with the ANC leadership. Buthelezi opposed the ANC's policies of armed struggle and economic sanctions.

In 1980, young people sympathetic to the ANC organized protests and school boycotts within KwaZulu. Buthelezi campaigned actively against these protests, and used paramilitary groups of his own young supporters to stop these protests. With the liberation movement irreconcilably divided by these events and ideological differences, the people of KwaZulu-Natal were forced during these early years to choose between the ANC and the Inkatha Freedom Movement (later to become the IFP). By aligning themselves explicitly with one or other political movement, people were guaranteed a degree of protection for themselves, their families, and their property. Whole communities were declared "no go zones" for opposition groups, and anyone living in those communities who did not publicly express allegiance to the appropriate movement was driven from his or her home by violence and intimidation. In this way, virtually the entire province of KwaZulu-Natal was divided into ANC and IFP areas.

> Residents from another section came over the hill and fired on Eugene's family, burning houses and driving them away, they had to run to the Indian area.

> The chief told them to leave the area, Lungile's father was killed, now she and her family have no home.

As the situation worsened, leaders within the ANC and IFP camps established and trained local paramilitary structures. Drawn largely from the ranks of adolescent men in the community, these structures were named self-defence units (SDUs) on the side of the ANC, and self-protection units (SPUs) on the side of the IFP. In 1990, as the conflict continued to escalate, the word "war" was used for the first time.

> Headlines trumpeted the news in huge bold print: "Natal on the boil"; "Thousands in impi attack";[3] " 'War' in Maritzburg!" . . . Among the public at large, and even in the editorial columns of certain newspapers, the prevailing reaction was one of bewilderment. (Kentridge, 1990)

Although the conflict is still not entirely over today, levels of violence have vastly diminished. To date, the conflict in KwaZulu-Natal has claimed approximately 15,000 lives. A further 25,000 people have been seriously injured and handicapped. As many as 500,000 people have been displaced from their homes and communities (Higson-Smith, 2002; Jeffery, 1997).

Intervention With Youth

One of the challenges of understanding youth conflict is the complex, multilayered nature of the phenomenon. Ecological models of society such as those first used by Bronfenbrenner (1979) and Garbarino (1985) are very useful in this regard. A four-level model of society is proposed, the four levels being the individual person, the small group, geographically defined communities, and society as a whole. To understand a social phenomenon such as youth violence, we need to understand it at multiple interdependent levels (see fig. 10.3).

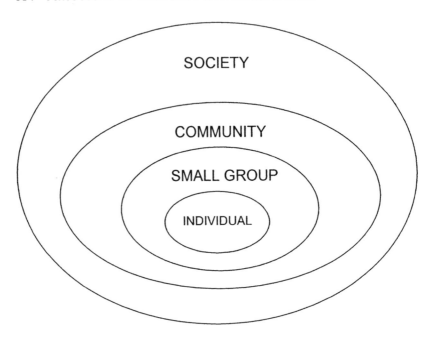

FIGURE 10.3 Systemic Model of Society

A brief case study illustrates this model. A young man who has become involved in a civil conflict as a member of a paramilitary group becomes involved in local peace initiatives. When things do not work out as he intended, he is accused of "selling out" to the enemy. Since other youths have been murdered for this "crime" in his community, such accusations are extremely frightening and traumatic (individual effects). However, such victimization is seldom restricted to the individual and very often family and friends are similarly threatened. In some cases, families are forced to protect themselves by turning against the individual or fleeing the community (small group effects). Such suspicion and threat within communities makes individuals very reluctant to be seen with people and agencies from beyond the community. This isolates the community from important developmental opportunities (community effects). Where this situation exists in numerous communities, social services, including health, welfare, education, and security, become compromised (societal effects).

At the level of the individual, we are concerned with the personal histories, beliefs, values, and psychologies of people. At the small group level, family dynamics, friendships, work colleagues, and the other most significant human relationships of our lives are of great importance. At the level of community we are concerned with neighbourhood dynamics, schooling, religious practices, sporting, and other social structures. Finally, the level of society involves the issues of international relations, economic differences, wars, and other macrolevel dynamics.

Going further in the analysis of the effects of civil violence on communities, we focus on each level in turn. If one lists all the different effects of civil violence at a particular level, one finds that it is possible to classify them all into two interrelated categories. The effects of violence at all levels are all to do with either *disempowerment* or *fragmentation* (Higson-Smith, 1999, 2002).

The word *disempowerment* has come to have many different meanings in different contexts and has therefore lost some of its usefulness. As I will use it here, disempowerment refers to the way violence prevents individuals, families, and other small groups, as well as community structures, from fulfilling their function or original purpose. For example, not having a safe place to play is disempowering to children, whose function is (in part) to play freely and develop to their full intellectual, physical, and emotional capacity. This is an effect at the individual level. When parents are caught up in basic survival strategies, they are disempowered in fulfilling their role as parents and guardians of the family. This is a small group effect. Similarly, when local political parties take over the role of ensuring the safety of the community (through paramilitary forces, "kangaroo courts", etc.), the local police are unable to carry out their intended function. This is a community-level effect. When seen in this light, a wide range of the effects of violence can be understood as disempowering in one sense or another.

Fragmentation refers to the breakdown that happens within individuals, small groups, and within and between community structures due to violence. When children are sent away from their homes to stay with relatives in safer communities, the family is fragmented (small group level). When community structures become so distrustful of outside service agencies that those agencies are prevented from working in the area, the entire community is fragmented (community level). Those effects of violence that are not disempowering are fragmenting.

When presented with a model of this kind, derived largely from "Western" styles of thought, it is worth asking whether there are meaningful connections to the experience of people who think in different ways. The following are the words of a 21-year-old South African man reflecting on his life.

> Violence affected me and my fellow youth, as the community is now divided. Those who got or have an education look down on youth who did not get an education. There is a great deal of tension between these two groups. The SAP [South African Police] had a hand in violence, and this resulted in me having a deep hatred of the police. Violence also resulted in us losing our education, losing our relationship with our parents, and I have to take part in some activities which are illegal. But I need the money. I need some sort of way to make a living. I see people who have something and I envy them and the only way to get it, to get where they are, is the illegal way. Envy and hatred is always a part of me. I know it's no use to cry over spoilt milk, over a mad situation, no use to fight to get what you want.

The words of African traditional healer Malidoma Some from Burkino-Fase sum up these ideas very elegantly: "there are two things that people crave: the full realisation of their innate gifts, and to have those gifts approved, acknowledged, and confirmed" (1998, p. 27).

Conceptualizing youth violence in terms of disempowerment and fragmentation provides us with a framework to understand these complex social dynamics. Similarly, by planning our interventions around the contrasting concepts of *empowerment* and *linking,* we can ensure that we consistently work in a therapeutic and developmental way (see fig. 10.4).

As described earlier, interventions must be multidimensional in order to impact effectively on this multidimensional phenomenon. A short list of potential interventions are listed in figure 10.5. However, an integrated intervention strategy must be devised for particular youth conflict issues in particular communities.

The Sinani Programme for Survivors of Violence (SPSV) has found that work with youth in small groups is highly effective and often neglected. This is because many young people are already organized into small groups of various kinds, including clubs, paramilitary units, and gangs. Also, small groups allow young people to support each other and develop interpersonal skills that will serve them well in the future.

Small Group Work: Structure

It is necessary and appropriate that youth groups be run on a "open" basis—in other words, that people are free to enter and leave the group as they like. It is acceptable to come to one or two group meetings in order to test the waters, and to bring friends to the group meeting. "Closed" groups tend to be exclusive, in that some people will always be prevented from becoming members of the

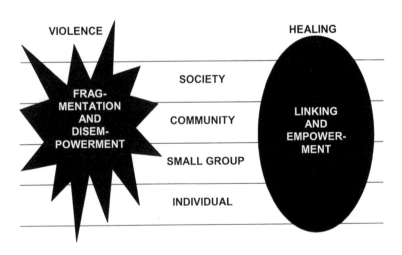

FIGURE 10.4 Linking and Empowerment

Individual	Small Group	Community	Society
• Education and training for employment • Career counseling • Trauma therapy • Life skills, especially communication, building relationships, managing frustration and anger, money	• Youth participation in civil society • Joint income generation • Community activism and service • Youth leadership development	• Local peacemaking work • Local employment projects • Recreation facilities • Intergenerational dialogues	• Policy to facilitate youth entry into labor force • Public awareness of youth concerns • Recognition of youth social contributions • Effective youth offender diversion

FIGURE 10.5 Overview of Youth Intervention Strategies

group. When this happens in a highly suspicious and fragmented community, the potential for increased conflict is raised, and community workers rapidly lose the trust of the people they are working with. It is common that youth groups in these communities will be closely monitored and that a couple of young people closely linked to the political leadership in the area will attend on an irregular basis.

Group Content

In line with the foregoing, the group members themselves determine the content of group sessions. Sessions deal with subjects that are important for meeting the challenges of adolescence, both those in a more stable and safe society and those of reaching adulthood in a society experiencing or recovering from civil conflict. Some important and common areas of work are as follows.

Managing feelings. It is common for adolescents to struggle with managing their own feelings. These struggles are magnified by the experiences of betrayal, exploitation, loss, and victimization that are part of civil conflict. Many of the young people in our groups are filled with sadness, rage, frustration, jealousy, and hopelessness. For the most part these feelings remain hidden, but they surface repeatedly to sabotage personal progress. Learning how to recognize and express these feelings safely and in an appropriate way is an important learning experience.

> I came to this workshop a very shy person carrying a lot of helplessness and hopelessness, but I feel I was being heard and taken seriously by other participants in the group. I felt I was ready to pursue a new life. (youth group member)

Negotiating relationships. Adolescence is also a time of negotiating and renegotiating relationships with peers, possible love partners, parents, potential employers, and other people within the community. When young people are burdened with all the destructive feelings outlined in the previous paragraph, the business of building relationships becomes extremely arduous. Furthermore, as a result of having spent many adolescent years within paramilitary structures or on the run, young people have often not had opportunities to develop these important life skills. When all strangers are regarded as potential threats, one does not learn how to start and sustain a conversation, express one's feelings honestly but responsibly, trust others and to be trustworthy, give and receive constructive feedback, and so forth.

Many young people in our groups fail to build the relationships necessary for their lives to progress in a healthy fashion. The group provides formal and informal learning opportunities. Formally, group sessions often include work such as "boys like . . . and girls like" (a debate around how to form relationships with people of the opposite gender), "my parents don't understand that . . ." (intergenerational relationship building), assertiveness training, and so forth. Informally, the groups put young people in a situation where they cannot help but build relationships with strangers (including group facilitators), other young people in the group, and—through youth projects—other people within their communities and beyond.

It is vitally important that, in order to be empowered, youth develop confidence in their ability to build relationships. This confidence comes from mastery, in other words, getting it obviously right, and through positive feedback from others. Youth workers are on hand to try to ensure that young people do successfully negotiate relationships and to help them recognize this when they do. Of course, this means working with some very difficult interpersonal dynamics as young people struggle to relate effectively, which can be extremely stressful at times. It is most important during this time that young people do not fail in their relationship-building attempts. While success and praise builds a sense of mastery, failure entrenches the sense of hopelessness and helplessness.

The benefit of work on managing feelings and negotiating relationships has become apparent in an unexpected way. One of the ways youth groups assist young people is by helping them identify opportunities to develop skills to enable them to generate their own income. Thus, many young men and women simultaneously attend youth groups and employment skills training courses. These courses are run by other agencies that specialize in that work and are linked to the KZN-PSV. Two chronic problems faced by employment skills training agencies is that of a high number of dropouts from their courses, and people completing their courses being dismissed from their new jobs. An evaluation of the training agency's work demonstrated that young men and women who were also involved in KZN-PSV's groups were better able to contain their frustrations and anger in the training courses and job situation. In addition, they were better able to develop supportive relationships with trainers and employers and to resolve problems before those problems resulted in them dropping out of the course or being dismissed from work.

Personal development and culture. Many young people are troubled by distress that originates in their life histories or current situations. Although this distress is often easily comparable with anxiety disorders (such as posttraumatic and acute stress disorders) and mood disorders (most commonly different forms of depression), it is unhelpful in the vast majority of cases to offer any kind of diagnosis to youth group members. Where mental health services are virtually nonexistent, little is gained from adding a stigmatizing label to existing problems.

As an alternative, the youth group can fulfil a number of different roles relating to mental health and ill health. First, the group provides a vehicle for emotional expression among peers and emotional support from them. In a sense, the group provides the setting for the "exposing to view" rituals that enable young people to recognize what has happened to them and to their communities, and to build a shared history. Second, the group provides a forum for talking about different ways of coping. Young people develop many strategies to cope with the pain of their past experiences and the reality of their current situations. Some are effective, and others are ultimately destructive. In group sessions, we talk about effective coping and share ideas and strategies. Third, the group allows for learning about emotional and mental health in a way that equips people to better manage their own situations. For example, some of the symptoms of traumatic stress, such as flashbacks, are associated in the popular perception with psychosis, or "madness." Discussions of what flashbacks are and why people experience them increases the possibility of control, and is thus empowering.

One group participant had the following to say about his mental health and the group:

> I get upset easily, I do not trust any one and have no confidence in myself. Emotionally, I'm upside down. . . . In the group I learn that I am not alone in such a situation. When I am alone I am self-blaming, self-hating, but as part of the group I can see a way forward.

Finally, the group provides an opportunity for young people to access individual counseling for themselves and the broader circle of people within the community with whom they interact. The SPSV employs two people whose main activity in the organization is assisting those people who, for whatever reasons, cannot be assisted in groups run within the community.

Adolescents more than any other component of South African society are caught between the diverse cultures of our country. Childhoods often have been rooted firmly in African traditional culture, but there has been exposure through education, the media, and personal contact with the "merchandising" of the West, with members of political parties struggling alternatively for a revival of traditional rulership or a multiparty democracy. These young people are simultaneously expected to value the traditional coming-of-age ceremonies, designer jeans, and freedom of speech. These examples are illustrative of the deep divisions in ideology and loyalty with which many young people are forced to contend. Naturally, the assumption that these people are the same as "Western" adolescents is false. However, it is important to note that the assumption that they are "African" is equally so. In fact, they are conflicted, multicultural, and acultural. Working with culture in this sense means grappling with the complex, often painful, and ultimately personal issues of identity, loyalty, and belief.

> The youth are carrying so much. I always forget how much they have been through, and each time I hear the stories I am shocked all over again. (SPSV staff member)

Skills training. Youth groups also include a range of skills development activities. These skills can be thought of as falling within three broad categories. The first category relates to personal skills (one of which, negotiating relationships, I have already discussed). Other personal skills include language skills, personal presentation, decision-making, stress management, and time management. Language is important, because these young people have missed out on developing their command of the English language. Good spoken English is a very important skill for finding employment in KwaZulu-Natal. Because youth do not have many opportunities to practice their English with fluent English speakers, they sometimes ask that group sessions be conducted in English.

The second category of skills involves actual training for employment. Many young people are lacking in skills due to the early disruption of their education. They need opportunities to develop skills to make them more employable. Without reasonable possibilities of earning an income and supporting themselves, it is virtually impossible for these men and women to make progress in their lives.

The SPSV does not have the technical or personnel capacity to offer employment skills training directly and so works in partnership with a range of other structures (mostly nongovernmental as well) that do offer training in a wide variety of work skills, including brick-laying, plumbing, electrical installation and repair work, tiling, painting, metal work, secretarial work, and computer skills. Acquiring these skills takes an enormous amount of commitment and concentration on the part of young people who have not participated in formal education for several years and are carrying the emotional baggage that results from years of civil conflict. The dropout rates are high, and even for those who do complete the training, the current employment situation in KwaZulu-Natal (indeed, in South Africa generally) is extremely problematic and appears to be worsening. However, with support and encouragement, we do see young men and women who have completed their training finding odd jobs that they use to demonstrate their ability, then getting short contract work, and eventually ending up in full-time employment. It is a bitter struggle to become economically self-sufficient, and the staff of the SPSV work hard to make young people aware of this from the very beginning.

Again it is important that youth are not led to believe that if they attend a certain training course then they will easily find a job and earn an income and then their life circumstances will improve swiftly. In reality, this is extremely unlikely, and when, after putting in an enormous amount of work under difficult circumstances, the young person's false expectations are not met, the feelings of betrayal and helplessness undermine any positive progress that he or she has made.

Young women often find themselves in a particularly difficult position with regard to employment skills. Zulu communities do not encourage women to search for jobs. "Women's work" is clearly defined and is largely restricted to household duties, child-rearing, and subsistence farming. For this reason, relatively few young women seek out job skills and employment for themselves. Those who do find themselves with fewer opportunities, since the training agencies tend to focus largely on construction-type work, and so they end up competing for work in an environment where employers favor men. In addition, these young women find themselves in opposition to their parents, elders, and community leaders. In these cases, their only support comes from the other young men and women in the youth group and the group's facilitators.

The third category of skills training involves those skills required to plan and implement community projects. As noted earlier, these young people are not in school and are not working, and so there exist few opportunities (with the exception of those on the battlefield) to demonstrate competence and ability. In order for people in this position to develop self-esteem they must be involved in something constructive. For this reason, the staff of the SPSV involve youth in community projects of their own choosing and design. These community projects have included raising poultry to generate income and making bricks for building houses, as well as organizing talent and beauty contests, film shows, and other events for young people in their community. Where possible, these projects generate enough income to send group members on work skills training courses and to meet other expenses that the group might incur.

Conclusion

In conclusion, through individual work, work in groups, and participation in youth projects, the community workers of the SPSV are striving to help young people develop their skills and the confidence to realize their goals, including returning their communities to peace. This is done through assisting them to master the challenges of adolescence and young adulthood (empowerment) and to form productive relationships with their peers, their families, and with people and organizations in their own community and the broader society (linking). The following is an extract from a poem by a young woman who is starting to reclaim her dignity and vision (Philisiwe Gomba, in Malange, McKay, and Nhlengetwa, 1996, p. 53).

> Who the hell are you to call us the lost generation?
> Where were you when we needed guidance?
> Where were you when we needed you to nourish our delicate minds?
> So we say, we were never lost, but ignored.
> We were never lost, but deprived. . . .
>
> The future is in our hands.
> Let us mould what is left of it,
> For we can make a difference.

Let us be a rolling stone and gather no moss
For it will cover our beauty.

Notes

1. *Sinani* is Zulu for "standing together."
2. "Necklacing" involved placing a car tire filled with petrol around a person's neck and lighting the petrol. This particularly violent form of killing was usually reserved for alleged spies and traitors to the liberation struggle.
3. "Impi" is a Zulu word referring to a unit of soldiers.

References

Andersson, N., Mhatre, S., Naidoo, S., Mayet, N., Mqotse, N.; Penderis, M.; Myburg, M., & Merhi, S. (2000). *Beyond victims and villains: The culture of sexual violence in South Johannesburg*. Johannesburg: Community Information and Epidemiological Technologies.

Archer, S. (1989). Defense expenditure and arms procurement in South Africa. In J. Cock & L. Nathan (Eds.), *War and society: The militarization of South Africa* (pp. 244–261). Cape Town: David Phillip.

Bronfenbrenner, V. (1979). *The ecology of human development: experiments by nature and design*. Cambridge, MA: Harvard University Press.

Coleman, M. (Ed.). (1998). *A crime against humanity: Analysing the repression of the apartheid state*. Cape Town. David Philips.

Evans, G. (1989). Classrooms of war: The militarization of white South African schooling. In J. Cock & L. Nathan (Eds.), *War and society: The militarization of South Africa* (pp. 283–297). Cape Town: David Phillip.

Garbarino, J. (1985). *Adolescent development: an ecological perpective*, Columbus, OH: Merrill.

Higson-Smith, C. (1999). "Linking" and "empowering": Key concepts for intervention following war and disaster. *Development in Practice, 9*(3), 39–48.

Higson-Smith, C. (2002). *Supporting communities affected by violence: A casebook from South Africa*. Oxford: Oxfam.

Jeffrey, A. (1997). The Natal story: Sixteen years of conflict. Johannesburg: South African Institute of Race Relations.

Kentridge, M. (1990). An unofficial war: Inside the conflict in Pietermaritzburg. Cape Town: David Philip.

Krug, E. G., Dahlberg, L. L., Mercy, J. A., Zwi, A. B., & Lozano, R. (Eds.). (2002). *World report on violence and health*. Geneva: World Health Organisation.

Malange, N., McKay, A., & Nhlengetwa, Z. (1996). On common ground. Durban: KwaZulu-Natal Programme for Survivors of Violence.

Matzopoulos, R., van Niekerk, A., Marais, S., & Donson, H. (2002). A profile of fatal injuries in South Africa: Towards a platform for safety promotion. *African Safety Promotion, 1,* 16–22.

Some, M. P. (1998). *The healing wisdom of Africa: Finding life purpose through nature, ritual and community*. New York: Tarcher.

Stamm, B., Stamm, H., Hudnall, A.C., & Higson-Smith, C. (2004). Considering a theory of cultural trauma and loss. *Journal of Loss and Trauma, 9,* 89–111.

Truth and Reconciliation Commission. (1998). *Final Report of the Truth and Reconciliation Commission: Vols. 1–5.* Pretoria: South African Truth and Reconciliation Commission. Available: http://www.polity.org.za/govdocs/commissions/1998/trc/index .htm.

CHAPTER 11

Becoming Visible Through the Lens of Violence

The Social Exclusion of Youth in Brazil

CLARY MILNITSKY

This chapter provides an account of the major factors that lead a large percentage of Brazilian youth to take up life on the streets, a place where they become highly vulnerable to violence and associated problems. It also describes some of the lessons learned from studies (Abreu e Silva, 2000; Abreu e Silva & Milnitsky-Sapiro, 2002; Boff, 2002; Kuchembecker, 2000) conducted as part of an ongoing action-research program designed to improve the conditions of street children. This project has involved the work of several professionals who perform socioeducational activities for governmental programs designed for children and youth in vulnerable conditions in Porto Alegre, a large city in southern Brazil. The challenges faced by this program raise important questions for theories of adolescent development. The factors affecting Brazilian youth most vulnerable to street life and all that it entails include processes of social exclusion and marginalization. Thus, a thorough account of the phenomenon of street children requires a sociological analysis of broad economic and societal trends, as well as a contextualized description of fundamental processes of individual identity formation (Violante, 1995; Carnegie Council on Adolescent Development, 1995). For this reason, the issues addressed in this chapter highlight the importance of adopting an interdisciplinary approach to understanding the underlying causes and developmental processes implicated in the lives of street youth. Such an interdisciplinary theoretical approach is also needed if we are to have an effective impact upon this very complex social problem.

As already mentioned, the situation of street children within Brazil is an acute problem. Accurate data about the numbers of children and adolescents who live on the streets in Brazil are hard to come by (Rizzini, 2004). Street youth frequently move to different *mocós* (places for hiding and sleeping), and from there, to different shelters or institutions (Instituto Brasileiro de Geografia e Estatística [IBGE], 2003). Nonetheless, estimates have been made of the numbers of street children through means of surveys and census data. The number of children between 10 and 17 years of age who work and live in the streets was estimated in 2002 to be about 250,000. This number represents roughly 1 out of every 20 of the working-class children of Brazil (IBGE, 2003). This is an alarming situation by any measure, and calls for public action.

Unfortunately, the prevailing models that have guided many of the interventions directed toward Brazilian street children have maintained that the condition of "being in the streets" is a choice made by the children. This attribution of street life as a choice has been accompanied by the view that engagement in street life is an indication of autonomy. This, in turn, has led to the misapplication of article 16 of the Federal Constitution and the Statute of Children and Adolescents, which protects the rights of children from the power of the state. Thus, many well-meaning public policies, such as the Programs of Social Education in the Streets founded in 1992, directed at street children have served to maintain the children at a subsistence level rather than to enable them to leave the street life. Our program has rejected this account of the motivations that lead children into street life. Instead, we have worked on the basis that social conditions, for which all Brazilians have shared responsibility, have left a large number of children with no option but life on the street.

In terms of developmental theory, the approach we have taken to understanding the challenges faced by street youth has employed an admixture, if not a complete integration, of theories of identity formation (Dolto & Dolto-Tolitch, 1993; Erikson, 1968; Rassial, 1997), depth psychology (Freud, 1958/1995; Rassial, 1997), and social-cognitive accounts of the development of moral and social reasoning (Turiel, 1983, 2002). Each of these approaches shares a view of the young person as actively engaged in the construction of a sense of self within a sociocultural and moral landscape. However, none of these theoretical approaches in isolation provides a sufficiently comprehensive framework for the work we hoped to undertake. Therefore, as we approached our effort to both research and to help to socially integrate these vulnerable youth, we set out to design a program that incorporated an interdisciplinary form of care that incorporated attention to basic physical, psychological, and educational needs (basic academics), with provision for sociomoral education as well. The question we constantly asked ourselves was how to fill in or compensate for the affective and cognitive gaps suffered in infancy and childhood by the so-called street children so that they might attain some better future as common citizens.

As we embraced the psychological accounts that provided a lens through which to understand and work with youth, we needed to also contextualize our approach to fit the specifics of adolescent development within contemporary Brazil. These factors include cultural and economic factors particular to Brazil, as well as transnational trends resulting from modern communications and a globalized economy that influence events within Brazil. In particular, we needed to adjust our thinking to address the atypical circumstances that form the life-world of street children. The following section outlines some of the ways transnational trends have impacted Brazilian society and culture and in turn, the life-world of street children. The next section takes up the ways in which contemporary media have altered the ways Brazilian adolescents and parents interact. This is followed by a discussion of how these currents in Brazilian culture influence the identity, social values, and behavior of young people who end up among Brazil's street children. The final sections outline the intervention program we have undertaken, and present the conclusions and recommendations that emerge from that effort.

Globalization, Contemporary Western Culture, and the Brazilian Context

The past half-century has been a period in which rapid changes in modes of transportation, communication, and commerce have converged to form a global economy. Along with this globalized economy has been the globalization of Western culture and the capitalist ideology that has fueled this economic integration. These macro trends have created a new set of developmental "universals" apart from the ontological changes captured by traditional developmental theories (Hall, 1997). In Vygotskian (Rogoff, 2003) terms, these transformations have altered the cultural tools and symbols that frame the development of contemporary youth. The contemporary context includes transnational values of consumerism and the corollary notion of disposable commodities that seeps into the construction of interpersonal relationships (Milnitsky-Sapiro, 1996). As a result, there is a potential for the application of the commodity metaphor to enter into social relations, particularly when applied to the social networks that would serve to protect the more vulnerable members of society (Abreu e Silva, 2000; Abreu e Silva & Milnitsky-Sapiro, 2002; Milnitsky-Sapiro, Cestari, & Giongo, 1996; Milnitsky-Sapiro & Tavares, 1993; Ruffino, 1995).

This emphasis on commodities exacerbates the fringe status of individuals living in poverty within what on the surface appears to be "the only acceptable way to live." Therefore, the families and children struggling to meet the most basic necessities cannot help but see themselves at at the fringes of society when all around them are signs of material comfort and objects of consumerism to be identified with. Official demographic census data within emerging nations such as Brazil now include indicators of social class defined by such consumer goods as the number of domestic appliances—superfluous or not (Berman, 1986; Lasch, 1987; Valsiner, 1989). Consumerism has an especially poignant effect upon the construction of identity in adolescence. In adolescence, the need to be identified as someone who belongs to a group in society becomes exacerbated by the need to use certain clothing such as hats, jeans, tennis shoes, and so on. The many faces of Benneton staring out from billboards in their stylish clothing are seen by not only the affluent of Europe and North America but also the poverty-stricken children and adolescents of Porto Alegre. Consequently, it is not difficult to imagine how stigmatized youth can feel under these life conditions (Milnitsky-Sapiro, Berman, Briones, & Kurtines, 1995).

Adolescence in Contemporary Brazil

One impact of globalization has been the expansion to Brazilian society of the contemporary Western cultural mandate to be and stay young—in body, mind, and behavior (Giongo, 1988; Milnitsky-Sapiro & Menegaz, 2002; Rassial, 1997). In order to accomplish this requirement, an adult needs to straddle "age boundaries." The Brazilian media currently presents most middle-class mothers and fathers as acting more as "friends" of their adolescent children than parents. The symbolic consequences of these role shifts are being studied in psychology. This recent work indicates that the impact of the blurring of generational lines ranges from young people lacking internalization of limits to forms of delinquency, such as "acting out" (Abreu e Silva, 2000; Abreu e Silva & Milnitsky-Sapiro, 2002; Giongo, 1988; Ruffino, 1995).

The blurring of generational boundaries compounds the already complex task of the adolescent transition from childhood to adult status and roles. Dolto and Dolto-Tolitch (1993) refer to the "lobster complex" as a metaphor for the physical and psychological transition that all adolescents traverse. The lobster can only grow by shedding its outer shell and surviving unprotected as it grows a new shell to accommodate its larger size. According to this metaphor, like the lobster, adolescents experience the loss of their childhood bodies, while at the same time trying to situate themselves in peer and family social milieus and roles that are simultaneously "nonchild and nonadult." In a culture in which the adults are not clearly demarcated as distinct from the youth, the process of locating oneself within this postchildhood period comes to be increasingly defined by commercial products and media stereotypes. This period of vulnerability, captured by Erikson (1968) and others (Milnitsky-Sapiro & Menegaz, 2001; Oliveira, 2001; Outeiral, 1994; Rassial, 1997; Ruffino, 1995) as an adolescent identity crisis, impacts working-class and poor children as well as the children of the Brazilian middle class. For those who face life on the streets, these transitions occur without the social support provided by home and school. The crosscurrents of contemporary Brazilian culture that are producing strains and stresses for youth growing up within middle-class surroundings are amplified for the young of the street, who now must negotiate the same period of vulnerability without the resources to compete for the material goods that define contemporary social identity. This is not to minimize the struggle the street children face merely to survive in the most basic sense of having enough food to eat and a safe place to sleep. However, much of the frustration and anger we see in such youth is compounded by the constraints their condition places upon their ability to construct social membership and a shared identity with mainstream adolescent culture.

Having described some of the broader contextual issues, I will now turn to a more detailed discussion of the conditions and subculture of Brazilian adolescent street children.

The Culture and Identity of the "Adolescents Who Live in the Streets"

The following discussion draws from our experience working with street children in Porto Alegre, the capital city of the relatively affluent and most southern Brazilian state of Rio Grande do Sul. The picture that follows, however, can be applied to most cities throughout the country. Ethnographic methods (Fetterman, 1998) employed in two different studies (Kuchembecker, 2000; Milnitsky-Sapiro, 1999) led to the conclusion that street life presents youth with social conditions and conflicts that almost inevitably lead them into patterns of crime and drug addiction. Perhaps the most salient factor is the psychological pain of being permanently exposed to the public sphere, with almost no privacy.

The children who enter street life tend to come from family circumstances that are unstable and often abusive. The mothers of street children most commonly have given birth to three or more children by different fathers (Milnitsky, Dutra, Coelho, & Correa, 1995). These women are frequently alcoholic and without regular employment. Generally, the birth father is missing, and a stepfather forms a transitory presence in the children's lives. These typically short-lived mother-"spouse" relationships tend to facilitate authoritative and abusive behavior by the "stepfathers" toward the children. The abuse suffered at the hands of the transitory "stepfather" and chaotic family ties are often the main reasons that these children run away from home.

Once they enter the streets, there is a noticeable, gradual transformation in their outward appearance that makes them easily distinguished from other young people (Kuchembecker, 2000). The newly arrived look better nourished, and better dressed. The stress of street life and the lack of consistent nourishment gradually leads to deterioration in their teeth and hair. If they remain in the street life for an extended period of time, they tend to be shorter in stature than other children of the same age. Their clothing is made up of discards worn previously by others, and is often oversized. The initial timid look of the recent arrival becomes "sharper." It also becomes difficult to guess their ages, because they tend to be sadder in appearance and shorter than other children. All of this combines to make the street child easily identifiable in the public sphere.

Their lifestyle is one of nomadic shifting from downtown locations to locations where there are makeshift shelters fashioned out of discarded lumber or available cardboard. As reported by Kuchenbecker and Milnitsky-Sapiro (2002), the instability of their prior home life and resulting fluidity of family attachments leads street children to approach strangers almost as relatives, who they call out to as "uncle" or "aunt" when begging for food or spare change: for example, "Do you have some change, "aunt," do you? I haven't eaten anything today" (João, 13 years old). The absence of adults creates a children's underworld, in which groups of youngsters band together in surrogate families (Milnitsky-Sapiro et al., 1995) generally with an older adolescent male in the role of "father" or group leader. This leader extracts payment from the daily take of his younger charges and punishes the children who try to hide some of the money they get. Most frequently, the leader "teaches a lesson" with a physical punishment, "so they don't forget" (Mauricio, 17 years old) (Milnitsky-Sapiro et al., 1995).

This life on the street is public, in that essentially all aspects of the children's lives are in plain view of the city's other residents. This creates a paradoxical situation in which the adolescent is without recourse to the sanctity of a home in which she or he can create the private space and personal domain requisite for normal identity formation (Nucci, Camino, & Milnitsky-Sapiro, 1996). At the same time, the constant public exposure results in a form of anonymity in which the street child becomes an invisible virtual "nobody" (Craidy, 1998). Being spectators of a publicly protected middle-class life through many gates and windows (of stores, shops, television shops, cars) makes the street children realize that they do not have much or anything to lose, when dealing with their lives or with the others as well, since to people "on the other side of this virtual space," they do not exist (Calligaris, 1993). Consider the following statement from an adolescent girl, Leci, that appeared in the August 2004 edition *Boca-de-Rua,* a newspaper produced in Porto Alegre for street children.

> We do what we can to survive and we don't have a time to stop working. During the day, we catch papers to sell to recycle, at night we wash cars until 2:00 am, when we go to the shelter, there are no beds left, then we stay in the street with all this winter cold. Then, the City Hall cleaning trucks come shooting the cold water and expelling everybody; I stand up and show them my ID, I tell them I am a citizen, they don't care. (América Latina Interconectada com Europa [ALICE], 2004)

As opposed to all who benefit from the transit between the spheres of the public and private, in which the streets serve as a functional place to anyone, the lack of privacy to the homeless children and adolescents makes them become virtual nobodies. The social representation of a home in all human societies portrays the image of privacy, warmness, and protection from nature and public life. In fact, one's home is a metaphor for oneself. According to Graciani (1997), the adolescents who live in the streets are nonadolescents, in the sense of the denial of their needs and rights and the exclusion of their human condition (because of their daily life in extreme circumstances, they are not allowed, as other youth are, to pass through an identity crisis related to issues of profession or belief). This public invisibility serves to insulate the public from its responsibilities to these children and exacerbates the negative consequences of street life for both the children and the public. Let us turn, then to a more in-depth discussion of this "invisibility."

The Invisibility of the Excluded

Hannah Arendt, in *The Human Condition*, discusses the phenomenon of the private sphere of life (the household), as opposed to the public sphere, or political realm. Distinctive elements before modernism, their limits became blurred by the emergence of the social realm, "which is neither private nor public, strictly speaking, [and] is a relatively new phenomenon whose origin is coincident with the emergence of the modern age and which found its political form in the nation-state" (1958/1983, p. 28). The concept of family belongs to the private realm but is also encompassed by the social realm, "because we see the body of peoples and political communities in the image of a family whose everyday affairs have to be taken care of by a gigantic, nation-wide administration of housekeeping" (p. 28). In which of these realms could we locate the "socially vulnerable children at risk," since they are actually excluded or exiled to a place that is neither private nor public but an invisible nonsocial realm?

Craidy explains that the street has a different meaning for the ones who are passing by or for people who have a direction such as going to work or walking in a promenade, while for the "street children" it is a space that gets redefined as one in which there are invisible walls they build for their privacy. Street children subvert the expected order, privatizing the public and carrying out in the streets the most intimate acts such as physiological needs, bathing, sleeping, etc." (1998, p. 21).

There are many elements that may be invoked to explain the tendency of the public to avoid interaction and even eye contact with "a repulsive side of ourselves as human beings," which the street children represent. Clearly, the involvement with street children evokes uncomfortable feelings among many members of the general public. For the children themselves, the emotional discomfort and privation of street life is often dealt with by recourse to drugs, and I turn next to this issue.

The Role of Drugs in the Context of the "Street Children"

This invisible population is aware of their exclusion from most aspects of citizenship, and although not always able to express their isolation in words, they demonstrate their awareness of their social status through antisocial acts of aggression and confrontation. They also cope with their pariah status through the use of drugs.

Drug use is pandemic among street children. Children enter into drug use as an aspect of their membership in a street fraternity, and as a means to experience pleasure and to deaden the pain of their more general plight. Paradoxically, the effort at escapism through drug use has brought public attention and some degree of visibility to street children (Kuchembecker, 2000). The socially disruptive effect of the drugs has brought the children attention from representatives of the municipal public health agency and public education specialists.

The most common drug among the street kids is *loló,* a solvent made originally for shoemaker's glue; while its chemical components vary, it acts as a central nervous system depressant. It is common to see street children with a clenched hand holding a dirty piece of fabric against their noses and mouths. That cloth (*paninho*) is soaked with the solvent loló (Milnitsky-Sapiro et al., 1995). In addition to loló, marijuana and cocaine are largely used. Cocaine is more popular than marijuana, and during the last 2 years, the "crack" form of cocaine has gained favor. "Crack" entails the use of hypodermic syringes and the sharing of needles, making HIV infection sadly common. Drug use among street children begins at alarmingly young ages. Kuchembecker (2000) reported that children (boys) as young as 9 and 12 are injection drug users, while children as young as 5 years old use loló. This precocity is also pointed out in another study working with this population. A separate survey conducted among street children in Porto Alegre indicated that 15.5% of the children and adolescents who were interviewed had begun to use drugs before 8 years of age, and 27.4% had begun to use drugs between the ages of 9 and 11.

The consequences of drug use, beyond the direct debilitation of addiction, include unwanted pregnancies and entry into prostitution in order to pay for the addiction (Kuchembecker, 2000). Beyond the psychological and social consequences, the emergence into a drug use leads the young person to construct a representation of life centered on "street-and-drug," as life themes, and as values. Young people's social and affective relationships, their plans, goals, and everything else, come to be subjected to these images as metaphors of life. As soon as these adolescents become drug-addicted, they become and feel more socially excluded—from school, family, and any possible work. They move closer to violence and organized crime, drug dealing, and prostitution. They expose themselves more and more to intervention by the penal system, or to some kind of violent death as a consequence of involvement in street crime and violence.

Having described some of the factors that account for Brazilian street children, and the dire consequences endured by these youth, I now turn to a discussion of an intervention program aimed at addressing the needs of these children.

Intervention in the Context of the Streets

As mentioned earlier, our approach entailed a break with the prevailing view of street life as a "lifestyle choice" and related modes of intervention solely through street-based programs. The medical and psychological needs of the children, ranging from acute mental health disorders to HIV infection, required a more intensive form of intervention, and a protective and caring environment as well. Working with the city government of Porto Alegre, we established Casa Harmonia, a transitional home for street children that provides basic health care, drug rehabilitation, and mental health services (Kuchembecker, 2000). At the time it was conceived (2000), the children were treated in this "casa," with the primary aim of offering the necessary holding period to overcome drug dependency and its traumatic consequences including homelessness and deprivation (Winnicott, 1984, 1963/1990). At Casa Harmonia, adolescents taken from the streets can be safely nurtured through the withdrawals associated with drug and substance abuse, as well as receiving medical treatment for HIV and other infections or disease conditions. The services provided by the institution include twice-weekly group therapy sessions conducted by one teacher and one psychologist. In addition to this standard group therapy process, the clients of Casa Harmonia participate in sessions of "motivational therapy," conducted by Adriana Kuchembecker, the institution's psychiatrist (see Kuchembecker, 2000). These motivational therapy sessions focus upon the personal identity, self-image, and values that undergird the young person's involvement in drug addiction. Breaking the bonds that tie these youth to drug addiction is the first and most essential step toward the process of moving street children toward a more self-fulfilling future.

Finally, the Casa Harmonia program provides street youth with occupational therapy and reintegration within the educational system. When possible, the staff endeavors to reconnect the children with their immediate and extended families. When this is not possible, or not in the best interests of the child, children are placed in permanent shelters. The steps taken by Casa Harmonia are proactive, and are a direct and aggressive response to the needs of street children. This represents a break from prior public policy, which tended to view the culture of street children as a benign variation of the diversity of lifestyles within a free and open society. At the present time, Casa Harmonia is included among the government-sponsored Centers of Psycho-social Attention for Drug Addiction. Resolving the basic conditions that are the root causes of the prevalence of street children, however, will require more than the best efforts of institutions such as Casa Harmonia. Ultimately, the solution lies with a more profound commitment of Brazilian society to address the factors of poverty, economic disparity, and social anomie that have allowed this problem to persist.

Conclusions

This chapter explored the factors that result in having 1 in 20 working and lower-class children enter life on the streets of Brazil's major cities. It also presented an overview of one intervention among several actions that different nongovernmental organizations (Boff, 2002) have been carrying out in partnership with Brazilian governmental sectors such as the departments of health and education. A conclusion to be drawn from the experiences and efforts of these various programs is the need for multidisciplinary and integrative forms of intervention. The needs of street children transcend the scope of the health professions, social service agencies, and educational institutions. Thus there is a need for the construction of institutions such as Casa Harmonia throughout each of the major cities in Brazil.

Even with such a concerted effort at treatment, the problem of street children will not be addressed until there is a commitment by the Brazilian policymakers and directors of social programs to reflect upon and take action around the root causes that lead so many young people to take up life on the streets. These are complex times, in which traditional cultural patterns and ways of life are being challenged by global forces that have redefined the nature of the family, the forms of work that might sustain family existence, and the boundaries that define national and cultural borders. Despite these complexities, it falls to everyone within a national community to respond to the needs of those least able to protect themselves from the forces of change that are at work across the globe. Our role as researchers is to try and provide some directions for how such responses can be made. This chapter is a small contribution to that larger endeavor.

References

Abreu e Silva, R. de. (2000). *Delinqüência juvenil e imagos parentais: uma interlocução na contemporaneidade* [Juvenal delinquency and parental imago: A contemporary dialogue]. Unpublished master's dissertation, Program of Social and Institutional Psychology, Federal University of Rio Grande do Sul, Porto Alegre.

Abreu e Silva, R. de, & Milnitsky-Sapiro, C. (2002, May 31—June 2). Adolescent violence: A Brazilian perspective on a contemporary Western society. Paper presented at *the 31st Annual Meeting of the Jean Piaget Society*, Chicago.

América Latina Interconectada com Europa [ALICE]. (2004, August). *Boca de Rua* (newspaper published by América Latina Interconectada com Europa [Project Latin America Interconnected with Europe for Digital Inclusion], a nongovernmental organization serving street children), p. 1.

Arendt, H. (1983). *A condição humana* [The human condition]. Rio de Janeiro: Forense-Universitária. (Originally published 1958)

Berman, M. (1986). Tudo que é sólido desmancha no ar: A aventura da modernidade [All that is solid melts into air: The experience of modernity]. São Paulo: Companhia das Letra.

Boff, A. (2002). *Crianças institucionalizadas: Um olhar psicanalítico sobre um programa de abrigamento em uma ong.* [Institutionalized children: A psychoanalytical approach to a shelter project in a nongovernmental organization]. Unpublished master's dissertation, Program of Social and Institutional Psychology, Federal University of Rio Grande do Sul, Porto Alegre.

Brasil Estatuto da Criança e do Adolescente [Statute of Children and Adolescents]. (1991). *Lei 8069/90* [Estatuto da Criança e do Adolescente (ECA)]. São Paulo: Atlas.

Calligaris, C. (1993). *Psicanálise e Sintoma Social* [Psychoanalysis and social symptom]. São Leopoldo, Brazil: Unisinos.

Carlini, E. A., Noto, A. R., Nappo, Solange, Galduroz, J.C.F., & Mattei, R. (1998). 4 levantamento sobre o uso de drogas entre crianças e adolescentes em situação de rua de seis Capitais Brasileiras—1997 [4th survey on drug's use by children and adolescents of six Brazilian state capitals]. São Paulo: Centro Brasileiro de Informações Sobre Drogas Psicotrópicas.

Carnegie Council on Adolescent Development. (1995). *Great transitions: Preparing adolescents for a new century* [concluding report]. New York: Carnegie Corporation.

Craidy, C. (1998). *Meninos de rua e Analfabetismo* [Illiteracy and street children]. Porto Alegre: Artes Médicas.

Dolto, F., & Dolto-Tolitch, C. (1993). *Palabras para Adolescentes: o el complexo de la langostra* [Words to adolescents: Or the lobster complex]. Buenos Aires: Atlântida.

Erikson, E. (1968). *Identidade: juventude e crise* [Identity: Youth in crisis]. Rio de Janeiro: Zahar.

Fetterman, D. M. (1998). Ethnography: Step-by-step (2nd ed.). Thousand Oaks, CA: Sage.

Freud, A. (1995). Adolescência [Adolescence]. *Adolescência: Revista da Associação Psicanalítica de Porto Alegre, 5*(11), 63–85. (Original work published 1958)

Giongo, A. L. (1998). *O "ficar" e sua função na adolescência: um estudo em uma escola de classe média-alta de Porto Alegre* ["Staying" and its function on adolescence: A study in a upper middle-class school of Porto Alegre]. Unpublished master's dissertation, Federal University of Rio Grande do Sul, Porto Alegre, Brazil.

Graciani, M.S.S. (1997). Pedagogia social da rua: Análise e sistematização de uma experiência vivida [Social pedagogy of the street: An analysis and systematization of an experience]. São Paulo: Cortez.

Hall, S. (1997). The centrality of culture: Notes on the cultural revolutions of our times. In K. Thompson (Ed.), *Media and Cultural Regulation*. London: Sage.

Instituto Brasileiro de Geografia e Estatística. (2003). [Brazilian Institute of Geography and Statistics]. Available: www.ibge .gov.br.

Kuchenbecker, A. (2000). *Uso de drogas entre meninos e meninas de rua no centro de Porto Alegre* [The use of drugs among homeless boys and girls in Porto Alegre's downtown]. Unpublished master's dissertation, Federal University of Rio Grande do Sul, Porto Alegre, Brazil.

Kuchenbecker, A., & Milnitsky-Sapiro, C. (2002). Uso de drogas entre crianças e adolescentes de rua: Mudando o enfoque da intervenção [The use of drugs among homeless children and adolescents changing the focus of the intervention]. Paper presented at the Third International Seminar on Toxics, Pernambuco, Recife.

Lasch, C. (1987). O mínino eu: Sobrevivência psíquica em tempos difíceis [The minimal self: Psychic survival in troubled times]. São Paulo: Brasiliense.

Melman, C. (1995). Haveria uma questão particular do pai na adolescência? [Could it be a particular question on the father in adolescence?]. *Adolescência, 5*(11), 7–24.

Menegaz, C., & Milnitsky-Sapiro, C. (2002). Capricho ou oráculo: representações na imprensa sobre adolescentes [Consulting the oracle: Do magazines shape Brazilian teen girls' behavior and values?]. *Revista de Ciências Humanas, 6,* 161–174.

Milnitsky-Sapiro, C. (1996). Desenvolvimento sociomoral e aspectos culturais do parentesco [Sociomoral development and cultural aspects of kinship]. *Psicologia: Teoria e Pesquisa,, 6,* 72–86.

Milnitsky-Sapiro, C. (1999). *Metodologia de projetos sociais: Teoria e prática* [Methodology of social program projects: Theory and practice]. Porto Alegre, Brazil: Relatório da FESC—PMPA.

Milnitsky-Sapiro, C., Berman, S., Briones, E., & Kurtines, W. (1995, March). Moral identity, moral education, and democracy: The Brazilian experience. Paper presented at the Annual Meeting of the Society for Research on Adolescence, Boston.

Milnitsky-Sapiro, C., Cestari, F. L., & Giongo, A. (1996, July). Practice of democratic dialogue in a public school in Brazil: A re-evaluation of rights, norms and obligations. Paper presented at "Morals for the Millenium," *Journal of Moral Education* Conference, Lancaster, UK.

Milnitsky-Sapiro, C, Dutra, L., Coelho, S., & Correa, C. (1995). Domains' distinction of social knowledge among street-kids. In *Proceedings of The American Educational Research Association Conference*. San Francisco: American Educational Research Association.

Milnitsky-Sapiro, C., & Menegaz, C. V. (2001). Capricho ou oráculo: Representações na imprensa sobre adolescentes. [Vanity or oracle: Media representations of adolescents]. In *Proceedings of First International Conference on Social Representation* (p. 117). Blumenau: Edifurb, 2001.

Milnitsky-Sapiro, C., & Menegaz, C. (2002, June 6–8). Consulting the oracle: Do magazines shape Brazilian teen-agers girls' behavior and values? Paper presented at the 32nd Annual Meeting of the Jean Piaget Society, Philadelphia.

Milnitsky-Sapiro, C., & Tavares, J. V. (1993). A violência urbana e rural contra a crianca no Brasil: Uma perspectiva interdisciplinar [Rural and urban violence against children in Brazil: An interdisciplinar approach]. *Humanas Revista do Instituto de Filosofia e Ciências Humanas, 16*(2), 91–107.

Milnitsky-Sapiro, C., Turiel, E., & Nucci, L. (2002, November 7–10). *The expectation for limits in adolescents' construction of autonomy.* Paper presented at the 28th Annual Conference of the Association for Moral Education, Chicago.

Nucci, L., Camino, C., & Milnitsky-Sapiro, C. (1996). Social class effects on northeastern Brazilian children's conceptions of areas of personal choice and social regulation. *Child Development, 67,* 1223–1242.

Oliveira, C. S. (2001). Sobrevivendo no inferno: A violência juvenil na Contemporaneidade [Surviving from Hell: Juvenile violence in contemporary times]. Porto Alegre: Editora Sulina.

Outeiral, J. O. (1994). Adolescer: Estudo sobre adolescência [Adolescents: Study on adolescence]. Porto Alegre: Artes Médicas.

Prefeitura Municipal de Porto Alegre. (1997). *Programa de atenção integral a crianças e adolescentes usuários de substâncias psicoativas* [Program of integral attention to children and adolescents users of psychoactive substances]. Porto Alegre: City Hall, Municipal Secretary of Health.

Prefeitura Municipal de Porto Alegre. (1998). *Drogas: Informação na Roda* [Drugs: Bringing in information]. Porto Alegre: Gráfica do DMAE.

Rassial, J. J. (1997) A passagem adolescente: da familia ao laço social [The adolescent passage: From family to the social ties]. Porto Alegre: Artes e Ofícios.

Rizzini, I. (2004). *Vida nas ruas—crianças e adolescentes nas ruas: Trajetórias inevitáveis?* [Life in the streets—children and adolescents in the streets: Unavoidable trajectories?]. Rio de Janeiro: PUC-Rio/Edições Loyola.

Rogoff, B. (2003). *The cultural nature of human development.* Oxford, UK: Oxford University Press.

Ruffino, R. (1995). Adolescência: Notas em torno de um empasse [Adolescence: Notes about an uncertainty]. *Adolescência, 5*(11), 41–46.

Turiel, E. 1983. *The development of social knowledge: Morality and Convention.* Cambridge, UK: Cambridge University Press.

Turiel, E. (2002). *The Culture of morality: Social development, context, and conflict.* Cambridge, UK: Cambridge University Press.

Turiel, E., Killen, M., & Helwig, C. (1987). Morality: Its structure, functions, and vagaries. In J. Kagan & S. Lamb (Eds.), *The emergence of moral concepts in young children* (pp. 28–36). Chicago: University of Chicago Press.

Valsiner, J. (1989). Human development and culture: The social nature of personality and its study. Lexington, Mass.: Lexington Books.

Violante, M. L.V. (1998). *A criança mal-amada: Estudo sobre a potencialidade melan cólica* [The non-cherhised children: A study on melancholic potentiality]. Petrópolis: Vozes.

Winnicott, D. (1984). *Deprivation and delinquency.* London: Tavistock.

Winnicott, D. (1990). *Moral e educação: O ambiente e os processos de maturação: Estudos sobre a teoria do desenvolvimento emociona* [The maturational processes and the facilitating environment] (3rd ed.). Porto Alegre: Artes Médicas. (Original work published 1963)

CHAPTER 12

Stories of Conflict and Development in U.S. Public Schools

COLETTE DAIUTE

Recounting an experience of conflict seems like an intensely personal act, especially for young people who have observed or participated in violent events. Nevertheless, when children tell or write stories about experiences of fighting, verbal abuse, and exclusion, these stories are social, even political, as well as personal. According to socio-historical theory, symbolic activities like storytelling, drawing, and role-playing echo and transform ways of being in a society. In this chapter, I discuss the significance of narrating conflict in research and practice. I explain how the process of storytelling is implicated in the events of conflict and the course of development related to those events. I also argue that assessing the nature, impact, and treatments of youth conflict requires a new understanding of the role of storytelling because development occurs in social discourse. The significance of this definition of storytelling (which I use interchangeably with "narrating") is that it offers insights about how people live their lives.

I will show how these processes come to life for children aged 7 through 11 and their teachers in the context of a violence prevention program in public schools in the United States. After a brief review of the social-historical nature of storytelling and a violence prevention curriculum that uses storytelling as transformative process (Walker, 1998), I illustrate the intricate mosaic that foregrounds the problems of society when we read stories as social scripts and the consequences for individuals when we read the same stories as personal. I offer examples to show how the intra- and interpersonal dimensions of conflict are intimately tied to intergroup conflicts.

Trends in Research on Youth Conflict in the United States

Previous United States—based research has identified individual and community patterns that place youth at risk for being involved in social conflicts and violence, such as: having aggressive characters; being raised in cycles of violence; living in extended neighborhoods with high concentrations of single-parent households; and belonging to families and institutions lacking material resources (Earls & Carlson, 1999; Greenberg, Lengua, Coie, & Pinderhughes, 1999; Sampson, Morenoff, & Earls, 1999; Widom, 1989). Case history research has used clinical interviewing methods to identify psychodynamic stresses in young people incarcerated for violent crimes (Garbarino, 1999). Scholars have also usefully applied developmental theory to examine socio-cognitive capacities (Selman, Watts, & Schultz, 1997) and personal characteristics (Arsenio & Lemerise, 2004) related to moral decision-making, interpersonal relationships, and behavior. Social factors include children's rejection and abuse by peers (Olweus, 1994), family members, and caretakers (Widom, 1989) as catalysts of cycles of violence.

Although previous research has identified some correlates of individuals' conflict behavior (Elliot, Hamburg, & Williams, 1998), an increasing number of researchers has identified the need to examine how social structures create youth conflicts. For example, some researchers posit that violence occurs in the context of injustice, like racism, sexual repression, and poverty, rather than in individuals (Foucault, 1988; Turiel, 2002; Wainryb, 1995). Consistent with these approaches, and on the basis of the assumption that conflict is integral to social systems, research can move away from creating profiles of antisocial youth to identifying social-relational dynamics that create the circumstances for conflicts, in particular for children identifying with economically and politically powerless groups in society. Socio-historical theory is an appropriate means for examining justice-sensitive developmental issues—like youth conflict processes.

Socio-historical theory (Vygotsky, 1978) provides a method for examining the development of individuals in society. From the perspective of this theory, the scholarly focus broadens from interpersonal conflicts to conflicts in society, creating a foundation for interpreting youth conflict in terms of social-relational dynamics, as well as individual subjectivities and capacities.

Leont'ev wrote:

> Personality originally arises in society . . . and [one] becomes a personality only as a subject of social relations. . . . The method of . . . dialectics requires that we go further and investigate the development as a process of "self-movement," that is, investigate its internal moving relations, contradictions, and mutual transitions so that its prerequisites appear in it as its own changing moments. (1989, p. 105)

According to this theory, the physical and psychological activities of an individual child are entwined with social history, so the child's character, capacities, and goals develop in terms of the salient relational dynamics of the time.

Storytelling is an activity that integrates the values and material circumstances in social history and individual lives. Focusing on the interdependent development of society and individuals reveals the political nature of experience.

Public contexts like schools exert power over individuals' expressions, and a socio-historical analysis of conflicts accounts for social-relational dynamics, like power struggles, material inequalities, or social exclusion in everyday discourse and activities. Acknowledging the political nature of experience in public schools then opens the way for inquiry into the political nature of symbolic communication like storytelling, the most common means of sharing experience in formal and informal settings. In the following sections, I develop two related ideas about conflict storytelling: first, that conflict storytelling is a developmental process, and second, that it is a political process.

Storytelling and Development

Scholars have argued that, beyond mere reporting, storytelling fosters the development of individuals and society (Bamberg, 1997; Hermans, 1997; Polkinghorne, 1991; Spence, 1982). Children become members of their cultures as they learn to think of the world and themselves in terms of scripts organized around the values of society (K. N. Nelson, 1986). Because storytelling is, moreover, a means of social positioning, addressed to audiences and to one's self, children, like adults, use it to perform identities and reflect on them (Bamberg, 1997; Daiute, Buteau, & Rawlins, 2001; Nystrand & Wiemelt, 1991). Physical events—a salient word, glance, movement, physical arrangement—are embodied in this interaction among narrator, audiences, and self-subject (Bakhtin, 1986). In this way, storytelling embeds institutional values, power relations, circumstances of the physical environment, and individual motivations (Harré & van Langenhove, 1999). Individuals' motivations bring social scripts to life as personal stories.

Over the past century, scholars have increasingly noted the developmental function of oral and written storytelling. Freud, for example, explained the importance of verbalizing dreams and fantasies as a talking cure that could "bring[ing] about the disappearance of painful symptoms of . . . illness" (Freud, 1909, p. 8). Clinical practices in this tradition also use nonverbal event representations like drawing, play therapy, and religious rituals (Apfel & Simon, 1996; chapter 13 here) to remedy traumas. Subsequent psychoanalytic theorists extended the role of narrating, as "aptly chosen reconstruction [that] can fill the gap between two apparently unrelated events and, in the process, make sense out of non-sense" (Spence, 1982, p. 21). More recently, narrative theorists have said that development occurs via processes such as valuation, defined as "anything people identify as a relevant meaning unit when telling their life story . . . including . . . a precious memory, a difficult problem, a beloved person, an unreachable goal, an unanticipated death of a significant other, and so forth" (Hermans & Hermans-Jansen, 1995, p. 15).

Especially when considering the sociopolitical nature of conflicts, one realizes that storytelling, like other symbolic representations, involves more than recounting facts. The facts—who did what to whom in what setting—may or may not be stated. Depending on their histories, intentions, and situational circumstances, narrators select the most salient among myriad possible facts. Since interpersonal interactions are governed by status and power relations, storytellers may suppress certain facts while foregrounding others. Some acts may seem worth recounting because they display courage, challenge, or some other valued quality. Storytellers may repress some acts that revive "unspeakable horrors" (Apfel & Simon, 1996) or that associate the storyteller with negative stereotypes (Daiute et al., 2001). Stories are, in summary, like other symbolic media, highly interpreted. In addition to this psychological and educational research, research on storytelling in disciplines like law has also explained that no purely factual accounts are possible (Amsterdam & Bruner, 2000).

The title of this chapter refers to "conflict stories" to express the idea that autobiographical (as well as fictional) storytelling is a creative process. The war story genre is prevalent across time and cultures, in part because of the developmental nature of reflecting on social experience, which then organizes future experience. After all, there would be no arguments, insurgencies, or wars if all parties perceived situations and events in the same way. War stories serve nations and individuals, and the business of creating the politically correct versions of these stories is serious indeed. The conflict stories I discuss in this chapter do not occur in the context of armed conflict but within the "war" of living with few material resources amid the riches in a country that is the military power of the globe, thus a national context harboring great inequalities.

Educators often ask children to share their personal experiences in school as a way to include their cultural experiences in classroom discourse, but we must also recognize how inequalities in educational contexts discriminate against the experiences of some children. In contexts where people have experienced intergroup conflicts, sharing experiences can be particularly contentious. When discussing personal experiences of conflict, for example, children living in neighborhoods where there are shootings in the streets or in homes where there is domestic violence are not likely to share such information, because they know it may shock or concern some people in a culturally heterogeneous societies, thus exposing them to exclusion or negative judgment.

Understanding Youth Conflict in a Violence Prevention Program

Numerous violence prevention programs are currently implemented in U.S. schools in response to reports of escalating school-based violence involving physical fights, assaults, and homicides in urban and, increasingly, suburban and rural settings (Henrich, Brown, & Aber, 1999). These programs are compelling as sites for analyzing the interaction between social forces and individuals' experiences of conflicts. A curriculum is based on institutional values that children as young as 7 can read and juggle with their personal motivations and goals.

The research I draw upon occurred in the context of a curriculum that promoted values of "love and freedom"—social understanding and coexistence through analyzing conflicts in terms of perspective-taking, empathy, and strategic resolution. Literature about discrimination provided a context for discussing conflict processes and individuals' roles in these conflicts. Two examples of such children's literature used in the study described here are *Angel Child, Dragon Child* (Surat, 1983), a story about Hoa, a recently immigrated Vietnamese girl who is the object of discriminatory teasing; and *Mayfield Crossing* (V. M. Nelson, 1993), a story in which the main characters are a group of African Americans in the 1960s South, where the small predominantly black middle school closes, requiring the students from that school to go to a mostly white school in another town. A teacher's guide for each literary selection suggested discussion questions and activities for analyzing conflict and role-playing resolution strategies via storytelling and writing activities. These activities were designed as opportunities for children to analyze social problems raised in the literary selections, to consider how such problems might apply to their own lives, and to imagine effective ways of dealing with such conflicts (Daiute, 2000; Walker, 1998).

Social Scripts and Personal Stories

Assumptions about conflict and resolution are defined by social groups and communicated via social scripts. Social scripts have also been referred to as dominant ideologies (Foucault, 1988); ways of knowing (Gilligan, 1982); cultural scripts (K. N. Nelson, 1986); and master narratives (Daiute & Lightfoot, 2004). Social scripts organize perception and action. Different social scripts may co-occur; they may be integrated, like plots and subplots; and they may clash—resulting in a story that appears incoherent. With experience, narrators use diverse social scripts appropriately and cleverly to remember, to guide their actions, and to persuade others. While social scripts generally serve an affiliative function, they may also be employed to resist expectations. In Western cultures, for example, a common conflict-related script is one in which adversaries resolve their differences and "live happily ever after." Members of groups within a society, however, identify with different scripts, like some privileged person's script that "everything will work out all right" or the feminist script that women are often used as scapegoats in problems like extramarital affairs.

A major goal of public school classrooms is to convey mainstream values via scripts. My colleagues and I analyzed values expressed by teachers and students in oral and written discourse during the violence prevention curriculum (Daiute, Stern, & Lelutiu-Weinberger, 2003). In this study, we identified curriculum values like understanding others, being kind, and reestablishing relationships gone awry. An example of such a value as expressed by one of the teachers is "These characters should find some way to get along, something in common" (p. 88).

Other values have to do with an individual's or a group's rights to respect and self-determination in antagonistic interactions, such as when a teacher stressed that a child coming to New York from another country has the right to dress in whatever way he or she pleases without being teased. Values relating to conflict resolution were also prominent in the curriculum materials and classroom discourse, as expressed by one teacher who pointed out to her class "There was ice existing between Raymond and Hoa, and what broke the ice?" (p. 89) and defined conflict in terms of the cold feelings antagonists sometimes have toward each other. Another teacher who, in contrast, emphasized perspective-taking, said "And the parents might look at it and say he's [been] hurting; the kids looked at it and thought something completely different" (p. 89), and "Someone want to tell us what it felt like?" (p. 89). Ultimately, this curriculum advocates a balance of connection and self-determination values.

Teachers' Scripts: Social Ideals

The analysis showed that teachers and children adopted a common general script in large group discussions in the classroom (Daiute et al., 2003). The script was generally that people sometimes have conflicts, but these can always be resolved through peaceful resolution processes like imagining the feelings of adversaries and "talking things out," which people in conflict have the responsibility to try. Not surprisingly, however, teachers identifying with diverse ethnic groups emphasized different versions of this script (Daiute et al., 2003). An introductory activity on conflict negotiation skills was for teachers to narrate their own personal experiences as "newcomers" to provide a model for children's conflict stories. These examples of newcomer conflict scripts demonstrate such differences.

The excerpt that follows is from a newcomer story by Mrs. Morales, an experienced third-grade teacher, who identified as Puerto Rican. As illustrated in this story, Mrs. Morales expressed some curriculum values, including examining social conflicts, escalation, and perspective-taking in verbal (rather than physical) contests to resolve their differences.

> I'm going to tell you a story first. At the end of it . . . you can ask me questions and I will answer them. . . . When I was about nineteen years old I was in college. . . . Yeah that was many moons ago [children laugh], actually it was twenty years ago [children try to guess how old the teacher is and they all joke good naturedly about this]. My college roommate Carmen and I decided to take a study [trip] to Puerto Rico and we were going to study there for a semester which is about four months. We left in August and then we were going to return some time in December. Okay, so our plane ride there was great. We were anxious to get there because you know this was Puerto Rico. . . . We were also excited about the trip, right?
>
> So our room, my room was shared with my roommate Carmen, but we also had to share the kitchen, the bathroom with other students that were there. There was a group of us from New York, there was seven of us, but the rest of the

students were from Puerto Rico. Now I am of Puerto Rican descent, and I was born in Puerto Rico, but I had never been there since I was a baby. Okay, and we started to have trouble with the girl students who were living in the boarding house. [Student says "because they were different"] Well, we all spoke Spanish, all of us, we spoke our New York Spanish, but we spoke and we understood. It's just that they didn't like us because we were from New York, and they didn't make us feel comfortable. They wanted us out, and in the middle of the night we actually had a fight. [Students say "oooooo."] It was not a fist fight . . . and we had to leave . . . because we were the newcomers.

In this story, as in her other interactions over the course of a school year, Mrs. Morales conveyed conflicts in terms of socio-historical factors like power relations and injustices far more than any other teacher. It makes sense that, as a self-declared member of a minority group, Mrs. Morales was quite clear about the importance of establishing one's identity, especially as the source of conflicts and as a potential barrier to conflict resolution. Mrs. Morales's relative lack of emphasis on specific resolution strategies was strikingly different from the emphasis in the curriculum and from some of her colleagues.

As illustrated in the story that follows, Mrs. White, an experienced third-grade teacher who identified as white, emphasized universal human qualities like kindness and personal responsibility to resolve conflicts.

I thought of one story that happened to me probably about, I would almost say about thirty years ago, and I thought it would be real good connection to this book, so let me tell you. I guess I was in my twenties. I had just graduated from college and I was a teacher. Oh, I wonder what the neighborhood is going to be like that I'm going to be teaching in, cause it is just as uncomfortable for teachers to come into a whole new class of twenty-five children that she doesn't know. . . . I called up the woman who gave me the job, the principal of the school, and . . . I asked her if they had a summer program there and then I also asked her if I could come by and then maybe meet some of the children that I might be teaching, get used to the school, find out what kind of books that they might have. She said, "Oh my goodness," we have too many kids in our summer program, and in fact we're looking for a teacher . . . come the next day, we're all going on a trip and then Thursday we will start you with your class. So the next day I went. Okay, I didn't really know anybody, so we were on a trip, and I sat down . . . on the bus . . . in the school bus, a yellow school bus. . . . Then I looked around and I noticed that I was the only white person on the bus. It had never happened to me before. All the children were, I think mostly . . . African American or Hispanic. All the teachers were African American or Hispanic, and I was the only white person, and somehow you know because in this country we are very aware of . . . I guess our race. I started to feel a little uncomfortable. . . . I was sitting on the bus and I said, "Okay, this is what I'm going to do is, I've got to start to feel comfortable." So I was sitting next to this little girl, and I just started to talk to her, and of course, I asked her her name. I asked her what grade she was in. I asked her what she liked to do in the summer, and then she asked me the same questions. She asked me my name. She asked me what class I was teaching. She asked me what I was doing for the summer, and then I started to talk to the other children on the bus. And then . . . when I got off the bus, I started to talk to the other teachers . . . and then I started to feel very, very comfortable.

Mrs. White's narratives, comments to students, and guidance of class discussions were overall more consistent with those of the curriculum than most of the other eight teachers in the study. Nevertheless, she emphasized values of empathy rather than ones that addressed differences of point of view, as was also suggested in the curriculum. Interestingly, teachers' unique implementations of the curriculum values, like those demonstrated in the foregoing stories by Mrs. Morales and Mrs. White, influenced their students' conflict stories (Daiute et al., 2003).

Students' Personal Stories: Cultural and Personal Transformations

Children's stories about personal experiences described a range of conflicts, from fights about toys to debates about fairness in jump rope games, emotional appeals about exclusivity in friendships, and intense reflections about physical and psychological fights. Like their teachers, children shaped their autobiographical stories in ways that conformed to a few major curriculum values, including perspective-taking and expressing peaceful conflict resolution strategies. Analyses also showed, however, that children's conflict stories conformed to scripts that were consistent by ethnic group identification as well (Daiute & Jones, 2003).

John, a 10-year-old student identifying as African-American, was asked to write about "a conflict or argument you or someone you know had" as an activity in his fifth-grade classroom. John's brief narrative about a conflict with a store manager expresses several social scripts emphasized in his teacher's implementation of the curriculum.

> One day I was walk in the croner store and manni [the store manager] said get out for no resana at all so I walked out of the store and maget was walking right behid me and he tryed to hit me so he hit me and I truned a round and I punched him in the face and he stared to cry. He was feeling bad and I was not so happy me self becaues I now that I could have talked it out and not punched him. He walked away crying. (Daiute, 2000, p. 211)[1]

Like Mrs. White earlier, John's teacher had encouraged her students to consider the thoughts and feelings of their adversaries in conflicts—as John did—and to attempt peaceful resolutions, like talking about conflict rather than escalating to physical violence. John's narrative, however, also echoed the script of discrimination-based surveillance familiar to young black males in public places (Cross & Fhagen-Smith, 2001; Gates, 1992). John describes the manager as chasing him "for now resana at all," and hitting him, in response to which he defended himself. John then also integrates an aspect of the violence prevention script emphasizing perspective-taking and compassion, ending with "he walked away crying."

John's way of describing this conflict is, moreover, consistent with how other children identifying as African American organized their conflict stories. For example, stories by children, like John, who identified as African American and children who identified as Latino/a portrayed individuals in conflicts as mutually responsible for those conflicts (although these two groups did so in somewhat different ways), while children who identified as white or European American portrayed conflicts in adversarial terms and as acts of aggression by one person against another (Daiute & Jones, 2003).

Rather than expressing conflicts as fights between individuals, African American children tended to describe conflicts as social systems. Stories by these children described characters in conflicts as equal and interdependent in terms of their rights and responsibilities. Conflicts often revolved around issues of injustice—like latent discrimination, as in John's story. Embedding conflict in social systems sometimes meant describing the rules that were broken or created in interpersonal conflicts, with characters appealing to authorities like parents, teachers, or older kids or to impartial systems like schedules, coin tosses, or moral reasoning (for example, one character pondered, "Why would someone hurt someone just for a ballfield?").

The following story, written by a boy in third grade who identified himself as African American, illustrates how conflict participants, including the author, rely on social systems.

> The bike fight
> One day me and my friend had an argument. We had an argument about my bike. He alwaysed hoged it allot and I never got to ride it. Since I never got to ride it we made a time schechuite [schedule]. He had it outside for 1 hour and I had it for 1 hour. (Daiute & Jones, 2003, pp. 192–193)

In this story, the author assumes a solution where he and his antagonist both have access to the contested resource—his bike. The narrator then comes up with an institutionalized solution—a schedule—to mediate conflicting desires for the bikes. The author acknowledges the differing perspectives, saying that his friend "hogged" the bike and referring to the injustice that he, the author, "never got to ride it," but he distributes justice to the needs of both participants.

Following a different cultural script, conflict stories by young authors identifying as Latino/a tended to focus on relationship issues, and conflicts were represented as repartee—back-and-forth conversations—among participants around issues like bonding, betrayal, and devotion. This process characteristically offered the perspectives of each participant and a friendly ending. For example, in the following story, the author and her best friend, Jimmy, engage in reciprocal pushing, getting mad, name-calling, stopping, saying sorry, and picking each other up. In addition to representing reciprocal actions, young

Latino/a authors also tended to solve conflicts through dialogue exchanging points of view rather than appealing to a mediation-like rules.

> Fight with My Friend
> One day Jimmy. Jimmy was Best Friend but now he [is not] my Best Friend Because he push me into the mud and I Push him water. and then we got Mad and called each other names he call me bad girl and I call him Pig. So we got into a Big Fight he Bushed me and I Push. and Bused him so then we stop each other and said Sorry. and then I pick him he pick me up So then we Became Best Friend agin. (Daiute & Jones, 2003, pp. 193–194)

Conflict stories by authors who identified themselves as white tended to situate the conflict outside the author, although the authors were represented as participants in a variety of ways. This perspective is conveyed in several ways: authors often portrayed themselves as victims of someone else's aggression or misunderstanding in an accident; played the role of fixer or judge; or told stories from the distance of time or emotion.

The following story by a girl identifying as white offers an elaborate description of the problem, its development over time, and the resolution. The author situates herself as the first-person participant in the conflict at a social distance from her interlocutor.

> Secrets: A while ago my friend Nicole and I had a fight that was larger than life, it was all about secrets. You see Nicole liked to take people over and tell them secrets in front [of] and about every one else. For a while this was okay, but soon it got out of hand, Nicole was telling more secrets than the entire population of Japan could in a year. If nobody was going to stop her I would! I felt as though I was carrying the world on my shoulders, but I told her calmly how I felt and she appeared to listen. I found out a couple of weeks later that she was acting, she was at it again, secrets, secrets, secrets, everywhere you looked, secrets, and Nicole behind each of there front doors. I couldn't take it anymore! Then one day Hannah told me about a really bad secret about me. I blew up right in her face, I made her promise never to tell a secret again, and she didn't for a while. (Daiute & Jones, 2003, pp. 194–195)

The author describes Nicole as the perpetrator of the conflict and situates the problem in Nicole to the point where "secrets" seems to symbolize Nicole. The author describes her own reaction indirectly, saying "it got out of hand." In turn, she depicts her involvement as taking the situation under control, pointing out that "If nobody was going to stop her I would!" This intervention is described as one of teaching Nicole rather than working with her to exchange views about the problem or work out a social resolution. The author's reflection ("I thought I was carrying the world on my shoulders") in fact characterizes the similarity we found across the texts by the white children on this task.

These examples illustrate how children as young as 7 organize the social world in ways that ally them to their diverse social groups. My analyses have also shown how children's stories (like their teachers') are sensitive to the immediate context and factors of status, goals, skills, and other diverse personal orientations.

The Politics of Storytelling

An analysis of differences between children's autobiographical and fictional narrating further supports my observation that storytelling is a social-political process. Storytelling may involve soul-searching, but it also is performance— meaning that audiences also influence narratives (Daiute, 2004). The premise of this comparison was that children might be performing for an audience in autobiographical tasks by shaping their experiences of conflict to curricular scripts while expressing more subjective perspectives in fiction. This is not to say that children would be lying, but that, like more experienced storytellers, they select conflict events or details of those events consistent with audience expectations.

While autobiography involves public exposure, fiction is in some ways a more private space. Fiction provides an author with a context for imagining de- sired circumstances, creating a best self, playing out what confuses or frightens the narrator, and telling the truth, even if at odds with the norm. When writing fiction, a youngster can for a moment distance from the pressures of institu- tional values and manipulate them for subjective purposes. For these reasons, children would want to conform to the values emphasized in a context where they spend a lot of their time, as they do in school. What we learn from the different values expressed in children's oral and written autobiographical and fictional stories is that, at very young ages, they become aware that some of their stories may be evaluated negatively, and this awareness has an impact on how they craft their experiences into stories. Those children identifying with discriminated minority groups, moreover, seem particularly astute about how they are perceived by others. My analysis identified curriculum scripts and more subjective, affective expressions to explore children's sensitivity to audience in autobiographical and fictional storytelling.

An analysis of 36 autobiographical and fictional conflict stories elicited twice a year from four children who participated in the curriculum over 3 years showed that children's autobiographical conflict stories were *performances* while the same children's stories about fictional characters involved in con- flicts were *centered* (Daiute, 2004). For this analysis, I defined "performed" stories as including relatively more clauses expressing curriculum values in the absence of personal affective expression and "centered" stories as those including relatively more clauses with representations of affective expressions and values not promoted in the curriculum (Daiute, 2004).

The following two narratives were written by 7-year old Eudora, who identi- fied as African American. The first story, "Me and Lerissa," echoes curriculum scripts about analyzing how conflicts get started, progress, and are resolved. Like "Me and Lerissa," children's autobiographical stories conformed to the curriculum emphasis on resolving conflicts peacefully, as Eudora did with her resolution, "Fine, I will do the computer."

Me and Lerissa
Me and Lerissa (my friend) had a disagreement because I wanted to do dolls and some thing else but she wanted to play on her computer but I said "why can't we just do dolls and she said" no. Fine I will do the computer. (Daiute, 2004, p. 117)

The story "Me and Lerissa" illustrates children's sensitivity to public scrutiny, as they consistently recounted personal experiences in conformity to values shared in school. Eudora's somewhat begrudging agreement, "Fine, I will do the computer," thus seems as though it could have been addressed to social pressures to tell the right kind of conflict story as well as to the adversary in her story.

In contrast, Eudora's story "Three," about fictional characters, expresses less social and more emotional states, which were not as prominent in the curriculum activities.

Three
One day when Jama saw Max and Pat jama felt very sad because she was alone. When it was getting late Jama was going home then when she was eating dinner she was thinking about her friends so after dinner she went to bed when she was going to bed she had a dream about her friend. On the next day she saw Pat and Max again and . . . (Daiute, 2004, p. 117)

This fictional narrative provides a foil for reading "Me and Lerissa." Notably different in the fictional narrative is the expression of psychological states, "sad," "thinking," "had a dream," "saw," attributed to Jama, who emerges as the protagonist. There is a whisper of curriculum values expressed in Jama's individual reflection and a whisper of an alternative to curriculum values with the lack of resolution. The emotional expression embodies a subjective voice that is silent in Eudora's more explicitly autobiographical piece. In this story, Eudora is not explicitly the subject and thus, as narrator, she can be a ventriloquist voicing her point of view through characters, and, like many other children, Eudora represented conflict differently across autobiographical and fictional narratives (Daiute, 2004).

When writing conflict stories with peers, children's expressions also contrasted dramatically with curriculum values and teachers' interpretations of the curriculum. For example, some children defied the curricular emphasis on peaceful resolution with comments like "We needed revenge" (Daiute et al., 2003, p. 96) when they recounted extensive violent episodes, stereotyping, and other classroom taboos. Two boys were enticed to prove their physical strength to the group of girls accusing them of not knowing how to fight, or fighting like "a chicken" (p. 96). Gradually, children in a group all began challenging and threatening each other, with phrases such as: "I would like to smack her [a few unclear words] own sister," "You need to be quiet 'cause you're scared of girls," "I scared of her? I would knock her down!" (p. 96). Other unique value expressions were phrased as less violent threats: "You are getting on my nerves," "Shut up," or "You're an idiot" (p. 96).

Another assumption that children challenged implicitly in their peer interactions was the focus on the equality of all perspectives and thus the possibility for resolution. It is not surprising that children from family backgrounds that have experienced discrimination might question universalist explanations that "everyone is really the same and can get along." A powerful interaction between two immigrant boys, one of Arab descent and one of western European heritage, illustrates how young people can critique mainstream society with some specific details that they do not express in the larger class discussion. "What a 'bad' country America is"; "America sucks, come on, America sucksa . . . it's not a good country, it has a lot of pollution, it does, I mean look at the manners they have"; "the bad language they have"; "yeah, the bad language, you can't even get used to them" (Daiute et al., 2003, p. 97). Even though this, like other examples, is not stated explicitly as a critique of curriculum values, it is precise and strong, coming from 9-year-olds.

Educators might want to discourage such interactions, but it is remarkable and important to observe how children conform to curriculum values in one context yet express very different values elsewhere. Fiction and fantasy stories are thus promising media for exploring contentious issues, for personal release, reflection, and initial steps toward mutual understanding and resolution.

Transformative Possibilities

As an interpretive process, storytelling is thus transformational. Simply changing facts in a retelling does not change events, but the portrayal of those events conveys the meaning of the events and thus defines causes, consequences, and future action. Certain facts, like wounds and death, are incontrovertible, but their explanations embody the human dimension of the facts—their meaning and significance. When narrators represent themselves handling challenging situations, whether true or not, this can be the basis for understanding or change. Even more important, perhaps, is that symbolic processes like narrating allow children to transform social situations, and in particular to address injustices, as seen in several of the foregoing examples. This balance of self-reflection and societal critique is notable in the stories presented here.

An intriguing measure of this transformative nature of storytelling is the link between certain narrative qualities and measures of behavior (Daiute & Buteau, 2002). An analysis of 316 narratives by 79 third- and fifth-graders, 158 narratives written in response to the curriculum-based fictional narrative task, and 158 narratives written in response to the autobiographical narrating task over a school year, addressed the question "How are shifts in social scripts in conflict stories related to shifts in reports of conflict behaviors?" Girls and boys—from European-American, Latino/a, African American, and Asian Americanbackgrounds, and recent immigrants (European, Caribbean)—who reported fewer behavior events at the end of the school year were also those whose narratives increasingly expressed curricular values like characters' mutual understanding and conflict negotiation strategies. This preliminary evidence of a relationship between narrative and behavior supports the idea that symbolic communication is an activity.

An example illustrates how the developmental function of writing presents itself. Dianna, a fifth-grader who identifies her race/ethnicity as Jamaican, was one of the children who reported fewer problem behaviors in the spring (2) than in the fall (10). Dianna's two autobiographical conflict narratives, presented here, show the kinds of changes in writing that are related to decreases in reports of problem behaviors. In the story she wrote in the fall, "My Conflict by: Dianna," wrote about a conflict with her friend Serena.

> My Conflict by: Dianna
> I had a conflict with my friend Serena in the park. She was calling me names and hitting me. I was walking away but she following me. But I was'nt calling her names to start with. I was feeling mad but a little sad, because of what she said to me. But I knew that it was not true. (Daiute & Buteau, 2002, p. 70)

This description of Dianna and Serena's fight is characteristic of stories children wrote earlier in the year, in particular the predominance of the description of author as victim of another's aggression. Dianna was called names, was hit, and felt bad. Dianna hints that she engaged in name calling, but only in retaliation: "I was'nt calling her names to start with." There is, moreover, no description of attempts to resolve the conflict. In contrast, Dianna's spring story, "The Fight," reports resolution strategies and a reflection about the conflict.

> The Fight
> My friend and I were whtching a movie and we saw the movie before so we played fight. I hurt her badly and she got mad so she hurt me badly and we had a fight. She hit me and I hit her back. She sat on me and I could not get out. I got out and kicked her she got hurt by my kick and she slapped me and I cry. I tried not to let her see. I could not stop. It hurt a lot, and I slapped her back and it did not hurt her at all. So we foght some more and I cried and I went home and she called and said, "Sorry. Fighting does not help." I said "Sorry." and made up. (Daiute & Buteau, 2002, p. 70)

Interestingly, Dianna reports that her friend was the one who initiated the conflict resolution by calling and apologizing. After Dianna responded in kind, they made up. The resolution strategy embeds a reflection on the conflict when Dianna's friend points out that "fighting does not help."

These stories by Dianna also illustrate what may be protective aspects of narrative writing. Narrative writing allows for the expression of aggressive and violent behavior, as illustrated by the more detailed and protracted fight reported in the spring story. Such psycho-social work involves emotional release and reflection and, in this case, is coordinated with social resolution. This may make an important, even life-saving, difference for a child at some point when a less resourceful orientation might involve her in interactions leading to irreparable harm. Such resourcefulness over several months requires institutional and social supports, and some children may have already known such approaches but had never had the opportunity to express them in school contexts.

Implications

While many in the field of psychology have overlooked creative symbolic processes, Hardt and Negri (2000), from the perspective of political theory, identify symbolic activity as central not only to interpersonal processes but also to global processes:

> Abstract social activity and its comprehensive power . . . is very powerful. It is the cooperating set of brains and hands, minds and bodies; it is both the non-belonging and the creative social diffusion of living labor; . . . it is intellectual energy and linguistic and communicative construction of the multitude of intellectual and affective laborers. (p. 209)

I hope to have shown in this chapter how narrating conflict is intellectual and affective labor by participants in classrooms reflecting on social values—perhaps one of the most important subjects in a democracy. If storytelling and writing are activities people engage in daily, those who work with and study young people can invite them to tell about their lives from diverse perspectives in diverse modes as a way to exert some influence on their own lives—first through reflection, which paves the way for action. Conflicts are, after all, embedded in the social fabric of communities, so researchers, educators, and clinicians must pay attention to the meanings young people make of conflicts. Stories of conflict embody those meanings and set the scene for future action.

I have argued that storytelling *is* a social interaction rather than merely *about* social interactions. As children are socialized to relationships via the storytelling process, they develop ways of interpreting and acting in conflicts and a wide range of human relations. The differences between children's autobiographical and fictional stories in public life reveal the complexity of their abilities to respond to diverse values about conflict across contexts like school, home culture, and peer culture and to personal concerns.

For these reasons, researchers, educators, and clinicians should be increasingly sensitive to the power of storytelling as a means not only of communication but also as guides for social relations. Those who work with children can invite them to participate in collaborative and individual storytelling and writing activities to learn more about conflict and resolution. The research discussed here also suggests that we should vary the nature of storytelling to include fiction as well as autobiography so that children can draw on a wide range of social and personal resources. Silencing the expression of conflict may make attempts to promote peace more artificial. Those of us doing this research have also found that creating stories in postwar contexts has for potential for the development of society, as well as for individual children involved in civic activities and reconstruction (Daiute & Turniski, 2004). As children write about conflicts in war-torn areas, their stories may be imaginative means to create new kinds of relations, at least in the interpersonal realm.

Note

1. Children's texts are presented with the original spelling, punctuation, and wording. Children created the texts in handwriting, and I transcribed them for print.

References

Amsterdam, A. G., & Bruner, J. (2000). *Minding the law: How courts rely on storytelling and how their stories change the ways we understand the law—and ourselves.* Cambridge, MA: Harvard University Press.

Apfel, R. J., & Simon, B. (1996). *Minefields in their hearts: The mental health of children in war and communal violence.* New Haven: Yale University Press.

Arsenio, W., & Lemerise, E. (2004). Aggression and moral development: Integration of the social information processing and moral domain models. *Child Development, 75,* 987–1002.

Bakhtin, M. M. (1986). *Speech genres and other late essays.* Austin: University of Texas Press.

Bamberg, M.G.W. (1997). Positioning between structure and performance. *Journal of Narrative and Life History, 7,* 335–342.

Cross, W.E., Jr., & Fhagen-Smith, P. (2001). Patterns of African American identity development: A life space perspective. In C. L. Wijeyesinghe & B.W. Jackson (Eds.), *New perspectives on racial identity development* (pp. 243–270). New York: New York University Press.

Daiute, C. (2000). Narrative sites for youths' construction of social consciousness. In M. Fine & L. Weis (Eds.), *Construction sites: Excavating class, race, gender, and sexuality among urban youth* (pp. 211–234). New York: Teachers College Press.

Daiute, C. (2004). Creative uses of cultural genres. In C. Daiute & C. Lightfoot (Eds.), *Narrative analysis: Studying the development of individuals in society* (pp. 111–134). Thousand Oaks, CA: Sage.

Daiute, C., & Buteau, E. (2002). Writing for their lives: Children's narrative supports for physical and psychological well-being. In S.J. Lepore & J.M. Smythe (Eds.), *The writing cure: How expressive writing promotes health and emotional well-being* (pp. 53–73). Washington, DC: American Psychological Association.

Daiute, C., Buteau, E., & Rawlins, C. (2001). Social relational wisdom: Developmental diversity in children's written narratives about social conflict. *Narrative Inquiry, 11*(2), 1–30.

Daiute, C., & Jones, J. (2003). Diversity discourses: Reading race and ethnicity in children's writing. In S. Greene & D. Abt-Perkins (Eds.), *Talking, reading, writing, and race: Contributions to racial understanding by literacy research* (pp. 178–200). New York: Teachers College Press.

Daiute, C., & Lightfoot, C. (2004). *Narrative analysis: Studying the development of individuals in society.* Thousand Oaks, CA: Sage.

Daiute, C., Stern, R., & Lelutiu-Weinberger, C. (2003). Contradictions in a violence prevention program. *Journal of Social Issues, 59*(1), 83–101.

Daiute, C., & Turniski, M. (2005, February). *Genres of co-existence: A case study in Croatia.* Paper presented at the National Council of Teachers of English Research Assembly, Columbus, OH.

Earls, F., & Carlson, M. (1999). Children at the margins of society. *New Directions in Child and Adolescent Development, 85,* 71–82.

Elliot, D. S., Hamburg, B. A., & Williams, K. R. (Eds.). (1998). *Violence in American schools.* New York: Cambridge University Press.

Foucault, M. (1988). Technologies of the self. In L. H. Martin, H. Gutman, & P. H. Hutton (Eds.), *Technologies of the self: A seminar with Michel Foucault* (pp. 16–49). Amherst: University of Massachusetts Press.

Freud, S. (1909). *Five lectures on psycho-analysis.* New York: Norton.

Garbarino, J. (1999). *Lost boys: Why our sons turn violent and how we can save them.* New York: Free Press.

Gates, H. L. (1992). *Loose canons: Notes on the culture wars.* New York: Oxford University Press.

Gilligan, C. (1982). *In a different voice: Psychological theory and women's development.* Cambridge, MA: Harvard University Press.

Greenberg, M. T., Lengua, L. J., Coie, J. D., & Pinderhughes, E. E. (1999). Predicting developmental outcomes at school entry using a multiple-risk model: Four American communities. *Developmental Psychology, 35*(2), 403–417.

Harre, R., & van Langenhove, L. (1999). Reflexive positioning: Autobiography. In R. Harre & L. van Langenhove (Eds.), *Positioning theory* (pp. 60 - 73). Malden, MA: Blackwell.

Hardt, M., & Negri, A. (2000). *Empire.* Cambridge, MA: Harvard University Press.

Henrich, C. C., Brown, J. L., & Aber, J. L. (1999). Evaluating the effectiveness of school-based violence prevention: Developmental approaches. *Society for Research on Child Development Social Policy Report, 8*(3). Ann Arbor, MI: Society for Research on Child Development.

Hermans, H.J.M. (1997). Self-narrative in the life course: A contextual approach. In M. Bamberg (Ed.), *Narrative development: Six approaches* (pp. 223–264). Mahwah, NJ: Erlbaum.

Hermans, H.J.M., & Hermans-Jansen, E. (1995). *Self-narratives: The construction of meaning in psychotherapy.* New York: Guilford Press.

Leont'ev, A. N. (1989). *Activity, consciousness, and personality.* Englewood Cliffs, NJ: Prentice-Hall.

Nelson, K. N. (1986). *Event knowledge: Structure and function in development.* Hillsdale, NJ: Erlbaum.

Nelson, V. M. (1993). *Mayfield Crossing.* New York: Avon Books.

Nystrand, M., & Wiemelt, J. (1991). When is a text explicit? Formalist and dialogical conceptions. *Text, 11,* 25–41.

Olweus, C. (1994). Bullying at school: Basic facts and effects in a school-based intervention program. *Journal of Child Psychology and Psychiatry and Allied Disciplines, 35*(7), 1171–1190.

Polkinghorne, D. (1991). Narrative and self-concept. *Journal of Narrative and Life History, 1,* 135–153.

Sampson, R. J., Morenoff, J. D., & Earls, F. (1999). Beyond social capital: Spatial dynamics of collective efficacy for children. *American Sociological Review, 64,* 633–660.

Selman, R. L., Watts, C. L., & Schultz, L.H. (1997). *Fostering friendship: Pair therapy for treatment and prevention*. New York: de Gruyter.

Spence, D. P. (1982). *Narrative truth and historical truth: Meaning and interpretation in psychoanalysis*. New York: Norton.

Surat, M. M. (1983). *Angel child, dragon child*. New York: Scholastic.

Turiel, E. (2002). *The culture of morality*. New York: Cambridge University Press.

Vygotsky, L. S. (1978). *Mind in society*. Cambridge, MA: Harvard University Press.

Walker, P. (1998). *Voices of Love and Freedom: A literacy-based ethics and prevention program*. Iowa City: Prescription Learning.

Wainryb, C. (1995). Reasoning about social conflicts in different cultures: Druze and Jewish children in Israel. *Child Development, 66,* 390–401.

Widom, C. S. (1989). Does violence, beget violence? A critical examination of the literature. *Psychological Bulletin, 106*(1), 3–28.

CHAPTER 13

Child Soldiers

Community Healing and Rituals in Mozambique and Angola

ALCINDA HONWANA

In this chapter, I analyze specific social and cultural notions of health, mental health, and healing as they apply, in particular, to child soldiers' reintegration into society in Mozambique and Angola. I will present a number of case studies from Mozambique and Angola, and I will then consider why such understandings and practices are fundamental to the well-being of these populations. The chapter is based on research carried out in Mozambique and Angola in the postwar periods, as people were trying to deal with and heal the social wounds of war.[1] These are two countries completely ravaged by war, with millions affected by it (refugees, displaced people, disabled people, orphans, widows, infant soldiers, abused girls, and so forth), and with very poor networks of modern health care systems (especially in rural areas), let alone psychological care. So, in this context, if any mental and psychological healing had to take place, it had to be based on local systems of health care. During my research, I was interested to know how mental health is understood by local people, how it related to the war, and what kinds of therapeutic strategies existed to deal with the social and emotional problems caused by a deep social crisis such as war. Near the end of the chapter, I offer several case studies of children's participation in ritual practices as a process toward their healing from the traumas of their war activities.

This chapter looks at the ways mental health and illness can be understood outside the framework of Western biomedical paradigms, in particular with the role of indigenous medicine in community healing, reconciliation, and reintegration in the aftermath of war in Mozambique and Angola. I will examine the ways individuals and groups deal with the social and emotional wounds caused by the drawn-out wars between the Popular Movement for the Liberation of Angola (MPLA) and the National Union for the Total Independence of Angola (UNITA) in Angola, and between the Mozambique Liberation Front (FRELIMO) and the Mozambique National Resistance (RENAMO) in Mozambique, and I focus on indigenous therapeutic strategies and healing mechanisms, such as treatments and cleansing and purification rituals carried out by diviners, healers, and healing churches, which in rural areas have often been the only mechanisms available to cope with death, illness, distress, and suffering and to restore health, peace, and harmony in the lives of individuals and groups in the postwar period.

This chapter is organized in three main sections: the first examines the issue of culture and mental health by looking at Western concepts of mental health as cultural constructions. The second section deals with local concepts of heath, illness, and healing in Mozambique and Angola, and highlights the role of the spirits of the dead in processes of causation and healing of ill health. Finally, the third section considers some of the therapeutic strategies employed by local populations in Mozambique and Angola to deal with mental distress caused by war. Community rituals to appease the spirits as well as cleansing rituals to purify polluted individuals are analyzed in this section.

The Context of Political Violence in Mozambique and Angola

In Mozambique, the war between the government and the rebel forces started in 1977 with the creation of RENAMO by the Rhodesian Central Intelligence Organization. With its economy devastated and development projects paralyzed, the country became increasingly dependent of foreign aid. As a result, the government decided to undertake far-reaching economic reforms, abandoning its former Marxist policies in favor of political and economic liberalization. In 1990, a new constitution was adopted, enshrining the principles of multiparty democracy. With its resources dissipated by years of war, the government was incapable of imposing a military solution to the conflict. As South African support decreased, following a process of internal reforms to end apartheid, RENAMO was also unable to sustain its war effort. With this military impasse, the possibilities of a political solution gained strength (Minter, 1994; Vines, 1991). Following several months of negotiations, the government and RENAMO signed their General Peace Agreement, in Rome in October 1992. The first democratic elections took place in October 1994; FRELIMO won these and formed a new government. Five years later, in the elections of 1999, FRELIMO renewed its mandate, though by a very narrow margin. The Mozambican conflict was one of the most brutal wars of its time. The social costs were enormous.

Its consequences for the civilian populations were catastrophic. Hundreds of thousands of Mozambicans died as a result of the war, about 5 million people were internally displaced by 1989, and more than 1 million became refugees in neighboring countries. Besides the many thousands of children who died as a direct consequence of the war, it is estimated that more than 250,000 children were either orphaned or separated from their families. School enrollments were reduced by an estimated 500,000, and medical facilities servicing approximately 5 million people were destroyed (Minter, 1994; Vines, 1991).

In Angola, UNITA was one of the anticolonial movements that had fought against colonial rule since the early 1960s, alongside the MPLA and the Popular Union of Angola—National Front for the Liberation of Angola (UPA-FNLA). After the 1974 coup in Portugal, which marked the end of the Portuguese colonial wars, the three Angolan nationalist movements engaged in a bitter internecine war to gain exclusive access to power. The MPLA emerged victorious, the UPA-FNLA faded in importance, and UNITA reconstituted itself with mainly U.S. and South African support, and continued its war against the MPLA government (Minter, 1994; Vines, 1991). UNITA portrays itself as anti-Marxist and pro-Western. In the height of the Cold War, the Angolan conflict directly involved South African and Cuban troops giving support to UNITA and the MPLA, respectively. The first chance for peace came in May 1991, with the signature of a cease-fire agreement between the government and UNITA. This cease-fire held until the elections in September 1992, the first democratic elections in the country's history. In these elections, deemed free and fair by the international community, the MPLA won a majority of the votes. UNITA refused to accept the election results, claiming electoral fraud, and Savimbi ordered his troops to return to war, restarting full-scale conflict in October 1992 (Minter, 1994; United Nations Development Programme [UNDP], 1997). This brutal and intense war lasted until 1994, taking a heavy toll on the civilian population—especially children. In November 1994, a new peace agreement was signed in Lusaka between the government and UNITA. In April 1997, a government of "National Reconciliation and Unity," which brought UNITA members as well as some from other political parties into the cabinet, was established. Peace didn't last long. In October 1998, following disagreements with the government, UNITA went back to war. Even before the renewed war at the end of 1992, the UN estimated that more than $30 billion had been lost during the Angolan conflict. It is estimated that in the 1992–94 war, more than 100,000 people died from war-related causes, the number of land mine victims rose to 70,000, and about 1.2 million people were displaced by September 1994 (Minter, 1994). According to the 1997 United Nations Development Programme *Report on Human Development in Angola*, about 280,000 people were living in neighboring countries as refugees, and approximately 1.2 million Angolans were internally displaced. The urban population rose by 50% in 1995, compared to a 15% growth in 1970. It is estimated that around 1 million children have been directly affected by the war, with more than 500,000 children dead. About half of the displaced population were children under 15 years of age. According to the UNICEF statistics for 1993, nearly 840,000 children were living in difficult circumstances (Minter, 1994). Thousands of children are unaccompanied, orphaned, or separated from their families, and many were dragged into armies and militia. In 1997, it was estimated that about 8,500 under-age soldiers would be demobilized by March 1997 (UNDP, 1997). About 10,000 were registered in the 1996–97 demobilization process. Indirectly, the war has affected many more children. Malnutrition has increased as a result of low food production and displacement. The deterioration of health care services during the war resulted in higher infant and child mortality rates. Many children were prevented from attending school, as a result mainly of displacement and destruction of schools.

Culture and Mental Health

In this section, I will start with an examination of the concept of culture and then see how culture and mental health relate to each other. The concept of culture has occupied the minds of social scientists for many generations. Anthropologists are particularly interested in the study of culture in their analysis of human social behavior and interactions in society (Swartz, 1998). Culture has been described as a

> set of guidelines (both explicit and implicit) which individuals inherit as members of a particular society, and which tells them how to view the world, how to experience it emotionally, and how to behave in relation to other people, to supernatural forces or gods, and to the natural environment. (Helman, 1994, pp. 2–3)

Therefore, culture is a "pattern of meanings" (Geertz, 1973) that shapes human experiences and provides a framework of understandings and beliefs that underpin people's life actions. Culture is about the rules and norms of a society and the ways in which these are enacted, experienced, and transmitted. Thus, culture cannot be static, as interpretations of rules and norms change over time and are constantly being re-created. Culture plays a crucial role in issues of health and well-being, since the processes through which people manage their afflictions are built on cultural perceptions.

The World Health Organization (WHO) defines health as not merely the absence of disease and infirmity but a positive state of physical, mental, and social well-being. This shows that mental health, or mental well-being, is part of health and cannot be dissociated from it. This definition goes beyond the Western biomedical tradition that separates body and mind. Dominant Western biomedicine is based on the premise that some afflictions are purely physical in nature (the domain of the body) and others are purely psychological (the domain of the mind). This dichotomy has a very long history that goes back to Descartes in the seventeenth century, when he articulated the split between the tangible body, which should be the concern of the field of science, and the intangible mind, the concern of the field of theology (Swartz, 1998).

This separation between mind and body is not made by many other medical systems that approach health and healing in a more holistic way. The WHO definition is in itself a negation of the Cartesian dichotomy, because it includes physical, social, and mental well-being in its notion of health. Even within biomedicine, this split is increasingly becoming unsustainable as biomedicine develops its understanding of social sciences.

Thus, mental health is part of the whole concept of health. As White and Marsella rightly asked, "What is "mental" about "mental health"" (1982, p. 85)? Indeed, in many cultures mental health is not perceived in isolation from the physical body and the social and natural environment. Rather, mental and physical health are understood to be interrelated: the mind influences the body as much as the body impacts the mind. In these cultures, there is a holistic approach to health and healing, as ill health is primarily perceived to be a social phenomenon that might be reflected on the body. Fainzang's (1986) study of concepts of health in Burkina Faso suggests that ill health is an event that marks an alteration in the normal course of life of individuals and groups. Divination is the method employed to "diagnose the social life," as it relies not on the physical manifestation of the affliction but rather on the social origins of it.

Mental health is thus closely linked to culture, because the ways people express, experience, and give meaning to their afflictions are tied to specific social and cultural contexts. Psychological distress and trauma have a social and cultural dimension. The manner in which people understand their afflictions is undoubtedly connected to beliefs about the origins of such afflictions. Such beliefs are central in devising appropriate therapeutic strategies for the alleviation and elimination of the afflictions. Because different cultures have different beliefs about causation and treatment of ill health, there will be differences in the way health and mental health are conceptualized and dealt with.

The main paradigms that shape aid and relief policies and interventions in African conflicts have been strongly informed by Western biomedical notions of health and illness. Such paradigms have often been imposed on societies that possess different worldviews and sociocultural patterns (Dawes & Honwana, 1996; Honwana, 1997). Because mental health is not a universal phenomenon, it is important to look for local knowledge about mental afflictions. It is this local knowledge that informs specific cultural understandings about the causes of ill health, including psychological distress, and about the effect that traumatic experiences and events might have on individuals and groups. Only through an understanding of local notions of mental health will it be possible to devise the appropriate programs to deal with it.

In Mozambique and Angola, for a variety of afflictions, patients often make recourse, in varying sequences of treatment, to both the hospital and the traditional healer or even the prophet of a religious denomination. Such a pluralistic approach to healing, combining several therapeutic strategies (Western, non-Western, pagan, religious, and the like) can be effective, although some obstacles to a pluralistic approach may occur due to lack of understanding of other cultural forms, and to the imposition of one to the detriment of others. When appropriately used, modern psychotherapies can be effectively used in conjunction with local concepts and therapies, as long as Western therapies are not be considered the rule—and, above all, local therapies should not be completely discarded, as I discuss further later in this chapter.

Mental Health as a Social and Cultural Construction

As mentioned earlier, dominant Western psychotherapeutic models are often seen as universal and applicable everywhere. However, this assumption has been challenged, as modern psychology is also a culturally constructed system. Modern psychology generally locates the causes of psycho-social distress within the individual, and devises responses, which are primarily based on individual therapy (Boyden & Gibbs, 1997). Thus, recovery is achieved through helping the patient deal with her or his intrapsychic world, and "come to terms" with the traumatic experience. Healing is mainly carried out in private sessions aimed at "talking out," and externalizing feelings and afflictions. As White and Marsella have pointed out:

> the use of "talk therapy" aimed at altering individual behavior through the individual's "insight" into his or her personality is firmly rooted in a conception of the person as a distinct and independent individual capable of self-transformation in relative isolation from particular social contexts. (1982, p. 28)

The approaches that are based on individual therapy and "talking out" methods have to a certain extent been fairly effective in Euro-American contexts. Such an effectiveness derives from the fact that these methods are rooted both in the biomedical conception of the self, framed by the philosophical premises of the Cartesian dichotomy, and in local ancient religious traditions, such as the institution of the confessional (Dawes, 1996). Also important is the fact that modern psychological therapy became part of the popular consciousness and is a form of "common sense" especially among the middle class. Although in modern psychotherapy there is a rise in interest in areas such as family therapy, community psychology, and behavioral public health, the dominant approaches are still centered on the individual self, as a unit in itself.

However, in other social contexts (such as Mozambique and Angola), there are certainly other forms of "common sense" routes to understanding the origins, manifestations, and treatment of mental health problems. In these non-Western settings, there are different conceptions of the self, and of the relationship between self and others (both the living and the dead). The self is not understood in isolation from the collective. Control and autonomy over one's body-mind and health transcend the boundaries of the individual self, as she or he can become ill due to someone else's intervention. The spirits of the dead, as well as some human beings, are often believed to be at the origin of a person's illness, death, and other misfortunes. In these societies, a great deal of importance is placed on the role that the spirits of the dead have in the processes of causation and healing of mental health problems. Here, the emphasis is placed not only on the individual self as such but also on the wider collective body, which can interfere and affect the health and well-being of the person, in ways that she or he cannot control. Therefore, in these contexts, an exclusive, or rather dominant, focus on the individual self would not take into account the role of the family and of the community in the causation and elimination of ill health (Honwana, 1997). I will come back to this discussion when examining local notions of health and ill health in Mozambique and Angola. I will next consider the application of posttraumatic stress disorder as a Western construct in non-Western contexts, using the examples of Mozambique and Angola.

Beyond Posttraumatic Stress Disorder

The concept of posttraumatic stress disorder (PTSD) represents a new discourse of trauma and its psychological sequelae that emerged in the 1980s in the United States (Bracken, Giller, & Summerfield, 1995). Many authors have studied the effectiveness of PTSD as a psychological model in non-Western societies (Bracken et al., 1995; Young, 1995; among others). PTSD was born out of trying to understand the experiences and problems faced by the American veterans of the Vietnam War. In this regard, it was conceived as an instrument to deal with psychological distress in men who left a situation of relative "normality," went into a traumatic experience (the Vietnam War), and then returned to "normality." That is why the prefix *post*.

What has happened in Mozambique and Angola, and in other ongoing conflict zones, especially in Africa, south Asia, and Latin America, is that the vast majority of adults and children we are dealing with today have lived most of their lives or were born during periods of conflict and social unrest. The armed conflicts in Mozambique lasted more than 15 years, and in Angola more than 20 years (recent reports indicate that UNITA has reenacted the war in certain areas of the country). Thus, for these people, violence and trauma is not *post*, but is rather current and very much part of their everyday life.

Nordstrom's (1997) work on war and violence in Mozambique stresses the fact that there the notion of violence should be understood well beyond the war itself—military attacks, the land mines, and other direct war situations. The notion of violence here is embedded in everyday life and touches on spheres like poverty, hunger, nudity, displacement, loss of dignity, and the like. In line with this argument, one can say that most people we have been dealing with in the aftermath of the war in Mozambique are still living under violent and potentially traumatic circumstances. Many refugees and displaced people returned to completely devastated villages where the houses and agricultural fields were burnt and schools, hospitals, factories, roads, and railway lines were destroyed. Many continue to live without the basic livelihood conditions (lack of food and clean water, lack of proper clothing to wear, lack of jobs and basic education, lack of proper shelter, and so forth)—not to mention the case of Angola, where the war has restarted after a period of cease-fire and peace agreements. In Angola, thousands of civilians have been once again plunged into full-scale armed conflict, and many young demobilized soldiers are being rerecruited into the military. Therefore, when applying Western psychotherapeutic models such as PTSD to other social and cultural settings, we need to be aware of local specificities and worldviews in order to adapt the models to the particular needs of the people. This is one of the ways of making their use relevant and more effective.

Another issue related to the application of PTSD concerns the healing therapies used to deal with it. As mentioned earllier, in the West, "talk therapy," in small or large groups, is one of the fundamental processes of coming to terms with the traumatic experience. However, studies on healing of war trauma in Mozambique and Angola have shown that recalling the traumatic experience through verbal externalization (talk therapy) as a means to heal is not always effective (Marrato, 1996). Because the person is not perceived to exist in isolation from the group, dealing with her or his intrapsychic problems will not be sufficient to eliminate the problem, especially if the origins of the affliction are believed to be "located" outside the person. Thus, treatment procedures should not only be focused on the intrapsychic problems of the individual but also should address those pesons or entities believed to be causing the problem. Instead of individual treatment sessions, rituals are organized to deal with these types of afflictions.

The rituals are full of symbolic meaning and draw on cultural beliefs and understandings of the problems at hand. They involve not just the patient and his or her immediate family but also neighbors, friends, passers-by, and the dead. In many of these rituals, people do not talk about what happened, and do not look back at the past. They would rather start afresh after performing the ritual procedures. These involve not necessarily verbal expression of the affliction but a series of symbolic procedures aimed at putting aside the traumatic experience. Many people believe that talking about the past (the trauma) can be equivalent to opening the door for the malevolent human beings or spiritual forces to intervene again.

This issue is also discussed by Summerfield (1999), when he points out that Cambodians do not share or talk about feelings and memories about the trauma of the Pol Pot years with foreigners. He mentions equally that Mozambican and Ethiopian refugees describe forgetting about the traumatic past as means of coping with it (p. 12). In the next section, I will develop this discussion by drawing on case material from Mozambique and Angola.

Local Concepts of Mental Health in Mozambique and Angola

In this section, I start looking at concepts of mental health other than the Western ones, by examining case material from Mozambique and Angola. I will first look at notions of health and ill health in general, because in these cultures, mental health is not separated from a general state of health and well-being. Given the centrality of spiritual agents in matters of health and healing in these two contexts, the role of such spiritual entities will need special consideration. Mental health as a collective matter is particularly important in moments of deep crisis, such as a war. So, I will analyze how the spirits of the dead who did not have a proper burial during wars are believed to be able to afflict people and cause mental illness. Finally, I examine the issue of social pollution by showing that individuals who have been in the war (both soldiers and civilians) are believed to be polluted by the "blood of the dead," and are seen as potential contaminators of their family relatives, and other members of the community.

Notions of Health and Ill Health

In southern Mozambique, people perceived health as being a natural state for all human beings. So to be unhealthy denotes abnormality, showing that some-where something is out of its normal place, that harmony is jeopardized. Health in this context is approached in terms of a life process rather than just in terms of a bodily process, and in this sense it acquires a broader dimension in com-parison to Western concepts. Thus, health is defined by the harmonious re-lationships between human beings and the environment (their surroundings), between them and the spiritual world, and among themselves within the en-vironment. Rather than being narrowly defined realms, the social (the spirits and the living) and natural worlds are united within a larger cosmological uni-verse. Thus, rain should fall at its ordinary time, crops should grow, people should not fall sick, and children should not die. If this harmonious state fails to come about, it is perceived to be the result of intervention of the malevolent forces. It can also be a sanction of the ancestral spirits for incorrect behavior, or of other spiritual forces. Therefore, the relationships among human beings, between human beings and the ancestral spirits, and between them and the environment have to be balanced so that health ensues. However, if they are disrupted in any way, the well-being of the community is jeopardized. In order to maintain this harmonious state of affairs, there is a complex set of rules and practices that govern society. Ill health is, therefore, considered to be primarily a social phenomenon, which results from an imbalance in these relationships. Traditional healing presents a holistic approach to health by combining both the social and the physical dimensions of the affliction in order to treat the person as a whole. Here there is an overall integration between body and mind, and the Cartesian dichotomy does not apply. The social imbalance in a patient's life is generally reflected in the physical body, and both dimensions are equally taken into consideration to restore the patient's health. The corollary is that healing is achieved through a double strategy: divination, which deals with the social causes of the patient's affliction and prescribes the rituals to repair it; and the physical healing that addresses the suppression of the bodily symptoms, through the use of herbal remedies.

Moreover, the individual is not seen as a singular entity but rather as part of a community. During the divination séance, the diviner carries out a careful ex-amination of the state of the patient's social relationships in the community (re-lationships with the living, with the spiritual world, and with nature) to achieve a diagnosis. The diviner—patient dialogue, developed during the consultation, represents a reciprocal learning process in which, as Jackson (1978) puts it, a process of "transference and counter-transference" of information occurs and brings them together. Thus, in this context the relationship between practitioner and patient becomes very close and enhances the cultural bonds between them.

In this regard, traditional healing can be extremely effective for dealing with mental illness.

Spiritual Agencies' Role in Health and Healing

In Mozambique and Angola, the ancestral spirits are part of everyday life action. It is believed that when an individual dies and the body is buried, the spirit remains as the effective manifestation of her or his power and personality. Thus, death is not the end of an individual's existence but rather marks the transition to a new dimension of life. Spirits of the dead take possession of a person's body and operate through him or her, exercising a powerful influence over the living (Honwana, 1996). The Supreme Being, or the Creator, is a remote divinity, which does not have a direct relationship with the community. People relate directly to the ancestral spirits with whom they share a combined existence, and interact in everyday life. The ancestral spirits are believed to be real entities whose action interferes with the life of human beings in society. They are the ones who protect and guide the communities. They promote fertility of the land and of women, good agricultural production, and good hunting and good relations among members of the group. They also protect them against misfortune, disease, ecological dangers, and evil, namely, witchcraft and sorcery. In short, the spirits care for the well-being of the communities. However, the ancestral spirits can also withdraw their protection and create a state of vulnerability to misfortune and evil intentions, or even cause maladies, to show their displeasure or anger with their descendants. They are believed to protect and give health and wealth to those who respect the social norms of the group, and to punish those who are antisocial, who act against the norms, which disrespects social order. Ill health can also be caused by the intervention of malevolent spirits manipulated by witches and sorcerers, or by the spirits of bitterness, those of individuals wrongfully killed or not properly buried. Communities venerate and worship the ancestral spirits through special rituals to propitiate them. In southern Mozambique, *ku pahla* is a verb that means "to venerate" or "to honor" the ancestral spirits. *Ku pahla* is a permanent way of paying respect to one's ancestors, and it is performed in multiple occasions such as: the birth of a child, before harvesting, during a meal, before a long trip, and the like. The performance of *ku pahla* gives individuals and groups a sense of security and stability that they need to carry on with their lives. It is this permanent liaison between the living and the dead that gives meaning to the existence of both the spirits and the community. Another way of establishing contact with the spirits is through possessed practitioners known as *tinyanga*. They are the intermediaries between the living world and that of the ancestral spirits, acting as mediums.

The War and the Spirits of the Dead

In Mozambique and Angola, there are local ways of understanding mental health. In both countries, people believe that mental illness is directly related to the anger of the spirits of the dead. In southern Mozambique, these spirits, called *Mipfhukwa*, are the spirits of the dead who are believed to have been killed unjustly, and who did not have a proper burial, with all the rituals aimed at placing them in their proper positions in the world of the ancestors. Thus, their souls are unsettled; they are spirits of bitterness. It is believed that these spirits have the capacity to afflict, by provoking mental illness and even death, those who killed or mistreated them in life. This revenge is also extended to the family of the killers, who have to pay for their relatives' behavior in the past. The *Mipfhukwa* spirits may also be nasty to passers-by, especially to those who cross their path. *Mipfhukwa* spirits are particularly important after a war, when soldiers and civilians are not appropriately buried. In fact, this phenomenon is often referred to as a result of warfare. Some of the elder participants in this research recalled that after the Nguni wars in southern Mozambique in the nineteenth century,[2] the spirits of the Nguni and Ndau warriors killed in this region away from their homes were not buried, and afflicted and killed many local families. The recent war between the government and RENAMO rebels is also believed to have "produced" many spirits of bitterness, which can cause mental problems or death to the living if not properly appeased. People were unanimous in stating that rituals for appeasing these spirits have to be performed in the places where battles occurred and many people died. These rituals are seen as vital to calm the spirits and place them in their proper positions in the spiritual world. These rituals are generally performed by traditional practitioners who have the capacity to "capture" and exorcise or appease these spirits.

The War and the Performance of Burial Rituals

In Angola, this is also a common phenomenon. In the areas were we carried out our research (Uige, Bie, Huambo, Moxico, and Malange) people mentioned that the spirits of the dead had to be appeased so that peace would ensue. Burial rituals for the dead are considered to be very important. Notwithstanding the importance of burial rituals, in difficult circumstances such as the war, in which many people died of unnatural causes, it becomes extremely difficult or almost impossible to bury the dead properly. Thus, the number of dead without proper burials in the postwar period is enormous, and people have to deal with that problem. People mentioned that soldiers who killed people and civilians who were present during killings are particularly vulnerable to insanity, which can be caused by the spirits of the dead they killed or saw being killed. This idea is discussed later in connection with the notion of social pollution. For now, let's consider some of the stories about the dead of the war that people shared with us, as follows.

> My mother was killed during the war, and because at that time there was no way of performing the burial, we did not do anything. After some time my daughter became very ill, and ordinary traditional treatment did not cure her illness. Later a kimbanda [spirit medium] told us that the spirit of my mother had possessed my daughter because since she died we did not do anything. After performing the

rituals the child's illness disappeared. (Mr. Lohali, Bie, Angola, interviewed by the CCF team in 1997)

During the war my father was killed. I did not perform a burial because I thought that in times of war there is no need for that. But, during the night I was unable to sleep . . . I was dreaming with my father telling me that "I am dead but I haven't reached the place of the dead; you have to perform my burial rituals because I can see the way to the place where other dead people are . . . but I have no way to get there." After I performed the rituals, and I have never dreamed of my father again. (Mr. Samba, Huambo, Angola, interviewed by the CCF team in 1997)

It is interesting to note in this statement that the dead father needed the rituals in order to make his way to his proper position in the world of the spirits. Despite seeing it, he could not get there. In this regard, an elderly traditional healer explained that when someone dies, it is imperative to perform the burial rituals, because without them access to the spiritual world can be blocked. So the unburied dead have to catch the attention of their relatives (through illness or dreams) and ask them for a proper burial, as in these two cases. In other circumstances, the spirits may cause illnesses (mental illnesses are very common) to their killers or relatives or even to passers-by, until the rituals are performed. I will examine some of these cases later. In times of war, most of the burial rituals that are performed happen in the absence of the dead body, as people most often receive the news of a relative's death by word of mouth. In such circumstances, burials continue to take place because it is believed that the spirits of the dead will "come with the wind" to join their kin for the ceremony. This view is expressed in Mr. Kapata's comment that "even when the person dies far away from home [and the dead body is not present] the spirit comes with the wind." The same idea was expressed by Mr. Marimba, who pointed out that even those who "died away from home need a burial ceremony. When they die far away their soul stays there unsettled. With the performance of the burial the soul comes with the wind and settles down."

The Notion of Social Pollution

In the rural communities, most people believe that individuals are potentially exposed to pollution in their contacts with other social groups and environments. Those who migrate across group boundaries, such as migrant workers, are particularly exposed to social contamination. This kind of contamination comes from being victims of witchcraft and sorcery, picking up unknown spirits, or being more vulnerable to illness in an unknown environment. Ecological conditions, too, may be a source of pollution (Ngubane, 1977).

Social pollution is an important factor in the context of postwar healing both in Angola and Mozambique. Pollution may arise from being in contact with death and bloodshed. Individuals who have been in a war, who killed or saw people being killed, are seen as being polluted by the "wrongdoings of the war." They are seen as the vehicles through which the spirits of the dead of the war might enter and afflict the community. These spirits may afflict not only to the individual who committed the offences but also the entire family or group. After the war, when soldiers and refugees return home, they are believed to be potential contaminators of the social body. The spirits of the dead, which might haunt them, can disrupt life in their families and villages. Therefore, the cleansing process is seen as a fundamental condition for collective protection against pollution and for the social reintegration of war-affected people into society (Honwana, 1997, 1999).

Case Studies from Mozambique and Angola

In this final section, I analyze some cases of different therapeutic strategies used in the postwar period in Mozambique and Angola. I discuss how individuals, families, and entire communities try to heal the social wounds of war through ritual performance. However, not everybody in these places performs rituals to appease the spirits of the dead. Such practices are, of course, more common in the rural areas, although they are also performed in urban settings. The closeness of the individual or the family to their cultural roots, the availability of health care alternatives, and religious and political affiliations are important factors in determining the ways in which people make decisions about the therapeutic or healing strategies to adopt (Honwana, 1998, 1999). In the postwar period, people perform various types of rituals. Some are aimed at addressing the problems of the community at large and are not centered on particular individuals. Others are directed toward healing particular individuals or families from pollution caused by the war. I will start by discussing the first category, which I call community rituals. Three cases are presented and analyzed. Second, I will examine rituals for former child soldiers who are trying to deal with what happened during the war (Honwana, 1999). An acknowledgment of the atrocities committed and subsequent break from that past is articulated through ritual performance.

Community Rituals

Case 1   After the war was over, traditional healers and diviners from Munguine in the district of Manhiça (about 100 km north of Maputo) were called to perform a ritual in the road that links the locality of Munguine to Manhiça. The ritual was needed because as soon as it got dark, nobody could use that road to get to Manhiça. Local people reported that as they approached the place they felt "something" beating them or heard voices sending them back or became blind and could not see their way to Manhiça. So they suspected that something was wrong in that place and requested the traditional practitioners' help. After analyzing the situation, the specialists decided to perform a ritual of divination to diagnose the problem. The ritual was performed at dawn in the presence of local chiefs, local government authorities, and the people of Munguine. The specialists performed *ku femba* (to catch the spirit) and identified the spirit of a

RENAMO commander killed in that place during the war. Then the spirit spoke through a medium. The spirit acknowledged that he had been afflicting local people because he wanted to go back to his place and have a proper burial. And in order to do so, the spirit requested some money and *capulanas* (local pieces of fabric) to take with him. The local population agreed to contribute money to give the spirit, and buy the *capulanas*. The chiefs and the government also gave a contribution. A week later, the spirit was caught again. A ritual took place in which the spirit was symbolically placed in the *capulanas* and tied together with the money. Then the whole thing was buried far away from Munguine. Some herbal remedies provided by the healers were also placed in the *capulanas* to avoid the return of the spirit. According to the local people, since then no more problems had occurred in that road.

Case 2   The town of Kuito is situated in the plateau of Bie in the central region of Angola. This town was severely affected by the 1992–94 war (the one that erupted when UNITA lost the general elections of 1992 to the MPLA). Thousands of people lost their lives in that "urban" war. Many of them died on the plateau as they tried to escape from military attacks, or look for food to eat. Until July 1997, many of the dead of the plateau remained there. Land mines prevented people from reaching the plateau to identify the dead and organize burial rituals. Many people in Kuito believe that things will not go well unless something is done to appease the dead and place them in the world of the spirits. Kutximuila and Aurora, two female healers from Kuito, said that the government should organize a big ceremony to honor the dead of the plateau. Their views were shared by the traditional chief of the area, who pointed out: "The government must think of having collective ceremonies to bury the bones of those killed in the war. . . . Here in Kuito many people died and no ceremonies were performed to appease their souls. Their souls are wandering about and can afflict anyone" (interviewed by author in 1997).

Case 3   In the aftermath of war in Angola, people from the areas of Huambo and Bie perform a ritual called *okusiakala ondalao yokalye,* which can be translated as "let's light a new fire." According to the local population, this ritual is performed after crises such as natural disasters, war, and other misfortunes of great magnitude. On the day of the ritual, every household extinguishes their old fires. The traditional chief, helped by traditional practitioners, lights a new fire, sparked out of the friction of two stones, in the center of the village. The people of the village are present to witness and participate in the ceremony. A portion of this new fire is distributed to every household so that all new fires have a common origin. The symbolism is simple but powerful: a burial of the past, a new start, a fresh beginning, and a rebirth of hope. These rituals are aimed at addressing the afflictions not of one person but of an entire community, which is being haunted by the spirits of the dead, or by the troubles caused by the war. In the case of Manhica, it was the spirit of the dead RENAMO soldier who afflicted the people; in Kuito, the fear of retaliation from the spirits of the dead of the plateau; and in the case of the new fire ceremony of Huambo and Bie, the need to break from the terrible past, and start afresh. In the first two cases, we are confronted with examples of failure to bury the dead. Both the RENAMO soldier and the dead of the plateau were not granted proper burials because of the war. Therefore, and as discussed earlier, people fear that peace and stability may be jeopardized. Traditional leaders and practitioners, who look after the interests of the community as a whole, generally officiate at community rituals.

Cleansing and Purification Rituals

In Mozambique and Angola, traditional healing for war-affected children, particularly former child soldiers, consists fundamentally of purification or cleansing rituals. Family members and the broader community attend these rituals. It is during these rituals that the child is purged and purified of the "contamination" of war and death, as well as of sin and guilt, and is freed from the retaliation of avenging spirits of those killed by him. These rituals are replete with symbolism whose details are distinctive to the particular ethnolinguistic group, but whose general themes may be common to all groups (Green & Honwana, 1999).

Case 1

> The day of his arrival, his relatives took him to the ndumba [the house of the spirits]. There he was presented to the ancestral spirits of the family. The boy's grandfather addressed the spirits, informing them that his grandchild had returned, and thanked the spirits for their protection, as his grandson was able to return alive. . . . A few days later, a spirit medium was invited by the family to help them perform the cleansing rituals for the boy. The practitioner took the boy to the bush, and there a small hut covered with dry grass was built. The boy, dressed with the dirty clothes he brought from the RENAMO camp, entered the hut and undressed himself. Then fire was set to the hut, and an adult relative helped out the boy. The hut, the clothes, and everything else that the boy brought from the camp had to be burned. A chicken was sacrificed for the spirits of the dead and the blood spread around the ritual place. After that the boy had to inhale the smoke of some herbal remedies, and bath himself with water treated with medicine. (fieldnotes, Mozambique)

This healing ritual brings together a series of symbolic meanings aimed at cutting the child's link with the past (the war). While modern psychotherapeutic practices emphasize verbal exteriorization of the affliction, here, through symbolic meanings, the past is locked away. This is seen in the burning of the hut and the clothes and the cleansing of the body. To talk and recall the past is not necessarily seen as a prelude to healing or diminishing pain. Indeed, it is often believed to open the space for the malevolent forces to intervene. This is also apparent in the following case from Uige (Angola).

Case 2

> When the child or young man returns home, he is made to wait on the outskirts of the village. The oldest woman from the village throws maize flour at the boy and

anoints his entire body with a chicken. He is only able to enter the village after this ritual is complete. After the ritual, he is allowed to greet his family in the village. Once the greeting is over, he must kill a chicken, which is subsequently cooked and served to the family. For the first 8 days after the homecoming, he is not allowed to sleep in his own bed, only on a rush mat on the floor. During this time, he is taken to the river and water is poured on his head and he is given manioc to eat. As he leaves the site of the ritual, he must not look behind him. (Honwana, 1998)

This case emphasizes the noninteraction with family and friends before ritual cleansing. The child is kept out of the village until the ritual is performed, and cannot greet people and sleep in his bed until the ritual proceedings are over. Also, as already mentioned, although children may be asked about war experiences as part of treatment, this is not a fundamental condition for healing. The ceremony aims at symbolically cleansing the polluted child and aiding him to put the war experience behind him, to "forget" (note the symbolism of being forbidden to look back, in the example from Uige). Food taboos and other kinds of ritual restrictions are applied. For example, in Uige the cleansed person must avoid fish and fowl for 1–2 months, after which the person must be reintroduced to the food by the traditional healer who officiated at the ceremony.

Case 3   The *Okupiolissa* ritual from Huila in Angola clearly shows the active participation of the community in these rituals, and stresses the idea of cleansing from "impurities."

The community and family members are usually excited and pleased at the homecoming. Women prepare themselves for a greeting ceremony. . . . Some of the flour used to paint the women's foreheads is thrown at the child, and a respected older woman of the village throws a gourd filled with ashes at the child's feet. At the same time, clean water is thrown over him as a means of purification . . . the women of the village dance around the child, gesturing with hands and arms to ward away undesirable spirits or influences. . . . They each touch him with both hands from head to foot to cleanse him of impurities. The dance is known as Ululando-w-w-w. When the ritual is complete, the child is taken to his village, and the villagers celebrate his return. A party is held in his home where only traditional beverages [are consumed]. . . . The child must be formally presented to the chiefs by his parents . . . the child sits beside the chiefs, drinking and talking to them, and this act marks his change of status in the village. (Honwana, 1998)

These cleansing and purification rituals involving child soldiers have the appearance of what anthropologists call rites of transition. That is, the child undergoes a symbolic change of status from someone who has existed in a realm of sanctioned norm-violation or norm-suspension (i.e. killing, war) to someone who must now live in a realm of peaceful behavioral and social norms, and conform to these. In the case just presented, the purified child acquires a new status that allows him to sit beside the chiefs and interact with them. Until the transition is complete (through ritual performance), the child is considered to be in a dangerous state, a marginal, "betwixt and between," liminal, ambiguous state. For this reason, the child cannot return to his family or hut, sleep in his bed, or perhaps even enter his village, until the rituals have been completed (Green & Honwana, 1999). Manifest symptoms associated with PTSD and related stress disorders reportedly disappear shortly after these ceremonies, after which the family, indigenous healers, and local chiefs direct attention toward helping to establish an enduring, trusting relationship between the traumatized child and family members, and with adults of good character. These ritual interventions are also intended to reestablish spiritual harmony, notably that between the child and his ancestral spirits, his family, and other community members. These healing and protective rituals do not involve verbal exteriorization of the experience as an important condition for the cure. Healing is achieved through nonverbal symbolic procedures, which are understood by those participating. That is why clothes and other objects symbolizing the past had to be burnt or washed away to impress on the individual and the group a complete rupture with that experience and the beginning of a new life. Recounting and remembering the traumatic experience would be like opening a door for the harmful spirits to penetrate the communities. Viewed from this perspective, the well-meaning attempts of psychotherapists to help local people deal with war trauma may in fact cause more harm than help. The performance of these rituals and the politics that precede them transcend the particular individual(s) concerned and involve the collective body. The family and friends are involved, and the ancestral spirits are also implicated in mediating for a good outcome. The cases presented here show how the living have to acknowledge the dead (the past), both the ancestors and the dead of the war, in order to carry on with their lives. The rituals are aimed at asking for forgiveness, appeasing the souls of the dead, and preventing any future afflictions (retaliations) from the spirits of the dead, closing in this way the links with that "bad" past.

Conclusion

I have argued throughout this essay that there are many ways of "seeing" things when it comes to mental health. Mental health and culture are intertwined, and every system of knowledge about mental health is culturally constructed. As Swartz points out, "we all make meaning of our lives in the light of our own experiences and those of the people around us" (1998, p. 260). As I have shown throughout this essay, in the cases of Mozambique and Angola, modern psychotherapeutic interventions are but a few among many ways of understanding and dealing with mental health in zones of ongoing conflict or its aftermath. These various systems of knowledge about mental health can complement each other. A pluralistic approach that brings them together in a creative and efficacious manner seems to be the most appropriate. The great challenge of mental health practitioners, and other aid and relief experts, is to be able to understand this diversity and be prepared to teach but, above all, to learn. Practitioners need to be able to move their own views and practices away from center stage and accommodate others, in order to achieve the best possible outcome. To illustrate this point, I will mention the example of the WHO smallpox eradication campaigns in India. According to Arnold (1985, 1989), several attempts to eradicate the disease proved to be unsuccessful, when biomedical knowledge about the disease was imposed to the population with complete disregard for their local understandings of it. Success only was achieved when attention was also directed to local worldviews and local medical knowledge. Biomedical treatment and vaccinations were then complemented with ayurvedic medical knowledge about the disease and with religious ritual prayers and offerings to Sitala, the goddess of smallpox among Hindu Indians. Considering that the majority of the Mozambicans and Angolans affected by the war are from rural settings, any attempts to help them have to take into account their worldviews and systems of meaning. This essay has suggested that local understandings of war trauma, of healing, and of community cohesion are vital, and need to be taken into account when dealing with populations affected by conflict and political violence. From the research undertaken in Mozambique and Angola, it is apparent that at the local level, families, as well as traditional chiefs and healers, are already engaged in these processes of healing the social wounds of war. They are not waiting for the government to bring in psychologists and other medical practitioners to solve their problems. They are using the means available to them to restore peace and stability to their communities.

Notes

My work in Angola was possible thanks to a Christian Children's Fund (CCF) consultancy in 1997–98. The Angola data presented in this chapter was collected both by myself and by members of the CCF team in Angola.

1. Angola and Mozambique were both colonies of Portugal, which acceded to independence in 1975, after a long period of armed struggle for national liberation. Both postcolonial governments adopted a Marxist orientation and socialist models of development. After independence, the opposition parties of the Mozambique National Resistance (RENAMO) and National Union for the Total Independence of Angola (UNITA) initiated a war against the Mozambique Liberation Front (FRELIMO) and the Popular Movement for the Liberation of Angola (MPLA) governments. In the case of Mozambique, RENAMO was created in 1977 by the Rhodesian Central Intelligence Organization, which was interested in sponsoring a rebel force within Mozambique in retaliation for FRELIMO's support of the Zimbabwe National Liberation Army and its Marxist policies. RENAMO was later taken over by South African Security Forces in 1980, in the same way that FRELIMO was also a strong support base for the African National Congress in the 1980s. In Angola, UNITA was one of the anticolonial movements that, alongside the MPLA and Popular Union of Angola (UPA) and the Angola National Liberation Front (FNLA), fought against colonial rule. However, with the end of colonial rule in April 1974, these three movements fought each other for control of the country. The MPLA emerged victorious, the UPA and FNLA faded in importance, and UNITA reconstituted itself, with mainly U.S. and South African support, and continued its fight against the MPLA government. See Vines, 1991; Minter, 1994.

2. In the nineteenth century, the Nguni broke from the Zulu state of Shaka and migrated toward Mozambique, conquering and dominating the peoples they encountered in their way. During this process, they subjugated the Ndau (a group from central Mozambique) and forced them south to work as slaves in the Nguni state of Gaza, which they established in the southern region after dominating the Tsonga. For more information, see Rennie, 1973; Liesegang, 1981; Rita-Ferreira, 1982.

References

Arnold, D. (1985). Medical priorities in nineteenth-century bengal. *South Asia Research* 5(2), 167–86.

Arnold, D. (1989). The body of the goddess: Smallpox inoculation and vaccination in nineteenth- to twentieth-century India. Unpublished manuscript, Department of Anthropology Library, School of Oriental and African Studies, University of London.

Boyden, J., & Gibbs, S. (1997). *Children and war: Understanding psychological distress in Cambodia.* Geneva: UN.

Bracken, P., Giller, J., & Summerfield, D. (1995). Psychological responses to war and atrocity: The limitations of current concepts. *Social Science and Medicine, 40,* 1073–82.

Dawes, A. (1996). Helping, coping and cultural healing. *Recovery and Cooperation on Violence, Education and Rehabilitation of Young People, 1*(5).

Dawes, A., & Honwana, A. (1996, December). Children culture and mental health: Interventions in conditions of war. In *Children, war and prosecution—Rebuilding hope* (Proceedings of the Congress in Maputo 1996). Maputo, Mozambique: Rebuilding Hope.

Fainzang, S. (1986). *L'interieur des choses: Maladie, divination et reproduction Sociale chez les Bisa du Burkina.* Paris: L'Hammatan.

Geertz, C. (1973). *The interpretation of cultures.* New York: Basic Books.

Green, E., & Honwana, A. (1999). *Indigenous healing of war-affected children in Africa.* Washington: World Bank.

Helman, C. (1994). *Culture, health and illness: An introduction for health practitioners* (3rd ed.). Oxford: Butterworth-Heinemann.

Honwana, A. (1996). *Spiritual agency and self-renewal in southern Mozambique.* Unpublished doctoral dissertation, University of London.

Honwana, A. (1997). Sealing the past, facing the future: Trauma healing in Mozambique. *Accord, 3.*

Honwana, A. (1998). *Okusiakala Ondalo Yokalye,* "Let us light the new fire": Local knowledge in the post-war healing and reintegration of war-affected children in Angola. Unpublished report for Christian Children's Fund.

Honwana, A. (1999). Negotiating post-war identities: Child soldiers in Mozambique and Angola. *Codesria Bulletin, 1 & 2.*

Jackson, M. (1978). An approach to Kuranko divination. *Human Relations 31*(2), 117–138.

Liesegang, G. (1981). Notes on the Internal Structure of the Gaza Kingdom of Southern Mozambique, 1840–1895. In J. B. Peires (Ed.), *Before and after Shaka.* Grahamstown, South Africa: Institute of Social Economic Research, Rhodes University.

Marrato, J. (1996, September). *Superando os efeitos sociais da guerra em Mocambique: Mecanismos e estrategias locais* [Addressing the social effects of the war in Mozambique: Local mechanisms and strategies]. Paper presented at the Fourth Congress of Lusophone Social Sciences, Rio de Janeiro.

Minter, W. (1994). *Apartheid's contras: An inquiry into the roots of war in Angola and Mozambique.* London: Zed Books.

Ngubane, H. (1977). *Body and mind in Zulu medicine.* London: Academic Press.

Nordstrom, C. (1997). *A different kind of war story.* Philadelphia: University of Pennsylvania Press.

Rennie, K. (1973). *Christianity, colonialism and the origins of nationalism among the Ndau of Southern Rhodesia 1890–1935.* Unpublished doctoral dissertation, Northwestern University.

Rita-Ferreira, A. (1982). *Fixação Portuguesa e historia pre-colonial de Moçambique.* Lisbon: Junta de Investigações Científicas do Ultramar.

Summerfield, D. (1999). In a training module.

Swartz, L. (1998). *Culture and mental health: A Southern African view.* Cape Town: Oxford University Press.

United Nations Development Programme [UNDP]. (1997). *United Nations report on human development in Angola.* Geneva: UNDP.

White, G., & Marsella, A. (1982). Introduction. In G. White & A. Marsella (Eds.), *Cultural conceptions of mental health and therapy* (p. 85). Dordrecht: Reidel.

Vines, A. (1991). *Renamo: Terrorism in Mozambique.* London: Indiana University Press.

Young, A. (1995). *The harmony of illusions: Inventing post-traumatic stress disorder.* Princeton, NJ: Princeton University Press.

CHAPTER 14

Building Citizenship in the Face of Violence

Opportunities for the Agency and Participation of Children in Colombia

ROGER A. HART AND ROCIO MOJICA

In many countries there has been a dramatic change recently in the way children are viewed by many of the agencies that work with them. One major change is the increasing recognition that vulnerable children actively contribute to their own survival and coping and that protecting children does not imply that we treat them as passive victims. This orientation to children was given an enormous international boost by the passage of the UN Convention on the Rights of the Child (CRC), which includes the rights of children to have a voice on all matters that concern them.[1] Colombia, a country that has long faced extremely high levels of violence, has been creatively developing new ways of building a more participatory culture of citizenship, including many new ways of working with children and youth (Alcaldia Mayor de Bogota, D.C., 2001; Instituto de Estudios Sociales y Culturales Pensar, 2002; Mockus, 2002; Robledo Gomez, 2003). This essay reviews these experiences and asks what potential these initiatives may have both for individual children and more broadly for the building of civil society. Most of the literature on participation of young people in war-affected countries concerns adolescence, but this essay deals with the entire age range, because this is an innovative aspect of Colombia's contribution. It has been written with the assistance of youth organizers working with war-affected children in the country who met in workshops organized by Save the Children/UK and UNICEF.[2]

Before discussing opportunities for participation, it is necessary to stress the critical importance of addressing poverty. Poverty and unemployment are generally believed to be the root cause behind why children join the army in Colombia and that for this reason all children involved in the conflict must be seen as victims even if they "volunteered" to fight (United Nations International Children's Fund [UNICEF], 2002b). Over 60% of the population in Colombia live below the poverty line. With this comes a great problem of inequity, exclusion, marginalization, and discrimination, which feed and exacerbate conflict and violence. No matter how much children are able to participate in their communities, they are unlikely to feel efficacious, and to become reliable and supportive members of community networks, if their basic environmental rights, like housing and water, are not fulfilled (2000; Bartlett, 2002; United Nations Centre for Human Settlements [UNCHS], 1996). The capital city of Bogota has improved dramatically as a civil society in recent years, with excellent services and public spaces, but there remains a large excluded population that lives from day to day on the informal economy (*Consultoría para los Derechos Humanos y el Desplazamiento Forzado* [CODHES] & Archdiocese of Bogota, 2000, p. 17). Too often the strategy of participation is discussed separately from issues of inequity and the need for a redistribution of resources and services. While we focus in this essay on participation, we believe that, in a larger view, both are necessary (Fraser & Honneth, 2003).[3]

The Problems of War, Violence, and Displacement of Children in Colombia

Children are affected in multiple ways by the armed conflict in Colombia (Bello & Ruiz-Ceballos, 2000). There are estimated to be 2.5 million internally displaced persons, approximately half of them under 18 years of age. There are over 11,000 child soldiers within the guerrillas and paramilitary forces, and many more children are used by the state as informants and for counterinsurgency propaganda activities. In 2000, approximately 600 children died in combat, and in 2001, more than 4,000 children died from violence ("Watchlist on Children and Armed Conflict," 2004).

While there is a need to continue to help those who are seriously traumatized to recover through individual interventions in a protected setting, it is increasingly recognized that even these children benefit from entering as soon as possible into everyday social settings where they can be actively engaged in meaningful change. Nearly 3 million children have been directly affected by the war, but it is generally believed by the government and the nongovernmental organizations (NGOs) that all 17 million children under 18 years old in Colombia have been affected by the war and need programs that will support them in facing this experience (UNICEF, 2002b).

Ex-combatant children have the greatest problems integrating into everyday life outside of war, having committed violent acts themselves. The government has a special national program for the 1,300 children currently released from fighting, but the program has had great difficulty in achieving their reintegration (Coalition to Stop the Use of Child Soldiers, 2005). In most cases, the children cannot return to their families or communities to find a space where they can be recognized and have a sense of belonging, because of the abuse and maltreatment that led them to leave in the first place, or because the conflict continues there. Furthermore, the reintegration of these children into any community life is hard because their sense of self and their behaviors are so tied to their roles in authoritarian military structures. The difficult challenge is to help them first gain the social competencies that will enable them to live in nonsegregated ways with other children. A great deal of attention is now being given to this group of children by researchers and program developers, though little research is yet published.

For children who have experienced or observed violence, there is a growing recognition that trauma has been thought of inadequately and that this has lead to interventions that focus too much on the individual (Ajdukovic, 1997). It is now being more broadly recognized that trauma should be seen also as a social phenomenon and viewed at the communal and societal levels, as in this book. Building from theories of resilience in children, most agencies in Colombia believe that children should be able to return to a normal community life as soon as possible.

Beyond the direct effect of violence, there are those children in families who have been forced to leave their homes and communities because of the conflict, often leading to family fragmentation (Bello, Cardinal, & Arias, 2002). Research has shown that symptoms of stress are more likely when a major trauma is followed by ongoing disruptions and uncertainty (Dawes, Tredoux, & Feinstein, 1989). The process often has fatally destructive effects on families and on the capacities of parents to raise their children because of the loss of work and the erosion of personal and family networks. Children who leave their rural homes also lose the daily rituals of participation or work with their families, their school network, and their sense of community. Continuity of experiences over time, and for some people, the attachment to a particular place, seem to be important to the development of self-concept and to the building of identity (Breakwell, 1986; Fullilove & Thompson, 1996).

These experiences with violence and massive disruptions set the stage for cycles of urban violence in poor neighborhoods. The children living in poor violent communities suffer from a general lack of trust among their peers, who are often in gangs or otherwise connected to local patterns of violence. This is often aggravated by "informant networks," whereby young people receive money from armed groups to spy and to spread rumors that set the community against itself. Families in displacement often prefer not to be identified as "displaced," in order to avoid a new persecution, and so children learn to be quiet. The following summary of an unpublished account by Martha Bello based on interviews with child domestic workers in the city of Cali illustrates how, with a climate of fear and loss of trust, there is a sad downward spiral of opportunities for children to have autonomy, participation, and dialogue within their families:

> Families often confine themselves to their farms. Children are prohibited by their parents from telling anything about what they do or say. Adults speak in front of the children, taking decisions that affect them all but without consulting them; they consider that the less children know the more secure they are. With the excuse of family security parents control their sons and daughters entire lives: where they go, whom they go with, and whom they speak to. The parents often isolate their children from their friends to avoid having them enter the armed groups, voluntarily or by force. As a result, children gradually develop a collective distrust and paranoia. In the period before the forced displacement, they experience the unfolding power of the armed forces in the form of individual acts of violence and the influence of weapons. Authoritarianism is naturalized and they learn to divide the world between "good" and "bad" persons. There are no state or private institutions that stand against the power of these groups or mediate between the groups and the community. The children are thus often in the middle of confrontations between armed groups, and they observe maltreatment and even murder, torture, fires, rapes and body mutilations. They have seen armed men threaten their families, steal their food and destroy their farms. These situations, distort their perception of justice and authority and the worth of living together in a community. They come to conclude that force determines the social order and that there are only winners and losers.
>
> Boys and girls who have lost a family member suffer even more, because they have to suffer the grief of death and feelings of revenge that they cannot rationalize. Added to their fears is the terror of not knowing what is really happening and why. The harassment of the armed groups typically occurs in a context that is in itself not favorable to children: the mother's subordination to the father's authority, the early assumption of responsibilities and the lack of play and recreation. When a family has no option but to run away to survive, the boys and girls are the last ones to know. Suddenly the children have to leave their homes, their pets, and their friends. They are not consulted; they are not able to choose what to take or to say goodbye to their relations. Sometimes families are obliged to give the children to relatives, further increasing their loneliness and anguish. (2004)

In their new urban community, displaced children and youth are commonly blamed for their own situation and treated as pariahs (Women's Commission on Refugee Women and Children [WCRWC], 2002; interview with Tailler de Vida (Workshop for Life) team, January 2003). Adolescent boys are the most excluded of displaced persons (CODHES, 2000). They are feared by the public, treated automatically as criminals by authorities, and largely ignored by those who run social programs. There is a tendency to confront them with authoritarian responses, but this strategy, of course, has the opposite effect, because it endorses violence as an appropriate strategy for dealing with everyday threats (Garbarino, Kostelny, & Pardo, 1992). Violence and criminality become their only avenues for participation, in gangs, as hired killers, and in the militia. Some paramilitary units are believed to be made up of at least 50% children. The high vulnerability of children in poor urban areas is illustrated by the neighborhood of Soacha in a marginal area of Bogota, with a murder rate for children under 17 years of 334 per 100,000, in comparison to a national rate of 83 per 100,000. They are killed because they are assumed to be supporters of armed groups, drug consumers, or involved in delinquency, bands, gangs, or just "vagos" (without a job) (Observatiorio de Manejo del Conflicto de la Universidad Externado de Colombia, 2004).

The Importance of Opportunities for Children's Agency and Social Cooperation

A number of different concepts are often merged in the literature under the term "children's participation," sometimes leading to confusion. All contemporary developmental theories of child and youth development are built centrally around the importance of children's agency. Opportunities to act with autonomy increase a person's sense of control and the predictability of one's environment, and such opportunities are basic to one's sense of well-being. People's perceptions of themselves as being effective has been called self-efficacy, which is in turn related to self-esteem (Bandura, 1997). In addition to opportunities for individual agency, children need to be able to act collaboratively with others. Opportunities for social cooperation can also contribute to building a sense of belonging to a community and to sharing with others in facing change and uncertainty. Because psychology has been largely divorced from social theory, these theories have generally not addressed differences in the availability of participatory opportunities for different groups of children (Burman,1994; James et al., 2000). We have already discussed how children's normal patterns of developing autonomy are often curtailed in violent settings because of the loss of a sense of security by both parents and children. Opportunities for cooperative activity with peers in a range of daily activities are also severely disrupted and require special efforts if they are to occur. There is often a loss of trust between peers, particularly when they live in or near a zone of conflict or gangs or they experience a large-scale influx of displaced persons from the war. For displaced children, there is the added problem of the loss of continuity over time. One possibly important solution to such loss of community might be for children to participate directly in the building of community in physical, material ways that help them to create a new shared sense of place. Participation with others in community-building projects may also help young people to believe that there are alternatives and hence that there is a future.

Group membership for these different age groups has different values, related to different developmental goals (Hart et al., 1996). Psychologists have written a considerable amount of theory on the development of identity, on the basis of research with children in Western countries (e.g., Erikson, 1980; Heath & McLaughlin, 1993). Children in the preschool and early elementary years are described as enjoying experimentation with social roles though play and opportunities for free play in a safe space, unpressured by time (Hart & Petren, 2000). Children from the age of about 8 through 11 are commonly characterized as being outward-looking and industrious as they pursue the development of what seem like independent identities (Erikson, 1980). In this late childhood period, groups are important settings for the development and demonstration of competencies and independence. During adolescence (from around 12 years of age) children have been observed to become more inward-looking and reflective (Erikson, 1980). They like to spend considerable time with their peer group working on the consolidation and differentiation of their identities. An important distinction between most adult—child interactions versus child-to-child ones is that they typically involve more one-way instruction, in contrast to the relatively flexible bidirectional quality of peer exchanges. Although some young people, of course, replicate the authoritative styles of adults, in general, mixed-age peer interactions can be particularly valuable in providing children with the chance to test their understandings and to adapt them to an ongoing situation (Hartup, 1983).

Given these developmental goals of children and adolescents, often all that is needed for social development is for adults to set the stage for the kinds of rich exchange that can occur when children participate with one another. There is, however, also a role at times for "guided participation" from adults or older children—interacting with children and structuring exchanges in ways that encourage autonomous development (Rogoff, 2003). It is interesting to note, however, that the participatory programs that are emerging all over Colombia are not coming from these theories of children's development but rather from practical experiences with the effectiveness of working in participatory ways with children and youth and from a desire to follow the guidelines of the CRC and the national mandate from the constitution to build a more participatory citizenship (Robledo Gomez, 2003). Since the adoption of the CRC by the UN in 1989, there has been a great increase in the degree to which many countries recognize the capacities of children as agents in their own development. The Latin American region can be said to be at the forefront of this "movement." This was not only because of the mobilization of government and NGOs in line with the goals of the CRC but also because of the prior influence of radical pedagogic theory in the region (Freire, 1970; Hart, 1992; Swift, 1992).

Different Settings for Children's Agency and Social Participation

In addressing opportunities for children's agency and social cooperation and how to expand them in Colombia, it is necessary to consider all of the relevant types of settings in the lives of children, from the family through educational and recreational settings to their public roles and involvement in mass movements. We will consider each of these in turn, reviewing their potentials and summarizing the state of the art.

The Family

In Colombia, families are typically highly authoritarian, and those that are under stress as a result of the conflict become even more so. Some parents find it necessary to protect their children from being influenced by neighborhood negative forces, like gangs, through punitive discipline, including physical assault (Scheinfeld, 1983). Psychologists told a delegation visiting displaced families in Colombia that "mothers try to limit their children's activities in order to protect them from recruitment or from turning to prostitution" (WCRWC, 2002, p. 21). The deepest and most effective strategy for building democratic behaviors in children would be to find ways to support more democratic processes within families, supporting them to become more participatory institutions, where children are seen as apprentices in learning to become effective members of the group rather than possessions to be molded through power and punishment. They would be trustworthy settings where children could discuss their fears and learn how to act in relation to violence. In this way, families would be a buffer to violence outside them and even a force of resistance to community violence.

Some programs for children in Colombia are now recognizing that families should be encouraged to enable children to be more involved in dialogues about the war, both to help them personally and as a way of building national resistance to violence. The Contructores de Paz (Children as Peacemakers) program, for example, is designed to bring discussions of the war home to the family (Alvarado & Ospina, 2001). Remembering and facing painful events in the community, or in the community they have had to leave, is increasingly promoted as the strategy for dealing with grief and fear, rather than protecting children by denying or pretending to forget such events. The term "representational competence" has been used to describe the observation that being able to make sense of traumatic or stressful events seems to be valuable in the resilience of children (Garbarino et al., 1992). Parents are also encouraged through discussion groups to watch news programs and to read and discuss newspaper reports with their children rather than avoiding them.

There is also a great deal of emphasis in local social welfare agencies on trying to reduce domestic violence. An example of the type of creative animation being used by government agencies are public events where large numbers of children "vaccinate" their parents against violence by pouring water from small sachets into their parents' mouths. In addition to this symbolic kind of action by children, there is also experimentation in a more fundamental way with participatory democratic development with very young children. Nuevo Voces Ciudadana ("New Voices of Citizenship"), a program of the Bogota city government, focuses on building democratic practices in the preschool classroom and, through collaboration with parents, in children's homes (Instituto de Estudios Sociales y Culturales Pensar, 2002; Departamento Administrativo de Bienestar Social el Distrito [DABS], 2003). The idea of working at the preschool level is a particularly innovative and exciting component of the Nuevo Voces program. Children learn more democratic scripts for such familiar events as arranging to eat and welcoming a stranger to the room, and they link this learning to their lives at home and in the larger community.

The goal of the Nuevo Voces program is to bring greater confidence and competence in citizenship among the two poorest social strata (Robledo Gomez,

2003). As in all societies, the power structure of Colombia has led to differences in the knowledge bases of the population, and the poorest classes have undoubtedly suffered from what Valsiner (2000) calls the "promotion of ignorance." Bogota's social welfare agency wishes to change this state of affairs by building the citizenship competencies of these two strata, but in the early phase of building this program, the emphasis seems to be on building the skills of participation rather than building people's capacities to gain access to and influence local government.[4]

Schools

Schools are the obvious place for a government to try to build the capacities of its citizens. All children need to feel that that they have a right to an equal role in the same physical place with other children and with a shared vision of positive goals for improvement and for the future. The structures and process used in schools should be microcosms of the kind of society the nation wishes to create. Schools are very important settings for learning about political power and how it can be differently organized and distributed. Even 5-year-olds entering school quickly develop a fairly accurate understanding of the roles of different people in schools (Emler, 1992). Research in experimental progressive schools has shown that children come to represent social systems differently; they come to understand that you can have authoritative systems that are not necessarily authoritarian ones and that you can achieve social consensus through discussion and negotiation. Unfortunately, the key principle of equity of educational opportunity is not met in Colombia. There is not a universal standard of 9 years of education, and many schools are chronically overpopulated. Private schools serve approximately 30% of primary schoolchildren and 45% of secondary schoolchildren, thereby reproducing patterns of poverty and inequity (WCRWC, 2002). Furthermore, teaching human rights is often seen as a "subversive act," and teachers are threatened and sometimes killed.

In spite of the pressures on teachers, there are many initiatives underway to have schools not turn their backs on the war but to make it a topic for the children to address directly. As one of the coordinators of the youth NGOs interviewed for this essay explained, "Children need ways to hear themselves speak about their fears." Special attention to opportunities for dialogue and self-expression are being given to schools that lie within zones of conflict in Colombia. Other large-scale initiatives are underway outside of these zones, but these programs are too often voluntary and after-school rather than fundamental to the training of all children (Bush & Saltarelli, 2000). Nevertheless, they are often good examples of how children can become active (e.g. Ospina, Alvarado, & Moreno, 1999). They not only have art classes and discussions but also plan local peace initiatives in their communities. There are also many important exercises in conflict resolution, but we know from research in the United States that these programs are not necessarily the value-free opportunities for children that they commonly claim to be (Daiute & Lelutiu-Weinberger, 2002). Open discussion about different values by all actors in learning communities is needed if the programs are to avoid cultural and class bias in their design. It appears that the "peace spaces" organized by schools in Medellín, which involve students, teachers, school authorities, and other members of the larger educative community, are of this kind. But individual programs are not likely to bring the kinds of deep changes that are needed to face and begin to transform a culture of violence. We cannot expect them to change day-to-day power relations, particularly in the context of conflict, where there is such a lack of trust.

The only way schools might be able to more deeply confront these problems is to contribute directly to the building of democratic culture. Colombia has long pioneered the highly democratic *escuelas nuevas,* or "new schools" (Torres, 1991). Children cooperate in their learning, are involved democratically in the everyday management of the school community and environment, and carry out investigations and take actions for the betterment of their larger community. With the growing interest in civil society in Colombia, there has been a burgeoning of research on the concept of social capital and how to promote it. In a very recent comparative study, those communities that had an escuela nueva were found to have significantly higher levels of social capital than those communities that did not (Forero-Pineda & Escobar-Rodriguez, 2004). But these schools are almost entirely in rural areas. The development of democratic models of schools has not yet gone beyond the experimental stage in cities, and so the majority of urban children in Colombia attend schools that are as authoritarian in structure as they typically are all over the world. It appears to be a difficult challenge to bring the lessons from small rural communities to the cities, but it is an important one to try (Hart, 2004).

The government of Colombia has in the past year created a national set of standards for evaluating citizenship in all school grades from grade 3 upward (i.e. all children above age 9) with an emphasis on active citizenship rather than traditional civics. Even though it is an admirable initiative, we should not expect too much of it, for it seems to be limited entirely to the content of curricula and makes no attempt to influence the structure of schools or their management. It is not likely to be effective to teach children about the potential of local participatory democracy inside structures that are largely authoritarian. But this national initiative is yet another sign of the earnest desire of the government to explore ways of bringing children centrally into the challenge of building a more civil society in the face of the conflict.

Informal and Supervised Activities in Safe Public Spaces

Typically, opportunities for children's societal participation are thought of only in terms of participation in programs. We need to be equally concerned with informal opportunities for social participation. For children who live in communities that have been disturbed by violence, there is a serious erosion of everyday opportunities for free play in public spaces, walking to school, or casual conversations with neighbors. In normal circumstances, children unself-consciously build community and a sense of identity with their peers and neighbors through joint everyday activities in public spaces (Hart, 2005; Hart et al., 1996; Hart & Petren, 2000). When fear leads children to retreat indoors, this informal kind of community-building dies. The city of Bogota has developed an ambitious and internationally recognized system of highly effective public spaces for adults, but there has not yet been much thought about how to specifically foster children's free access to public space. Some other countries have learned that in violent communities, "safe neighborhood" programs can be created, where community organizations for children convince local businesses to serve as sites for children to retreat to in times of danger (Bartlett, Hart, de la Barra, & Missair, 2000; UNICEF, 2004a, 2004b).[5] Residential areas can also be designed to enable residential communities to better observe the movements of people who might threaten their children, and in this way make their neighborhoods more "defendable." These are solutions that can be most effectively achieved by communities if they are supported by their local governments. For example, the government of Northern Ireland has established the Irish Play Board in Belfast, with a large full-time staff and budget to win the battle for peace on the streets of Belfast and other northern cities. Safe communities should not become segregated neighborhoods or "gated communities." No matter how culturally homogenous, a community should not be closed to people of other persuasions. The same principle applies to play and recreational programs; there should not be separate programs for particular populations, like displaced children or families (Bartlett et al., 2000).

Play offers an important means for children to establish a sense of control over difficult circumstances (Garbarino, Scott, & Faculty of the Erikson Institute, 1989; Hart & Petren, 2000). The important quality in planning and designing a play environment is that it allows for a broad range of play and different types of opportunities for children to initiate their own actions and exercise control over the environment (Chawla, 1987; Chawla & Heft, 2002; Hart, 1976, 2002). This is no doubt important to supporting a person's perception of his or her self-efficacy and self-esteem (Bandura, 1997). Colombian researchers report that

> displaced children are subjected to physical spaces which are completely different to those they had before. The possibilities for running and playing freely are greatly reduced when the whole family is packed into one bedroom, and the social and urban environment is drastically modified. (UNICEF, 2004b)

In poor urban communities, green space disappears as families are forced to use all of the available space for dwellings. Young children's contact with nature is often romanticized but there are clear benefits to enabling children to have spontaneous contact with the natural world, and green space offers the greatest kind of diversity of play resources for young children (Hart, 2005; Nabhan & Trimble, 1994). Recent research has even suggested that green space contributes to the reduction of violence in communities (Kuo, Bacaicoa, & Sullivan, 1998).

Children living in war situations or in settings with extreme violence can benefit from play programs, both to shield them from painful experiences or to deal with their painful experiences, sometimes collectively. The essential quality of these programs is that children are enabled to initiate their own activities, with adults as supporters rather than directors (Hart & Petren, 2000). Sometimes it is not possible for children in dangerous communities to find safe space outdoors for play and recreation, and so NGOs have created safe play zones where children can engage in large motor play, pretend play, and dramatic storytelling. These kinds of play spaces are particularly valuable in enabling staff from children's agencies to observe children in a sustained way in different social settings in order to learn whether there are some children in need of special care. Because there are too many children affected by the conflict for the NGOs to try to evaluate them all individually, some programs instead build the capacity of community members to observe children and adolescents in play with each other. In these normalized play settings, it is possible for them to help child care professionals to identify which children are having social difficulties that require special intervention.

The experiences of those nations that have created community centers for the support of families and children living in poor neighborhoods might be relevant to war-affected children. They often include a safe place for children to meet and play that goes well beyond the simple benefits of child care relief for parents. These centers enable a kind of collective socialization of children that has obvious potential for the development of community consciousness. The same center can serve multiple functions: a base for parent meetings; a place for teenagers to hang out and make their own plans; an information center; and so on. It is notable that the Save the Children model of family center in the United Kingdom emerged from playgroups for children in poor urban areas in the 1970s and 1980s. Save the Children stresses that center-based family support should not be viewed within the crisis-oriented model of intervention, offering "therapeutic" help to families and children, but rather should be seen as fundamentally about community development. Centers of this sort have been found to be particularly effective if they are located next to places offering basic services for adults and spaces for community development meetings.

Participatory Organizations and
Programs for Children and Youth

The most obvious setting for introducing participatory opportunities for children and youth is in out-of-school programs. These commonly do not have the constraints of schools and have long been seen as places for the recreational, social, and moral development of children. But these traditional youth organizations do not offer high degrees of autonomy and opportunity for children to develop the skills of social cooperation. Unfortunately, like most countries, Colombia does not yet have many organizations that are self-managed by children or young people (see Hart & Rahjbhandary, 2003). They do, of course, have youth leaders, and there is a strong tendency in Colombia, as in the United States, to equate the term *participation* with the term *leadership* rather than emphasizing participation for all. While Colombia now has hundreds of programs for war-affected children that are somewhat participatory in how they involve children, these programs are rarely designed in a collaborative way with the children and young people and rarely involve young people in their monitoring or evaluation (see Sabo, 2003). Art, dance, and music are common ways that older children and youth come together in their communities to work through their feelings with each other. They also sometimes prepare performances or exhibits for presentation to the larger community, providing a source of pride and a route to the building of community identity. For example, Batuta is a children's band program in many cities that began in the poor neighborhoods of Medellín with the expression "When you hold a violin in your hands you'll never hold a gun." Nonetheless, as with all countries, most of these programs seem to be less participatory than they need to be, particularly with adolescents. When researchers talk with adolescents about how they would like to be with each other, they find that they are keen to find opportunities to come together in their own time, with adults supporting them, but on the sidelines (Hart et al., 1996). Depending on the age of the child, there is certainly a role for skilled adults with children, but the emphasis should be on animating and facilitating their participation.

There are many in Colombia who would like to replace the old models of hierarchic youth organizations with new democratic ones, but it is difficult, given the context of authoritarian, violent, communities. There is a tendency for many persons to feel that when young people speak of their "rights" they are engaging in revolutionary language and that they should rather speak of "duties." The youth organizers have to be savvy regarding patterns of power and hierarchic control of youth in their communities. For example, none of the armed groups like to see young people behave autonomously, have long hair, stay out late at night, or wear short minidresses. They disapprove even more of homosexuality and drug consumption. Whenever any kind of child or youth organization is formed in a community, it will be attacked from different directions, often leading youth workers to be afraid to organize. Furthermore, some communities have resisted supporting the training of young people because they feel that armed groups will want to recruit these "leaders" into their forces. The ideal training program for participatory youth programs would be about the facilitation of cooperative activity rather than "leadership," but this might be too subtle a distinction for the reactionary tendencies in our workshop discussions with youth organizers from NGOs.

In spite of these problems, and the great pressures on youth from gangs, with the attraction of money from drug trafficking, some youth organizers help groups of young people to organize in participatory community youth centers. These centers are conceived as alternatives to violence, where youth can be key actors of social development and can be recognized by their families and communities as subjects, as voices to be heard and taken seriously. It is a powerful democratic lesson for adolescents to discover that they can share in the running of an organization that is so strong because of its collaborative structure that it can resist the normal forces that require them to show allegiance to one gang or another. Sometimes they work with their communities to develop highly collective projects that present a wall to those who would want to recruit them to fight. Tailler de Vida (Workshop for Life) is an NGO that works with displaced adolescents aged 13 to 18 years. Some of these are young people who have been involved with violence. There is a double goal here—to help combatants rehabilitate and to prevent other children from being recruited. Art, in the form of wall painting, rap, theater, and dance, is central to most of their projects. They create theatre from their own life experiences and take these to their communities and to other settings. The NGOs report that making videos like "This War is Not Ours and We-re Losing it!" has been particularly effective for the young people's attempts to reclaim a space for themselves—though, sadly, many adults are afraid to attend their performances.

Some of the NGOs in our research workshops for this essay concluded from their observations of many years of great national expenditure on programs for adolescents in Colombia that it would be more effective to involve youth in intergenerational community programs of recovery and reconstruction of their communities, rather than marginalizing them as a separate age group. This can often be achieved by bringing youth initiatives into preexisting community organizations. Intergenerational programs also enable youth to have needed dialogues beyond their own age group. Life story methods have been found to be a particularly effective, like the one used in the Conciudadeno (Common Citizens) project in Medellín, where women meet weekly with adolescent boys and girls. There are also important advantages to including children as well as youth in community organizations. Traditionally, governments all over the world have created youth programs in response to violence. But if they only support this age group, they will always miss the preadolescent years during which young people become disaffected! Furthermore, research in recent years has demonstrated the value of young people being able to work together in mixed age groups, for the social development of both the young and the older participants (Gauvain, 2001; Rogoff, 2003).

Again it must be noted that beyond the building of local community solidarity, youth need to be able to connect to trusted governmental structures. A recent qualitative series of studies by a coalition of four youth groups in the district of Aguablanca, in Cali, concluded: "the lack of institutional presence in many of the neighborhoods, the history of clientelism and the marked distrust felt towards the police and other state institutions, suggests that links to external groups and institutions are severely limited" (Associacion Arte y Cultura [GEAC] & Asociación de Mujeres Activas por un Futura Mejor, 2002, p. 156).

Other Participatory Activities

Beyond the fundamental importance of participatory group process with peers, NGOs have found that children, both combatants and victims, often want to share their stories with a larger audience. There has been a wide range of ways of involving war-affected children in media in Colombia but with little critical perspective on their impacts on children. At one end of the extreme are the makers of news reports and films who use children in their stories and manipulate them to appear as the world wants to see them, as poor and vulnerable victims and not much else. At the International Conference on War Affected Children in Winnipeg in 1999, most of the journalists showed interest in interviewing only young people from those countries who had had the most recent and the most horrific experiences (Cockburn, 2000, p. 32). The young people complained that when they told one of the media representatives of their desire to speak about their roles and their solutions to problems, rather than outlining the horrors they had seen, they said "that was not very interesting" and terminated the interview (32).

Documentary filmmakers have a potentially important role to play in giving children a larger voice to air their experiences, but they are also not usually aware of how to work with children. For example, the makers of the HBO television special *Children in War* did not feel it necessary to address the impact of the filmmaking experience on the children in any detail, because psychologists had told them it was fine as long as they got children to "openly talk about their war-related experiences" (Raymond & Raymond, 2000, p.11).[6] Recently three ex-combatant children have spoken about their lives as guerillas on Colombian television. It had a sensational impact on the issue of child soldiers in the country, but there has been no published report of whether the impact of this experience was beneficial to the young people, if it possibly brought greater risks than benefits to them, or how it affected their sense of self and their right to privacy (United States Agency for International Development, 2003).

At the other end of the continuum are the much more appropriate opportunities for children to produce their own media. Making newspapers is a common feature of many of the programs for war-affected children in Colombia, but there are other ways of enabling children to get their own messages out with integrity. Examples have already been given of community theatre. Radio also offers great potential because many different children's groups can tape shows, at low cost, but so far, they usually seem to be designed to involve very small groups of children or youth (Harburg & McCrum, 1994; WCRWC, 2002).

International exchanges can offer some special opportunities for children and young people to grapple with their difficult circumstances. It seems that when a national situation has been politically charged in complex ways for a long time, young people from overseas can often serve as more open, receptive audiences than young people from the same country. International dialogue can also offer young people an increased capacity to challenge, reformulate, and refine their thinking and to learn new strategies of coping and acting. One good example is the exchange program of South African youth from poor, violent communities in South Africa with youth in the very large poor community of Aguas Blancas in Cali (Grant, 2004). These groups of young people are attempting to build community involvement programs in their respective communities and are measuring their impacts on social capital in the two communities over a 3-year period. Involving the young people directly in the collection and analysis of the data for the evaluation of the scheme is important, for it stresses to the young people the seriousness of their efforts to change the community and recognizes their capacities as competent actors in the enterprise in a way that is usually reserved for program managers and outside experts.

There are many participatory programs in Colombia that enable children to become active in peace promotion. The largest of these was a national campaign called the Children's Movement for Peace (Cameron, 1998, 2001; *Soldiers of peace*, 1999). Although this was by all accounts an important event in the country, it is not at all clear that "movement" was the correct term for it. While there was no doubt child initiation in the earliest stages of this program, it seems to have all the indications of having become a "social mobilization" of children by adults, and in particular by the mass media. This is not necessarily a bad thing, for there can be benefits to children's involvement in large-scale campaign even if they are initiated by others. But the conceptual distinction between self-initiated participation and social mobilization by others is an important one, and there are values to being explicit about it (Hart, 1992). A council of children was formed to coordinate the national events, but all but two of the fifteen children were from the capital, Bogota. Nevertheless, the council was able to promote specific coordinated actions for thousands of children to engage in. Before the "movement," there had been a lot of local organizations in all areas of the country, not only in the conflict areas. Many NGOs and UNICEF saw the value of connecting these efforts and organized a national gathering of children near Bogota in 1996. CNN covered this event and built it into a major media campaign. Five children were profiled as leaders, stressing their charismatic role more than the efforts of thousands locally.

A national referendum, called Vote for Peace, developed out of this national movement or mobilization. This caught the imagination of the country and was apparently important in inspiring an adult movement for peace and influencing the peace negotiations. It is now worthwhile to look back at this and ask whether this was an ideal way of building on the efforts of children. The greatest problem with large-scale mobilizations of people is that they are inevitably short-term in nature. They happen when the initiators plan them to happen and often do not have any sustained follow-through. It is very clear from reading the moving narratives of the child leaders of the movement for peace that the availability of local settings for engagement were the critical factor enabling them to become positive social actors for peace (Cameron, 2001). The key criterion in evaluating this movement then would be whether local groups were energized by these national events and continued to function with greater effectiveness and whether new local ones were started.

Conclusions

Colombia is gradually moving toward a new way of seeing children and their capacities that may have important consequences for the future of the nation. Many people who work for children in Colombia, both in government and in

NGOs, believe that taking into account the way violence is reproduced in their society is fundamental to finding a long-term solution to the conflict and that treating children as citizens with the capacity to be involved in dialogue and change is critical. The very many different local programs through which both NGOs and government agencies have been providing opportunities for children to work together in participatory ways are probably more effective than large-scale mobilizations of children for changing how young people are seen. Although youth workers are often accused by right-wing militias of preparing the young for revolutionary activity, there seems to be a more dominant attitude in the country that sees young people's active engagement in local affairs, and even their outspokenness on matters of violence and war, as positive. Given this complex range of responses, there is a need for new cultural norms allowing youth to emerge gradually and authentically through effective demonstrations of their success rather than through large-scale mobilizations and confrontation.

Unfortunately, the number of participatory programs is still small, and, given the authoritarian structure of most families, it will take many years for these ways of thinking to become deeply embedded in the culture. There is also a danger that the rhetoric of participation has grown faster than the reality of what the programs can offer. For example, in spite of constitutional changes that called for more participatory local governance, there are still few functioning local participatory government structures to enable young people to use their skills to help connect their communities to formal government.

An even more fundamental barrier to the potentials of participatory programs for confronting violence is poverty. Building relationships and constructing community and civil society, which are central to the recovery from violence, will not be possible if poverty is not addressed at the same time. The city of Porto Allegre, Brazil, has demonstrated that it is even possible for municipal governments to bring participatory budgeting process down to the community level, with young people having a specific part of the budget under their responsibility (Guerra, 2002). This requires not only participatory competencies in the population but also governmental structures that the poor can work through. Unfortunately, in Colombia, this seems to commonly not be the case with the poorest two social classes, for the most local institutions of government, the Junta Accion Communal, are generally not trusted, open, transparent structures.

Finally, the lack of evaluation is a great weakness in the movement for child and youth participation in Colombia. The movement for children's right to participate has happened so quickly internationally that the academic community has not caught up. It is not enough to argue that the new self-determining and participatory ways of working with children are superior to the traditional authoritarian and leadership models for building a culture of peace. If Colombia is to be successful in its experimentation with young citizenship, we urgently need to build a comprehensive program for the systematic evaluation and development of new initiatives. Without such a program, the new trends described in this essay will remain the interesting but losing side of the great ideological divide in how Colombians think of their children and their future.

Notes

1. This essay follows the CRC in using the term "children" to refer to all persons aged 18 years of age or under. For an introduction to the CRC and children's participation, see Hart, 1992, 1997; de Winter, 1997; Willow, 2002.

2. The Colombian office of UNICEF generously organized a workshop of NGOs working with children affected by the armed conflict in Bogota to discuss the issue in 2003. Save the Children/UK organized a similar discussion group of NGOs in 2004.

3. This is related to the theoretical debate over the recognition of people versus the redistribution of resources as the appropriate strategy to achieve social justice (Fraser & Honneth, 2003).

4. It could be argued that the poor are no worse, and are probably better, at the skills of social participation than middle-class families. The distinction between "cognitive social capital" and "structural social capital" is probably relevant here (Krishna & Shrader, 2000). Only so much can be done by enabling citizens to build community when there is a lack of community-level structures of governance with transparent decision-making processes and accountable leaders.

5. See also www.childfriendlycities.org.

6. Question posed to the director by one of the authors at a screening of *Children in War,* United Nations, New York City, 2000.

References

Ajdukovic, D. (1997). *Trauma recovery training: Lessons learned.* Zagreb: Society for Psychological Assistance.

Alcaldia Mayor de Bogota, D. C. (2001). *Bogota para vivir todos del mismo lado.* Available: www.univerciudad.net/Bogota en datos.

Alvarado, S. V., & Ospina, H. F. (2001). *Concepciones politicas y transformaciones de actitudes frente a la equidad en niños y niñas de sectores de alto riesgo social del eje cafetero* [Political conceptions and transformation of attitudes in children from areas of resk in the coffee-growing region]. Manizales, Colombia: CINDE and the University of Manizales.

Associacion Arte y Cultura, Fundación Grupo Experimental de Alternativas Culturales, & Asociación de Mujeres Activas por un Futura Mejor. (2002). Exploring youth and community relations in Cali, Colombia. *Environment and Urbanization, 14*(12), 149–156.

Bandura, A. (1997). *Self-efficacy: the exercise of control.* New York: Freeman.

Bartlett, S. (2002). *Children's rights and the physical environment.* Stockholm: Radda Barnen.

Bartlett, S., Hart, R., de la Barra, X., & Missair, A. (2000). *Managing cities as if children matter: Children's rights, poverty and the urban environment.* New York: UNICEF.

Bello, M. (2004). *Unpublished report on displaced children.* Save the Children/UK, Bogota.

Bello, M., & Ruiz -Ceballos, S. (Eds.). (2000). *Conflicto Armado, Niñez y Juventud* [Armed conflict, children and youth]. Bogota: Universidad Nacional de Colombia.

Bello, M. N., Cardinal, E. M., & Arias, F. J. (Eds.). (2002). *Efectos psicosociales y culturales del desplazamiento* [Psycho-social and cultural impacts of displacement]. Bogota: Universidad Nacional de Colombia.

Breakwell, G. (1986). *Coping with threatened identities*. New York: Methuen.

Burman, E. (1994). *Deconstructing developmental psychology*. New York: Routledge.

Bush, K. D., & Saltarelli, D. (Eds.). (2000). *The two faces of education in ethnic conflict: Towards a peace building education for children*. Florence: UNICEF.

Cameron, S. (1998). *Making peace with children*. Bogota: UNICEF.

Cameron, S. (2001). *Out of war: True stories from the front line of the children's movement for peace in Colombia*. New York: Scholastic.

Chawla, L. (1987). Childhood place attachments. In S. Altman (Ed.), *Place attachment* (pp. 63–86). New York: Plenum.

Chawla, L. (2001). *Growing up in an urbanizing world*. Paris: UNESCO.

Chawla, L., & Heft, H. (2002). Children's competence and the ecology of communities. *Environmental Psychology, 22,* 201–216.

Coalition to Stop the Use of Child Soldiers. (2005). Available: www.child-soldiers.org.

Cockburn, G. (2000). *Meaningful youth participation in international communities: A case study of the international conference on war-affected children*. Winnipeg: Canadian International Development Agency.

Consultoría para los Derechos Humanos y el Desplazamiento Forzado. (2000). *This is not our war: Children and forced displacement in Colombia*. Bogota: UNICEF.

Daiute, C., & Lelutiu-Weinberger, C. (2002). Negotiating violence prevention. *Journal of Social Issues, 59*(1), 83–101.

Dawes, A., Tredoux, C., & Feinstein, A. (1989). Political violence in South Africa: Some effects on children of the violent destruction of their community. *International Journal of Mental Health, 18*(2), 16–43.

Departamento Administrativo de Bienestar Social el Distrito. (2003). *Proyecto nuevas voces ciudadanas: Experiencia de intervención pedagógica* [the new voices of citizenship program: Commentary on an educational innovation]. Bogota: Author.

de Winter, M. (1997). *Children as fellow citizens: Participation and commitment*. Oxford: Radcliffe Medical Press.

Emler, N. (1992, Summer). Childhood origins of beliefs about institutional authority. *New Directions for Child Development, 56,* 65–77.

Erikson, E. (1980). *Identity and the life cycle*. New York: Norton.

Forero-Pineda, C., & Escobar-Rodriguez, D. (2004). *School rules and democratic behavior and the peaceful social interaction of Colombian children*. Unpublished manuscript. Available: www.isnie.org/ISNIE02/Papers02/foreroescobar.pdf.

Fraser, N., & Honneth, A. (2003). *Redistribution or recognition? A political-philosophical exchange*. London: Verso.

Freire, P. (1970). *Pedagogy of the oppressed*. Harmondsworth, UK: Penguin Books.

Fullilove, M., & Thompson, M. (1996). Psychiatric implications of displacement: Contributions from the psychology of place. *American Journal of Psychiatry, 153*(12), 1515–1523.

Garbarino, J., Kostelny, K., & Pardo, C. (1992). *Children in danger: Coping with the consequences of community violence*. San Francisco: Jossey-Bass.

Garbarino, J., Scott, F. M., & Faculty of the Erikson Institute. (1989). *What children can tell us: Eliciting, interpreting and evaluating information from children*. San Francisco: Jossey-Bass.

Gauvain, M. (2001). *The social context of cognitive development*. New York: Guilford Press.

Grant, E. (2004). Mental health and social capital in Cali, Colombia. *Social Science and Medicine, 58*(11), 2267–2277.

Guerra, E. (2002). Citizenship knows no age. *Environment and Urbanization, 14*(12), 71–84.

Harburg, C., & McCrum, S. (1994). *We are on the radio*. London: Child-to-Child Trust.

Hart, R. (1976). *Children's experience of place*. New York: Wiley.

Hart, R. (1992). *Children's participation: From tokenism to citizenship*. Florence: UNICEF.

Hart, R. (1997). *Children's participation: The theory and practice of involving young citizens in community development and environmental care*. New York: UNICEF.

Hart, R. (2002). Containing children: Some lessons on planning for play in New York City. *Environment and Urbanization, 14*(2), 135–148.

Hart, R. H. (2004). Las Escuelas Nuevas y el desarrollo sostenible. In *Proceedings of the International Conference on Escuelas Nuevas, Armenia, Colombia*. Bogota: Fundacion Volvanos a la Gente.

Hart, R. (2005). The landscapes we make for children. *Child, Youth and Environmental Studies, 1*(1), 53–64.

Hart, R., Daiute, C., Iltus, S., Sabo, K., Kritt, D., & Rome, M. (1996). *Child and youth development through community participation and children's developing capacity to participate*. New York: Children's Environments Research Group, City University Graduate School.

Hart, R., & Petren, A. (2000). The child's right to play. In A. P. a. J. Himes (Ed.), *Children's rights: Turning principles into practice* (pp. 107–122). Stockholm: Save the Children.

Hart, R., & Rajbhandary, J. (2003). The children's clubs of Nepal: A democratic experiment. In K. Sabo (Ed.), *Youth participatory evaluation: A field in the making* (pp. 61–76) (New Directions for Evaluation, No. 98). New York: Jossey-Bass.

Hartup, W. W. (1983). Peer relations. In E. M. Hetherington (Ed.), *Handbook of child psychology* (pp. 103–196). New York: Wiley.

Heath, S. B., & McLaughlin, M. W. (1993). *Identity and inner city youth: Beyond ethnicity and gender*. New York: Teachers College Press.

Instituto de Estudios Sociales y Culturales PENSAR. (2002). *Camino Hacia Nuevos Ciudadanías*. Bogota: DABS.

James, A., Jenks, C., & Prout, A. (1998). *Theorizing Childhood*. Cambridge, UK: Polity Press.

Krishna, A., & Schrader, E. (2000). *Cross-cultural measures of social capital: A tool and results from India and Panama* (Social Capital Initiative Working Paper Series No. 21.). Washington, DC: World Bank.

Kuo, F. E., Bacaicoa, M., & Sullivan, W. C.(1998). Transforming inner city landscape: Trees, sense of safety and preference. *Environment and Behavior, 30*(1), 28–59.

Mockus, A. S. (2000). *Bogota culta y producta, con justicia social: Programa de gobierno visionario 2001–2003*. Available: www.idct.gov.co/Cultura Ciudadana.

Nabhan, G.P.A., & Trimble, S. (1994). *The geography of childhood: Why children need wild places*. Boston, MA: Beacon Press.

Observatiorio de Manejo del Conflicto de la Universidad Externado de Colombia. (2004). Unpublished manuscript. Universidad Externado de Colombia, Bogota.

Ospina, H. F., Alvarado, S. V., & Moreno, L. L. (1999). *Educación para la Paz* [Education for peace]. Bogota: Cooperativa Editorial Magisterio.

Philippine Educational Theatre Association. (1984). *Children's theatre teacher's manual*. Manila: Philippine Educational Theatre Association.

Raymond, A., & Raymond, S. (2000, January/February). The making of children in war. *International Documentary*, 10–11.

Robledo Gomez, A. M. (2003). Inclusión, nuevas ciudadanas y ética del ciudadanías [Inclusion, new citizens and the ethics of citizenship]. In Departamento Administrativo de Bienestar Social el Distrito (Ed.), *Inclusión social y nuevas ciudadanías* [Social inslusion and new citizenship]. Bogota: DABS.

Rogoff, B. (2003). *The cultural nature of human development.* New York: Oxford University Press.

Sabo, K. (Ed.). (2003). *Youth participatory evaluation: A field in the making* (New Directions for Evaluation, No. 98). New York: Jossey-Bass.

Scheinfeld, D. (1983). Family relationship and school achievement among boys of lower-income urban black families. *American Journal of Orthopsychiatry, 53*(1), 127–143.

Soldiers of peace: A children's crusade. (1999). [Television broadcast]. Atlanta: Cable News Network.

Swift, A. (1992). *Brazil: The fight for childhood in the city.* Florence: UNICEF.

Torres, R. M. (1991). *Escuela Nueva: Una innovación desde el estado* [The new school: An innovation for the state]. Quito, Ecuador: Instituto Fronesis/Libresa.

United Nations Centre for Human Settlements. (1996). *An urbanizing world global report on human settlements.* Oxford: Oxford University Press.

United Nations International Children's Fund. (2002a). *Sowing mines, harvesting death.* Bogota: UNICEF Colombia.

United Nations International Children's Fund. (2002b). *The war's children.* Bogota: UNICEF.

United Nations International Children's Fund. (2004a). *Child friendly cities.* Available: www.childfriendlycities.com.

United Nations International Children's Fund. (2004b). *Hacia la construcción de una ciudad mas amable y justa* [Toward the construction of a more friendly and just city]. Bogota: UNICEF.

United States Agency for International Development. (2003). Office of transition initiatives: Hot topics—Colombia. Available: www.usaid.gov.

Valsiner, J. (2000). *Culture and human development.* Thousand Oaks, CA: Sage.

Willow, C. (2002). *Participation in practice: Children and young people as partners in change.* London: Children's Society.

Watchlist on children and armed conflict. (2004, February). Available: www.watchlist.org.

Women's Commission on Refugee Women and Children. (1999). *Untapped potential: Adolescents affected by armed conflict.* New York: Author.

Women's Commission on Refugee Women and Children. (2002). *Unseen millions: The catastrophe of internal displacement in Colombia.* New York: Author.

PART IV

GLOBAL PROCESSES
INVOLVING YOUTH

Introduction to Part IV

A city like this one makes me dream tall and feel in on things. Hep. It's the bright steel rocking above the shade below that does it. When I look over strips of green grass lining the river, at church steeples and into the cream-and-copper halls of apartment buildings, I'm strong. Alone, yes, but top-notch and indestructible—like the City in 1926 when all the wars are over and there will never be another one. The people down there in the shadow are happy about that. At last, at last, everything's ahead. The smart ones say so and people listening to them and reading what they write down agree: Here comes the new look. Look out. There goes the sad stuff. The bad stuff. The things-nobody-could-help stuff. The way everybody was then and there. Forget that. History is over, you all, and everything's ahead at last.

—Toni Morrison, *Jazz*

In the first chapter of this part, William Cross, Jr., examines youth conflict in the African American community in the United States. Cross's historical analysis provides support to what Toni Morrison describes near the beginning of her novel *Jazz:* how each generation suffering from conflicts hopes it has seen the end of injustice. Each generation then realizes, whether through the aesthetic irony of narrative, or thorough political analysis, that patterns of conflict repeat, although new versions of conflict involve young people in different ways.

Cross offers a historical analysis of what happened to inner-city black communities and their youth in New York when production in the industrial sectors was moved to other countries and adults started losing jobs. He notes that the false promise of globalization—to replace old jobs with new ones—was not realized, and the absence of job opportunities in the mainstream economy resulted in increasing involvement of low-income black Americans and their youngsters in the underground economy and drug trade. Drawing on alarming

267

data on school tracking and dropouts, as well as increasing suicide rates and homicide, as the number one cause of death in the community, the author points to truncated developmental trajectories of black youth.

Drawing from his extensive ethnographic fieldwork in another part of the world, in the Niger Delta, Charles Ukeje in his chapter describes ongoing protests of the local community against the practices of the multinational oil companies and repression and violence of the state. Ukeje illustrates how youth movements and violence in the region have been deeply embedded in the historical, economic, and political context of Nigeria by tracing Nigeria's colonial, postcolonial military, and postmilitary civilian phases in history. Analyzing the complexities of the ongoing Nigerian conflict from the perspectives of multinational oil companies, local communities, and young people, Ukeje argues that youth movements are integral to relations among diverse stakeholders of national resources in conflict with the multinational companies. He offers ideas for transforming the current inequities and lack of access to social and educational mobility and reengaging youth as leaders in social issues using nonviolent methods.

In the final chapter of the book, Jocelyn Solis points to another negative outcome of globalization—transnationalization of communities in search of financial stability. In particular, Solis discusses her work with the Mexican community in New York, examining Mexican young people's experience of their identity in relation to the identities thrust on them by their political and economic status as undocumented immigrants in the capitalist system of the United States. Drawing on her work with Mexican immigrant youth in a community-based organization in New York, Solis notes that it is important to focus on individual experiences. She argues convincingly that psychological analyses can complement sociological and political analyses and can be incorporated in the study of youth violence and conflict in transnational communities to offer specific ideas for intervention.

These three authors describe international processes. Together, these chapters focus, in particular, on legacies of political-economic injustices framing young people's violence against mainstream institutions and the existing order. Compared to earlier parts, these scholars' analytic lenses offer the broadest view, examining international processes of migration, exploitation of local communities by multinational corporations, and global exploitation of human resources. They explain how economic interests of powerful nations and corporations affect local life among immigrant children and families in New York City, youth in the oil-rich delta of Nigeria, and generations of people across ghettos in the United States. Each narration of global economic interests reveals the personal toll resulting from impersonal exchanges. This part brings the sensibilities of diverse social science disciplines—social psychology, political science, and developmental psychology—to the analysis of youth conflict in the age of globalization. They offer hope that rather than repetitions and revisions of the cycles of conflict, possibilities exist to interrupt these patterns and truly realize youth's dream of ending injustices.

CHAPTER 15

Globalism, America's Ghettos, and Black Youth Development

WILLIAM E. CROSS, JR.

Globalism is associated with the movement of jobs and industry from one country to another, and from 1955 to the present, hundreds of thousands of industrial sector jobs were shifted from the United States to various countries across the globe. In theory, globalization works when new jobs become available to replace the old. This essay describes what happened to inner-city black communities and their youth when the promised replacement jobs never materialized. The absence of a mainstream economic presence in the ghetto has given rise to a thriving underground economy anchored by the drug trade. While the trade itself can be analyzed from a rational, business perspective, the violence and community chaos linked to the trade plays havoc with black child and youth development. The article reviews how clinical psychologists and psychiatrists have taken the concept of posttraumatic stress disorder (PTSD), once solely associated with psychological reactions to wars outside the United States, and applied it to the emotional states of inner-city black children and youth who have experienced, witnessed, or possess firsthand knowledge about the violence and chaos linked to the underground economy. In addition, the history of the social struggles of white ethnic groups in the United States is revisited, as a way of gaining insight into what worked to effectuate social mobility for white groups trapped in poverty at earlier points in U.S. history. However, such lessons have been for naught, because when similar programs are put forth as part of the solutions to contemporary poverty, charges of socialism and the need to limit big government blunt any steps in that direction. Finally, hip hop culture, the organic voice of poor black youth in the United States, has been selected and assimilated by youth cultures across the globe as the model for expressing discontent, resistance, and struggle against systemic poverty found in Japan, Germany, England, South Africa, and elsewhere. However, despite its vast cultural influence and associated industries that annually generate billions of dollars in sales, salaries, and commissions, the hip hop movement has little influence and poses practically no threat to the larger social order. To the contrary, the reverse has happened, in that key aspects of the movement have been commodified and absorbed, materially speaking, into the very global economy hip hop originally sought to contest.

At the writing of this essay (spring and summer 2004), groups, organizations, schools, and universities, as well as leaders from all walks of American life, were holding meetings, seminars, and conferences to ponder the fulfilled and unmet promises of the 1954 United States Supreme Court school desegregation decision. The termination of the racial caste system in the United States, a system that marginalized black people across every of sector of American life for the period covering 1900 to 1960, prepared the way for the explosive rise of the black middle class, from the 1960s to the present. However, not every black person was able to take advantage of the new situation. If half of the black population moved forward and upward between 1954 and 2004, a significant fraction became ensnarled in the so-called underclass. For many blacks, the spiral downward shows no signs of ebbing, and as recently as the spring of 2004, over 50% of all black men between the ages of 16 to 64 living in New York City were unemployed (Scott, 2004). Currently, more black men are in prison than college, and at the high school level, black youth are disproportionately funneled into special education and lower track classes. Eventually, far too many drop out of high school altogether (Fine, 2001; Orfield, 2004). Homicide, often related to gang wars and the drug trade, is the leading cause of death for black men living in poverty (U.S. Department of Justice, 2001).

In addition to being the year of the momentous Supreme Court decision on school desegregation, 1954 also marked a turning point in U.S. economic history. At the time, few people inside or out of the black community could appreciate that the American economy was showing early signs of change such that anyone, including blacks, with a high school education or more would be absorbed into one of the expanding layers of American society that included technologies, pharmaceuticals, financial services, education, medical care, prison construction, military operations, and the service industries. However, for the same time period, that is, 1954–2004, men and women of the working class would see their take-home wages dramatically shrink, as the other half of the American economy, the *industrial sector,* literally closed shop and moved offshore (Kitwana, 2002). Between 1954 and 2004, millions of decent-paying union jobs with good medical and health benefits simply disappeared from America's borders, as something called "globalization" took hold. It has been estimated that the earning power of the American working class and working poor has shrunk precipitously since the 1970s (Reich, 1991). Between 1973 and 1986, the average real income of black men dropped almost 50% (Coontz, 1992). In the white community, jettisoned workers were labeled unemployed or redundant workers, but in the black community a more colorful and ideologically tainted term evolved, and blacks were defined as the underclass, a term suggestive of *self-created* poverty (Cross, 2003).

The ability of the Republican Party and the Radical Right to racialize the discourse on poverty—make poverty a racial rather than systemic issue—has been America's most successful way of not dealing with poverty. In a masterful scheme that turned the discourse on poverty upside down, America convinced itself that rather than a changing economy, the poor were their own worst enemy and poverty programs and safety-net assistance, such as welfare and aid to families with dependent children, were actually attenuating the problem (Murray, 1984). The analysis suggested that (1) there was no relationship between the disappearance of the industrial sector and welfare dependence; (2) poverty resulted from poor people making bad career choices; and (3) either for cultural or biogenetic reasons, black people were particularly vulnerable to welfare entanglement. With great fanfare, America divested itself of programs designed to help poor people (H.R. Rep. No. 3734, 1996), and because propaganda made it appear that blacks were more dependent than other groups on welfare, the new welfare schema, which forced the poor to accept low-paying, dead-end jobs in the expanding service industry, was also said to "solve" the peculiar problems of "black" poverty. Hidden by the smoke of the Far Right's war on poverty was the connection between the disappearance of well-paying working-class jobs and the expansion of the global economy.

It is somewhat disingenuous to suggest that the American economy became globalized from the mid-1950s onward. From the perspective of black people, contact with Europeans has been one global nightmare after another. The 400-year slave trade linked trade between Europe, Africa, and North and South America; the 1884 Berlin Conference on Africa saw Britain, France, Portugal, and Germany take control of Africa's riches, followed by the rise of the racist state of South Africa; all these developments were all part of global exploitation of blacks by whites. Perhaps it is more accurate to note that not a new globalism but a new *phase* of globalism has driven from America's shores the types of well-paying jobs that once made the quality of life of America's working class the envy of the world.

Creation of the Black Underclass

American blacks, along with Native Americans, have been disproportionately damaged by the most recent phase of globalization, and inner city "ghettos" have been turned into slums. Between the 1930s and the early 1950s, the federal government, in cooperation with the state and local governments, as well as both the banking and real estate industries, passed laws and established housing and lending policies that resulted in racial ghettos of privilege for whites and spatial-residential isolation and marginalization for blacks (Massey & Denton, 1993). The density of black ghettos has always been beyond comprehension, but as long as the majority of the population was employed, blacks found ways to convert their conditions into levels of humanity never intended by those who would spatially isolate them. After World War II, as the GI Bill helped white working-class men transcend social-class barriers and enter the middle class, blacks became the *workers of choice* (Dickerson, 1986). With restrictive immigrations laws of the 1920s still in place—laws that limited the inclusion of new workers from many non-European countries—the late 1940s and 1950s became the golden era of black working-class life.

Discrimination and racism, inadequate schools, police brutality, and the everyday hassles of what Denton and Massey (1993) call the American version of "apartheid" were omnipresent in the inner cities of the forties and fifties; however, employment helped make possible strong churches and parallel social institutions such as the "black" YMCAs. Black sports teams, stellar jazz and blues figures, and a list of racial heroes stirred the daydreams of many black youth. Crime and violence were part of ghetto life before globalization, but in the grand scheme of things, these negative dynamics were manageable and limited in scope. School attendance and achievement motivation matched that to be expected of any working-class community, even though the perennially underfunded school system servicing blacks seemed intent on crushing black aspirations (Homel, 1984). Oppositional identity (Ogbu, 2003), or the tendency to reject values of white society as well as mainstream black culture, was practically nonexistent, and the lure of street life, while ever-present for some black youth, was a nonstarter for most. Street gangs flourished from time to time, but stable black family life, employed black men, and a vibrant black culture muted the draw of gangs and any inclination toward rejecting traditional black culture (Cross, 2003).

In many ways, black communities of preglobalization days were places of hope and positive energy, waiting to be triggered by first the Civil Rights movement (circa 1954–65) and later the Black Consciousness movement (circa 1965 to the mid-1970s). These movements did not inject positive energy into the black community; rather, each transformed omnipresent positive dynamics into specific political, cultural, educational, and economic objectives (Van Deburg, 1992). Blacks became explicitly ideological, and though black rage and anger would add to the motivational fuel of either movement, it is critical to understand that the overall thrust was, first, that of a request (Civil Rights movement) and then a demand (Black Power movement) for *inclusion* (Cross, 1991; Van Deburg, 1992). The former operated via an assimilationist framework (let us in so we can be like you) and the later a more pluralistic orientation (let us in and be prepared to make changes in yourself and the white community).

The Watts Riot of 1965 signaled the beginning of the end of the Gandhian assimilationism advocated by the movement for nonviolent change of Martin Luther King, Jr., and in the face of increased black assertiveness and militancy, America's shift toward racial justice quickened (Dickerson, 1986). Between 1965 and 1967, racial riots or black rebellions spread across the American urban landscape. In the aftermath of the assassination of King, a national report on the causes of rioting forecast a structural split within the black community (National Advisory Commission on Civil Disorders, 1968) and the categories *middle class* versus *underclass* seemed to capture this split. The Kerner Report showed that one cluster of black youths and adults were able to take immediate advantage of the educational and employment gains won by the Civil Rights and Black Power movements, and, over time, emerged as the new and expanded black middle class. The other cluster was depicted less clearly. The report could not decide whether this second group was as motivated as the first but better suited for working-class life or was an unprepared, overly hostile, and alienated cohort doomed to be bypassed by the gains of the movements. The same kind of intellectual waffling could be found in the so-called Moynihan Report (1965) on the black family a few years earlier. At one point, the Moynihan Report accurately spotted the negative change in job prospects for working-class men and women as a central problem, but its weak-kneed recommendation was not to challenge society to provide jobs and a hope for the future but to encourage black youth to join the army. More than the Kerner Commission, which flirted with a call for an internal Marshall Plan, Pat Moynihan turned away from any recommendation about creating jobs or calling for massive jobs projects, as was done during the depression, with the building of the Triborough Bridge in New York City or irrigation structures linked to the Tennessee Valley Authority (Federal Writer's Project, 1939). Instead, redundant black workers were castigated for inventing their own redundancy. Victim-blaming notions such as the culture of poverty or black biological inferiority replaced clear-headed analysis based on systemic dynamics (Kihss, 1970).

In alarmist language suggestive of an invasion from Mars, both the Moynihan Report and the Kerner Commission depicted the tens of thousands of rural black folk migrating from the southern region of the United States to the urban centers of the North as a challenge to urban governments (Gardner & Sanford, 1969). These simple, rural black folk—poorly educated and novices to modern economic realities—were proof positive of the success of the southern region's 60-year scheme (from circa 1900 to 1960s) to *deliberately underdevelop* its black citizens across all aspects of modern American life (social, economic, political, cultural, and educational). Thus, they were not "illegal" aliens, and they were most certainly not from Mars; these were citizens of the United States of America, whose faces and credentials carried the imprint of 60 years of systemic racial oppression in the states of Mississippi, Georgia, North and South Carolina, Louisiana, Alabama, Texas, Tennessee, Arkansas, Missouri, and Virginia (Anderson, 1988).

In neither the Kerner Report nor the Moynihan Report is there any serious discussion on how and why black migrants were *socially produced* in the South between 1900 and 1960. Consequently, there was no call for a "Federal Commission on Reparations for Blacks Paid by the Southern States." Nor was there a call to action by the federal government for a 10-year plan of federal projects and activities, as was done during the depression to assist whites who were unemployed. Nor was there a call for a federally sponsored and southern-supported *truth and reconciliation commission* that would allow the southern region to find a way out of its denial of collective criminalization and terrorism. Such ideas were thought radical, un-American, socialistic, and communistic. Consequently, all that America had learned from its experiences with the GI Bill, the Levittown housing experiments and federal housing loan guarantee programs, and the Works Progress Administration projects (such as the Triborough Bridge Program or the Tennessee Valley Project) never informed a blueprint for *really* helping black people. Such ventures not only "saved" white workers from poverty but also promoted home ownership, stabilized (white) family incomes, made possible movement to the suburbs and life beyond inner-city congestion and density, and, most important of all, made possible the jump from working-class existence to the doorsteps of middle-class life through affordable and assessable public higher education. These "social programs" of the 1930s, 1940s, and 1950s that transformed the social status of hundreds of thousands of whites from working-class to middle-class suddenly became radical and off-limits when the discussion shifted to ways the United States might assist the social mobility of its long-oppressed black citizens.

In place of suggesting that systematic forces had helped shape the current credentials of black migrants, both the Kerner Commission Report and especially the Moynihan Report pinned the problem not on the southern states, not on the shrinking employment base, not on changes in the economy, not on the failure to provide reparations, not on the absence of a federally coordinated plan of action that would link employment and housing for adults and families, not on public figures like Robert Moses of New York City, who would build 200 public parks and amazing swimming pools in white neighborhoods throughout New York City and only two ill-equipped and poorly managed parks for Harlem and East Harlem, not on Mayor Richard J. Daley, Sr., who would oversee the building of skyscraper housing projects in Chicago that were designed for maximum isolation of poor blacks from white communities and easy patrol and control by a mostly white police force. Rather, poor black people were castigated for being undereducated, for being poor, and for acting in non-middle-class ways (Coontz, 1992). *Symptoms of poverty* became the units of analysis, and soon a "theory on the culture of poverty" was put forth and the action of choice became benign neglect (Valentine, 1978).

In the absence of a federally coordinated internal Marshall Plan, as was done to revive Europe after World War II, poor black people were placed at the mercy of the trends and whims of the market economy (Jaynes & Williams, 1989). Starting in 1955, gaining momentum in the mid-1960s, unveiling itself as an explicit business strategy by the 1970s and 1980s, and gaining rapid pace in the aftermath of the 1973 oil embargo, heavy industry, which between 1900 and the late 1950s had provided full-time employment to working-class men and women with an eighth-grade education or less, shut operations within the United States and replaced them with new factories in other parts of the world. Ironically, these new "offshore" factories would employ workers with "less" formal education than that of the black adults left behind in the United States.

Consequently, the quality and education level of the working-class workforce within the United States was *never at issue*. Rather, lower wages could be paid to nonunion, poorly educated workers from other parts of the world, as compared to the high wages and high benefits companies would be forced to pay the same caliber of worker, here, in the United States. In a manner of speaking, the new freedoms and new possibilities linked to the struggles of the 1950s and 1960s positioned many blacks to enter the middle class. But for their brethren whose sights were on the backbreaking but well-paying jobs at nearby factories and heavy industries, freedom came too late. This is the splitting captured by the Kerner Report, and this is the splitting that Pat Moynihan twisted into a victim-blaming framework.

American society closed ranks across class lines. The Kerner Report would be forgotten, Moynihan would become a hero for helping middle-class and wealthy people become blind to the connection between poverty and systemic forces, the Far Right would rewrite history and make invisible the socialist origins of the Triborough Bridge and the Tennessee Valley Authority, and poor people would be depicted in the mass media as their own worst enemy. The authors of *The Bell Curve* would proclaim America an opened society (Herrnstein & Murray, 1994) where anyone with the right stuff (e.g., genes) could succeed and those with bad genes would filter down to their rightful and "natural" place at the bottom of the social order. Poverty programs, designed to *transition* poor people into jobs that in reality no longer existed, were declared the true cause of poverty. In a thinly veiled effort to cut off monies from social programs that it might be absorbed for "better use" by the market economy, class warfare against the poor was openly embraced, and in a massive disinvestment of the poor, safety net programs were obliterated by the Personal Responsibility and Work Opportunity Reconciliation Act of 1996. Moynihan's earlier suggestion of a policy of benign neglect, in effect, became the law of the land, and in its wake emerged the so-called underclass.

From Ghetto: The Creation of the Black Underclass

Most residents of black ghettos are average Marys and Joes who get up each morning, greet their children, send them off to school, and leave soon thereafter for work (Valentine, 1978). But with the dramatic downturn in jobs, many of their neighbors have been forced to reinvent themselves, economically speaking, and the *underground economy* has become an attractive option. As noted earlier, between 1973 and 1986, young black men and women suffered a 50% drop in real income. As long as poor and redundant able-bodied black youth and workers live and breathe, they will struggle to fill the void; the men call it surviving and hustling or "street-life" (Payne, 2004; Valentine, 1978). Repeating a pattern first set by Irish, Italian, and eastern European Jewish immigrants of the 1920s and 1930s (Kavieff, 2000), who, in the midst of the Great Depression, turned bootlegging, gambling, and prostitution into employment opportunities (around 1930 in the Detroit area, 30% and higher of all employed white males were engaged in some facet of the underground economy, second in importance only to the auto industry), blacks began to organize around the illicit drugs of their day, which, following Prohibition times, had shifted from alcohol to marijuana, heroin, designer drugs, and cocaine. A major problem with powder cocaine is that it is simply too expensive for poor folks to afford. In the spirit of capitalism, drug entrepreneurs invented a way to reduce powder cocaine into something called crack cocaine, and vials of crack were priced at a fraction of the cost of powder coke.

Crack cocaine revolutionized the trade, and between 1975 and 1995, the crack trade spread like wildfire through black communities. Issues of territory and distribution were "negotiated," and gang violence, beatings, and murder became tools of the trade (Butterfield, 2005). Again, such behavior is not particularly new or unique, and people are quick to forget that violence and murder were the mainstay of white ethnic gangs in the white ethnic ghettos of an earlier time. Recall, for example, New York City's Jewish- and Italian-run Murder Incorporated, Detroit's Jewish Purple Gang, and the Italian Mafia of New York, Chicago, and elsewhere. As gruesome and heartless as many blacks have become within the context of the drug wars, few can match the horrific St. Valentine's Massacre, in which Italian gang members shot down seven members of an Irish gang in Chicago on February 14, 1929 (Allsop, 1970).

Taking a page from these earlier prototypes of the underground economy, young black men organized themselves around gangs and negotiated and fought for control of the trade or underground economy. As the adult market for the trade became saturated, the focus turned to younger users, and just as there were alcohol-free zones placed around schools during the heyday of the bootlegging trade in the 1930s, so too have drug-free zones been set up around black schools in our modern episode of underground economics. In the same way that protracted alcoholism can have destructive social consequences, crack cocaine is extremely debilitating to one's self, one's family, and sectors of the community. Bootleggers did not have to be concerned that "one drink" would lead to alcoholism; in fact, they counted on many people having a few drinks now and then. Things are different with the drug trade and the addictive power of crack cocaine. Just one "experiment" with crack can result in addiction. Consequently, the trade and its infamous crack houses turned sections of the ghetto into slum areas, and this, added to the negative effects of long-term unemployment, is an ongoing cancer to the community as a whole.

The emergence of the black gangs and the drug trade paralleled the rise of the Far Right in America, and the draconian response fashioned to checkmate the drug tidal wave reflected a fascist mindset (Gonnerman, 2004). The Far Right's answer was to arrest more people, increase the length of sentencing, and build more prisons. Knowing that many users and dealers were from their own white middle class and wealthy neighborhoods, the mostly white legislators understood that they had to differentiate penalties. The scheme that emerged turned on whether the infraction involved powder versus crack cocaine and might just as well have been called "penalties for white versus African American use and distribution of drugs" (Duster, 1997). Harsh and mandatory penalties were linked to crack-based infractions, and minimal and negotiated sentencing was possible for other forms of drug crime. Before the new laws took effect, blacks were likely to receive 6% longer sentences than whites for similar infractions, but after the laws were passed, the sentencing differential became 93% (Tonry, 1996). In 1983, Virginia reported that 63% of incarcerations involved white criminals, and only 37% blacks and minorities. Just 6 years later, in the shadow of the state's new drug laws, the figures reversed to 34% and 65%, respectively (Duster, 1997). These figures capture the *racialization of drug laws* for states across the United States, and are all the more amazing when one realizes that in absolute terms, and for the same period, drug use was higher in white than in black and Latino communities.

States such as Florida, which helped wipe out the ballots of thousands of black voters in the 2000 presidential election, took the opportunity to tack on a *lifetime penalty* to the drug laws, namely, that persons from Florida convicted of a felony drug violation lose the right to vote within the state for the remainder of their lives (Manza & Uggen, 2006). In commentaries about the number of black people and black men in particular who serve time in prison and have criminal records, the racialization of the laws is played down, and a finger is pointed at black men, themselves, for making the wrong "personal" choices (Manza & Uggen, 2006).

Not long ago it was the men from Italian, Irish and, to a lesser extent, low-income Jewish neighborhoods who filled America's prisons, but over time, many ethnic white "ex-cons" found their way into the mainstream economy (O'Connor, 1997). Fast-forwarding to contemporary times, the prison-related AIDS epidemic points to a different outcome for black men, and, as it turns out, for their girlfriends and wives as well. Prison officials know that while in prison men have sex with men, and this trend has not changed just because the prisoners are black. However, prison systems across the land will not distribute condoms to prisoners (Harding & Schaller, 1992). In a surrealistic morality play built on a foundation of hypocrisy and denial, the certainty of infection and death is favored over the appearance of promoting promiscuity. It would be bad enough if the story stopped at the steps of the prisons and the men who inhabit them (Younge, 2004). Today, 64% of new AIDS cases among women involve black women, even though they make up only about 15% of the female population in the United States (Centers for Disease Control, 2002). The major source of their infection is black men returning from prison (Edwards, 2001). Consequently, in real time, the ripple effects of imprisonment and the spread of AIDS has become as great a problem as the original lack of jobs that triggered this Faustian cycle in the first place. In the black community, there has always existed some degree of hope for each and every ex-con, for in the spirit of Malcolm X, there is always hope that the individual will find a way to transcend his circumstances, even after having acquired the label *black ex-con.* Today, hope that a personal metamorphosis or identity transformation (Cross, 1991) might turn an ex-con's life around has been replaced with the fear of the inevitability of death from HIV infection.

Implosion

Instead of pathology, involvement in street-life reflects rational strategies for survival and a chance for the good life—no matter how short-lived (Payne, 2004). Ethnographic studies of the drug trade show that the quality of leadership, reticulation of distribution networks, concerns for employee incentives and disincentives, quality control concerns, and overall organizational dynamics involve a business sense that is at odds with mainstream America only insofar as the products being processed and sold are illicit drugs (Adler, 1989; Williams, 1989). Of course, reliance on violence as the ultimate form of conflict resolution also places the venture at odds with the larger society. In examining the mindset, soul, and personality of the average street Brother or Sister, one discovers not a twisted mentality, a mangled soul, or a psychopath who defies recognition as a member of the human family—rather, he or she is more often than not rather mundane and "average" (Payne, 2004). However, alongside such rationality and practicality one also finds the bitter fruit of nihilism, chaos, and a sense of hopelessness.

On occasion, the nadir of existence in the slum sectors of the ghetto creates a chasm between black youth and all others. In the need for money, food, and attention, two young black men entered, in Queens, New York, a Wendy's (fast food chain) restaurant where one of them had once worked. They pushed five employees into a back room, as part of the robbery. Each potential "witness" was murdered by a shot to the back of the head, and the two escaped with $2,400 and hamburgers (*Two suspects*, 2000). Or there is the biracial woman in her late teens who, having been raised in an all-white community, travels to Chicago to find adventure and intimacy with a *real* black man; she finds her mate at a party, and they venture out to his car. The sex becomes rough, and in trying to forcibly sodomize her, he squeezes her neck too tightly, and she dies (Powers, 2002). Or the killer aims his gun as he drives by a rival gang member, but one of the bullets kills a little boy who is just sitting at the window's edge, looking wide-eyed and happy at the world beyond his windowpane (Gettleman, 2004; Loftis, 1997). Along with rational behavior, protracted unemployment also engenders chaos and episodes of utter hopelessness and meaninglessness. In interviews (Glasgow, 1981) with young black men from extremely poor circumstances, it is simply not uncommon for them to respond to the question Where will you be by the time you reach your 25th birthday? with the answer "I don't know, I will probably be dead." In the black community, suicide was once considered a form of craziness practiced only by whites, but in 2004, the Centers for Disease Control reported that since 1980, the suicide rate for young black males has increased dramatically. Beyond the psychology of the individual, entire cities become engulfed in the chaos and despair. Reporting in the *New York Times* on recent trends in Camden, N.J., Jeffery Gettleman (2004) noted that, in a city of 79,000 covering only 9 square miles, there were 53 homicides, 800 aggravated assaults, 750 robberies, 150 acts of arson, and more than 10,000 arrests during a 12-month period covering most of the year 2004.

The Progeny of Redundant Workers:
Black Youth Development

I noted earlier that between 1900 and the early 1960s, the social and political policy of white-dominated southern states was to underdevelop their black
citizens. State-sanctioned segregation and policies of white preference and fa-
voritism are said to have ended in the aftermath of the Civil Rights movement
and the Black Consciousness movement. However, under the guise of *benign
neglect,* the themes of segregation, unequal treatment, constrained and limited
access to the larger society, as well as outright social, economic, and educational underdevelopment, are evident just below the surface. This is particularly true within the field of education. Although the constitution of every state
declares that all children will be accorded equal educational resources and a
quality education at public expense, few states actually distribute school funding equitably (Fine et al., 2005). In fact, there is tremendous, organized resistance to the equitable distribution of tax dollars for public education (Kozol,
1991). What makes the school equity issue so intriguing is that "education" is
presented as the singular vehicle for poor people to effectuate social mobility.
While parents must contend with periodic or protracted redundancy, underemployment, or employment without health care benefits and access to quality
and affordable child care, their progeny are too often enveloped in a school
experience that is inherently less than it could be, given the larger society's
resistance to educational equity, to say nothing of the fact that many in society
think children of color are inferior in the first place.

Inner-city schools specialize in *arrested development* by oversubscribing
black students to special education and vocational education tracks and providing minimum access to college prep classes (Boykin, 2002; Fine et al., 2005;
Haney, 2002). This steering of black education away from academic competition and sustained success even affects the black middle class. In a study of over
9,000 students, black American, Afro-Caribbean, and Latino students, whose
parents were college educated or more, were far less likely to be in AP/honors
courses than was true of white and Asian American students whose parents
were college educated (Fine et al., 2005). Likewise, while white and Asian
American students report greater teacher support, when they are in AP/honors
classes, as opposed to lower track classes, African American, Afro-Caribbean
and Latino students are consistently less likely to perceive teachers as responsive and supportive, regardless of tracking status (Fine et al., 2005). Finally,
inner-city kids and black boys, in particular, experience more frequent disci-
plinary actions and suspensions from schools (Haney, 2002).

One can find within the black community traditions and incentives that help
some black youth discover and take ownership of pathways leading to mainstream acceptance and success (Eccles, 2004). For others, the pressures of poverty, the need to be practical about one's life chances, and the mere existence
of the underground economy shape alternate definitions of "how to make it."
Living in poverty can make initiation into the underground economy seem "nat-

ural" and "normal." This can lead law enforcement to see black youth involvement in the drug trade as an unavoidable consequence of the inner-city environment, while the same behavior in white youth is processed as a "mistake" correctable by and worthy of a second chance. In a case study about three small-time drug dealers, two white students are depicted as having distributed small amounts of drugs in their high school days in New York City, an activity they continued together in college. The other figure was a young black male who was the dealer for the two white students both in college and when they attended high school in New York City. Upon being caught, the two white students were persuaded to help entrap the black youth, in exchange for a lighter sentence and a chance to have their court records sealed such that any future search of their personal histories would reveal no history of a criminal past. Whereas the exchange between the two white college students and the black youth always involved less than 2 grams of coke, the state police had the two white students request delivery of 2.5 grams of coke, which is a class A-1 felony carrying a mandated *minimum* sentence of 15 years to life. The black youth was successfully entrapped, and he was sentenced to 7 years to life, while the white dealers spent no time in jail and received a "second chance." When the reporter for the story visited the black youth in prison, he found him sitting at a table in an empty visiting room.

> He wears the standard inmate uniform plus a pair of New Balance sneakers. It is easy to tell that not long ago he was a cocky [black] teenager—the sort of kid who thought he could beat the system by selling drugs, making a lot of money, and never getting caught. (Gonnerman, 2004, p. 35)

Perhaps the journalist might have expanded his last commentary to show that black teens bring their energy, enthusiasm, motivation, organization skills, interpersonal talents, daring, and bravado to the underground economy. They are developing youth trying to make crime satisfy their otherwise *normal* developmental needs (Spencer, 2000). That is, they are acting out "normal" developmental tendencies, but the avenues for their enactments are constrained to that which is socially marginal. They are kids trying to become men and women through challenging activities that are, at best, high-risk ventures leading to incarceration and a lifelong criminal record. No sealed court records, no second chance. Their work within the higher layers of the drug distribution organization exposes young people to the more ruthless side of the trade. Seeing and participating in the violence of the trade has had its negative ripple effects in the black community. To begin with, drive-by shootings and gang-related violence cause mothers to keep their children at home, causing their children to lose valuable time in school (Libman, 1993). Concern for safety and a heightened sense of vigilance can constrict a young child's sense of adventure and exploration. We generally imagine positive youth development taking place in safe and nurturing environments, but the opposite is often true in the inner city. Hypervigilance and a pressing sense that one is not safe can lead to depression and suicidal ideations (Kinchin, 2005). Most ominously, the number one cause of death for young black males is drug-related homicide. For those who live and survive, more will end up in prison than in college.

Nancy Boyd-Franklin and A. J. Franklin have written extensively on black youth development, and most instructive are the terms they employ to depict (black) development. They claim that their book, *Boys into Men: Raising Our African American Teenage Sons* (2000), is a *survival guide* written for parents, teachers, social workers, and counselors whose task is to help black teens negotiate the *mine fields* of the teenage years. For example, black teens are often targeted by police, and this has led to such dangers as DWB, or *driving while black*. If pulled over by the police, Boyd-Franklin and Franklin instruct black teens to (1) place one's hands in full view atop the steering wheel on the dashboard, (2) avoid making any fast moves, such as reaching for one's wallet or grabbing a shiny cell phone that the police might mistake for a gun, and, by all means, (3) do not talk back. Each of these points is grounded in history, because in the past black young people have been beaten or shot by the police during the course of what began as a "simple" traffic violation.

Clinical psychologists and psychiatrists have turned to the study of child and youth development in war-torn countries to better comprehend the trauma they see in kids and teens from the inner city (inner-city PTSD). Were it not enough that the stress of poverty can cause them to encounter physical, verbal, and sometimes sexual abuse at the hands of their guardians and kin, black children and adolescents are also forced to negotiate far too frequently the *homicidal* death of a relative, playmate, friend, or school associate (Foy & Goguen, 1998; Sanders-Phillips, 1997). Consequently, the knowledge and experience needed to treat postwar trauma disorders have found application in the treatment and counseling of black kids from the inner city. In a study conducted at an inner-city primary care health clinic (Lipschitz, Rasmusson, Anywan, Cromwell, & Southwick, 2000), 90 females between the ages of 12 and 20, mostly (88 %) African American, shared their experiences with community and family violence: 85% reported witnessing community violence; 55% had witnessed shootings; 39% had witnessed stabbings; 13% had witnessed homicides; 4.5% reported having been stabbed or shot themselves; 36% had used weapons; 24% had been arrested; and 20% had spent time in jail. With regard to family violence, 67% had heard about the homicide of a friend or family member; 32% had witnessed abuse at home; 16% had experienced abuse at home; 11% had experienced sexual abuse at home; 30% had experienced sexual abuse outside of the home, and 10% had been raped. Not surprisingly, 13% could be diagnosed with current PTSD, 11% with partial PTSD, and the dominant posttraumatic stress symptoms were psychological distress related to reminders of the trauma event; avoidance behavior toward people or places related to the trauma event; recurrent, intrusive thoughts; and a hypervigilant mindset. Girls and young women with full, as compared to partial or no, PTSD experienced greater depression, higher rates of substance abuse, more frequent suspension from school or school failure, and more frequent encounters with the law leading to arrests. Recall that, since 1980, the suicide rate for young black boys has dramatically increased, from its generally low rate of years past.

Urban Poverty and the Hip Hop Movement

Bakari Kitwana, in his amazing book *The Hip Hop Generation* (2002), argues that the sector of the black populace most deeply affected by globalization, loss of jobs, and the downward spiral of black working-class life was born between 1965 and 1984; they reached late adolescence and early adulthood in the 1980s and 1990s, during the emergence, apex, and stasis of globalization. Both as an expression of reportage and resistance, this generation found reason to communicate and amplify its hopes, dreams, anger, outrage, humor, and, most important, its "blight" through hip hop culture. In the face of a society that denies its social class dynamics, hip hop, rap, and gangsta rap music became the CNN of the ghetto, with searing, brutally frank, and mind-bending lyrics that provocatively caught the attention of many who originally never intended to listen so intently. Through hip hop culture, the underclass and the poor attempted to expand the audience participating in discussions linking poverty, crime, unemployment, and street-life. In short order, the internet and other technologies helped hip hop connect youth from Japan, Germany, South Africa, and France (Yarmouth, 2004). As an expression of resistance and rebellion, it has even been appropriated by the children of the white middle class within the United States, who, through the purchasing of clothing, shoes, CDs, and DVDs that bear the hip hop imprint, drive a multibillion-dollar hip hop "industry" (Kitwana, 2002). Some would argue that the global economy, once a target of hip hop agitation and protest, has, paradoxically, commodified and thus co-opted many aspects of hip hop (Kitwana, 2002).

In a recent retrospective looking back at 30 years of hip hop, Greg Tate (2005) notes that, for all its high-profile "stars" and rappers, the message of hip hop has been no more successful than the results of 30 years of academic research in changing the larger society's agenda on how to deal with poverty. Tate also notes that most of the wealth generated by hip hop never finds its way back to inner cities, and many of the people who run the industry—managers, technicians, lawyers, accountants, publicists, and others—were not born in, do not currently live in, and do not invest in inner cities. An example of the "contradictions" reflected in the hip hop movement is that much of the "authentic" hip hop clothing and shoes are made outside of the United States in low-wage nonunion sweatshops—the essence of what hip hop, supposedly, opposes.

In the year of its 30th anniversary—that is, 2004—hip hop was witness to the election of George W. Bush to his second term as president of the United States. His election can only be understood as a setback to the socioeconomic agenda implicit in the hip hop movement. The year 2004 also revealed that hip hop's basic message about what conditions are like in the inner cities has yet to gain a consensus, even among blacks themselves. If anything, the reverse is true, in that some observers are using hip hop culture to denigrate the image of the hip hop generation, and point not to the link between systemic forces and poverty but to the negative and supposedly self-inflicted "habits" of poor people themselves. Nothing demonstrates this more pointedly than a speech given by the internationally renowned black comedian Bill Cosby. The occasion was a commemoration of the 50th anniversary of the 1954 *Brown v. Board of Education* school desegregation decision jointly sponsored by NAACP and Howard University on Monday, May 17, 2004, in Washington D.C., at Constitution Hall. Cosby, in addition to his iconic status within U.S. popular culture, has a doctorate in education and has contributed millions of dollars to historically black colleges. He and former president Jimmy Carter were honored with special awards. In his acceptance speech, Cosby missed the opportunity to call for an internal Marshall Plan, reparations for slavery, job projects on the order of the Tennessee Valley Authority or the Interstate Highway Projects, or a demand that the right to vote be returned to black ex-felons. Instead, Cosby launched into a vicious and furious verbal attack on the hip hop generation:

> Ladies and gentlemen, the lower class economic people are not holding up their end in this deal. These people are not parenting. They will buy things for their kids [like] $500 sneakers . . . and won't spend $200 for Hooked on Phonics. They're [black kids] standing on the corner and they can't speak English. I can't even talk the way these people talk: "Why you ain't" or "Where you is" . . . And I blamed the kids until I heard the mother talk. And then I heard the father talk. . . . Everybody knows it is important to speak English except these knuckleheads. . . . You can't be a doctor with that kind of crap coming out of their mouths! (Dolgin, 2004, p. 3)

At another point, Cosby trivialized why so many black youth are in prison by stating:

> These are not political criminals. These are people going around stealing Coca-Cola. People getting shot in the back of the head over a piece of pound cake and then we run around and we are outraged, [saying] "The cops shouldn't have shot him." What the hell was he doing with the pound cake in his hand? (King, 2004; *New York Times*, 2004)

In his diatribe Cosby reduces poverty to weak culture, distorted values, "bad" parenting, and poor personal choices. At every step, he blames the poor for not doing their part to take advantage of the positive outcomes of the 1954 desegregation decision and the struggles by black people for greater educational equity that followed in the aftermath of the decision. He essentially revisits Pat Moynihan's tangle of pathology thesis on black family functioning and suggests that in the absence of that old bogeyman called white racism, poor blacks have managed to make a mess of their lives. Cosby was attacked in the press, but there were many who came to his support (Dolgin, 2004). More important, his remarks did little to raise the level of discourse on the role of systemic forces in the reproduction of poverty and the so-called underclass. If anything, his "insights" helped move the analysis further to the right and contested both the ideology and solutions put forth by the hip hop movement.

The Cosby controversy reveals a chasm not so much between the have and have-not sectors of the black community, for it must be recalled that Cosby's origins were working-class. Much of his discourse is shaped not by his current positionality—that is, a person of wealth and means—but his recollections of what it meant to be born poor and socialized in a working-class black community in the era before the hip hop generation. Cosby's youth was framed by what I earlier called the golden era of black working-class life (circa 1945–65; Cross, 2003). He experienced poverty, he was shaped by racism, but he also was immersed in a segregated community during a time when employment for black men and women was commonplace, and jobs for black teens within the fringes of the mainstream economy were easy to come by. Black family structure was intact (more than 70% of black families were intact between 1900 and the late 1960s), Joe Lewis was champion, Jackie Robinson was making waves in baseball, Richard Wright's *Native Son* and Ralph Ellison's *Invisible Man* were bestsellers, and Miles Davis signed with Columbia Records and produced *Kind of Blue*. There was nothing romantic about the pre—hip hop period, and sections of every black ghetto were slumlike in their conditions, but in a general sense, segregated black ghettos were teeming with vitality, hope, aspiration, and a sense of proactive and positive struggle, and this is especially true of the period from 1945 to 1965. As noted earlier, the Civil Rights and Black Power movements sprang from the pre—hip hop era.

The hip hop era is the post—Civil Rights and post—Black Power experience as told by those for whom redundancy or underemployment is the norm, such that by the spring of 2004, 50% (and in some places more) of the black men living in urban areas of the United States are unemployed! The material conditions of the hip hop era cannot sustain the quality of life of an earlier era, when poverty and segregation, *plus employment,* went hand in hand. The ghetto today has been turned into a slum, in that poor, segregated, unemployed, and underemployed persons are spatially isolated—literally cut off from everyday contact with mainstream America. Cosby's remarks suggest that he, as well as many other blacks, simply cannot comprehend just how dramatic are the differences between black ghettos of the hip hop era and black ghettos shortly after World War II.

In summary, the hip hop movement is important because at its best, it helps convey a graphic picture and narration of the everyday struggles of poor and racially oppressed black people. It has become a model that poor people from other parts of the world use to communicate their predicament. Ironically, it has even become a vehicle of adolescent protest and identity search for white middle-class youth far removed from the ghetto. It is a multibillion-dollar global enterprise, although the dollars generated seldom circulate within and across the low-income black communities that, ironically, gave birth to the movement in the first place. Despite its cultural energy and importance, hip hop has not made a dent in the thinking of those who over the course of the next four years (circa 2004–2008) will be in a position to enact programs that could generate well-paying jobs accessible to the able-bodied urban poor. And if the Bill Cosby controversy tells us anything, it is a long way from winning the propaganda war over how people should understand what it means to be poor, urban, black, and unemployed.

Solutions

How does one counter the loss of jobs, globalization, and America's tendency to racialize the discourses on poverty, crime, and violence? I am personally persuaded by Derrick Bell's thesis that America is *incapable* of solving what is essentially a solvable problem (Bell, 1993). We are living in the age of the Far Right, and its commitment to minimize public expenditures while maximizing the flow of capital and resources into the free market means that even tried-and-true programs and policies—that worked in the past to assist white ethnic groups to escape poverty and lower-class stagnation—will not be applied to problems of poverty in the present. The repair and rehabilitation of our roads, bridges, and tunnels, the building of new urban school facilities, the repair and modernization of sewage and sanitation systems across the country, the repair and refinement of our water supply systems are but a few examples of multi-year projects that could stimulate employment for thousands of the currently unemployed black (and white) people, while producing products, services, and activities that add value to the life of all Americans, just as the building of the Triborough Bridge, the Tennessee Valley System, and the construction of the interstate highway system did in the past. With these projects engaging black adults, the stage would be set to explore new and progressive educational interventions, to capture the attention of the children of black communities. However, education ventures aimed at black youth will not work if we do not *first* change the meaning of life for parents and significant adults—that is, make them a part of the larger social order through meaningful jobs that pay a living wage and provide health benefits. We could do these things and more, but we will not—especially if the objective is to help black people. It appears we would rather build prisons in the rural areas of most states, since prison construction and employment related to the operation of prisons is helping to solve two problems. First, it answers the question What do we do with redundant black workers? Second, it provides employment for unemployed white workers in depressed areas outside America's urban centers, where most new prisons are built.

If America has used prisons to solve the poverty problem, it will be interesting to watch how it responds to the new redundant workers from the professional and highly educated ranks. Between 2004 and 2015, estimates suggest that 3.3 million white-collar positions will be lost from America's shores (Cassidy, 2004). Some point out that on balance, outsourcing will have more of a positive than negative effect on the United States economy, by creating more jobs than are lost. However, these "new" jobs may not be filled *by the same people* who lose their $100,000-plus jobs to outsourcing (Cassidy, 2004). Because the highly educated persons have more political clout, there is a better chance that the voicing of their pain will not fall on deaf ears. It is ironic that attempting to meet the needs of middle-class workers whose jobs have been outsourced will likely further distract politicians and planners from efforts to solve poverty problems linked to the permanent loss of jobs at the manufacturing level.

References

Adler, P. (1989). *Wheeling and dealing: Ethnography of an upper-level drug and smuggling community.* New York: Columbia University Press.

Allsop, K. (1970). *The bootleggers and their era.* Garden City, NJ: Doubleday.

Anderson, J. (1988). *The education of blacks in the South, 1860–1935.* Chapel Hill: University of North Carolina Press.

Bell, D. (1993). *Faces at the bottom of the well: The permanence of racism.* New York: Basic Books.

Boyd-Franklin, N., & Franklin, A. J. (2000). Boys into men: Raising our African American teenage sons. New York: Dutton.

Boykin, A. W. (2002, February 7–9). Commentary as part of panel entitled "The Achievement Gap: Description, Cause, and Solutions," Annenberg Conference on the Achievement Gap, Brown University.

Butterfield, F. (2005, January 16). Guns and jeers used by gangs to buy silence. *New York Times,* pp. 1, 22.

Cassidy, J. (2004, August 2). Winner and losers, the truth about free trade. *New Yorker,* pp. 26–30.

Centers for Disease Control. (2003). *CDC HIV/AIDS surveillance report, 2003 (Vol. 15).* Atlanta: U.S. Department of Health and Human Services.

Coontz, S. (1992). *The way we never were.* New York: Basic Books.

Cross, W. E., Jr. (1991). *Shades of black.* Philadelphia: Temple University Press.

Cross, W. E., Jr. (2003). Tracing the historical origins of youth delinquency and violence: Myths and realities about black culture. *Journal of Social Issues, 59*(1), 67–82.

Dickerson, D. C. (1986). *Out of the crucible: Black steelworkers in Western Pennsylvania, 1875–1980.* Albany, NY: State University of New York Press.

Dolgin, J. (2004). The Cosby controversy: The limited response to the rhetoric of Bill Cosby. Unpublished research paper, Graduate Center, City University of New York.

Duster, T. (1997). Patterns, purpose and race in the drug war: The crisis of credibility in criminal justice. In C. Reinarman & H. G. Levine (Eds.), *Crack cocaine in America* (pp. 260–287). Berkeley: University of California Press.

Eccles, J. S. (2004, March 5). Ethnicity, race, and gender as contexts for development. Paper presented at Tenth Biennial Meeting of the Society for Research on Adolescence, Baltimore, MD.

Edwards, T. (2001, October). Men who sleep with men: Aids risk to African American women.

Fine, M. (2001). *Framing dropouts.* Albany, NY: State University of New York Press.

Fine, M., Bloom, J., Burns, A., Chajet, L., Guishard, M., Payne, Y., et al. (2005). Dear Zora: A letter to Zora Neale Hurston 50 years after *Brown. Teachers College Record, 107,* 496–528.

Foy, D. W., & Goguen, C. A. (1998). Community violence—related PTSD in children and adolescents. *PTSD Research Quarterly, 9*(4), 1–6.

Gardner, J. W., & Sanford, T. (1969). *One year later.* New York: Praeger.

Gettleman, J. (2004). Camden's streets go from mean to meanest. *New York Times*, p. B1.

Glasgow, D. G. (1981). The underclass. New York: Vintage Press.

Gonnerman, J. (2004, June 30–July 6). A question of justice: Three young men, two coke deliveries, one prison sentence, pp. 31–32, 35.

Haley, A. (1964). *The Autobiography of Malcolm X.* New York: Ballantine Books.

Haney, W. (2002). Revealing the illusions of educational progress: Texas high-stakes testing and minority student performance. In Z. F. Beykont (Ed.), *The power of culture: Teaching across language difference* (pp. 25–52). Cambridge, MA: Harvard Educational.

Harding, T. W., & Schaller, G. (1992). HIV/AIDS policy for prisons or prisoners? In J. M. Mann, D. J. M. Tarantola, & T. W. Netter (Eds.), *AIDS in the World* (pp. 761–769). Cambridge, MA: Harvard University Press.

Herrnstein, R., & Murray, C. (1994). *The bell curve.* New York: Free Press.

Homel, M. W. (1984). *Down from equality: Black Chicagoans and the public schools 1920–1940.* Urbana: University of Illinois Press.

H.R. 3734, Cong., Cong. Rec. (1996) (enacted).

Jaynes, G. D., & Williams, R. M., Jr. (1989). *A common destiny: Blacks and American society.* Washington, DC: National Academy Press.

Kavieff, P. (2000). *Organized crime in Detroit, 1910–1945.* Fort Lee, NJ: Barricade Books.

Kihss, P. (1970, March 1). "Benign neglect" on race proposed by Moynihan. *New York Times*, p. A1.

Kinchin, D. (2005). *Post traumatic stress disorder: The invisible injury.* Oxford: Success Unlimited.

King, C. I. (2004, May 22). Fix it, brother. *Washington Post*, p. A27.

Kitwana, B. (2002). *The hip hop generation.* New York: Basic Books.

Kozol, J. (1991). *Savage inequalities: Children in America's schools.* New York: Harper-Collins.

Libman, G. (1993, October 27). Fenced in by fear of gangs, drive-by shootings and drugs, a growing number of parents say violence is forcing them to keep their kids safe at home. *Los Angeles Times,* p. E1.

Lipschitz, D. S., Rasmusson, A. M., Anywan, W., Cromwell, P., & Southwick, S. M. (2000). Clinical and functional correlates of posttraumatic stress disorder in urban adolescent girls at a primary care clinic. *Journal of American Academy of Child Adolescent Psychiatry, 39,* 1104–1111.

Loftis, C. (1997). *The boy who sat by the window: Helping children cope with violence.* Far Hills, NJ: Small Horizons Press.

Lowenstein, R. (2005, January 16). A Question of numbers: Since establishment of social security in 1935, government actuaries have been crunching data and projecting the future of the system—why don't they see a crisis looming? *New York Times Magazine*, pp. 41, 47, 72, 76–78.

Manza, J., & Uggen, C. (2006). *Locked out: Felon disenfranchisement and American democracy.* New York: Oxford University Press.

Massey, D. S., & Denton, N. A. (1993). *American apartheid: Segregation and the making of the underclass.* Cambridge, MA: Harvard University Press.

Moynihan Report. (1965). *The Negro family: The case for national action.* Washington, DC.

Murray, C. A. (1984). *Losing ground.* New York: Basic Books.

O'Connor, T. A. (1997). *The Boston Irish.* Boston: Little, Brown.

National Advisory Commission on Civil Disorders [Kerner Report]. (1968). *Report to the president of the United States on the causes of urban riots in the United States.* Washington, DC: U.S. Government Printing Office.

Ogbu, J. (2003). *Black students in an affluent suburb: A study of academic disengagement.* Mahwah, NJ: Erlbaum.

Orfield, G. (2004). *Dropouts in America: Confronting the graduation rate crisis.* Cambridge, MA: Harvard Education Publishing Group.

Payne, Y. (2004). Black men and street life as a site of resiliency. *Critical Psychology, 4,* 109–122.

Powers, K. (2002). Murder by the lake. *Savoy, 2*(4), 58–62.

Reich, R. (1991). *The work of nations: Preparing ourselves for twenty-first century capitalism.* New York: Knopf.

Sanders-Phillips, K. (1997). Assaultive violence in the community: Psychological responses of adolescent victims and their parents. *Journal of Adolescent Health, 21,* 356–365.

Scott, J. (2004, Februrary 28). Nearly half of NYC black men jobless. *New York Times,* p. B1.

Spencer, M. B. (2000). Identity, achievement orientation and race: "Lessons learned" about the normative developmental experiences of African American males. In W. Watkins, J. Lewis, & V. Chou (Eds.), *Race and education* (pp. 100–127). Needham Heights, MA: Allyn and Bacon.

Tate, G. (2005, January 4). Hiphop turns 30: Whatcha celebratin for? *Village Voice.*

The wide variations in black-white educational gap in America's largest cities. (2004). [Special issue]. *Journal of Blacks in Higher Education, 44.* Available: www.jbhe .com/news_views/40_black-white_education_gap.html.

Tonry, M. H. (1996). *Malign neglect: Race, crime, and punishment in America.* New York: Oxford University Press.

Two suspects in Wendy's shooting arrested [Television broadcast]. (2000). Cable News Network.

U.S. Department of Justice. (2001). Justice Programs, Bureau of Justice Statistics, homicide rates by race, 1976–2000. Available: www.ojp.usdoj.gov/bjs/homicide/ race.htm.

Valentine, B. (1978). *Hustling and other hard work: Life styles in the ghetto.* New York: Free Press.

Van Deburg, W. L. (1992). *New day in Babylon.* Chicago: University of Chicago Press.

Yarwood, J. (2004). Deterritorialized blackness: (Re)making colored identities in South Africa. Unpublished research paper, Graduate Center, City University of New York.

Younge, G. (2004, April 6). Black women in US 23 times as likely to get AIDS. *Guardian,* p. 12.

Williams, T. (1989). *The cocaine kids: The inside story of a teenage drug ring.* New York: Da Capo Press.

CHAPTER 16

Youth Movements and Youth Violence in Nigeria's Oil Delta Region

CHARLES UKEJE

Although the area was eventually subdued with gunboats, the colonial history of the coastal communities in the present-day Niger Delta of Nigeria was punctuated at every stage by stiff resistances against foreign incursions and the imposition of Pax Britannica. The past 1 1/2 decades have opened another unprecedented chapter of sustained grassroots social action, violent conflicts, and anarchy in that region. At the heart of the present version of social convulsion are allegations that almost 5 decades of irresponsible oil field practices have left an unpleasant legacy of abject poverty among inhabitants (Ojo, 2002; Ukeje, 2004). During the first decade after independence, protests by Niger Delta communities—who by a twist of fate constitute minority ethnic groupings within the larger Nigeria federation—were over perceived political marginalization and subordination. Hence there were demands for the creation of more states as the only way to bring government closer to the people, and vice versa (Isumonah, 1998; Osaghae, 2000). The various minority ethnic groups that were aggrieved for one reason or another were satisfied with using nonviolent methods to persuade government to listen to them.[1]

Unfortunately, these nonviolent methods of persuasion failed to achieve the preferred results. Instead, they led to a steady deterioration of relationships, especially between oil communities and government/multinational oil companies (Ukeje, Adetanwa, Amadu, & Olabisi, 2002). The strains in relationships, in turn, paved the way for widespread violent protests on the part of communities; and what has been referred to as a bizarre and frightening accumulation of terror practices by the government to subdue restive communities. Initially, scholarship focused on investigating the vicious cycles of protest and repression at the community and national levels (Naanen, 1995; Osaghae, 1995; Welch, 1996). Recently, however, there has been a shift in orientation toward critical reflections on the specific impacts of this vicious cycle on different demographic and socioeconomic categories, and how these groups perceive and react to them. For instance, there is a growing harvest of literature indicating that different social (low-income, middle-income, and high-income), demographic (children, young people, adults), sexual (male, female), and spatial (urban, semiurban, and rural areas) groups feel the pinches, contradictions, and crises associated with oil-based accumulation of wealth differently (Obi, 1997a; Ibeanu, 2001). This chapter interrogates how young people are implicated by, and reacting to, these different crises traceable to the convoluted character and political economy of crude oil production in Nigeria's oil delta.

Whether the focus is on the internationally known Ogoni or Ijaw struggles, or those by a plethora of other ethnic groups, it is difficult to deny that the activities of young people are shaping and giving clarity to mass protests and violence in the Niger Delta (Ukeje, 2001b). The argument here is that the youth movement and violence in the region are deeply embedded in the historical-economic-political context of Nigeria, starting with colonial, postcolonial military, and postmilitary civilian society (Nwabueze, 1999). It is important to highlight some of the most salient trajectories, aspects, and flashpoints of these experiences. Essentially, then, what this chapter points us toward is the urgent need to transcend the frequent, often nauseating, supposition that young people in the oil region are a bunch of social pests with an insatiable appetite for "blind violence," as one notable Nigerian political scientist explicitly claimed (Gboyega, 1997, p. 177). What are the prevailing narratives around youth movement and violence—from the perspective of oil communities, government, multinational oil companies, and the young people themselves? By interrogating the complexities of the youth movement and violence, this chapter also hopes to suggest pragmatic lessons that can form the basis for qualitative public policy interventions for reengaging young people in non-violent and more constructive ways of social action.

Footnoting Violent Conflicts in the Oil Region of Nigeria

In Africa, where the power and authority of the state is unusually intrusive, excessive, and writ large, even the most pedestrian social changes are closely interwoven with the mis/fortunes of the state. It is clearly outside the scope of this essay to elucidate why this is so, and what implications it portends for societies in the continent. The important point to make is that the wholesale adoption of the colonial regime of law and order by successive governments in the postindependence era ensured that governance was patently antipeople and antisociety; invariably an instrument of alienation, marginalization, and exclusion of the vast majority of the people. Whatever channels through which the ordinary citizenry, therefore, sought to articulate their individual and collective grievances and aspirations about governance were thwarted and foreclosed with brute force. Those in power at the same time maintained a measured and aloof distance from the people on whose behalf they claim to govern. By the time critical segments of the population started demanding a voice on how they should be governed, the postcolonial state responded in kind by evoking a fearsome regime of authoritarianism marked by crude harassment, intimidation, repression, incarceration, extrajudicial murder of militant opposition figures and groups, and bad governance. Habitually, the public space was emptied of its meaning, content, purpose, vibrancy, sanity, tolerance, and so on. It became a site for making claims and counterclaims between the governed and their governors.

This scenario is most vivid in the Niger Delta, where long years of neglect and underdevelopment have unleashed an unprecedented level of anger and social frustration among different communities. The earliest version of popular movement and insurrection occurred in February 1966 when a group of young students and activists drawn predominantly from the Ijaw ethnic group—under the banner of the Niger Delta Volunteers Force (NDVF)—instigated the short but infamous Boro Revolution, named after its leader, Isaac Adaka Boro. The "revolution" had occurred against the backdrop of what the militant young people perceived as gross economic, political, and social injustices perpetuated by the dominant ethnic groups, who exploit their vantage positions in government to subjugate minority ethnic communities in the Niger Delta. Although the principal clamor was for the creation of more states and the allocation of greater proceeds from crude oil sales to the Niger Delta, the revolt paralyzed oil production activities and nearly brought the government down. Obviously, today, the Boro Revolution continues to provide the mythical platform and basis for defiant political expressions by Ijaw and non-Ijaw young people (and communities) in that region (Ukeje, 2001a).

The groundswell of resentment, anger, and violent social actions in the 1990s has a character strikingly similar to that of the previous ones—except, of course, for the fact that it was accentuated by economic and political factors that never existed before. One was the inability of government to effectively manage and cushion the debilitating impacts of neoliberal economic prescriptions under the Structural Adjustment Program (SAP) (Ihonvbere, 1993; Obi, 1997b). For the most part, neglected oil communities suffered a double jeopardy from the harsh side effects of poor oil field practices and of SAP. Another factor had to do with the elevation of the language of politics into that of violent contentions along ethnic, religious, and political lines under the military. One legacy of the long and painful years of military rule was that the space for popular civic participation in governance was severely curtailed (Soyinka, 1996). The annulment of the results of what is generally acknowledged as the freest presidential election ever held in the country, in June 1993, was the proverbial last straw.

An unintended outcome of military rule was that it also provided a crucible out of which militant civil society groups (coalescing around peasants, students, workers, intellectuals, journalists, retired military officers, and urban dwellers) spread and radicalized themselves. Presenting themselves as prodemocracy, pro—human rights, proenvironment and pro—minority rights groups, they became resolute in clamoring for the reopening and reexpansion of the democratic space and respect for the wishes of the majority.[2] At the same time, elements within these groups also reactivated their ethnic networks, fearing that the scuttling of the democratization process by the military would fuel smouldering embers of ethnoreligious conflicts in the country. The annulment especially paved the way for the spread of militant ethnic movements in different parts of the country; beginning with the formation of the Odua People's Congress (OPC) in the Yoruba-speaking southwest, where Chief M.K.O. Abiola was from, to challenge perceived wrongdoings by the military oligarchy in denying him his popularly earned presidential mandate. Other militant ethnoregional groupings soon emerged: the Arewa People's Congress (APC) in the north, the Movement for the Actualization of the Sovereign State of Biafra (MASSOB) in the southeast, and the Supreme Egbesu Assembly (SEA) in the south-south Niger Delta region.

Within the oil region, several ethnic and subethnic groups also began to mobilize themselves; believing that the only language the government and multinational oil companies understand was that of militancy, instead of the *siddon look* ("sit-down-and-look") approach of the past. It began with the struggle by the Ogoni people under the banner of the Movement for the Survival of Ogoni People (MOSOP)[3] but then spread to every corner of the Niger Delta. Undeterred by state-sponsored terrorism, many oil communities have adopted politicized social action and violence as the preferred methods for attracting attention to their plights, while asking penetrating questions about their place and stake in the badly executed nation-state project called Nigeria (Osaghae, 1995). Because these popular community initiatives are couched in socially appealing identity overtones, the search for solutions not only becomes tortuous but also portends grave dangers for domestic peace and stability in Nigeria (Soyinka, 1996; Maier, 2000).

The Youth Movement and Violence in the Oil Region

The youth factor has had much less attention in debates about conflict in Africa, yet it may take over from ethnicity as a consideration of more general future importance in a continent with such a high proportion of young people potentially alienated from wider civil society by failures of educational systems and employment opportunities. (Richards, 1997, p. 159)

Although this observation was made in the context of the sociopolitical culture of young people and how that played a key role in the spontaneous outbreak of bloody civil wars in Liberia and Sierra Leone (Furley, 1994; Richards, 1994; Abdullah, 1999), it appropriately applies to most other African countries that are grappling with social complications arising from the persistent failure of past and existing educational and employment schemes for young people (El-Kenz, 1996; O'Brien, 1996; Richards, 2002). Again, this is truer in the Niger Delta, where young people have been at the crux of each and every social action over the years. Although the last decade and a half have witnessed the proliferation of several youth movements under different names and guises, they all pledge support to the same agenda of socioeconomic and political emancipation of their communities and peoples. Some of them have pan—Niger Delta coverage, such as the Youth's Association of Professionals for the Emancipation of the Niger-Delta, Niger Delta Izon Youth Collegiate Leadership (reportedly a coalition of 47 militant youth groups), the Niger Delta Youth Leaders Forum, and the Niger Delta Frontline Front. Others promote more parochial ethnic interests, such as the National Youth Council of Ogoni People (NYCOP), the Ijaw Youth Council (IYC), the Ijaw National Youth Movement, Federated Niger Delta Ijaw Communities, Federated Ijaw Youth Congress, National Union of Izon Youths, Isoko National Youth Movement, Mboho Mparawa Ibibio of Akwa Ibom state, to mention only a few. It is impossible to know their exact number, not only because these youth groups spring up by the day but also because their membership usually overlaps. What is common to them, however, is the close familiarity with a complex repertoire of strategies, not just for drawing attention to typical "bread-and-butter issues" but for agitating against the corporate misdemeanors of oil companies and neglect by successive governments in the country.

These youth movements can be distinguished from earlier ones in terms of their more daring exploits, modus operandi, membership, organizational skills, and resources. They have transformed from amorphous and discrete movements into visible and vibrant militant groups, often with substantial organizational capabilities and mobilization skills. Because of the appealing social messages they carry, many of them have succeeded, through aggressive recruitment drives, in attracting new and committed members from diverse backgrounds, education, and training. Against popular myth, therefore, many of these movements are now led by well-educated and experienced activists who are conversant with the language and methodology of grassroots mobilization on a range of important issues. These new generation youth movements have also joined forces with wider civil society groups on burning national issues, such as calls for a sovereign national conference, review of the revenue allocation formula, restructuring of Nigeria's wobbling federalism, and increased spending on social welfare . At the same time, they have been able to transcend their geographic locations by taking their struggles into the larger national and global domain, aided by easy access to the global media (print, electronic, and internet), networking with international governmental and nongovernmental organizations engaged in human, environmental, minority, and cultural rights advocacies, and using their former members, loyalists, and supporters in the diaspora to sustain sympathy. Finally, unlike their predecessors, many of the contemporary youth movements have developed stronger moral and utilitarian justifications for violence by locating their actions in the context of larger global movements on issues affecting disenfranchised groups. Understanding the different logics that drive youth militancy and violence, therefore, requires an acknowledgment of the complex dynamics that young people are daily confronted with—both from within and outside of their immediate domain—and an understanding of how they de/construct these realities and social circumstances by engaging and negotiating with the Nigerian state and multinational oil companies for better opportunities.

The general trend in the literature is to underplay and misrepresent the *raison d'être* for militant youth movements and their purpose in embarking on violence. One particularly prominent strand suggests that young people lack the social and political consciousness to forge alliances that can promote genuine developmental transformations outside the framework identified and imposed by the older generation. This point of view is very critical of the existence, utility, and staying power of youth movements, especially in terms of constructing and promoting an alternative social and political vision for disengaging or liberating their communities from the infinite contradictions of underdevelopment. The deficit in this approach is that it ignores the critical and autonomous agency of young people by preferring to treat youth militancy as episodic, unstructured, and counterproductive to societal growth and development (Caputo, 1995; Comaroff & Comaroff, forthcoming). The truth, of course, is that the agency of young people is central to understanding whatever social changes—slow and painful as they may seem—are taking place in the contemporary Niger Delta.

I mentioned earlier that young people played prominent roles in the minority nationalism projects of the Ogoni and Ijaw ethnic groups in the Niger Delta in the 1990s, as in many other ethnic and subethnic groups in the region. In the Ogoni case, the National Youth Council of Ogoni People (NYCOP) became prominent because of the growing frustration among its ranks with what was generally perceived as the progovernment attitude of their overall leadership within the umbrella organization, MOSOP (Naanen, 1995). As far as these young people were concerned, the activities of their leadership were becoming too self-centered, treacherous, and inimical to community clamors for ethnic self-determination, greater resource allocation from the federal government and greater control of oil resources, and inclusive participation in the political affairs of the country. Although he was a strong figure in the discredited leadership of MOSOP, Ken Saro-Wiwa saw and exploited this growing frustration and spirit of militancy among the wider ranks of Ogoni youths. Ijaw nationalism also received a similar impetus with the emergence of a semiautonomous youth movement, the Ijaw Youth Council (IYC)—an umbrella organization of hundreds of youth associations and groups spread over six states on Nigeria's Atlantic seaboard, where Ijaw people (reputed to be the fourth largest ethnic group) mostly live (Ukeje, 2001a). Whereas the IYC served as the political and intellectual platform for articulating the interests and concerns of Ijaw youths, the "military" arm of Ijaw nationalism is still the Supreme Egbesu Assembly, popularly called the Egbesu Boys.[4] As was the case between MOSOP and NYCOP, the IYC became prominent against a similar background of frustration with the reactionary postures of the leadership of the parent group, the Ijaw National Council (INC). Eventually, the more pro—status quo traditional elites within MOSOP and the INC lost the initiative—not necessarily power and influence—to their younger generations. Cashing in on this generational shift, the much younger, educated, and popular leaders who took the mantle of leadership opted to rely more on youth groups, either by co-opting existing ones or by creating new wings. Whatever option(s) the new leaders chose, they were conscious that identifying with young people and mainstreaming them into the broader community struggle for the development of self-determination was a worthwhile step in the right direction. This was true particularly in the sense that the young people can momentarily form themselves into an exuberant crop of politically conscious movements that serve community causes in different capacities, including taking up arms, when desired, against the government and oil companies.

It is obvious that the emergence of the NYCOP, the IYC, the Egbesu Boys, and the surplus other militant youth movements in the oil region are either part of broader ethnocommunal movements or autonomous in relation to them. Either way, however, the cultural contents and dimensions of youth protests and violence must not be ignored. In fact, at the same time that most of the youth groups flourishing in the contemporary Niger Delta were doing so in response to excruciating socioeconomic, political, and environmental circumstances, the vocabulary of their grievances is firmly anchored on cultural symbols, values, traditions, and memories of gallant struggles. This is demonstrated by their heavy reliance on an inventory of cultural folklores, images, symbols, and invocations that other kith and kin recognize and share. Culture, therefore, performs powerful instrumentalist and facilitative functions in helping inhabitants of oil communities to absorb and process new and radical ideas and identities, and to use them to secure (or advance) group identities and interests. Unfortunately, the centrality of culture in understanding the etiology of community mobilization and conflict analysis has not received the attention deserved in public policy and in the literature (Warren, 1993).

Collective political action and violence are usually not a spontaneous, unilateral projection of people experiencing discontentment (Welch, 1980). In fact, they often have value-added undertones that can only be captured by looking at the cumulative, experiences that people live through on daily basis or over a period of time. The proliferation of youth movements and violence must therefore be understood as a metaphor for gauging social disaffection and powerlessness against a system that is both disempowering and alienating, in terms of access to subsidized socioeconomic opportunities, particularly qualitative education and gainful employment (De Boeck & Honwana, forthcoming; Durham, 2000; El-Kenz, 1996). By employing unorthodox violent methods, therefore, youth movements seem to have reconciled themselves to the fact that the Nigerian state is *autistic*, and as such requires some kind of shock therapy before it can come to terms with its own inherent inadequacies and insensitivities to doing the bidding of the ordinary citizenry.[5] This metaphor for powerlessness, and the menu of responses adopted by youth movements to negate them, is further complicated by the steady demonopolization of state power and authority, such that the state can no longer lay effective claim to monopoly of power and mechanisms of coercion because many oil communities are also able to muster sufficient resources to acquire firepower to defend ethnic interests. Paradoxically, on each occasion when the state attempts to subdue restive communities and militant youth movements, it is inadvertently also signaling a loss of the capability and claim to the right to allocate values authoritatively without recourse to repression.

Of course, there are other contradictory narratives about the youth movement and youth violence in the oil region that are worth highlighting for the significant outcomes they portend for social stability and development in the Niger Delta. It is popular in public policy, and some academic, circles to brand young people who participate in aggressive social actions as a bunch of half-baked and jobless young people for whom violence is a cheap escape from the meaninglessness of life and the drudgery that is pervasive in the oil communities (Gboyega, 1997). They are seen as a nuisance for holding government and oil companies to ransom with cheap blackmail. Among oil companies, the pervasive impression is that militant young people lack the education and skills to work in the oil industry, and that the few with higher degrees earned them in the liberal arts and social sciences—based disciplines instead of the sciences and engineering. Under this circumstance, as oil companies claim, the best that can be done for the young people is to put them on the company payroll as casual, daily, paid workers or, in extreme cases, retain them as ghost workers who receive some stipend from oil companies on a monthly basis in return for an informal commitment to protect oil installations. The vital point that the oil companies seem to have overlooked is that the argument that they are behaving as responsible corporate citizens toward host oil communities is inexcusable and unconvincing if after decades of their operations, they still cannot boast of community development approaches that produce a significant pool of employable young people or indigenes to work for them. On those rare occasions when multinational oil companies carry out sincere and critical self-assessments of the social impacts of their operations, they are confronted with the bleak fact that their corporate actions fall far short of their corporate mission statements.[6]

Although unemployment is a major crisis throughout Nigeria, the situation is particularly chronic in the Niger Delta, where the young people believe they have been denied access to job opportunities in the oil industry through an unwritten but deliberate policy of exclusion. On every occasion when young people mobilize themselves against oil companies, it is on matters that have to do with their inability to receive support from oil companies in terms of formal educational and vocational training and employment opportunities. Part of their complaint is that the recruitment policies of multinational oil companies operating in the Niger Delta are biased against host oil communities in general, and young people in particular. These are very serious allegations that could not go away overnight, given how contagious the grievances among young people— most especially those who had the benefit of higher education but remain unable to find jobs many years after graduation—have become. The cumulative result of the exclusion of young people in the oil communities from gainful employment in the oil industry is that they see the companies as affecting their daily lives in hopeless ways yet pretending to be unconcerned. As it usually turns out, most young people in oil communities end up finding out the painful way that they are subjected to the "dual processes of disconnection from institutions revolving around production, consumption and community life, and the social and psychological experiences of disempowerment accompanying this disconnection." In this context, the "actual experiences of life on the margins are . . . continuing sources of much anger and anxiety on the part of those young people so marginalized" (Wyn & White, 1997, p. 122; Wyn & White, 2000).

Because militant young people are in actual fact products and reflections of the society in whose crucible they are painfully coming of age, even the most simple and procedural issues that can easily be resolved through dialogue and negotiations can be expected to degenerate into protest and violence.[7] Pestieau warned of the dire consequences of jumping to hasty conclusions and making reckless generalizations about youth militancy and violence, instead encouraging scholarship and public policy that would look "beyond the impatience, the bursts of fury or the high excitement in order to understand the inability to come to terms with the limited possibilities offered by prevailing circumstances" (1992, p. 194). In a similar context, Tarrow insisted that "for people whose lives are mired in drudgery and desperation, the offer of an exciting, risky and possibly beneficial campaign of collective action may be a gain" (1996, p. 19). Violence, in this situation, is the cheapest option in collective political action, specifically because it costs far less to prepare for and perhaps also because it is much easier for marginalized local groups to implement (1996, p. 103).

It is important to factor in another issue that is germane to the ups and downs of the youth movement and violence in the oil region, mostly relating to the notion and limitations of space or boundaries. To begin with, youth activism is erroneously captured as a phenomenon that is in situ or localized and therefore without external inputs, dimensions, and ramifications. At least in the Niger Delta, it is no longer contestable that the notion of boundary—for example, between rural-urban spaces—is now anachronistic. If this is accepted, what follows is not just to demystify the popular claim that rural dwellers lack political consciousness but also that such binary categories can only be taken with a pinch of salt, given the cross-flow of persons, knowledge and ideas, and resources between these complementary spaces. In practical terms, youth movements in oil communities have been well served by a plethora of other youth-led human, environmental, and minority rights advocacy groups springing up in different parts of the country and beyond.

That youth movements receive intellectual, logistical, and sometimes financial support from sources other than those within their immediate localities is also not open to contention. What is becoming quite apparent is that better endowed and better exposed rights-based organizationsin other parts of Nigeria and elsewhere are also now providing youth movements in rural oil communities with ideas, resources, expertise, information, logistics, and best practices, to be able to mobilize appropriate consciousness and activism. Although these rights groups frequently serve as mouthpieces for youth movements in the Niger Delta, it is not difficult to discern a qualitative improvement in the language and practice of community mobilization among the leadership and the rank and file of youth movements in poor oil communities. As territoriality and space in physical senses become less of a constraint, many youth movements in the oil region are also beginning to learn from the experiences of their peers in other different communities, and forging alliances with others far and wide. The best testament to this trend—which, admittedly, is far less to visible to many observers—is the ability of Ijaw young people to network among themselves across the six coastal states where people of Ijaw ethnic extraction are found, despite the constraint of human locomotion and geography (Ukeje, 2001b).

Through a process of social diffusion, using digital media, young people are also able to externalize their grievances and protests and to receive external support from global rights movements. In launching themselves into the international limelight, youth movements in the Niger Delta also receive active support from an increasing number of their peers who have access to better facilities and resources available abroad and through the information superhighway. It is important not to ignore these transboundary networks and linkage transactions in galvanizing support and encouragement for local youth movements that are competing for public attention and sympathy with better endowed adversaries: the state and multinational oil companies.

Although they are considered adversaries, many communities and youth movements still rely on the structures of incentive and reward cleverly put in place by multinational oil companies and the state to survive. While they hardly accept this fact or the blame that comes with it, multinational oil companies are as responsible for this acute dependence on them by young people and by oil communities, covered up under the subhead of corporate social responsibility. Over the years, multinational oil companies have perfected the art of using money to settle the most ordinary problems, using money to divide the ranks of oil communities, and using money to sponsor different groups against the other. The invidious labyrinth of graft and corruption put together by multinational oil companies, in the belief that these were the only ways they could appease host communities, have proved advantageous only to a tiny segment of the population of these communities. Thus, when community and youth movements embark on protest and violence, such may in fact be reactions to an attempt by oil companies to alter, disrupt, stall, or completely hinder the smooth functioning of the existing structure of reward. As was rightly pointed out by a former expatriate executive of Shell, who angrily resigned his appointment from the environmental unit of the company, "too many promises and disappointments in the past have exhausted the patience and the confidence of the people" (van Dessel, 1995, p. 29).

The foregoing situation has sharpened young people's perceptions of the older generation as manipulative, greedy, subversive, and conservative. It has also caused such intergenerational disagreements and conflicts between young people and the older generation whom they hold accountable for their miserable social predicaments. In this climate of intragroup differences and suspicions, the older generation (consisting especially of traditional rulers, contractors to oil companies, political elites, and community leaders) seems to have reluctantly accepted that their fear of young people is the beginning of wisdom. In one particularly sad instance, a traditional ruler was brutally murdered in

Ewveni, an oil community in Delta State, for allegedly embezzling 6 million Nigerian naira paid to the community by an oil company. He was reportedly tied to a motorcycle and dragged around town until he bled to death (FGD Opinion leader, Ughelli, personal communication, April 15, 2000).[8] This sort of action informs the fear that only if genuine efforts are made to repair the generational fault-lines can the looming social anarchy be averted.

The increasing susceptibility of young people to criminality—not necessarily militancy for the sake of social emancipation and development—has become another source of growing concern in the Niger Delta. Youth criminality in the region has manifested in acts of sabotage directed at oil installations and production facilities, the taking of company staff as hostages and demanding ransom before they are released, brutal acts of arson and murder, and so on. Although there is a thin line between youth militancy and criminal brigandage, an alternative paradigm for understanding youth criminality, which, in itself, is sometimes blown out of proportion by media sensationalism, is to point to the fact that it occurs in reaction to the ominous dark sides of neoliberal economic reforms and globalization (Ake, 1995; Aina, 1996; Gedley, 2001; Muller, 1986). For many developing countries undergoing painful neoliberal forms and transitions from one-party authoritarian rule and controlled economies to multiparty democracy and laissez faire, the processes have been distinguished by the intensification of coercion, conflict, polarization, domination, inequality, exploitation, and injustice, not the sugary "benefits" of interdependence within the global village (Aina, 1996, p. 11). In such countries, the period of "youthhood" is unduly elongated, thus forcing many young people to depend on immediate and extended families for subsistence and survival (Wallace & Kovatcheva, 1998, pp. 16–17). Usually affected by circumstances beyond their control, therefore, young people are inadvertently catapulted into a dangerous social anonymity that comes along with political and economic disenfranchisements that are known to be provocative sources of disorder and violence in many countries.

It is important to understand that the introduction and socialization of young people into this anonymous and dangerous social reality is often prompted by a chain of factors, beginning with a sharp decline in, and stoppage of, family (household) incomes. It is equally important to bear in mind that such a process also has the tendency of accelerating the weak and tenuous relationship between young adults and their families as the latter find it difficult, if not impossible, to function effectively as the basic social unit of responsibility and protection. In turn, this degeneration has led to the erosion and adulteration of the central notion (and the ascribed functions) of family in the traditional African context, as communities find it increasingly burdensome to care for immediate families, not to mention extended relations. A fallout from this is what Ly claimed is the "eclipse of those traditional forms of solidarity that large kinship groups had generated and sustained" (1988) over decades on the continent (Katz, 1998; MacDonald, 1997).

An important caveat to mention before the concluding remarks that follow is that even though uneducated and poor young people may have a higher propensity for embracing social actions with a violent orientation—after all, a hungry man is an angry man—their social predicaments are insufficient reasons for them finding violence attractive. There seems to be a mental black box within which several pieces of information are logged and processed, social conditions evaluated and internalized, and several stages of cognitive transformations must be overcome before such categories of young people can assertively embrace violence as a preferred alternative. Perhaps, then, the rising incidence of youth violence can be traced to the fact that as many youngsters attain social puberty, they are confronted with the fact that they do not have the enabling environment and fiscal wherewithal to live through this crucial stage successfully. It follows that the anger and frustration of many young people may, in fact, be a result of an unnecessarily delayed transition to adulthood. De Boeck and Honwana (forthcoming) made the point very well that the period where childhood stops and youth starts, or where youth ends and adulthood begins, are not the same everywhere; these vary across and within societies and cultures. As their transmutation to adolescence is deferred or outrightly subverted, many youngsters in the oil region discover multiple and complex layers of economic, social, political, and cultural ambiguities they have little or no control over—ambiguities that can scuttle their dreams and life ambitions.

Conclusions

The continuation of state-sponsored repression under the present civilian rule suggests, with regard to the Niger Delta, that little has changed, despite the end of military rule. It will be recalled that during his inauguration address on May 29, 1999, President Olusegun Obasanjo vowed that his administration would respect, restore, and protect the fundamental human rights of the Nigerian citizenry and, specifically, find a lasting solution to the problems of underdevelopment in the Niger Delta. The arrowhead of the administration's intervention is the controversial Niger Delta Development Commission (NDDC). Now, with President Obasanjo in his second term of office, the optimism that followed this open commitment has dissipated completely, only to be replaced by unbridled continuation of state-sponsored repression.

Perhaps there is some sense in drawing unique lessons from how most traditional African societies responded to and addressed youth-related problems of the nature that is acutely prevalent in contemporary Niger Delta. As Ly reminds us, "traditional African society managed to integrate youth by assigning it specific tasks in the village collectivity. The social integration of African young people was assured by what was in effect a kind of community youth policy" (Ly, 1998, pp. 152–153). Most modern interventions ostensibly directed toward young people have not achieved the desired results because they rely on policies that are not thoughtfully conceived before implementation. The shortfall in existing government policies aimed at empowering and mainstreaming young people is demonstrated by the erroneous conviction that matters affecting young people are also coterminous with those of women, rural development, sports and recreation, and so forth. If nothing else, placing youth issues under any of these ministerial portfolios as previous governments have done demonstrates a lack of direction and incoherence in government. Indeed, only recently the incumbent government established a ministry to cater for women and youth affairs. There is also a dangerous gap between those values a country/society professes and those that are obtainable. At the heart of the youth problem in the Niger Delta, as in many African countries, is the fact that while development is extolled as a social virtue, governments are inadequately prepared to offer young people an enabling environment in which they can strive for, and attain, development (Human Rights Watch, 2002).

Notes

1. The different methods for airing grievances included writing petitions, sending high-powered delegations to present complaints to relevant authorities, resorting to expensive litigations in court, occasional nonviolent demonstrations, and so on.

2. The cumulative impact of this clamoring prompted the statement credited to the information minister, Professor Jerry Gana, that "the violent military dictatorships in the country over the years had turned the populace into an angry lot ready to fight over the slightest provocation" (*The Guardian Online*, May 2, 2000).

3. Mr. Saro-Wiwa and eight of his Ogoni colleagues were hanged in November 1995 by the military junta of General Sanni Abacha.

4. In Ijaw folklore, Egbesu is the god of war. There is a lot of mystery surrounding this cultlike group, whose members, it is claimed, usually swear allegiance to the god Egbesu. They are also known to seek his guidance and protection before they embark on missions targeting oil companies and government interests. Other lesser known militant arms of the IYC are the Federated Niger Delta Izon Communities (FNDIC), the Niger Delta Volunteers Force (NDVF), the Niger Delta Resistance Movement (NDRM), and the Membutu Boys, to name the notable ones.

5. The shock therapies have ranged from the forced seizure and vandalization of oil installations to the taking of oil company executives and staff as hostages, the vandalization of government properties, direct confrontations with state security apparatuses, general lawlessness, and so on.

6. See *Community Spokesman*, January 25, 2002, p. 4.

7. In an incident in the Olugbobiri oil-producing village, a situation degenerated into violence after young people demanded mere clarifications on a proposed road project in the area that they alleged was altered by the oil company without proper consultation with the local people.

8. A different figure was reported in "Delta Youth Abduct three Shell Officials," 2000, p. 7.

References

Abdullah, I. (1999). The role of youths in conflicts. In A. Palm (Ed.), *The role of youth in conflict prevention in Southern Africa*. Finland: Kauhava. Available: www.katu-network.fi/suomi/pdf/YOUTH%20REPORT.pdf.

Adibe, C. E. (1994). Weak states and the emerging taxonomy of security in world politics. *Futures*, *26*(5), 490–505.

Aina, T. (1996). *Globalization and social policy in Africa: Issues and research directions* (Working Paper Series 6/96: 11). Senegal: CODESRIA.

Ake, C. (1981). *A political economy of Africa*. London: Longman.

Ake, C. (1995). The new world order: A view from Africa. In H. Hans-Henrik and G. Sorenssen (Eds.), *Whose world order? Uneven globalization and the end of the Cold War* (pp. 19–42). Boulder, CO: Westview Press.

Anene, J. C. (1959). The foundations of British rule in Southern Nigeria, 1885–1891. *Journal of the Historical Society of Nigeria*, *1*(4).

Asiegbu, J. U. J. (1984). *Nigeria and its British invaders, 1851–1920: A thematic documentary history*. New York: NOK.

Bayart, J. (1993). *The state in Africa: The politics of the belly*. London: Longman.

Beckman, B. (1985). Neo-colonialism, capitalism, and the state in Nigeria. In H. Bernstein & B. K. Campbell (Eds.), *Contradictions of accumulation in Africa* (pp. 71–113). Beverly Hills, CA: Sage.

Boubakar, L. (1998). The present situation of youth in Africa. In J. Kuczynski, S. N. Eistendadt, L. Boubakar, & S. Lotika (Eds.), *Perspectives on contemporary youth* (pp. 152–153). Tokyo: United Nations University.

Callaghy, T. M. (1989). Internal and external aspects of repression by a lame Leviathan: The case of Zaire. In G. A. Lopez & M. Stohl (Eds.), *Dependence, development and state repression*. New York: Greenwood Press.

Chabal, P. (1994). *Power in Africa: An essay in political interpretation*. New York: St. Martin's Press.

Caputo, V. (1995). Anthropology's silent "Other": A consideration of some conceptual and methodological issues for the study of youth and children's culture. In Amit-Talai, Vere, & Wulff (Eds.), *Youth cultures: A cross-cultural perspective* (pp. 19–42). London: Routledge.

Comaroff, J., & Comaroff, J. (forthcoming). Reflections on youth, from the past to the postcolony. In F. De Boeck & A. Honwana (Eds.), *Makers and breakers, made and broken: Children and youth as emerging categories in postcolonial Africa*.

De Boeck, F., & Honwana, A. (forthcoming). Children curbed in Africa: agency, identity and place. In F. De Boeck & A. Honwana (Eds.), *Makers and breakers, made and broken: Children and youth as emerging categories in postcolonial Africa*.

Delta youth abduct three Shell officials. (2000, April 5). *Guardian*, Lagos, p. 7.

Dike, K. O. (1956). *Hundred years of British rule in Nigeria, 1851–1951*. Lagos: Nigerian Broadcasting Corp.

Dike, K. O. (1962). *Trade and politics in the Niger Delta, 1830–1885*. Oxford: Clarendon Press.

Dudley, B. (1973). *Instability and political order: Politics and crisis in Nigeria*. Ibadan, Nigeria: Ibadan University Press.

Durham, D. (2000). Youth and the social imagination in Africa. *Anthropological Quarterly*, *73*, 3–4.

Elaigwu, I., & Gowon, J. (1985). The biography of a soldier-statesman. Ibadan, Nigeria: West Books.

El-Kenz, A. (1996). Youth and violence. In S. Ellis (Ed.), *Africa now: People, policies and institutions*. London: Heinemann.

Fatton, R. (1992). *Predatory rule: State and society in Africa*. Boulder, CO: Lynne Rienner.

Furley, O. (1994). Child soldiers in Africa. In O. Furley (Ed.), *Conflict in Africa*. London: Taurus Academic Press.

Gboyega, A. (1997). Nigeria: Conflict unresolved. In I. W. Zartman (Ed.), *Governance as conflict management: Politics and violence in West Africa* (p. 177). Washington, DC: Brookings Institution Press.

Gedley, J. (2001, August). Globalization and its impact on youth. *Journal of Future Studies, 6*(1), 89–106.

Herault, G., & Adesanmi, P. (Eds.). (1997). *Youth, street culture and urban violence in Africa.* Ibadan, Nigeria: French Institute for Research in Africa.

Human Rights Watch. (2002, October). *The Niger Delta: No democratic dividend.* News release.

Ibeanu, O. (2001). Healing and changing: The changing identity of women in the aftermath of the Ogoni Crisis in Nigeria. In S. Meintjes & T. Meredeth (Eds.), *The aftermath: Women in post-conflict transformation* (pp. 189–209). London: Zed Books.

Ihonvbere, J. O. (1993). Economic crisis, structural adjustment and social crises in Nigeria. *World Development, 21,* 141–153.

Ihonvbere, J. O. (1994). The state and underdevelopment in Nigeria. In J. O. Ihonvbere, *Nigeria: The politics of adjustment and democracy.* London: Transaction.

Ikime, O. (1997). *The fall of Nigeria: The British conquest.* London: Heinemann.

Isumonah, A. V. (1998). *Oil and minority ethnic nationalism in Nigeria: The case of the Ogoni.* Unpublished doctoral dissertation, University of Ibadan.

Katz, C. (1998). Disintegrating development: Global economic restructuring and the eroding ecologies of youth. In T. Skelton & G. Valentine (Eds.), *Cool places: Geographies of youth culture* (pp. 130–144). London: Routledge.

MacDonald, R. (1997). Youth, social exclusion and the millennium. In R. MacDonald (Ed.), *Youth, the "underclass" and social exclusion* (pp. 167–197). London: Routledge.

Maier, K. (2000). *This house has fallen: Nigeria in crisis.* London: Penguin Books.

Muller, H. (1986). Youths as a force in the modern world. *CSS &H, 10,* 237–260.

Naanen, B. (1995). Oil-producing minorities and the restructuring of Nigerian federalism: The case of the Ogoni People. *Journal of Modern African Studies, 32*(1), 65–75.

Nwabueze, G. (1999, June 2). Contextualizing the Niger Delta crisis. *CASS Newsletter,* p. 2.

Obi, C. I. (1997a). Globalization and local resistance: The case of Ogoni versus Shell. *New Political Economy, 2,* 1.

Obi, C. I. (1997b). Structural adjustment, oil and popular struggles: The deepening crisis of state legitimacy in Nigeria (CODESRIA Monograph Series). Dakar, Senegal: CODESRIA.

O'Brien, C. D. (1996a). A lost generation? Youth identity and state decay in West Africa. In R. Werbner & T. Ranger (Eds.), *Postcolonial identities in Africa* (pp. 55–74). London: Zed Books.

Ojo, J. B. (2002). *The Niger Delta: Managing resources and conflicts* (Research Report No. 49). Ibadan, Nigeria: Development Policy Centre.

Olorode, O. (1988). Imperialism, neocolonialism and the extractive industries in Nigeria. In O. Olorode, W. Raji, J. Ogunye, & T. Oladujoye (Eds.), *Ken Saro-Wiwa and the crises of the Nigerian state* (pp. 1–35). Lagos: Committee for the Defence of Human Rights.

Osaghae, E. E. (1995). The Ogoni uprising: Oil politics, minority agitation and the future of the Nigerian state. *African Affairs, 94,* 325–344.

Osaghae, E. E. (2000, Spring). From accommodation to self-determination: Minority nationalism and the restructuring of the Nigerian state. *Nationalism and Ethnic Politics, 7*(1), 1–20.

Oyerinde, O. (1998). Oil, disempowerment and resistance in the Niger Delta. In O. Olorode, W. Raji, J. Ogunye, & T. Oladujoye (Eds.), *Ken Saro-Wiwa and the crises of the Nigerian state* (pp. 55–70). Lagos: Committee for the Defence of Human Rights.

Pestieau, J. (1992, May). Powerlessness and individualism. *International Social Science Journal, 132,* 193–175.

Richards, P. (1994). Rebellion in Liberia and Sierra Leone: A crisis of youth? In O. Furley (Ed.), *Conflict in Africa* (pp. 134–170). London: Taurus Academic Press.

Richards, P. (1997). *Fighting for the rain forest: War, youth and resources in Sierra Leone.* Oxford: Heinemann.

Richards, P. (2002). Youth, food and peace: A reflection on some African security issues at the millennium. In T. Zack-William, D. Frost, & A. Thomson (Eds.), *Africa in Crisis: New challenges and possibilities* (pp. 29–39). London: Pluto Press.

Soyinka, W. (1996). *The open sore of a continent: A personal narrative of the Nigerian crisis.* New York: Oxford University Press.

Soremekun, K. (2004, Fall). The Warri crisis: A case of three in one. *ACAS Bulletin, 68,* 20–23.

Tarrow, S. (1996). *Power in movements: Social movements, collective action and politics.* Cambridge, UK: Cambridge University Press.

Ukeje, C. (2001a). Oil communities and political violence: The case of Ijaws in Nigeria's Delta region. *Journal of Terrorism and Political Violence, 13,* 4, 15–36.

Ukeje, C. (2001b). Youth, violence and the collapse of public order in the Niger Delta of Nigeria. *Africa Development, 26*(1 & 2), 337–366.

Ukeje, C. (2004). *Oil capital, ethnic nationalism and civil conflicts in the Niger Delta of Nigeria.* Unpublished doctoral dissertation, Obafemi Awolowo University, Ile-Ife, Nigeria.

Ukeje, C., Adetanwa, O., Amadu, S., & Olabisi, A. (Eds.). (2002). *Oil and violent conflicts in the Niger Delta* (CEDCOMS Monograph Series No. 1). Ile-Ife: Obafemi Awolowo University Press.

van Dessel, J. P. (1995). *The environmental situation in the Niger Delta, Nigeria.* [Internal position paper]. GreenPeace, Netherlands.

Wallace, C., & Kovatcheva, S. (1998). *Youth in society: The construction and deconstruction of youth in East and West Europe.* London: Macmillan Press.

Warren, K. B. (Ed.). (1993). *The violence within: Cultural and political opposition in divided nations.* Boulder, CO: Westview Press.

Welch, C. (1980). *The anatomy of rebellion.* Albany: SUNY Press.

Welch, C., Jr. (1996). The Ogoni and self-determination: Increasing violence in Nigeria. *Journal of Modern African Studies, 33*(4), 635–649.

Wyn, J., & White, R. (1997). *Rethinking youth.* London: Sage.

Wyn, J., & White, R. (2000). Negotiating social change: The paradox of youth. *Youth and Society, 32*(2), 165–183.

CHAPTER 17

Transborder Violence and Undocumented Youth

Extending Cultural-Historical Analysis to Transnational Immigration Studies

JOCELYN SOLIS

The current focus in U.S. research on globalization and its local effects on nations draws primarily from the sociological analysis of changing economies, politics, and immigration patterns. While the rapid exchange of resources, commerce, and information are also effects of globalization that are generally deemed positive, there is a series of negative outcomes that must also be addressed by social science research in the United States. Around the world, undocumented immigration enables the infringement of human and legal rights. These infringements are violent consequences of economic globalization that are the result of foreign investment from politically dominant countries, such as the United States, that benefit from the pool of human and material resources of less economically powerful nations. Such economic and political polarization of groups has been studied as an outcome of globalization (Sassen, 1991). Today, especially, economic policies such as the North American Free Trade Agreement (NAFTA) favor the United States economy and already wealthy Mexican investors by cheapening the cost of labor rather than favoring the Mexican workers who provide the labor (Sassen, 1991).

I have been interested in studying Mexican immigration in relation to youth violence, a phenomenon I take to be a related outcome of globalization in the United States, particularly in such new receiving areas as New York City, where the uneven distribution of economic resources favors the United States and disfavors the working-class Mexican population. The majority of undocumented Mexican immigrants have come to New York in search of financial stability (Smith, 1998). As the number of immigrants returning home decreases and the number of Mexican nationals living abroad increases, the impact of remittances on the Mexican economy is significant: it is the source of the country's third largest national income (Smith, 1998). However, workers who are maintained in low social rungs enable this economic growth in Mexico; often feeling forced to leave their home country, undocumented immigrants take life risks by entering the United States to find low-paying work.

The transnationalization of the Mexican population in New York is generally taken to be a complex process of undocumented migration, settlement, and (sometimes) return to the home country (Smith, 1996, 1998). The formation of a transnational Mexican community in the United States has been studied from the sociological perspective in terms of the economic impact of remittances on Mexico, and through the symbolic incorporation of those abroad in their cultural practices in the home country (Smith, 1996, 1998). In this chapter, I argue that studies of transnationalization in the United States are divorced from the particularities of individual lives. Especially in the form of personal, psychological understanding and development, I offer that the inclusion of the individual within transnational studies is possible. I discuss how the cultural-historical approach in psychology can be used to study phenomena of globalization, such as the formation of transnational communities, especially to complement sociological and political understanding of immigration in the context of Mexican young people's experiences of violence in the United States

Similarly, traditional psychological and developmental theories tend to ignore social structures in favor of universal, mental mechanisms that do not consider diversity or political context as factors that play central roles in youth studies, or in the development of human activity and consciousness more broadly. This chapter attempts to illustrate how cultural-historical theory is a potentially integrative means of analysis in the study of transnational immigration and youth violence by drawing from research I conducted in a community-based Mexican organization in New York City, Asociación Tepeyac, which defends the human rights of undocumented immigrant youth.

Immigration and Youth Violence

Asociación Tepeyac is a community-based organization working at the grassroots with Mexican immigrants in New York. Founded in response to the needs of a rapidly growing, largely undocumented population, its primary mission is to defend the human rights of immigrants and advocate for their legalization in the United States. As I have been a participant observer of the organization for over 4 years, my arguments in this chapter draw from extensive ethnographic fieldwork, public documents, interviews, and youth projects I have conducted there.

Because much of the Mexican immigrant population in New York is relatively young, their education, social and cultural upbringing, and experiences have been a major concern in Tepeyac's cultural and educational programs, which include English tutoring, computer literacy, and after-school projects. Such programs are seen as a preventive means of engaging Mexican immigrant youth in constructive activities that will deter their participation in gangs and alcohol or substance abuse. As I have argued elsewhere, Mexican immigrant youths' involvement in violent activities can be explained as an outcome of structural conditions that enable cycles of violence to emerge (Solis, 2003). Mexican youth become undocumented immigrants as a result of conditions of poverty that force them out of their country and discriminatory U.S. immigration policies that draw them into new situations of prejudice and exploitation. Consider the following excerpt from an article in Tepeyac's monthly newsletter in which the executive director expresses this analysis:

> For a group of immigrants who are oppressed, without the right to complain, without the right to say they are being exploited, mistreated, paid unfairly, without a union to help enforce their rights, the anger, frustration, rage, indignation accumulate inside, and when a person is drinking and is uninhibited, all that negative force is liberated; but it is liberated negatively, against those who are not even the causes of our troubles. That is why alcoholism and drug addiction become more dangerous in a community of immigrants who are exploited and repressed. (as cited in Solis, 2002, p. 271, my translation)

From such a human rights perspective, the history of work with immigrant youth suggests that without a sense of entitlement to fair treatment, access to basic human rights, or public representation in their favor, many undocumented youth are at risk for becoming violent, joining gangs, or abusing substances (Solis, 2002). Such activities, in turn, are detrimental to the communities in which they live and to the relationships they foster. As a means of circumventing this development, Asociación Tepeyac maintains a high public profile, especially in New York's Spanish-language media, and includes in its services labor advocacy for those immigrants who are exploited, unpaid, or mistreated in their places of work.

In my own research with Mexican children and teens (Solis, 2002), I found that regardless of their own immigration status, both U.S. citizens and undocumented children were aware of uneven relations of power that victimize members of their families and communities. Moreover, their own experiences as immigrant and minority children exposed them to prejudices in school that they could articulate in terms of race, ethnic, and language discrimination (Solis, 2002). Although such awareness can serve the development of young people's critical consciousness, if they do not have proper means with which to address the injustices that affect them, the outcomes for such youth may be violent retribution toward those who stand in a weaker position of power, for example, a younger sibling or a peer (Solis, 2003). The same holds for gender relations, especially among young couples (Solis, Bonil, & Garcia, 2002). Immigrant women become victims of domestic violence by partners whose hard labor, low wages, and social invisibility produce frustrations that are channeled into the excessive consumption of alcohol and spousal abuse in the privacy of their homes. While such channeling of gendered aggression is culturally tolerated in Mexico, the structural conditions of undocumented immigration contribute to its reproduction or intensification in the United States (Solis et al., 2002).

While youth violence exerts itself in many ways, an underlying basis for its emergence in Mexican communities in New York rests on structural conditions of immigration that make the problem transnational. By implication, the responsibility to address youth violence rests across nations on both individual and social levels. Both individual (mental) and social (policy) changes are needed to intervene in the formation of violent young people. Integrating transnational immigration studies into psychological analyses can offer a means of thinking about the design of intervention and youth services for individuals affected and affecting societies across borders. To illustrate this concept, I will first discuss valuable insights researchers can draw from the transnational immigration literature to understand youth violence.

Violence in the Context of Transnational Mexican Migration to New York

Transnational studies, in contrast to globalization studies, are useful to researchers of human development because they focus on changes to the local practices of individuals in society. While globalization studies seek to understand how economic, political, and cultural changes restructure the power of nations in the world, transnationalization is understood more locally as the study of social processes and practices of migrant populations across nations that are the result of global capitalism (Glick Schiller, Basch, & Blanc-Szanton, 1992). Recent books on transnational studies in New York (Cordero-Guzman, Smith, & Grosfoguel, 2001; Jones-Correa, 1998) attempt to anchor such processes in activities where particular uses of territories, the formation of communities, and new forms of sociopolitical participation characterize them. For instance, the use of video and electronic communication, cable television, and electronic money transfers, along with decreasing airfares, simplifies and quickens the formation of transnational communities (Foner, 2001b). To understand social changes brought about by immigration, technological advances in society, and particular economic flows, consideration of the current context in which migrants live is primordial.

Global migration to New York is a historic phenomenon. The emergence of current transnational communities in New York is a result of the city's key economic positioning in the world, yet transnationalization is not a new trend (Foner, 2001a). In the United States, New York received the highest and most diverse number of immigrants in the 20th century (Cordero-Guzman et al., 2001). Although New York was the main port of entry to Europeans in the early part of the century, changes to the 1965 immigration laws also changed the primary site of entry to the southern border, enabling greater immigration from countries other than Europe. Latin American immigration has increased significantly since this time, and has maintained New York as a primary destination city. Mexican immigration to New York catapulted in the 1980s and 1990s following severe economic crises in Mexico and increasing job availability in New York City (Smith, 1996). New York is historically an immigrant city, and its multicultural demographic makeup has surely also facilitated the growth of its recent immigrant populations (Foner, 2001a), including Mexicans.

Nevertheless, immigrant incorporation is generally a difficult process, and for the first generation, transnational ties are usually thought to help mitigate the transition into a new society, maintain membership to the home community, and perhaps even enable permanent return to the home country. Much of the focus on youth in the immigration literature has centered on issues affecting the second generation, such as cultural assimilation, racial identification, and educational attainment. Especially when considering the social standing of minorities, these processes of incorporation are characterized by the difficulties that minority and immigrant youth face (Portes, 1996; Smith, 2001; Waters, 1994). This literature has not addressed some important questions, including whether transnational ties become weaker in the second-generation youth; whether the nature of these ties increases or decreases the difficulties of incorporation of the first- and second-generation immigrants; and how immigration status intersects with such processes (Foner, 2001b).

For instance, in their review of assimilation theories, Alba and Nee (1997) comprehensively discuss findings on the large-scale factors that seem to ensure the successful incorporation of immigrants and their children in U.S. society. Some of the measures of successful incorporation or cultural assimilation of immigrants are their socioeconomic, educational, linguistic, and residential mobility (Massey & Denton, 1992). Immigrants, and especially their second-generation children, are said to assimilate successfully as they learn English, achieve a higher education, and move to middle-income homes. Such broad-scaled work on immigrant assimilation and incorporation rarely discusses the processes by which such outcomes are reached, including the activities of young people that interact with structural barriers like racial discrimination or immigration status. Analyses could do much more to discuss how structural barriers keep some immigrants from becoming upwardly mobile, or how these barriers are overcome by others. Moreover, assimilation studies analyze the successful incorporation of immigrants and their children from the top down; they consider how well these populations attain social mobility as this is prescribed by U.S. society, rather than by the cultural groups under study. Portes and Zhou (1993), for example, have documented patterns of downward, "segmented" assimilation, whereby some immigrant and second-generation young people incorporate themselves into a U.S. "underclass" of oppositional minorities. Particularly when studying the assimilation of second-generation youth, this kind of analysis can make unsuccessful assimilation seem like a result of young people's personal failure to develop positively in society. The danger in presenting such outcomes divorced from their processes is that the explanations implicitly fall on the individual's actions or psychological states rather than on his or her interactions with structural conditions from which psychological states emerge (Solis, 2002).

In addition, research based on assimilation theories rarely describes whether and how nondominant groups that belong to an "underclass" alter the structural conditions of mainstream society for their successful integration. The literature overlooks how immigrants and their children align themselves within, above, or beyond larger, societal ideologies of success. Cordero-Guzman et al. (2001) also critique this literature because it ignores a key process of immigrant incorporation and assimilation: racialization. In his research on the transnational Mexican community in New York, Smith (2001) argues that New York Mexican young people's social mobility is contingent on race relations and gendered access to higher education and varying strands of the work force. He speculates that the Mexican population occupies an ambiguous position in the racial hierarchy in the United States, and that the varied educational and economic mobility of the second generation can be explained by this ambiguity in their racial identification and the population's growing representation by both government and nongovernment organizations in the city. Nonetheless, an important issue affecting second-generation youth concerns their involvement in youth gangs and violent behavior that often is related to their unambiguous racial and ethnic memberships. Smith says that recent Mexican immigrants are quite young, and instead of entering the workforce directly, some "enter the schools, the *sonidos* [dance parties], and other arenas as adolescents and undergo a secondary socialization that can have varied, and sometimes highly negative impacts on their futures" (p. 283). He goes on to explain the increase in youth gangs because of the abuse Mexican youth encounter in school by other groups, and recent immigrant youths' imported experience with urban gangs in Mexico.

On the other hand, the rise of Mexican youth gangs has been visible historically across U.S. cities. Diego Vigil (2002) describes how racial confrontations and social distancing of Mexican immigrants in Los Angles into isolated neighborhoods and substandard housing led to the marginalization and formation of youth gangs in Los Angeles in the early part of the twentieth century. He says that the "community dynamics that created gangs and shaped gang members stemmed from the nexus of immigration, rapid industrial and capitalist development, and poor urban planning" (p. 106). Citing Hazlehurst and Hazlehurst (1998), Vigil concludes that youth street gangs have been known to develop transnationally because of migration. Similarly, in New York today, Mexican immigrant and second-generation youth are socially and politically marginalized, caught in the lower end of a changing global economy. They lack resources or the legal status necessary to access institutions of power.

Such consideration of historical and structural social conditions that explain the link between immigration and youth violence is a contribution of the transnational immigration literature. Moreover, the notion that Mexican immigration may continue while the second generation grows simultaneously makes their continued marginalization and participation in violent behavior a real possibility (Fouron & Glick Schiller, 2001). This should be a cause for concern not only to the United States but also to Mexico, because the research has demonstrated that youth violence, in light of the effects of immigration, transcends borders and can become transnational (Castro, 1981; Hazlehurst & Hazlehurst, 1998; Lomnitz, 1978; Vigil, 2002).

Apart from such discussions of structural conditions, much of this literature alludes to psychological states that accompany immigration and the development of marginalized youth. As I mentioned earlier, discussions of "downward" assimilation are laden with values about what constitutes success in U.S. society, and implicitly attribute responsibility and fault to individuals. In other literature, recent immigrants are described in terms of psychological, affective states (Ainslie, 1998); they withhold sentiments of belonging and loyalty to their home country—which may, in fact, motivate or justify their participation in home communities while abroad (Fouron & Glick Schiller, 2001). Such affective states and identity processes may even favor migrants' eventual return to the home country (Foner, 2001b). Marginalized immigrant youth are also described in psychological terms as feeling isolated (Vigil, 2002), contributing to their participation in street gangs (Solis, 2003). Similarly, the upward or downward mobility discussed in studies of immigrant and second-generation assimilation is really about the directionality of human development of these groups. In spite of such important consideration of affective states like motivation to succeed, sense of self and belonging, or desire to return that connect to immigrants' actions in both sending and receiving countries, the transnational immigration literature does not tend to draw its analyses from psychological theories or from studies of human development.

I argue that transnational immigration studies have much to learn from systematically analyzing psychological factors, just as the psychological literature has much to gain from studies that seriously consider social, cultural, and political conditions and processes. I propose that cultural-historical theory can be extended to serve as a method to achieve this much-needed complementarity between social and psychological analyses, and is generative of means of intervening in youth violence.

A Cultural-Historical Analysis of Immigrant Youth Violence

Cultural-historical theory provides this link by drawing from multiple histories: those of society and individuals. The life histories of immigrant and second-generation youth need to be studied systematically alongside analyses of the structural conditions in which their histories are situated. In this section, I describe how this particular theoretical framework serves these purposes and can lead to practical means of intervention in multiple social contexts of human development. This description is an important contribution of this chapter, as the application of historical analyses to youth violence has not been previously addressed as such by the developmental literature or in studies of transnational migration.

Scribner's theoretical analysis (1985) of Vygotsky's uses of history proposes that psychological phenomena can be studied along several levels of history.

These levels include simultaneously the history of the species, the history of individual societies, the life history of the individual, and the history of a psychological system. I argue that this multidevelopmental organization, especially along the latter three types of history is valuable to studies of transnational migration and youth violence. To understand the development of violent youth, it is necessary to see how both societal and personal histories become integrated. Societal history represents the wider, large-scale institutional changes in immigration and economic policies and patterns, while an individual dimension of historical analysis represents personal history, including local, individual practices that are unique, in this case, to immigrant and second-generation youth. Thus, while transnational migration studies document the history of migrants' practices in society, a cultural-historical analysis of youth violence would push further the study of individual history (ontogeny). Moreover, the integration of both societal and individual histories is seen in the formation of a psychological system, with a history of its own, that mediates between the individual's mental and material activity.

Cultural-historical theory poses a dialectical integration of the history of societies and individuals by locating material or cultural tools that give rise to a psychological system. Thus, in order to understand how and why certain behavior develops, one would have to locate the cultural tools available in society that are used by individuals in practical activity. In addition, this theoretical framework permits human development to be both multidirectional and functional. The possible permutations of development are endless, if one considers that the interactions between social and personal histories are variable and contingent on what is culturally available. This theoretical notion is consistent with social-psychological work (Deaux, 2000; Sampson, 1989) and poststructuralist notions of human development (Henriques, Hollway, Urwin, Venn, & Walkerdine, 1984) that deemphasize universality in favor of variability and diversity.

Further, the Vygotskian notion of activity, especially goal-directed, practical activity, is captured in the dialectical relationship between the outer, social world and the individual's consciousness. Vygotsky's Marxist psychology tells us that human mental functioning is never solely internal to an individual, but is always developing in a dialectal relationship with the social world. Practical activity, or human goal-directed behavior, is mediated by cultural tools that function to reorient one's activity, transforming it from material activity to mental activity, which is then exercised on the material, social world (Vygotsky & Luria, 1994). Leont'ev (1978) also says that the tooled structure of human activity is found in its implementation in a social system of interrelationships with other people. Human cultural activity involves the manipulation of resources and structures already made available by society historically as tools that help one mentally and materially to reach a particular goal. Therefore, a psychological tool develops from cultural artifacts and mediates between individuals' cognitive and material functions (Vygotsky, 1978).

Vygotsky's explanation of the development of thought (1986) exemplifies these principles best. As the child is exposed to and participates in language (which is culturally created), she or he comes to acquire the language of her or his world in a functional sense; social, external speech becomes personal, allowing the child to use words to think aloud and plan future actions when involved in practical activity. In time, this "egocentric" speech is transformed into inner speech or thought, which serves for planning coordinating actions on the world. In this way, language is a cultural tool transformed into signs, a symbol system developing from the actual social practices and relationships that gave it its meanings; eventually, the symbolic system mediates between the individual's outer social world and inner consciousness through practical, meaningful, and intentional activity.

I would like to draw a theoretical parallel between the cultural-historical development of thought and language to the development of consciousness and violent behavior by arguing first that violence preexists individuals. Violence has been available historically for individuals, groups, and nations to reach their own goals, such as the constitution or preservation of power, and the enforcement of one's ideas, decisions, or policies. As such, violence can be thought of as a cultural, mediational tool. In the histories of Mexican immigrant youth, violence is experienced personally and enabled through structural, institutional forms: poverty, racial discrimination, and immigration status. To understand whether external, social predispositions toward violent behavior become internal, symbolic means for immigrant youth to achieve their own goals, one would have to analyze young people's personal histories to examine whether violence carries psychological functions. If cultural forms available to them mediate immigrant young people's goals, is violence somehow functional to their development? What does violence allow immigrant youth to do? Is violence a practical means of interacting with others?

The method I devised to apply socio-historical theory to the analysis of youth violence was to represent conditions and injustices in nested spheres of activity influencing young migrants' lives. My review of the political-economic history (cited briefly earlier for purposes of this essay) revealed the dynamics of ongoing Mexican migration to the United States, along with the continued and worsening maintenance of policies that have allowed families to languish in undocumented status, while the United States economy has benefited from their labor. Positing such injustices as violence in the public sphere, I then did a case study of a transnational institution to make explicit the processes and issues of interaction between the state and the Mexican community from a human rights perspective. My analysis of the values and activities at Asociación Tepeyac consisted of detailed discourse analyses of a total of 16 of the bulletin issues of the association's newsletter, *Popocapetl*; interviews with principals; my participant observation as a volunteer in the organization between 1999 and 2002; and my work with 16 young people aged 5–16 in an after-school literacy program. Over the 10 meetings, a core group (2 boys and 3 girls) attended most consistently. In addition to gathering data from those activities, I interviewed the mothers of the core five young people who participated in Asociación Tepeyac to gain insights about transitions into the more private sphere of the family. Focusing ultimately on the sense that young people made of their experience of undocumented identity, I worked with the young people on literacy skills by creating a booklet to help young people in Mexico who would be making the journey to the United States. Across the archival, observational, interview, and textual data produced from these interactions, I identified cultural tools—or the children's ways of expressing their identities in relation to their group activities and the identity expressions across the many public spheres I described earlier.

Following from such questions in my research on Mexican children and youth's experiences of violence, I found that aside from the institutional violence to which such boys and girls were exposed, they also participated in interethnic, intraethnic, and reactive types of physical violence (although none were actively involved in gangs). More important, such activity seemed to carry out certain psychological functions related to relations of power in U.S. society and the young people's own ability to exert power over others (Solis, 2003). I proposed elsewhere that Mexican young people's violent behavior carried out at least two mental functions: (1) to defend oneself affectively (e.g., protecting one's self-esteem), and (2) to develop a dominant identity in a hierarchical relationship (e.g., male—female; recent immigrant—established resident). Others believe that the involvement of Latino youth across a variety of contexts (Europe, El Salvador, Guatemala, and Brazil) in gangs arises as a type of social membership that counteracts their social isolation, especially in densely populated areas where young people are exposed to crime, often as victims (Clinard, 1960, 1968; Shaw & McKay, 1942; Vigil, 2002). Thus, there is increasing recognition in the literature that young people's involvement in violent circles has some social and psychological benefits (see other chapters in this book as well). The cultural-historical analysis that led to this conclusion extends the transnational migration literature's relation to youth development by positing that although violent behavior may not be fully functional externally, it maybe mentally functional for some young people under some circumstances.

In the role of aggressors rather than targets of abuse, Mexican young people's violent behavior may be goal oriented in a psychological sense. Mexican youth who are socially marginalized are made to feel inferior. In order to counteract such feelings of inferiority and the development of low self-esteem, poor self-confidence, and self-doubt, Mexican youth may exert their own power over others through whatever means are readily available to them, such as interpersonal violence toward women, children, or those of racial, ethnic, and language groups deemed socially inferior. The development of oppositional identities has social origins (Cross, 1995) yet is not functional to the ideals of U.S. society, as the assimilation literature suggests (Portes & Zhou, 1993). However, this cultural-historical analysis also suggests that an oppositional identity may be functional in the personal development of immigrant and second-generation minorities as a means of protection from psychological harm and instantiation of power originating from social inequalities. In contrast, the "successful" assimilation of these young people into mainstream U.S. society can carry the psychological cost of personal alienation from their families and communities. While cultural-historical theory does not explicitly address power relations in society, it is a necessary component of psychological analysis. In addition, multihistorical analyses of transnational migration and immigrant or second-generation youth provide important insights concerning the preventive mechanisms that are needed across sites of human development to deter the formation of violent youth, which I discuss in the next section.

Transnational, Social, and Psychological Limits to Youth Violence

Greater undocumented immigration from Mexico paradoxically means both cheap labor that enhances the United States economy, and increased pockets of poverty, with all of their social perils. Given the fact that the community is transnational, this also means greater amounts of remittances to enhance the Mexican economy. Now that Mexican-U.S. dual nationality is possible, there has been talk of enabling Mexicans to vote from abroad. Mexico's move toward democratic elections was exemplified in its last presidential election, when a new party finally took the presidency away from the Institutional Revolutionary Party's stronghold of 72 years. Currently, the country's strongest parties have been campaigning in the United States. This is a phenomenon occurring in other transnational populations, such as the Dominican diaspora on the island and in New York (Pessar & Graham, 2001).

In my own experience working with Mexicans in New York, I have witnessed such actions on the part of government officials pertaining to all of Mexico's major political parties who approach Mexican organizations in the city. Interested in the affairs and issues affecting Mexicans in the United States, they must also know that the transnationalization of the Mexican community enables communication of the political choice of migrants abroad to families remaining at home. While undocumented Mexicans in the United States would benefit from political representation through more direct means, and may express feelings of loyalty to their home country, many also feel that they were expelled from it, forced to leave due to conditions fostered and maintained by government actions. At worst, the development of violent personal behavior arises from conditions of inequality present in both U.S. and Mexican societies and, thus, transcends borders. Transnational consideration of government policies and reforms that address their role in fomenting youth violence would be a much-needed, structural preventive method. When migrant youth and the children of immigrants become violent, what is it that society wants to represent to them? What message is intended?

In addition, the creation of safe social spaces that counteract structural forms of violence need to occur locally. The preventive methods of such community-based organizations as Asociación Tepeyac in creating constructive educational activities and social events where alcohol is prohibited are useful, yet need to be better planned to become enriching. Others who supervise sites of youth activity must also be informed of the role they play in the directionality of human development. As Smith notes, Catholic priests have closed their dance halls and gyms to Mexican young people because their activities were becoming dangerous. This aggravates the situation by "moving the social encounters these young people have out of supervised areas and into the street" (2001, p. 291). While young people need safe social spaces for their activities in order to prevent violent behavior, there are still too many keepers of such spaces who are ill informed about the Mexican community and about how violence within it develops. Rather than become avoidant of the problem, much more work is needed on the level of intervention that will address directly Mexican young people's psychological burdens and conflicts that lead to violent behavior.

Teachers, facilitators of community programs, youth counselors, and others who work directly with immigrant and minority youth need to be knowledgeable about processes of human development in the context of greater social relations of power and inequality. It is not sufficient to counsel young people around psychological matters outside of these broader parameters. By taking culture and history as points of departure to understand the experiences of these young people, professionals can begin to explore structural sources of violent behavior. Keeping in mind the cultural-historical analysis laid out earlier, such professionals can facilitate changes to the goal structure of young people's actions: they must help them find new cultural means of reaching their objectives while preserving their dignity and affective integrity. They must also be capable of detecting how young people interact with predominant ideologies and persons in higher positions of power in society. Methods of intervention must allow young people to examine their institutional memberships and exclusions, and enable them to think critically about sources of tension and psychological conflict beyond the immediate and the personal.

For example, in my research I have encountered undocumented, second-generation young people who demonstrate contempt for higher authorities (Solis, 2003). They tell of racial/ethnic battles and confrontations with peers and teachers in school, police in their neighborhoods, and less directly with immigration, the authorities who nonetheless have a say in whether these young people can eventually work legally or have access to an affordable college education. These immigrant young people need counseling programs that enable them to confront their feelings toward authorities in power as well as toward themselves. They need to learn to question whether their sense of self-worth has been diminished and inferiority has been internalized on the basis of arbitrary criteria (such as race, gender, or immigration status) communicated through mechanisms of power such as the popular media and government policies that affect their lives. Rather than use violence to react, immigrant young people should be supported to find other means of responding to structural violence by becoming conscious of the social processes by which power is wielded, and by finding proactive, nonviolent forms of contestation.

Immigrant youth who became undocumented as small children when their parents decided to migrate and who have grown up in the United States are the target of violence when undocumented immigrants are treated like criminals, persecuted on the border, restricted from activities and rights that others take for granted, and made to feel unworthy of improved economic conditions in the United States, economic conditions that they help to create through their labor yet are constantly reminded they do not deserve. The extent to which undocumented Mexican parents can provide better opportunities for their U.S.-born children is also questionable. These young people also need to find means other than violence to respond to their victimization, and discover a sense of agency to guide their use of proactive means of changing abuse and unequal treatment that they face. The existence of structural inequality and interpersonal violence is a global commonality. Youth professionals and young people themselves need to be aware of the ways violence can be depersonalized within the particulars of their everyday interactions with citizens, institutions, others with whom they identify, and those with whom they do not. Young people living in circumstances characterized by violent identity labels like "illegal" must develop cognitively, socially, and emotionally *through* those labels. Denial of the existence and burden of these labels exacerbates the plight of these young people and the communities they serve.

Note

For more information, the organization may be contacted by email at Popocateptl@Tepeyac.org.

References

Ainslie, R. C. (1998). Cultural mourning, immigration, and engagement: Vignettes from the Mexican experience. In M. M. Suárez-Orozco (Ed.), *Crossings: Mexican immigration in interdisciplinary perspective* (pp. 283–300). Cambridge, MA: Harvard University Press.

Alba, R., & Nee, V. (1997). Rethinking assimilation theory for a new era of immigration. *International Migration Review, 31*(4), 826–874.

Castro, G. L. (1981). *El Cholo: Origen y desarrollo* [El Cholo: Origin and development]. Mexicali: Universidad Autonoma de Baja California.

Clinard, M. B. (1960). Cross-cultural replication of the relation of urbanism to criminal behavior. *American Sociological Review, 25,* 253–257.

Clinard, M. B. (1968). *Sociology of deviant behavior*. New York: Holt.

Cordero-Guzman, H. R., Smith, R. C., & Grosfoguel, R. (Eds.). (2001). *Migration, transnationalization, and race in a changing New York*. Philadelphia: Temple University Press.

Cross, W. E. (1995). Oppositional identity and African American youth: Issues and prospects. In W. Hawley & A. Jackson (Eds.), *Toward a common destiny: Improving race and ethnic relations in America* (pp. 185–204). San Francisco: Jossey-Bass.

Deaux, K. (2000). Surveying the landscape of immigration: Social psychological perspectives. *Journal of Community and Applied Social Psychology, 10*(5), pp. 421–431.

Foner, N. (2001a). Introduction: New immigrant in a new New York. In N. Foner (Ed.), *New immigrants in New York* (pp. 1–31). New York: Columbia University Press.

Foner, N. (2001b). Transnationalism then and now: New York immigrants today and at the turn of the century. In H. R. Cordero-Guzman, R. C. Smith, & R. Grosfoguel

(Eds.), *Migration, transnationalization, and race in a changing New York* (pp. 35–57). Philadelphia: Temple University Press.

Fouron, G. E., & Glick Schiller, N. (2001). The generation of identity: Redefining the second generation within a transnational social field. In H. R. Cordero-Guzman, R. C. Smith, & R. Grosfoguel (Eds.), *Migration, transnationalization, and race in a changing New York* (pp. 58–86). Philadelphia: Temple University Press.

Glick Schiller, N., Basch, L., & Blanc-Szanton, C. (Eds.). (1992). *Towards a transnational perspective on migration: Race, class, ethnicity and nationalism reconsidered.* New York: New York Academy of Sciences.

Hazlehurst, K., & C. Hazlehurst. (Eds.). (1998). *Gangs and youth subcultures: International explorations.* New Brunswick, NJ: Transaction.

Henriques, J., Hollway, W., Urwin, C., Venn, C., & Walkerdine, V. (Eds.). (1984). *Changing the subject: Psychology, social regulation and subjectivity.* London: Methuen.

Jones-Correa, M. (Ed.) (1998). *Between two nations: The political predicament of Latinos in New York.* Ithaca, NY: Cornell University Press.

Leont'ev, A. N. (1978). *Activity, consciousness, and personality.* Englewood Cliffs, NJ: Prentice-Hall.

Lomnitz, L. (1978). Mechanisms of articulation between shantytown settlers and the urban system: *Urban Anthropology* 7(2): 185–205.

Massey, D., & Denton, N. (1992). Racial identity and the spatial assimilation of Mexicans in the United States. *Social Science Research, 21,* 235–260.

Pessar, P. R., & Graham, P. M. (2001). Dominicans: Transnational identities and local politics. In N. Foner (Ed.), *New immigrants in New York* (pp. 251–273). New York: Columbia University Press.

Portes, A. (1996). *The new second generation.* New York: Sage.

Portes, A., & Zhou, M. (1993). The new second generation: Segmented assimilation and its variants. *Annals of the American Academy, 530,* 74–93.

Sampson, E. E. (1989). The challenge of social change for psychology: Globalization and psychology's theory of the person. *American Psychologist, 44*(6), 914–921.

Sassen, S. (1991). The global city: New York, London, Tokyo. Princeton, NJ: Princeton University Press.

Scribner, S. (1985). Vygotsky's uses of history. In J. Wertsch (Ed.), *Culture, communication and cognition* (pp. 119–145). New York: Cambridge University Press.

Shaw, C., & R. McKay. 1942. *Juvenile delinquency and urban areas.* Chicago: University of Chicago Press.

Smith, R. C. (1996). Mexicans in New York: Membership and incorporation in a new immigrant community. In S. Baver & G. Haslip-Viera (Eds.), *Latinos in New York: Communities in transition.* Notre Dame, IN: University of Notre Dame Press, pp. 57–103.

Smith, R. C. (1998). Transnational localities: Community, technology and the politics of membership within the context of Mexico and U.S. migration. In M. P. Smith & L. E. Guarnizo (Eds.), *Transnationalism from below* (pp. 196–238). New Brunswick, NJ: Transaction,

Smith, R. C. (2001). Mexicans: Social, educational, economic, and political problems and prospects in New York. In N. Foner (Ed.), *New immigrants in New York* (pp. 275–300). New York: Columbia University Press.

Solis, J. (2002). *The (trans)formation of illegality as an identity: A study of the organization of undocumented Mexican immigrants and their children in New York City.* Unpublished doctoral dissertation, City University of New York.

Solis, J. (2003). Re-thinking illegality as a violence *against,* not *by* undocumented Mexican immigrants, children, and youth. *Journal of Social Issues, 59*(1), 15–31.

Solis, J., Bonil, S., & Garcia, G. (2002, November). *Mexican women's community response to domestic violence: A sociocultural analysis of migration, gender, and violence.* Paper presented at the Hominis Intercontinental Convention, Havana.

Vigil, D. (2002). Community dynamics and the rise of street gangs. In M. M. Suarez-Orozco & M. M. Paez (Eds.), *Latinos: Remaking America* (pp. 97–109). Berkeley: University of California Press.

Vygotsky, L. (1978). *Mind in society: The development of higher psychological processes.* (M. Cole, V. John-Steiner, S. Scribner, & E. Souberman, Eds.) Cambridge, MA: Harvard University Press.

Vygotsky, L. (1986). *Thought and language* (A. Kozulin, Trans.). Cambridge: MIT Press.

Vygotsky, L., & Luria, A. (1994). Tool and symbol in child development. In R. Van der Veer & J. Valsiner (Eds.), *The Vygotsky reader* (pp. 99–174). Oxford: Blackwell.

Waters, M. C. (1994). Ethnic and racial identities of second generation Black immigrants in New York City. *International Migration Review, 27*(4), 795–820.

Epilogue

From Conflict to Development

The typical developmental pathway through youth—however that is constructed in diverse locations—may not be through violent conflict, but the chapters in this book have shown how in contexts across the globe young people are involved in dramatic conflicts that are, in many ways, inescapable, and thus a normal part of life. Circumstances in the world at the beginning of the twenty-first century may present more challenges to young people than ever before in history, or those of us concerned with the plight of young people may simply have better means of monitoring and reflecting on these challenges, as we have done in this book. Whichever is the case, we have illustrated how conflicts arising from disagreement, injustice, and competition are occurring worldwide. We suggest, based on these case studies, that scholars, educators, and clinicians working with youth consider conflict as a normative activity. This epilogue notes a few of the major areas for ongoing research and, eventually, practice with young people.

The authors have shown here, chapter after chapter, how social, political, and economic circumstances, in their contexts, engage young people in conflict and violence directly or create fertile ground for youth involvement in conflict, whether because of national tensions, injustices, neglect, or lack of resources. Circumstances like allowing people to live in poverty while corporations, elite groups, and the government make money off local resources, recruiting abandoned children into armed conflict, allowing economic injustices to sustain rifts among ethnic groups, and tolerating youth-against-youth violence, for whatever reasons, all point back to society. These essays have described cycles of conflict over power struggles, resources, and identity claims that affect young people's ability to thrive and contribute to their families, communities, and nations in positive ways.

The experiment here, to analyze youth conflict beyond individual youth, his or her family, and culture, has offered descriptions of national and regional troubles, contexts for informing research on youth conflict and insights that could guide work on young people's behalf. Since we have provided ample overview of the contexts and processes of youth conflict in the general introduction and part introductions, we will use this epilogue to highlight two ideas for ongoing research and practice around youth conflict—the idea that youth conflict is a practice, and the idea that young people develop through meaningful participation in the broader society, although that participation may be negative as in conflict.

Youth Conflict Is a Social Practice

On the basis of these case studies, we propose that youth conflict is a social practice—an activity that is embedded in a cycle of opportunities locally, nationally, and globally. The more prevalent the conflict activities, the more normative we would have to say they are. By pointing out how political, economic, and social contexts create the circumstances for youth conflict, the chapters in this book have offered models for future research to explore this idea. To gain greater clarity and specificity about how participation in youth conflict is a normative practice worldwide, researchers across more international contexts could shift the perspective in their inquiries away from the close-up sphere of an individual young person's character and abilities to the societal spheres where children and youth experience and interact with those around them and with the values and systems that define their lives.

Our analysis of the social, political, and economic causes of youth involvement in conflict does not completely absolve young people of their responsibilities to behave with respect for the physical and psychological lives of others. That youth problems begin with social and political forces beyond their sphere of activity doesn't mean that there are no abnormal or immoral young people. Nevertheless, the circumstances described in these chapters—wars, poverty, lack of adult support and protection, competition for material and social resources—are fertile ground for participation in conflict, posing special challenges for those whose resources and power are most limited. Future research could further examine such circumstances as they occur in other contexts and the social roles that young people play in those other contexts.

Participatory Development

As was highlighted in the introduction and part introductions, the authors of this book offered insights about psycho-social processes, intergroup processes, interventions, and international processes. Across those processes, youth participation emerges as a powerful force. The authors have recounted how broader societal processes set the scene for young people's participation in armed conflict, fighting, bullying, exclusion, and disrespect that cause harm. Authors also explained that harmful means of participation could be ameliorated by making possible positive means of participation. A major challenge for ongoing theoretical and practical research is to examine the notion of "participatory development" emerging from these observations. If we see that in contexts worldwide, Western and non-Western, in relatively wealthy and relatively poor countries, young people participate in society through negative conflicts (serving in wars, carrying out societal values by disciplining peers through collective bullying or discrimination, etc.), then we could analyze how such participations affect young people's development positively and negatively. Such analyses could further illuminate dynamics in the community and national spheres that responsible adults should be in a position to change.

In addition, those analyses could identify the motivational processes of conflict and transform those into productive and imaginative activities in programs fostering young people's positive participation in society. The authors of these chapters have, for example, explained how the need for survival, recognition, social connection, and determination of self and society play a role in young people's involvement in institutions, which could be official public institutions like school and government or unofficial institutions involved in dividing society. Future research examining youth conflict in terms of political, economic, and social dynamics could examine such processes more closely and check for alternative proposals. In addition to the motivating aspects of conflict, like those mentioned earlier, inescapable factors, like threat, humiliation, and injustice, also provoke and require young people's response that is sometimes violent. These processes merit further examination and, ultimately, community and national action for amelioration.

Future research can build on these observations by exploring the nature and effects of participation as a developmental process. Questions to guide such research include: In what contexts and manifestations do young people engage in conflict in order to receive physical or psychological support that is otherwise not available? What do we learn about participation as a developmental mechanism from contexts where young people serve social roles as physical or psychological fighters? What are the similar and different processes organizing social conflict and social development? How, in particular, do social connection, self-determination, and societal influence function across conflict activities and practices to promote reconciliation, rebuilding, and healing?

Limits of the Volume

As an initial step toward transnational understanding of youth conflict and development, this book also has limitations. The insights and supporting studies are not necessarily representative of each local context or the global interactions placing young people in harm's way. The diversity of perspectives on youth conflict and development offered by our case studies makes comparison difficult, so the crosscutting themes and insights are hypotheses worth exploring in future research, especially in closely monitored contexts of practice. While we present a rich array of contexts, there is still a limit to the number of countries represented, and in terms of regions, there is a notable lack here of countries primarily identified as Arab or Scandinavian. Although we offer case studies from most of the other continental regions, there are only one or two for each area, thus in no way representing its full diversity. Because we considered a broad range of manifestations of youth conflict, these case studies offer insights about the lives of females as well as males, but males still tend to be overrepresented in research on armed conflict, bullying, and street violence. There is, moreover, complexity we have missed by focusing on conflicts manifested interpersonally rather than as victimization, as in rape or mass murder (for example, school shootings). Since the conflicts we discuss had been identified as salient manifestations in their contexts, psychological exclusion, which in some areas is more typically a female-gendered practice, has not been a focus.

In the introduction to this book, Daiute pointed to the myth of childhood innocence in the context of the sometimes ugly reality of today's world. In closing, we propose that young people are precious to their families, their cultures, and their nations not so much for their innocence, which seems impossible to sustain in the contemporary world, even though maintaining innocence may remain an ideal goal. Families, cultures, and nations should, instead, consider young people precious for their participation. Toward the goal of nurturing youth to participate in positive ways, we must develop our theories and practices with respect for young people's ability, insight, contribution, and humanity, which cannot be separated from that of the adult world. In promoting participation by youth in society, we may, moreover, be able to foster understandings about connections that can strengthen research and development.

Index